The Image of Venice

FIALETTI'S VIEW AND SIR HENRY WOTTON

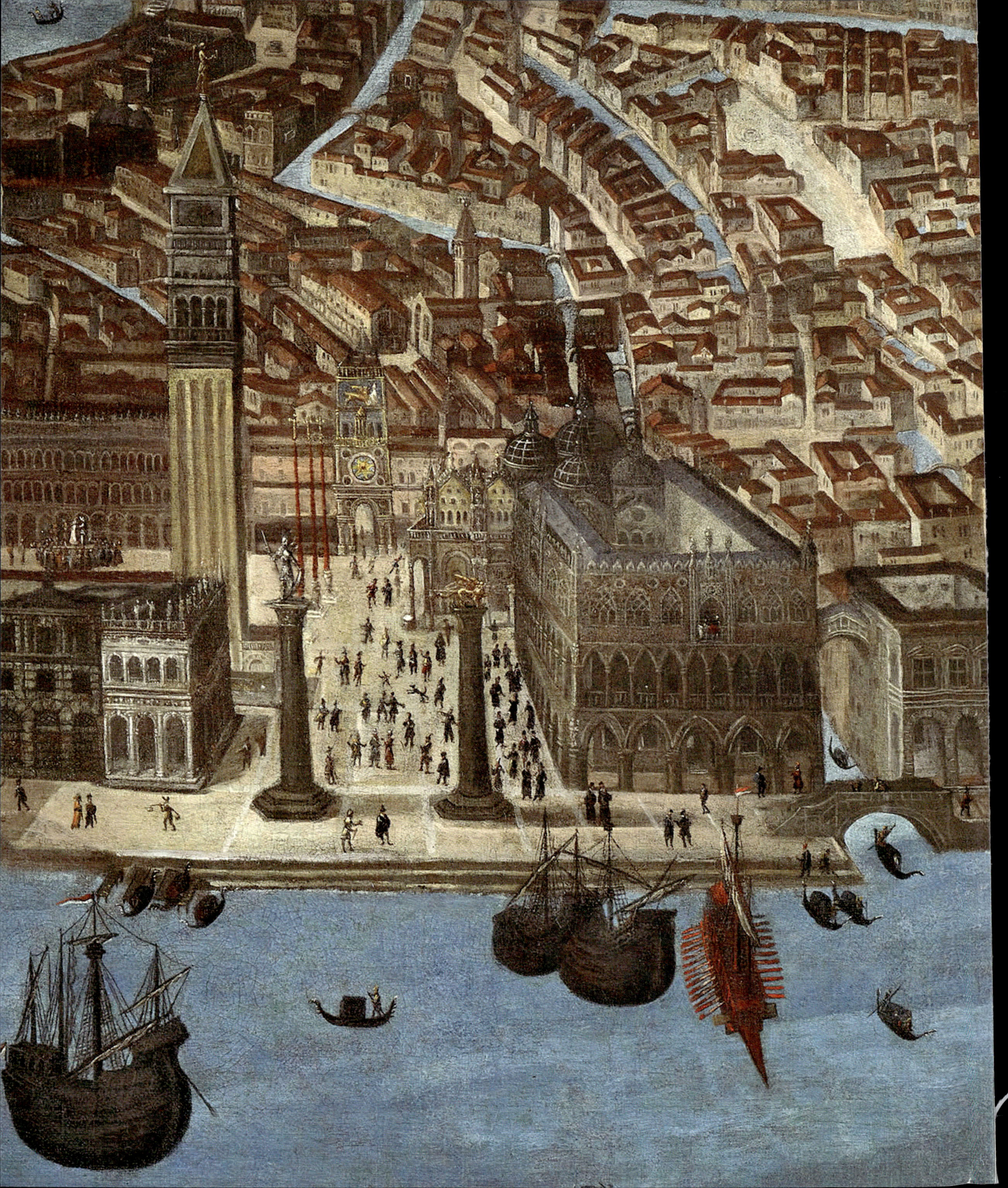

The Image of Venice

FIALETTI'S VIEW AND SIR HENRY WOTTON

DEBORAH HOWARD AND
HENRIETTA MCBURNEY

with contributions by

CHRISTY ANDERSON • RUTH BUBB
ANDREW HOPKINS • DANIEL MCREYNOLDS
ALLISON SHERMAN • LAURA WALTERS

Paul Holberton publishing

A catalogue record for this book is available from the British Library

ISBN 978 1 907372 48 3

Produced by Paul Holberton publishing,
89 Borough High Street, London SE1 1NL
www.paul-holberton.net

Designed by Laura Parker
www.parkerinc.co.uk

Printed by E-Graphic, Verona
www.e-graphic.it

JACKET Fialetti's *View*, detail
FRONTISPIECE Fialetti's *View*, detail of the Piazzetta di San Marco

CONTENTS

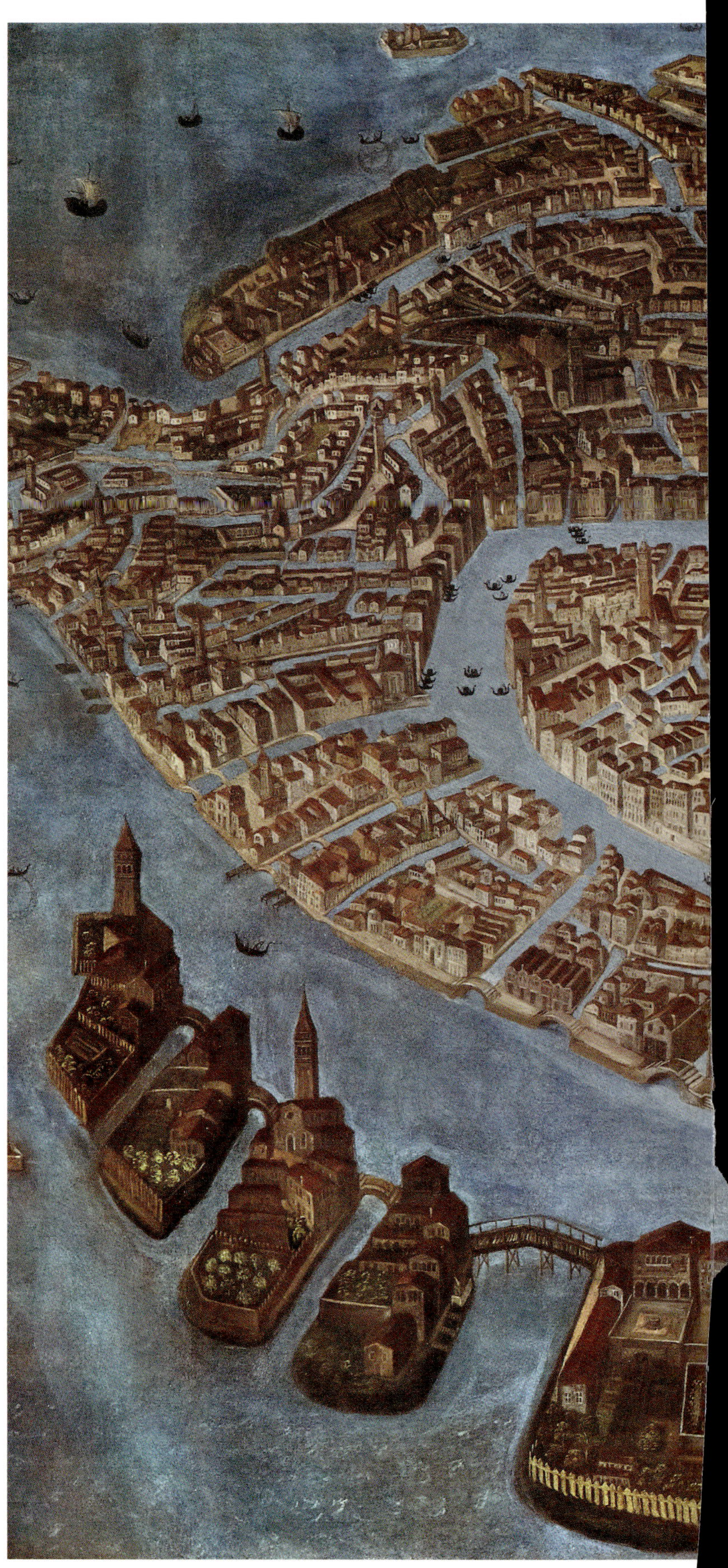

1

Odoardo Fialetti, *View of Venice*, signed and
dated 1611, oil on canvas, 200 x 425 cm
Eton College

Of all my predecessors, the one I would most like to have known, with the possible exception of Montague Rhodes James, is Sir Henry Wotton. Henry Savile might have been more learned and much richer, Thomas Smith more powerful at Court, while the College undoubtedly owes the most to William Waynflete, but Wotton by all accounts had the most wit, the most charm, the most developed sense of taste. Robert Boyle said that he was "not only a fine gentleman himself, but very well skilled in the art of making others so". Izaak Walton, who was both a friend and his biographer, used to go fishing with him on the river at Eton. He quotes him as "saying often, he would rather live five May months than forty Decembers" – as any fisherman would. He was one of the first to introduce Palladio to the English, and was as effective an ambassador to Venice as that subtle republic would allow, at a time when the Protestant north had some hope of persuading Venice to go one step further than its habitual hostility to Rome by actually joining them in alliance – always, I suspect, a vain hope. He lived dangerously – just escaping the fall of the Earl of Essex, for whom he had worked, and the wrath of the King when he made his famous joke about the mendacious purpose of an ambassador. His portrait, in the pose of a melancholy scholar, inviting us to join him (via a word bubble) in doing philosophy, hangs to my great pleasure in my dining room.

Wotton was also a great collector, on behalf of himself, his king, Lord Salisbury, and a good many others. This book describes, analyses and explains one of his most interesting purchases, and one of his greatest benefactions to Eton and indeed to England – Fialetti's enormous depiction of Venice which now hangs in Election Hall in the College. It has recently been wonderfully restored, thanks to the Friends of the Eton College Collections and the skill of Ruth Bubb, one of the contributors to this book. Hanging as the focal point of the British Museum's brilliant Olympic Year Exhibition *Shakespeare: Staging the World,* it became known to the public more widely; this book, will, I hope, make it even more accessible, as well as contributing to scholarly discussion surrounding it. The Provost and Fellows of Eton are most grateful to our former Keeper of Fine and Decorative Art Henrietta McBurney for her initiative, as for much else, in bringing together, with Professor Deborah Howard, leading scholar of the architecture of Venice, the specialists included in this volume. Our gratitude also goes to Old Etonians, individuals amongst the Friends of our Collections, members of The Venice in Peril Fund, and others, too, for enabling this publication to take place.

WILLIAM WALDEGRAVE
Provost of Eton

THE PUBLICATION OF THIS BOOK has been made possible thanks to the generosity of many people. Amongst these is a number of Old Etonians, some of whom, as Collegers in their time, remember Fialetti's *View* hanging on the walls of College Hall where they ate their meals each day. It was due to funds from the Friends of the Eton Collections that the View was conserved in 2010; individuals amongst the Friends have continued their association with Fialetti's painting by subscribing to this volume, some very generously indeed. We are also delighted that several members of The Venice in Peril Fund have helped us to realise this book, a demonstration that the ties between Venice and England which Sir Henry Wotton did so much to establish are still strong. We are most grateful to all these subscribers, as well as to other individuals listed below and some who have wished to remain anonymous, for their invaluable support of this project.

Major donors
The Lord Phillimore OE (CD'OG, PSS 63)
  & Lady Phillimore
Mr & Mrs T.W. Sanderson

Benefactors
Francis Carnwath OE (FJRC 58)
Mr & Mrs J.H.W. Christofferson
Mr & Mrs J. Derrick
Mr Hamish & Mrs Sophie Forsyth
Mr & Mrs Robert Hayes
Henry Hayter OE (GWN, PSS 56)
Nigel Jaques OE (DCW 54)
Jonathan Keates
The Lord Lloyd of Berwick OE (KS 48)
Jeremy Lloyd OE (RCM 60)
Michael Mackenzie OE (CAI 74)
Mr & Mrs Peter Robinson
Cameron Rose Hon OE
Mr & Mrs J.S. Thomas
Mr & Mrs Peter Thomson
Alex van Someren OE (JWR 82) & Carol Atack
Lord Waldegrave OE (AJM, RDM 65)
  & Lady Waldegrave

Subscribers
David Adshead
Julian Baughan OE (RCM, KS 61)
Mr & Mrs H.C. Bennett
Rufus Bird OE (DAE 92)
Simon Boyd OE (MNF 67)
Jeremy Bray OE (RMAB, DSS 75)
Charles Byam-Cook OE (PSS 63)
Ian Cadell OE (RJNP 58)
Frances, Lady Clarke
Mrs Jane Clay
Ellen Cornelissen
Professor Paul & Dr Fiona Cornish
Mr & Mrs C.I.H. Cross
John Farmer OE (PSS 53)
Lord Charles FitzRoy OE (CNCA 74)

Dr Emily Gowers
Professor Norman Hammond
  & Professor Jean Wilson
Robert Hanbury OE (RDFW 58)
Anthony Hanson OE (EPH, RMAB 63)
Charles Harding OE (DPS 70)
Mrs Enid Hardy
Mr & Mrs D.W.R. Harrington
Richard Haslam OE (FWH 63)
Dr Jonathan & Dr Gwen Holliday
Professor Deborah Howard
Mrs Susannah Kelly
Mr Peter Kerruish OE (GIB 66)
  & Mrs Kerruish
Richard Lebus OE (JDRMcC 67)
Mr & Mrs D.E. Long
Dr John Long
Lady Iona Mackworth-Young
Scott Mandelbrote OE (WHM, KS 86)
Bill Masser Hon OE
Toby Motley OE (CEDC 61)
Peter Ratzer
Charles Rickett OE (GIB 66)
Sir William Rollo OE (CWW 73)
  & Lady Rollo
Mr & Mrs Christopher Rowell
Lord Sassoon OE (CAI 73)
Mrs Felicity Strong
Mrs Jacqueline Tarrant-Barton
Brian Thornton OE (HKP 55)
Antti Kalevanpoika Vauhkonen
Mr & Mrs G. Versteegh
Richard Walford OE (JA, DH 78)
Sasha Walicki OE (MAG 13)
Mr & Mrs Peter Watkins
Amy Wehle
Ralfe Whistler OE (ACB-R, FJAC 48)
Major Tom Wills OE (FJAC 58)
and those who have chosen to remain
  anonymous

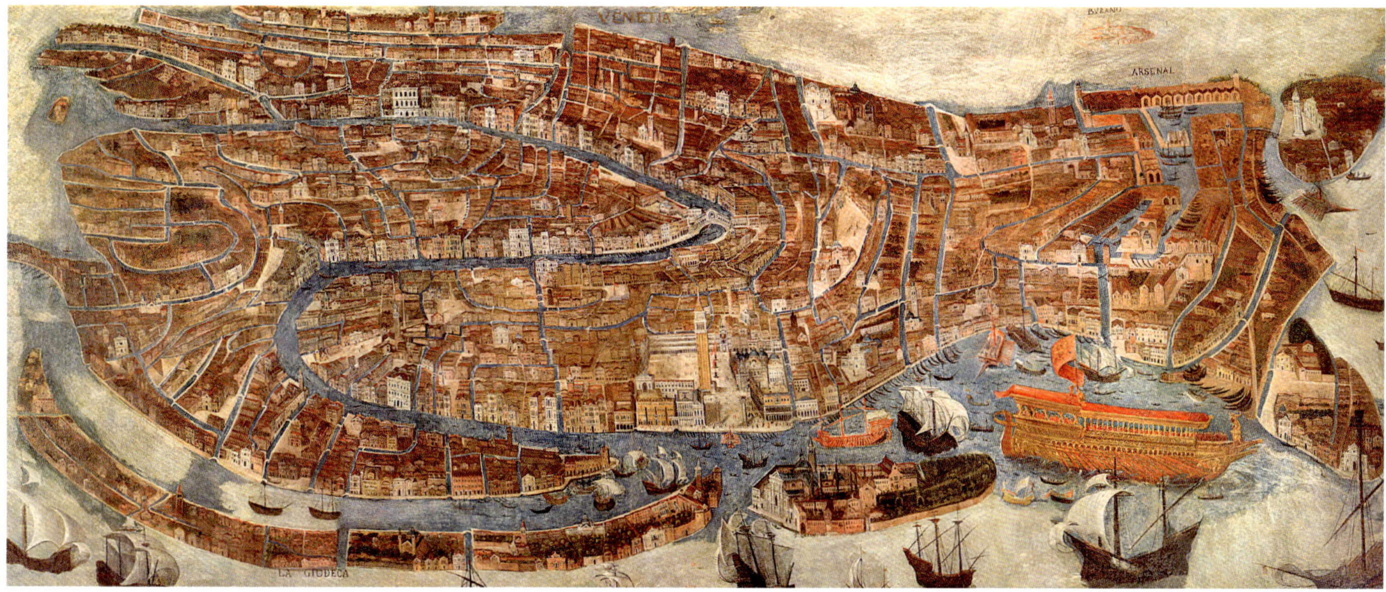

As well as investigating the making of Fialetti's pioneering work of art, the sources for its imagery, and its role in the career of Henry Wotton, the book investigates as many aspects of this distinctive view of the townscape of Venice as possible, drawing together the work of historians of art, architecture, religion, politics and society.

Fialetti's View: *fiction and reality*

Fialetti's great painted canvas is the earliest of a series of very large painted views of Venice produced in the first half of the seventeenth century,[5] although great urban panoramas had already been made in other parts of Italy, such as Mantua and the Vatican.[6] Two views of Venice painted not long after that of Fialetti invite comparison with it: one, attributed to Gian Battista Arzenti, probably painted in 1620–30, adopted a more improvised layout (fig. 4), whereas Joseph Heintz the Younger in 1648–50 reproduced the format of Jacopo de' Barbari's woodcut rather precisely, taking a higher viewpoint than Fialetti (figs. 5, 7). Each artist included recent structures that seemed to be of particular interest, but in each case the choice was different. Depicting the city on Ascension Day, Arzenti paid special attention to the *sestiere* of Castello in the eastern part of the city, as well as some of the new palaces on the Grand Canal (fig. 6). Heintz inserted Palladio's churches of San Giorgio and the Redentore (strangely missing from Fialetti's *View*, as we shall see), as well as the still newer church of Santa Maria della Salute.[7] Much later in the century, after 1682, an unidentified artist painted another large view of Venice, over four metres wide, now in Bern.[8]

To assess the fidelity of Fialetti's map we need, first of all, to understand the genesis and urban form of Venice itself. As Chapter 2 of this book shows, the creation of the city involved a sustained programme of land reclamation. This arduous process led to the perception

1. Introducing Fialetti's View of Venice

DEBORAH HOWARD AND HENRIETTA MCBURNEY

THE CITY OF VENICE holds a special place in the global imagination. This book explores the history of one of its largest surviving depictions, which has remained almost unknown to the wider public since its creation four centuries ago. Signed and dated 1611, the painting is the work of a notable early seventeenth-century Bolognese artist, Odoardo Fialetti (fig. 1).[1] His huge bird's-eye view of the watery townscape is enlivened by tiny vignettes of Venetian life. Eight square metres in size, this remarkable painting is a *tour-de-force* among depictions of cities.

In 1636 the painting was given to Eton College by the former British ambassador to Venice, Sir Henry Wotton. Over the centuries it was known only to pupils and masters at the school and their visitors, its surface obscured by layers of grime. Restored by conservator Ruth Bubb during 2010–11, Fialetti's painted bird's-eye view has emerged as a striking work of real artistic merit. Its prominent position in the British Museum's *Shakespeare* exhibition in the summer of 2012 brought it to the attention of the general public for the very first time.[2]

Our book sets this remarkable picture in the context of view-painting in Venice from Gentile Bellini to Canaletto, and attempts to find out more about it. Who was Odoardo Fialetti? What new evidence about the work has arisen from the recent conservation? How realistic was the view? Was it based on first-hand observation or collated from other views in paint and print? Who might have commissioned the image? How and why did Wotton acquire Fialetti's *View*, and what led him to donate it to Eton?

Sir Henry Wotton (fig. 2) was a notable figure in early seventeenth-century English culture. Appointed in 1604 and again subsequently, he became the first British ambassador to reside in Venice. He wrote an influential treatise on architecture, which offers valuable insights into his personal response to the townscape of Venice. From 1624 to his death in 1639 Wotton was Provost of Eton, and is buried in the College chapel. He seems to have collected works of art while in Venice, and in his will he bequeathed to Charles I four portraits of doges attributed to Fialetti (see Chapters 7 and 10 below).[3] Yet many questions surround his involvement with the Eton *View of Venice*, and his contribution to architectural debates in early Stuart England has been little explored.

The arrival of this huge picture in England marks a crucial stage in the transmission of culture between Venice and the British Isles. This was a momentous period in the history of the Venetian Republic. Over the centuries, the Serenissima had forged a precarious strategy of independence from the Catholic Church, seeking to retain control over local religious affairs. Matters came to a head in 1606, when Pope Paul V placed the Republic under interdict. Wotton's personal interest in the affair is clear from the fact that he acquired a portrait of the leader of the Republic's inflexible stance, Fra Paolo Sarpi, for Lord Salisbury (see fig. 102).[4] As this book will suggest, aspects of Fialetti's *View* seem to reflect a particular religious standpoint.

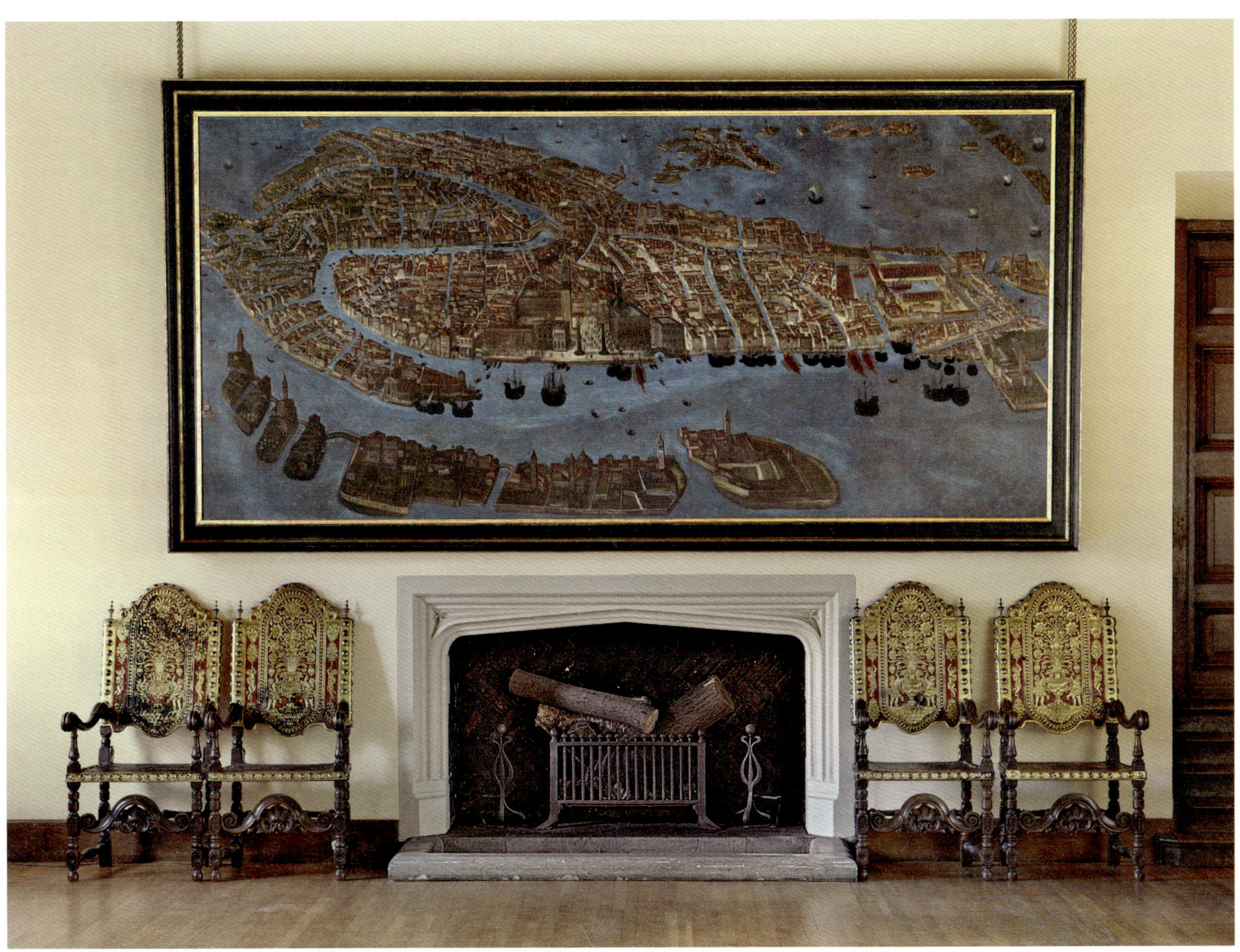

3
Eton College, Election Hall, south wall,
showing Fialetti's *View* (see fig. 1)

ACKNOWLEDGMENTS

We are grateful to a number of people at Eton College for their support of the book. Lord Waldegrave, present Provost of Eton, has contributed the Foreword. Penny Hatfield, former College Archivist, Charlotte Villiers, Exhibitions and Outreach Co-ordinator, Lynn Sanders, Print Room Assistant, and Jackie Tarrant-Barton, Secretary of the Old Etonian Association, have given much help and support in different ways. Justin Nolan, Secretary of the Friends of the Collections, encouraged a lively interest in the book amongst the Friends.

The beautiful photography of the Fialetti *View* was undertaken while the painting was in the British Museum by Prudence Cuming photographers, London. Roddy Fisher kindly undertook photography of material at Eton and further photography was done by Dennis Wallis.

The editors and authors are grateful to the staff of the following institutions for their help and support in preparing the material for the book: Art Resource (Liz Kurtulik); Biblioteca Nazionale Marciana, Venice; the Bodleian Library, Oxford; the British Library (Permissions and Reproductions); the British Museum, Department of Prints and Drawings (Sheila O'Connell); Cameraphoto Arte, Venice (Piero Codato and Giorgio Santuzzo); the Hamilton Kerr Institute, University of Cambridge; Museo Correr, Venice (Archivio Fotografico); National Library of Sweden (Reprographic Services Department); the National Maritime Museum (Pieter van der Merwe); Peterhouse, Cambridge (Scott Mandelbrote); the Royal Collection (Karen Lawson, Agata Rutkowska, Adam Sammut, Chris Stevens and Lucy Whittaker); Trinity College, Cambridge (Sandy Paul); the University Library, Cambridge (Rare Books); and The Venice in Peril Fund.

Special thanks are due to Christina Anderson, Karen Hearn, Robert Hill, Maartje Van Gelder, Christopher Rowell and Timothy Wilks, who kindly read draft chapters and made valuable suggestions.

We are grateful to numerous other scholars, colleagues and friends who have generously shared information and given encouragement. These include: Eric and Poppy Anderson, Louise Anderson, Emma-Louise Bassett, Matteo Casini, Ian Cadell, Nicola Christie, Tracy Cooper, Brendan Cole, Frances, Lady Clarke, Francisca Crommelin, Sue Cruikshank, David Dallas, Filippo de Vivo, Patricia Fortini Brown, Jeremy Garfield-Davies, Giorgio Gianighian, Richard J. Goy, Lucy Gwynn, John Guinness, Karen Hearn, Anthony Hobson, Yolande Hodson, Jonathan Keates, Mary Laven, Catherine MacLeod, Joanna Marschner, Michael Meredith, Paola Pavanini, Paul Quarrie, Sarah Quill, Barley Roscoe, Juergen Schulz, Desmond Shawe-Taylor, Rebecca Tessier, Dora Thornton, Lilah Wayment and the late Charles Young.

DEBORAH HOWARD AND
HENRIETTA MCBURNEY
Cambridge, November 2013

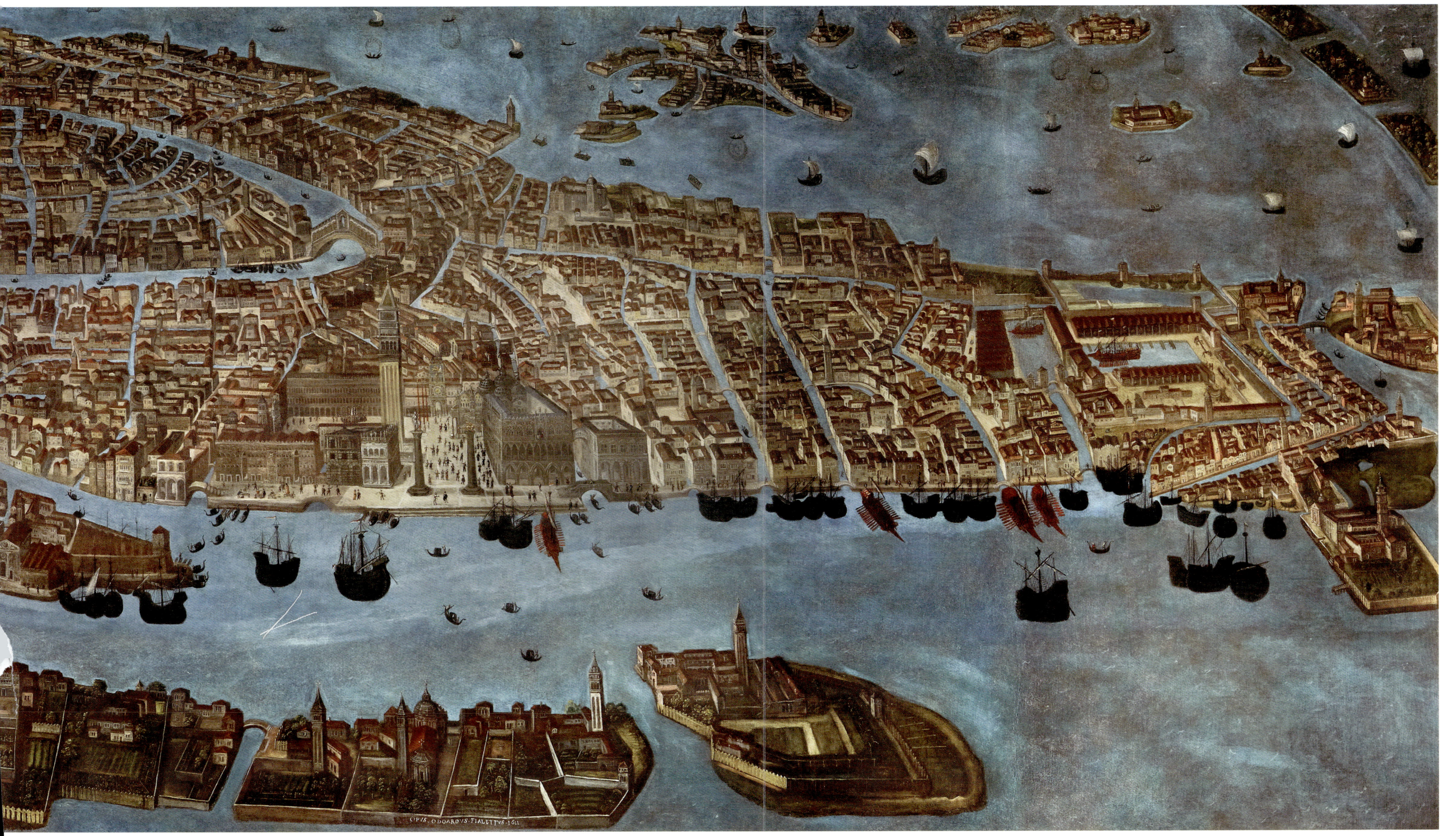

OPVS · ODOARDVS · FIALETTVS · 1611

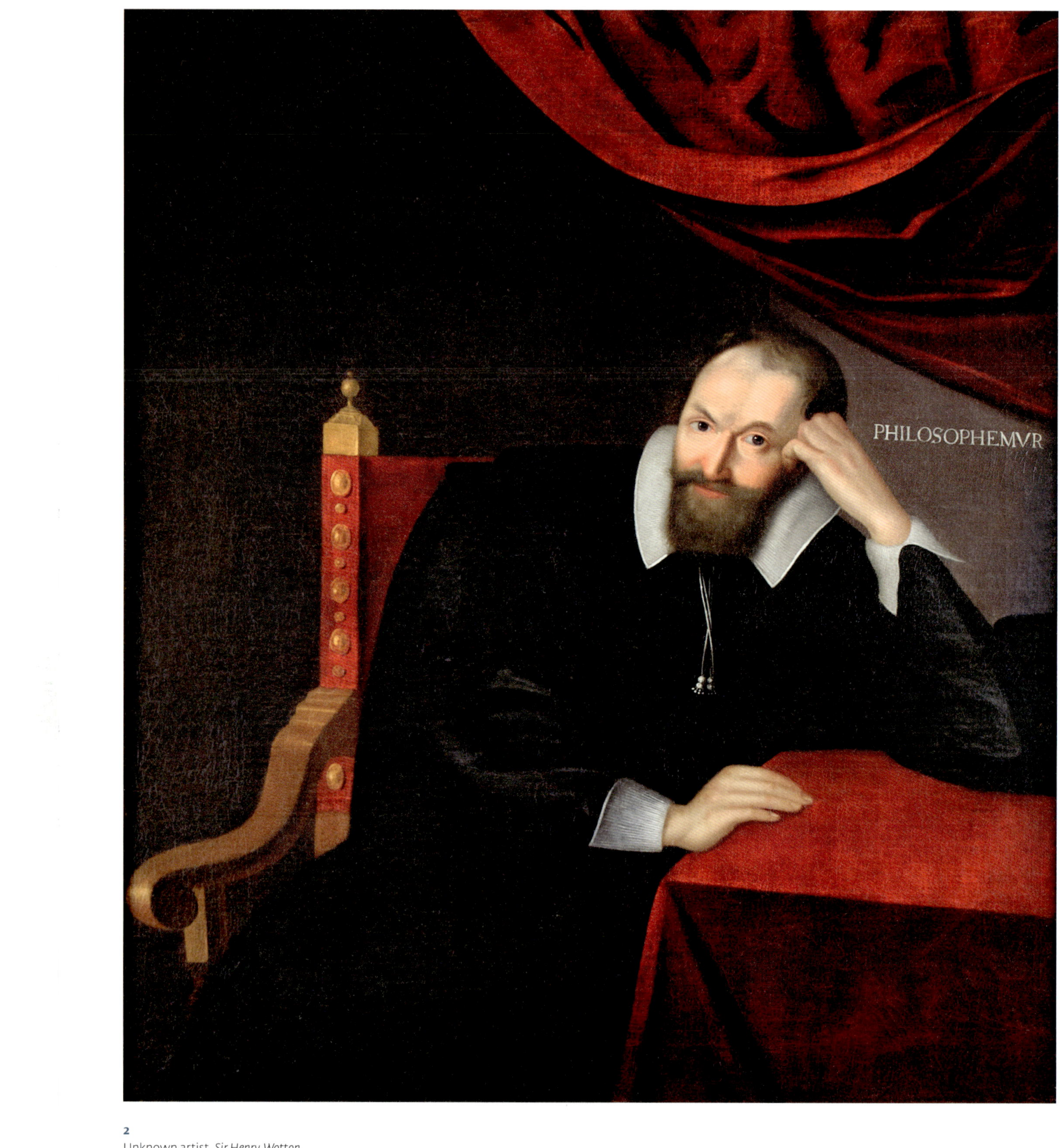

2
Unknown artist, *Sir Henry Wotton*,
c. 1625, oil on canvas, 128.5 x 111 cm
Eton College

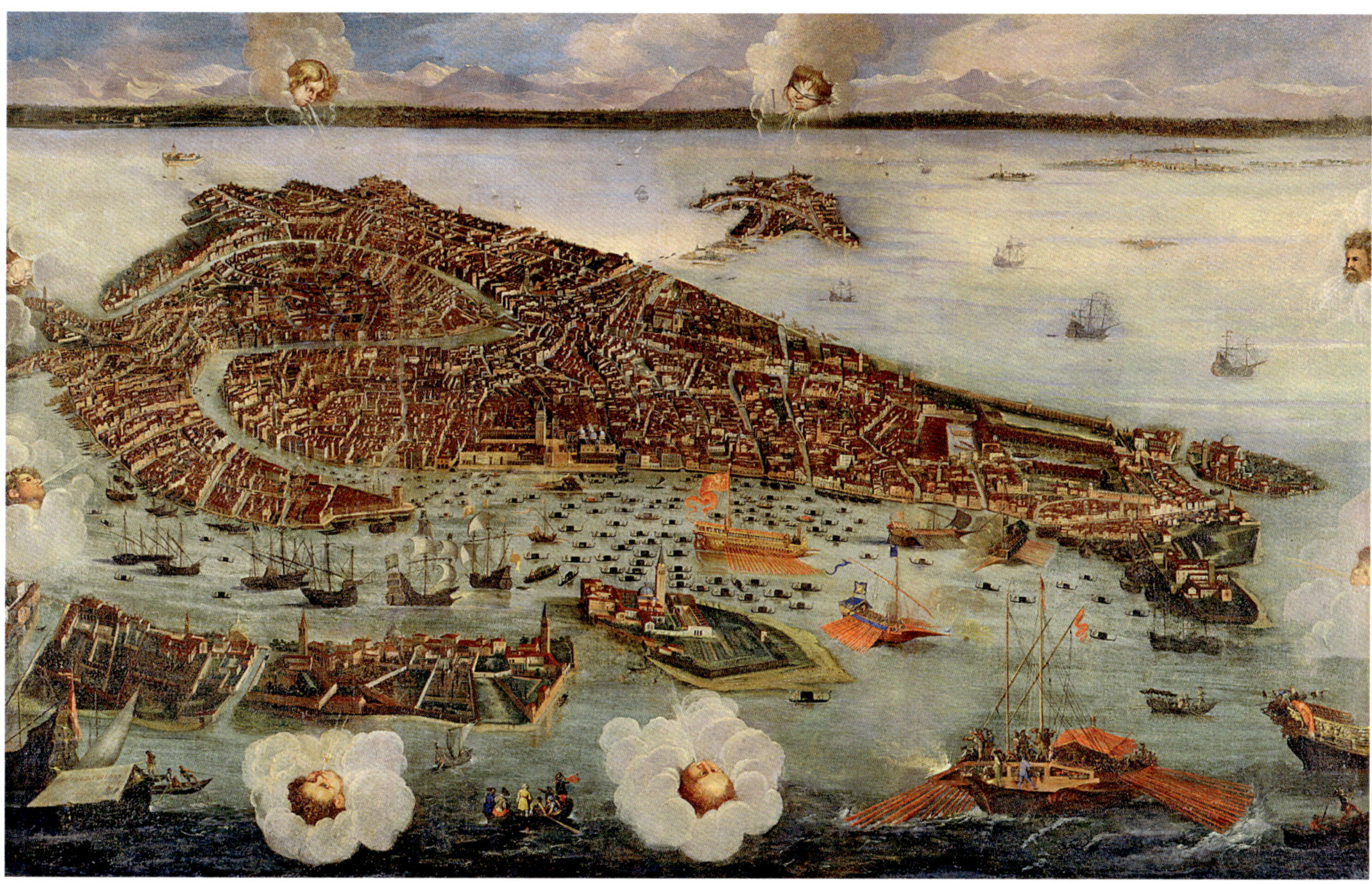

of Venice as a miraculous apparition rising from the waters of the lagoon.[9] Thus the challenging amphibious site engendered a deeply rooted fascination with the appearance of the townscape, inspiring meticulous descriptions in both text and image. During the meteoric rise of the Venetian printing industry over the course of the sixteenth century, these verbal and visual depictions proliferated, as Allison Sherman recounts. As a result, the widely circulated published representations became just as familiar as the city itself and created an alternative reality in the European mind.[10]

The slippery passage of recognisable features between maps and views and the real townscape conferred a flexible identity on Venice. Shapes and forms that seemed familiar from printed images might not exist in reality, but came to be regarded as essential landmarks. When Fialetti's *View* is compared with the real topography of Venice, many surprises emerge. Yet, to condemn the image for blatant inaccuracies would be to miss the point of its creation and subsequent impact.

In many respects, as Andrew Hopkins shows, the artist was cavalier in his depictions of famous buildings,

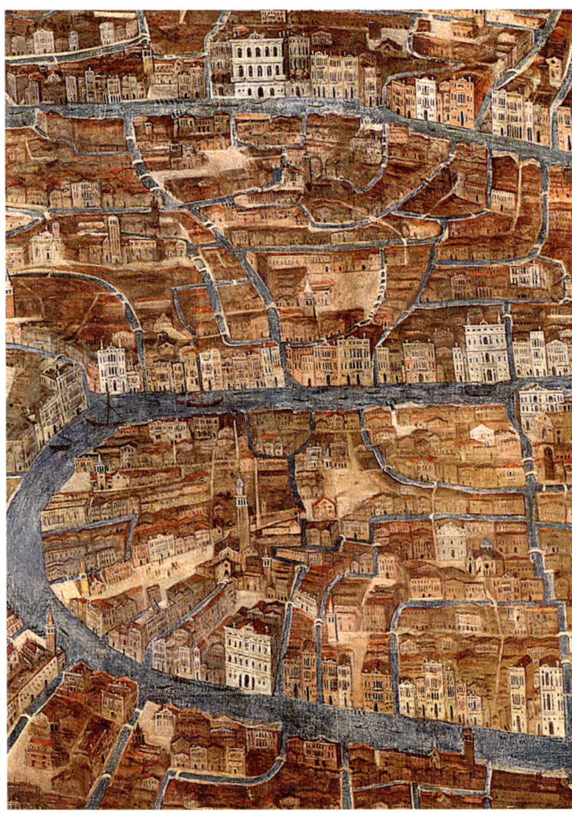

such as the newly constructed Zecca (Mint) and Library in Piazza San Marco. These major works of the Florentine architect Jacopo Sansovino are so inaccurately represented in the *View* that one wonders if Fialetti were merely painting them from memory. Yet they are instantly recognisable, the deviations from reality giving them a reductive simplicity that evidently served the purpose. As a printmaker of renown, Fialetti had easy access to the stocks of mapmakers, publishers and printers, and could use print collections as sources for reference in his studio.[11] Jacopo de' Barbari's bird's-eye view, first published on six huge sheets in 1500, provided the basic layout and many of the essential details (fig. 7), while other elements were updated using later variants of de' Barbari's view, such as that by Bernardo Salvioni published in 1597 (see fig. 51). Strangely, Fialetti represents the Rialto market as it is shown in Jacopo de' Barbari's view of 1500, ignoring its rebuilt appearance

7
Jacopo de' Barbari, *Bird's-eye-view map of Venice*,
woodcut on six sheets, 134.0 x 280.8 cm
London, British Museum

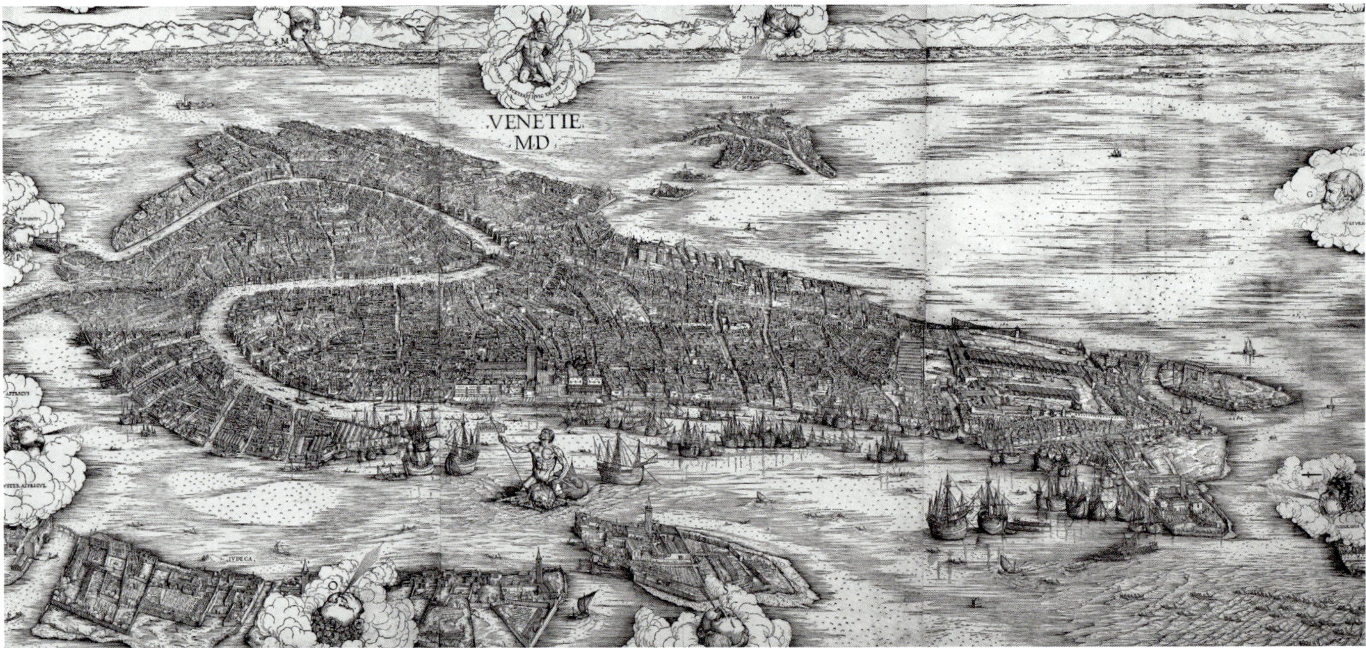

following a fire in 1514 (see figs. 85, 86). Anyone who visited the market would know its actual state, yet de' Barbari's depiction had become so familiar that it seemed instantly recognisable. At the same time, two of the latest additions to the townscape – the Bridge of Sighs and the Rialto Bridge – are carefully inserted into the (by now outdated) template of de' Barbari (see figs. 75, 84).

Some oddities in Fialetti's *View* seem to suggest clues about its patronage. For instance, as Hopkins shows, Andrea Palladio's two masterpieces, the churches of San Giorgio Maggiore and the Redentore, are completely ignored. It would appear, therefore, that the unknown patron was not a particular admirer of Palladio – or at least did not monitor the details of representation. San Giorgio is carefully copied from Jacopo de' Barbari's view made over a century earlier, although the whole church and much of the monastery had been rebuilt from the 1560s onwards. Indeed the monumental white classical façade of San Giorgio – visible across the water from Piazza San Marco – was completed in the very year of the execution of Fialetti's *View* (see figs. 77, 78). Perhaps even more surprisingly, the new church of the Redentore, founded in 1577 after a terrible plague epidemic, is absent, whereas the relatively modest Jesuit church on the opposite bank of the Giudecca canal is given exaggerated prominence (fig. 8). When one remembers that the Jesuits had been expelled from Venice following the Interdict of 1606, this is a curious choice – one that seems to suggest Jesuit or at least pro-Catholic sympathies in the patron. Fialetti's own religious affiliations give no clue, for in his series of engravings of the dress of the main Catholic religious orders (see figs. 57, 58) he gives equal treatment to the Jesuit order and to the Capuchins, who officiated at the Redentore. Some possible patrons among art agents and collectors are discussed in Chapter 7.

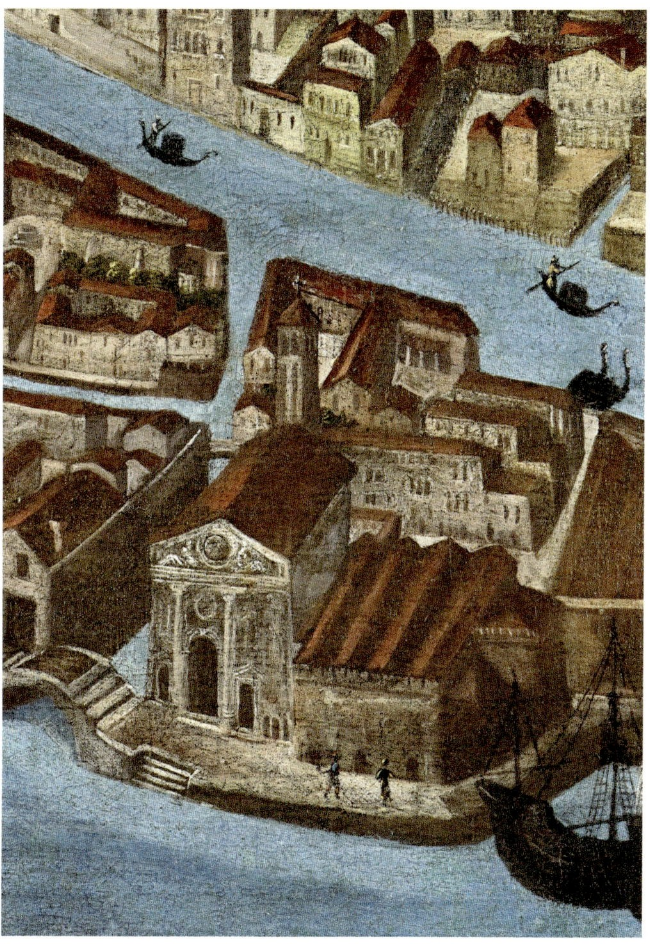

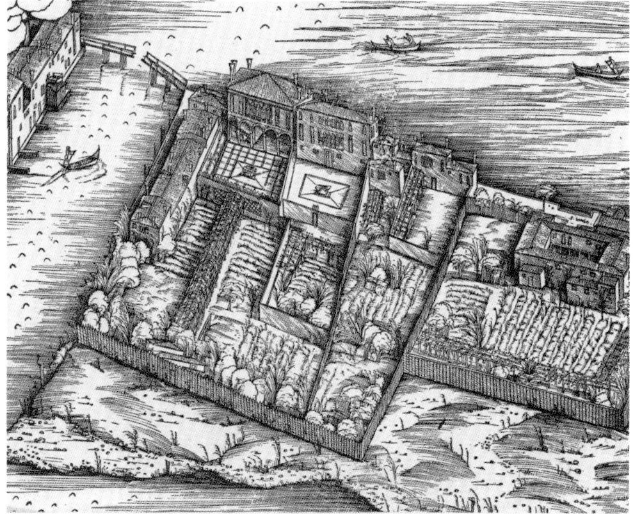

Fialetti's artistry

A number of essays in this volume discuss how, in his *View*, Fialetti borrowed from earlier map- and view-makers, above all, of course, from de' Barbari's woodcut. There is further discussion, especially by Hopkins, of the selectiveness of Fialetti's updating of the landmarks of the city, ignoring new buildings altogether or indicating their contemporary appearance in an abbreviated or shorthand way. In using and adapting the work of others to create his *View*, Fialetti was following a recognised practice, one described by Giovanni Battista Armenini, who in his drawing treatise stated that artists could borrow to create something original.[12] Fialetti adapted and combined elements from his models to create his own portrait – or *ritratto* – of the city, and the skilful ingenuity with which he does this is one of the hallmarks of his style.[13]

His *View* has variously been described as a 'view', 'bird's-eye view', or 'map', none of which terms is entirely accurate. To use more precise cartographic terminology, Fialetti, following the model provided by de' Barbari, adopts a 'high-oblique' view; that is to say his viewpoint is high (rather than medium or low), but without being vertical, in which case he would have created a map (or an aerial view) without the use of perspective.[14] Unlike de' Barbari, however (and indeed the other view painters of the period, Arzenti and Heintz), Fialetti varies the scale, painting the area of San Marco on a larger one than the rest of the city. The effect

of its buildings appearing more prominent than those of the surrounding townscape is to draw the eye in to the area of St Mark's, emphasizing its 'stage set' qualities and inviting the viewer to 'enter' into this part of the city and its drama. In the same way, Da Ponte's new Rialto Bridge is given prominence by being depicted on an enlarged scale (both the Piazzetta San Marco and the Rialto Bridge had appeared in vignettes in Salvioni's map of *c.* 1597). The features of the Giudecca, being in the foreground of the painting and therefore closest to the viewer, are shown in greater detail than other parts of the city. The spectator looks down into ordered plots with squares quartered by paths, some with a simple fountain or well in the centre, tunnel arbours and pergolas, and orchard trees trained against walls (fig. 10). Here Fialetti follows de' Barbari (fig. 9) very closely, but transforms the woodcut template into a vivid, coloured scene.

In a conscious adaptation of the de' Barbari model, Fialetti populates that artist's empty stage with figures – tiny vignettes of bystanders, gondoliers, street-traders and actors. Naturally the main activity is in the most public arena, the Piazza and Piazzetta of San Marco, and here courtesans, foreign dignitaries wearing turbans, merchants, and others meet, converse, promenade and cluster around a theatrical show (fig. 11). While some of these would seem to be of Fialetti's own invention, Giacomo Franco's *Habiti d'huomini et donne venetiane* (1610) clearly provided the models for others. A leaping dog, reminiscent of one shown racing across the Piazza in front of the Doge's Palace in one of Franco's plates, adds to the movement and bustle (figs. 12–13). On the Molo in front of the Mint the figures with objects spread out on trestles appear to be merchants with their wares or money-changers, or possibly lawyers with their stalls for drawing up contracts (fig. 16). A man in long robes and a turban standing on a low platform may be a mountebank with a small figure, perhaps a dwarf, close by; two

10
Fialetti's *View*, detail showing villas
and gardens on the Giudecca

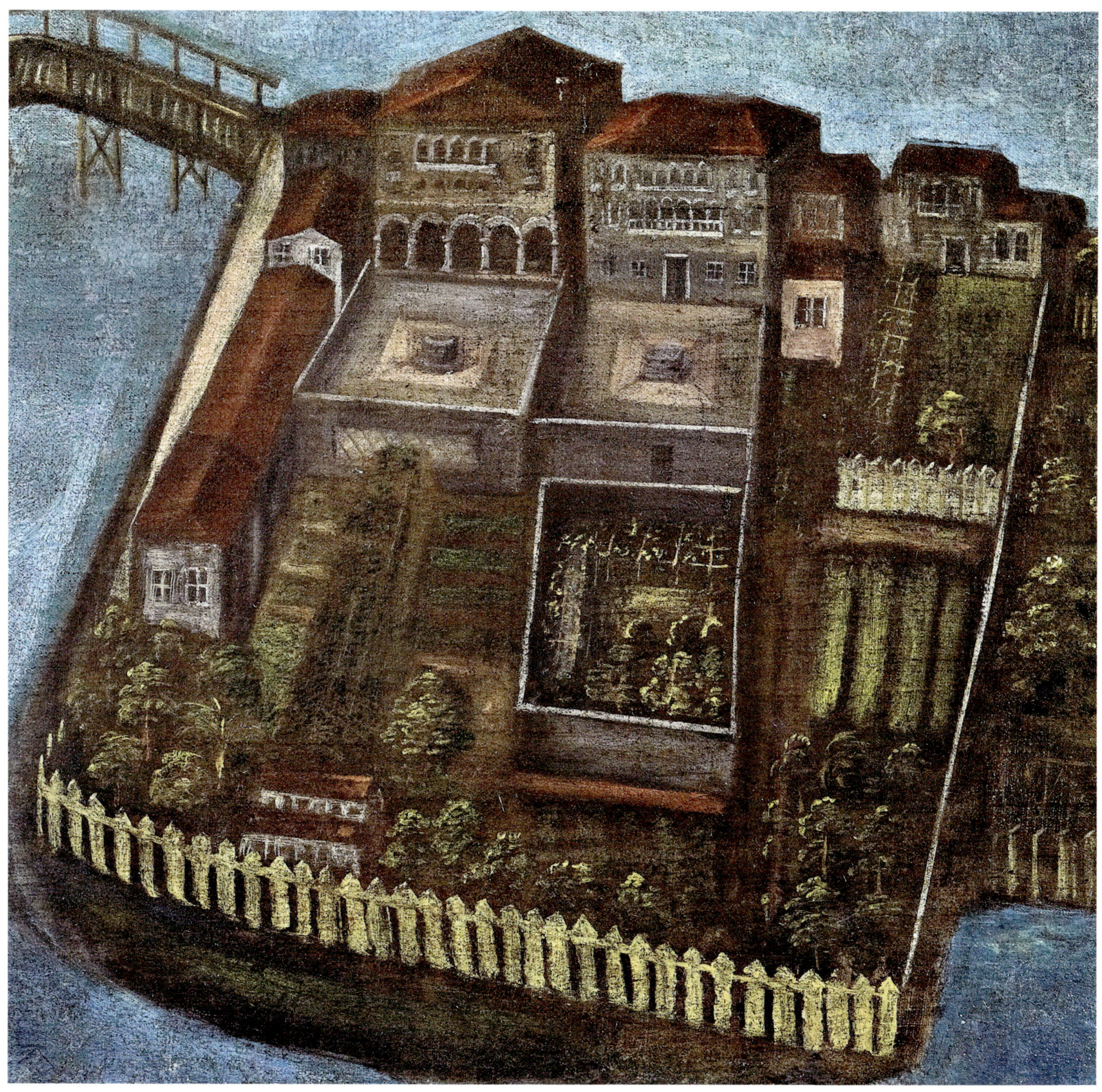

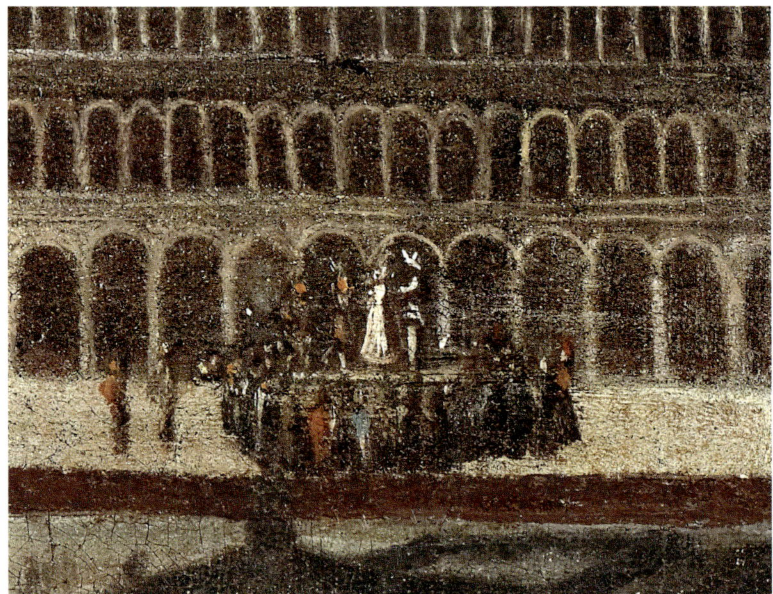

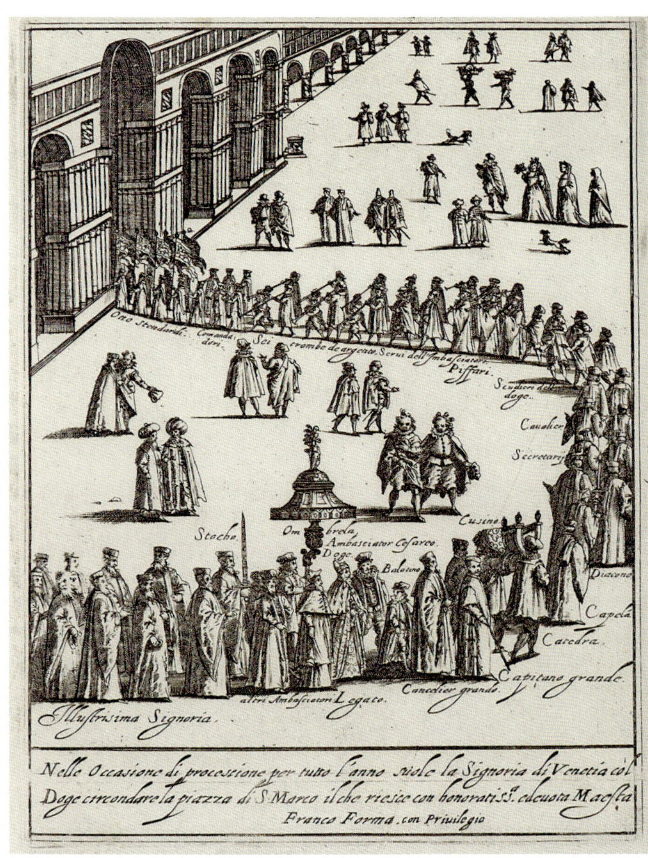

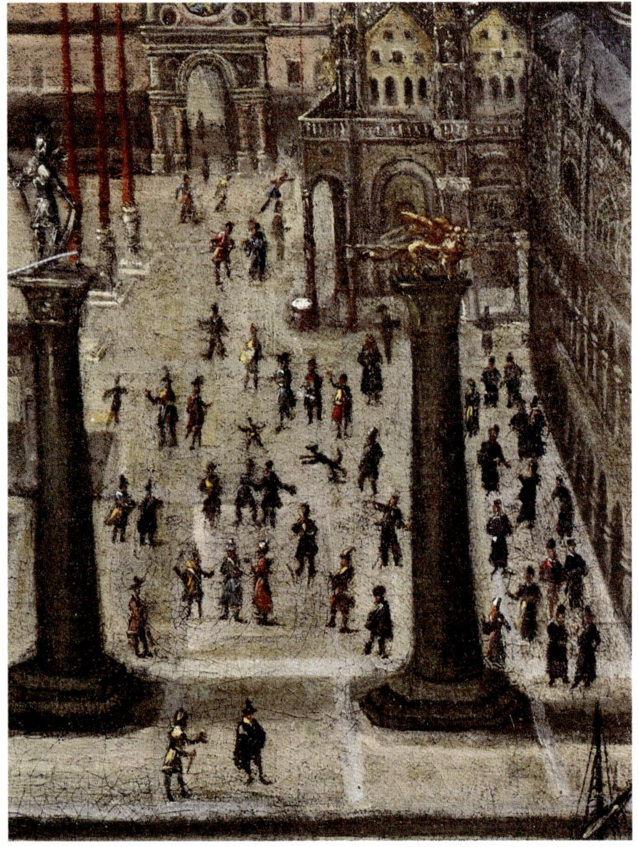

   DEBORAH HOWARD AND HENRIETTA MCBURNEY

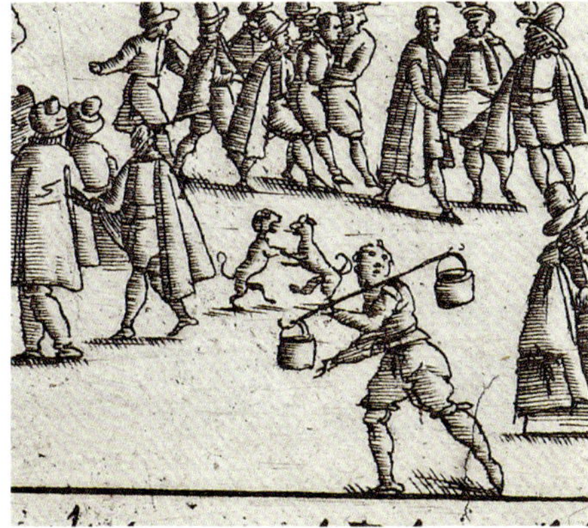

14
Giacomo Franco, *Nelle occasione di processione …
[nel]la piazza di S. Marco*, etching from *Habiti d'huomini et
donne venetiane*, Venice, 1610, detail showing a man with
buckets on a yoke

15, 16
Fialetti's *View*, details showing a man with buckets
on a yoke, and commerce on the Molo

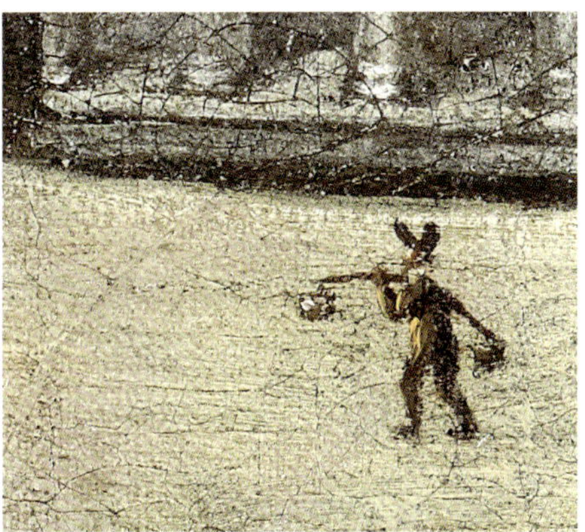

tradesmen with baskets or buckets hung either end
of yokes echo again a detail in one of Franco's scenes
(figs. 14 and 15), as does another carrying his load on his
head. A splash of red on the façade of the Doge's Palace
draws the eye to two figures on the balcony.

Human activity appears elsewhere in the city,
where people promenade on *rive* (fig. 75), look out from
the arches of the Rialto (see fig. 85), and hurry across
Campo Santo Stefano (fig. 17). The many varieties of
watercraft shown in the lagoon and on the canals are
equally populated by gondoliers, sailors, rowers and
passengers. The ships (*navi*) consist mainly of three-
masted merchantmen of 'carrack' form; some smaller
single-masted square-riggers (originally called *coche*,
this rig being derived from earlier northern 'cogs');

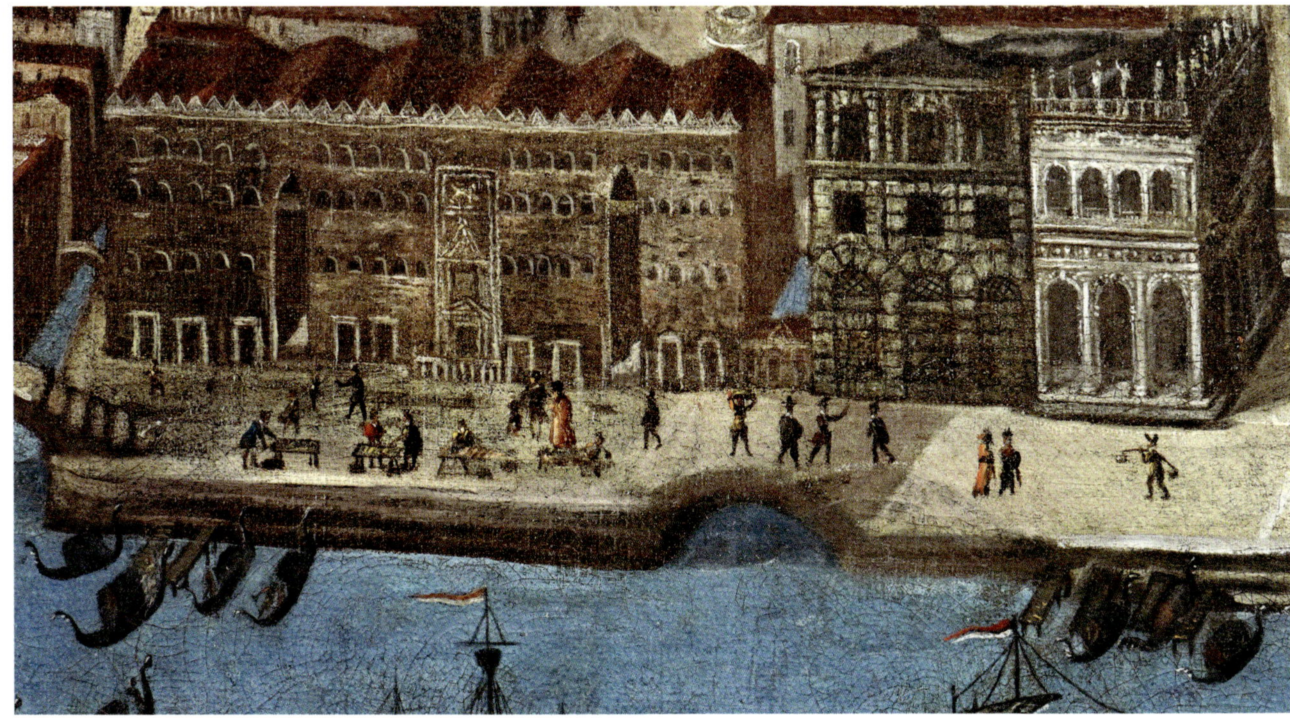

war galleys (mostly single-masted although there is one two-master); and different types of gondola.[15] The influence of Franco's engravings can be seen in the covered gondolas, where grander passengers can be glimpsed protected from the weather in the cabins or *felze* (figs. 18 and 19). The other boats are quite old-fashioned for the date of the painting. These elements, too, can be seen to have been taken from the earlier sixteenth-century printed views, particularly Pagan's 1559 view for the 'carracks', many seen end-on, giving their distinctive round appearance (*navi rotonde*); the galleys, meanwhile, were apparently taken un-adapted from Forlani's 1566 view, so that even

though Fialetti shows them all moored – in front of the Doge's Palace on the Molo and further to the east along the Riva degli Schiavoni and Ca' di Dio and in the Arsenale – they are depicted with their oars out, not stowed (fig. 89). In the Arsenale shipbuilders are at work at their saw benches with a half-built *nave rotonda* nearby, and boats can be seen laid up in sheds. The stylized images of fishermen with their circular nets – some containing fish – spread out in arcs from their boats, are, as Bubb points out, taken from Pagan's 1559 *View* (figs. 45, 64). Just as Fialetti, in his landscape prints, shows labouring farmers and peasants who provide not only human interest but a sense of scale in the natural

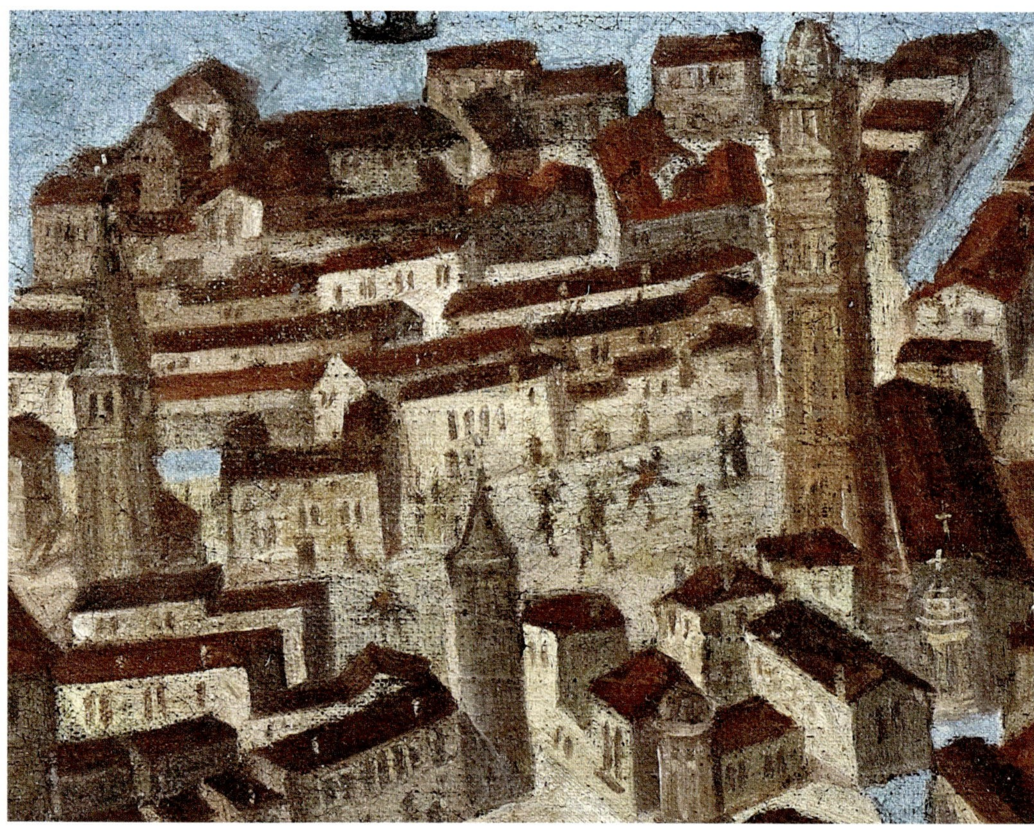

  DEBORAH HOWARD AND HENRIETTA MCBURNEY

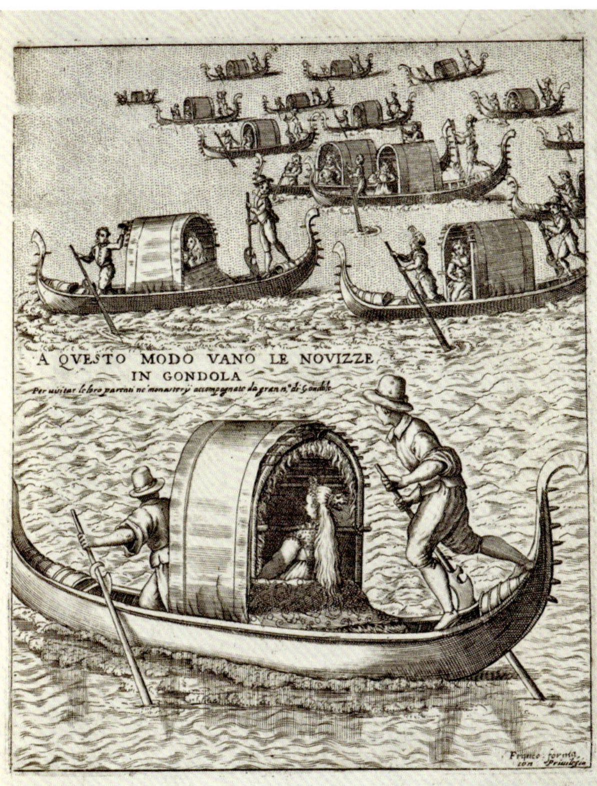

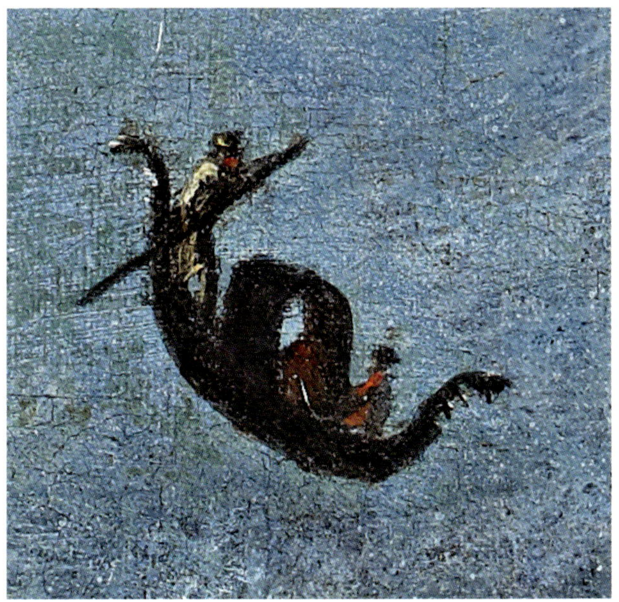

world (see figs. 60, 61), so the figures he adds to the artificial landscape of the Venetian archipelago help create the impression of a peopled stage, where human activity of every sort is taking place in and around the buildings, squares, bridges and boats that make up the extraordinary cityscape.

An important dimension of Fialetti's *View* was obliterated when the areas of water were covered with overpainting at a later stage in its history.[16] As Bubb reveals, Fialetti employed two different pigments of blue – indigo and smalt – in varying tones in order to re-create the varying depths and patterns of the water channels of the lagoon (fig. 1). In this way he gives the water a distinctive character of its own. Further revealed under the overpainting were wispy touches of very light blue paint applied over the darker blue pigment, indicating movement on the surface of the water – a technique which was to become familiar in the works of the eighteenth-century *vedutisti* such as Guardi and Canaletto (figs. 20 and 21). But as the first to produce such 'bird's-eye' views of Venice in colour, Fialetti had no model to follow and his innovative interpretation of the water as part of the essential spirit of the city is one of the most dramatic aspects of his creation.[17] In none of the earlier portraits of the city had the interdependence of the water and architecture been so vividly conveyed.

In 1608, Wotton described a portrait of Doge Leonardo Donà which he had sent from Venice to Robert Cecil, Earl of Salisbury, as "done truly and naturally but roughly *alla Venetiana*".[18] While he does not specify the artist, it has generally been assumed that Wotton had commissioned the likeness from Fialetti,[19] just as the four portraits of doges acquired for his own collection have, following Wotton's own attributions, traditionally been attributed to Fialetti (figs. 93, 97–100).[20] Even though we cannot verify Fialetti's authorship of the portrait he sent to Cecil,[21] Wotton's description of its style of execution

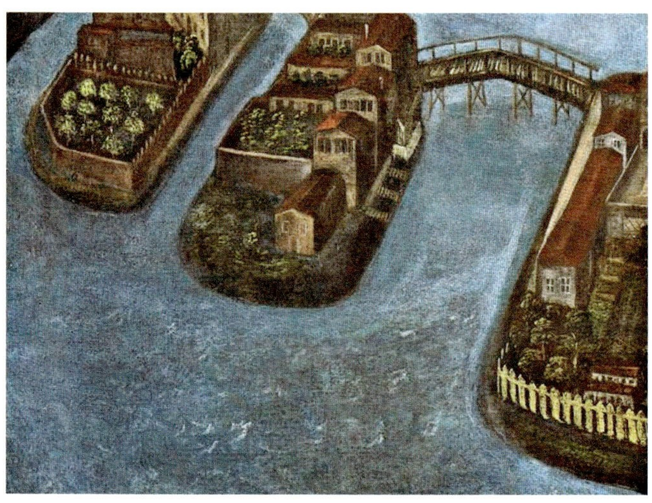

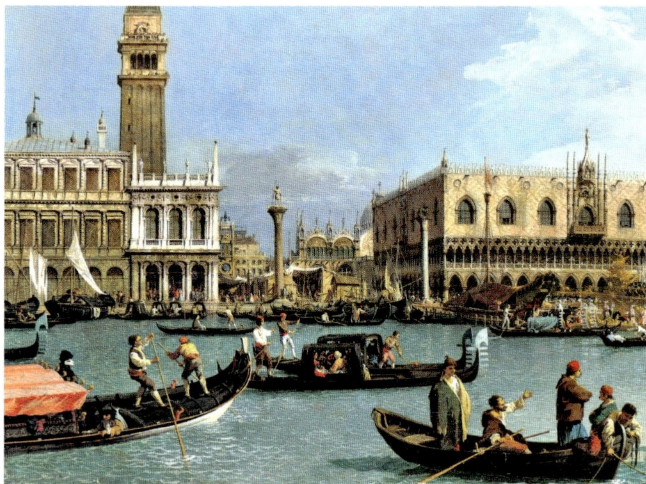

seems to fit Fialetti's as we know it from his *View*, from the handful of his paintings in Venetian churches and from the large body of his etchings.[22] Further describing the portrait of Doge Leonardo Donà, Wotton notes that it should "be set at some good distance from the sight", suggesting an impressionistic handling rather than one with a meticulous rendering of detail.[23]

Such characteristics could well be applied to Fialetti's painted *View of Venice*, which demonstrates his "free sketchiness", and execution "in a forthright, relatively unsophisticated way".[24] In it, as we have seen, he ingeniously puts together elements taken from earlier and contemporary printed views and scenes of Venetian life to create his own portrait – or memorial – of the city. Topographical accuracy was not his aim; rather he imbues the physical forms – both man-made and natural – with vitality and expressiveness to capture the unique essence of the "city that seems to float".

NOTES

1   For a brief summary of Fialetti's career, see
    F. Benvenuti, 'Fialetti, Odoardo', *The Dictionary
    of Art*, ed. J.S. Turner, 34 vols., London, 1996, XI,
    p. 51. He was inscribed in the Venetian painters'
    guild from 1604 to 1612; see E. Favaro, *L'arte dei
    pittori in Venezia e I suoi statuti*, Florence, 1975,
    p. 151. Two unpublished dissertations discuss
    Fialetti's career: S. Canella, 'Odoardo Fialetti,
    1573–1638', tesi di laurea, Padua University,
    1974–75 (supervisor: Rodolfo Pallucchini); L.M.
    Walters, 'Odoardo Fialetti: The Interrelation
    of Venetian Art and Anatomy, and his
    Importance in England (1573– c.1638)', PhD
    thesis, University of St Andrews, 2009
    (supervisor: Peter Humfrey); see further
    Chapter 4 by Laura Walters in this book.

2   J. Bate and D. Thornton, *Shakespeare: Staging
    the World*, exh. cat., London, 2012, pp. 148–49,
    291. Fialetti's *View* was mentioned in L. Pearsall
    Smith, *The Life and Letters of Sir Henry Wotton*,
    Oxford, 2 vols., 1907, II, p. 210. It was first
    published by M. Azzi Visentini, 'Ancora
    un'inedita pianta prospettica di Venezia in un
    dipinto di Odoardo Fialetti per Sir Henry
    Wotton', *Bollettino dei musei civici veneziani*, 35/1,
    1980, pp. 19–25; she remarked (p. 19) that it
    was "astonishing" that the work had not before
    received scholarly attention. The view was
    again mentioned and illustrated in F. Panzarin,
    'Il collezionismo inglese a Venezia nel Seicento:
    Henry Wotton letterato, agente, collezionista,
    mecenate e il suo rapporto con Odoardo
    Fialetti, *Arte in Friuli, Arte a Trieste*, vol. 20,
    2000, pp. 37–60, on p. 38, and p. 43, fig. 5.
    In 1990 it was lent to the exhibition *Leonardo
    e Venezia* at the Palazzo Grassi, Venice (G. Nepi
    Sciré, P.C. Marani *et al.*, *Leonardo e Venezia*, exh.
    cat., Palazzo Grassi, Venice, pp. 420–21).

3   See Chapter 7.

4   R. Hill, 'Art and Patronage', in M. Keblusek and
    B.V. Noldus (eds.), *Double Agents: Cultural
    and Political Brokerage in Early Modern Europe*,
    Leiden, 2011, pp. 28–29. On Wotton's reaction
    to the Interdict, see Chapter 8 below.

5   M. Azzi Visentini, 'Venezia in una sconosciuta
    veduta a volo d'uccello del Seicento', *Antichità
    viva*, 18/4, 1979, pp. 31–38.

6   M. Bourne, 'Francesco II Gonzaga and Maps
    as Palace Decoration in Renaissance
    Mantua', *Imago Mundi*, vol. 51, 1999, pp. 81–52;
    F. Ceccarelli and N. Aksamija (eds.), *La Sala
    Bologna nei Palazzi Vaticani: Architettura,
    cartografia e potere nell'età di Gregorio XIII*,
    Venice, 2011; on European city views in general
    see C. de Seta (ed.), *L'immagine della città
    europea dal Rinascimento al secolo dei Lumi*,
    exh. cat., Museo Correr, Venice, 2014.

7   Azzi Visentini, 'Venezia in una sconosciuta
    veduta', p. 31, claims that Heintz omits the
    Redentore, but in fact he shows both the
    Zitelle and the Redentore on the two
    easternmost islands of the Giudecca.

8   This fine painted view, 190 x 410 cm, now in the
    Abegg-Stiftung of Riggisberg, Bern, is based
    on Merlo's woodcut view of 1660, with later
    insertions. See Azzi Visentini, 'Venezia in una
    sconosciuta veduta', *passim*.

9   A recent study of this perception of the
    miraculous qualities of the city is D. Savoy,
    Venice from the Water, New Haven and London,
    2012.

10 See B. Wilson, *The World in Venice: Print, the City
    and Early Modern Identity*, Toronto, Buffalo and
    London, 2005.

11 Fialetti published some of his etchings himself,
    but also worked for other print-sellers in
    Venice, such as Justus Sadeler. See M. Bury, *The
    Print in Italy 1550–1620*, exh. cat., London, 2001,
    pp. 174–75.

12 G.B. Armenini, *De' veri precetti della pittura*,
    Ravenna, 1586. Inigo Jones, for example, was
    known for his use of other artists' prints in
    creating his stage sets.

13 Jessica Maier discusses the shared terminology
    of *ritratto* for city as well as human portraits: 'A
    "True Likeness": the Renaissance City Portrait',
    in *Renaissance Quarterly*, 65, 2012, pp. 711–52.

14 Yolande Hodson (written communication)
    kindly provided the terminology she has
    adapted from air photography to describe

antiquarian cartography. The Italian terms
'*veduta prospettica*' (perspective view), '*pianta
prospettica*' (perspective plan/map), and '*pianta
topografica*' (topographical plan) are equivalent
to medium-low oblique view, high oblique
view, and map or aerial view.

15 Pieter van der Merwe (written communication)
    kindly provided information on the watercraft.
    He notes that "by this time galleys were using
    mainly enforced labour which were rowed
    '*a scaloccio*' – that is three men on one bench
    with one oar, requiring less skill than the
    earlier practice of three men, each with an
    oar, on one bench '*alla sensile*'".

16 Possibly applied in the mid nineteenth
    century: see p. 143 below.

17 Ironically it was this pioneering aspect of
    Fialetti's *View* that was the very element
    covered over, reducing the painting in the
    process to a flat, somewhat lifeless scene.

18 Pearsall Smith, *Life and Letters*, I, pp. 419–20.

19 See Chaney, *Evolution of the Grand Tour*, 2007,
    p. 207.

20 See Chapter 7 for the re-attribution of these
    portraits.

21 Disappointingly, as with the majority of works
    sent by Wotton to Salisbury, the portrait of the
    doge cannot be traced in Salisbury's collection:
    see S. Bracken, 'The Early Cecils and Italianate
    Taste', in Edward Chaney (ed.), *The Evolution of
    English Collecting: The Reception of Italian Art in
    the Tudor and Stuart Periods*, New Haven and
    London 1993, pp. 201–19, at p. 208 (noting that
    "puzzlingly, of those [paintings] which can be
    directly traced to [Wotton], none appears in
    the inventories taken in Salisbury's lifetime");
    Hill, 'Art and Patronage', p. 32.

22 Fialetti's works are discussed by Walters in
    Chapter 4.

23 See discussion of portrait of Doge Grimani
    (fig. 97) on p. 104.

24 For these descriptions used of Fialetti's
    etchings see S.W. Reed and R. Wallace, *Italian
    Etchers of the Renaissance and Baroque*, exh. cat.,
    Boston, 1989, pp. 248–51.

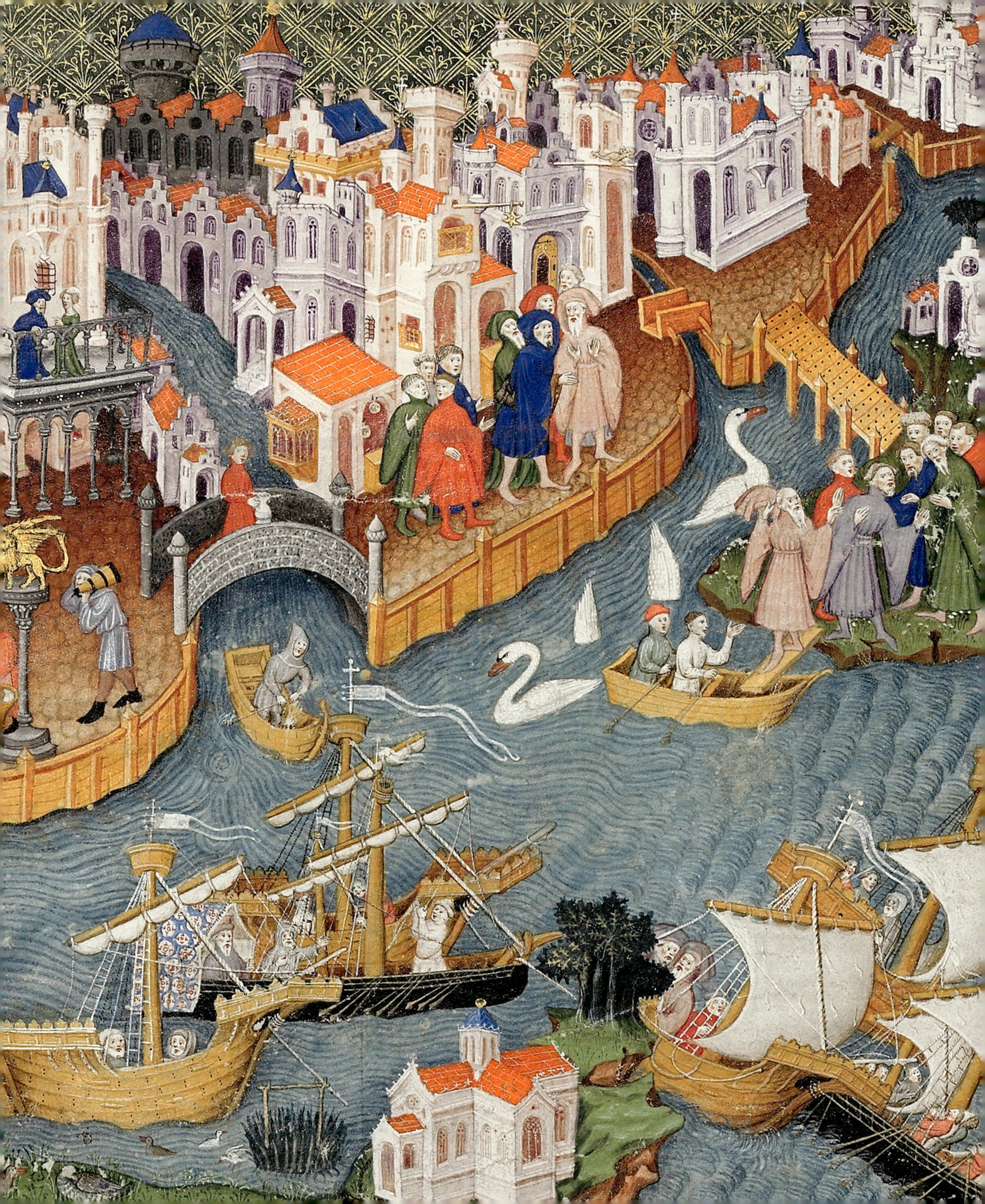

2. Venice: Reality and Representation

DEBORAH HOWARD

As we sailed further on, we found before our eyes the famous, great, wealthy and noble city of Venice, the mistress of the Mediterranean, standing in wondrous fashion in the midst of the waters, with lofty towers, great churches, splendid houses and palaces. We were astonished to see such weighty and such tall structures with their foundations in the water.
(German pilgrim Felix Faber, 1483)[1]

BORN FROM THE WAVES LIKE VENUS, Venice has always seemed a miraculous apparition, but in fact the site is largely a man-made creation. The city lies in a shallow lagoon, protected from the sea by the *lidi*, or long sand-spits, now best-known for their beaches. The area was already inhabited in Roman times. The early dwellers settled on an archipelago of small marshy islands, separated by large tracts of open, shallow water.[2] As the Roman Empire disintegrated during the fifth century, an influx of refugees from the mainland swelled the population. Early chronicles date the foundation of Venice to the year AD 421, on 25 March, the Feast of the Annunciation to the Virgin. This foundation myth propagated Venetian pride in their Roman ancestry – some versions of the legend even claimed Trojan origins.[3] The city also evolved a rich iconography incorporating attributes of the Virgin Mary, as well as those of classical deities such as Venus, Mercury and Neptune.[4]

In AD 537, the Roman official Cassiodorus remarked that the Venetians lived on a diet of fish like "aquatic birds, now on sea, now on land" and made their living

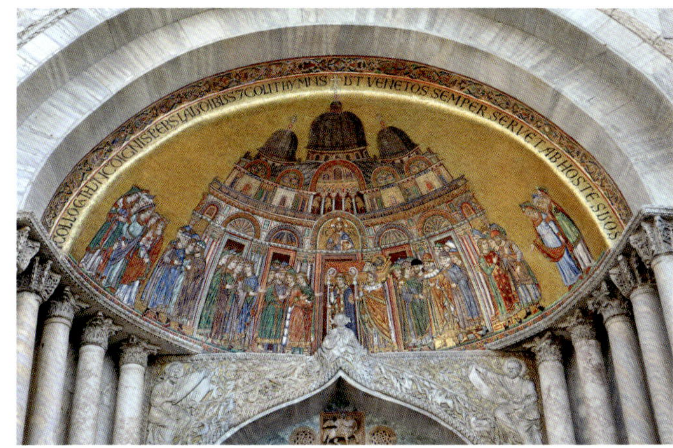

23
The Arrival of the Body of St Mark in Venice in AD 828/29, mosaic, 13th century, above left-hand portal of façade, Venice, San Marco

by extracting salt from the sea.[5] By the seventh century, when the cathedral of Torcello was founded, Venice was a distant colony of the Byzantine Empire. As Mediterranean trade expanded the settlement grew, thanks to the sheltered moorings and the easily defended site.[6] The acquisition of the body of St Mark, smuggled out of Alexandria by merchants in the year AD 828/29, suggests that the presence of Venetians in Eastern Mediterranean ports was already commonplace (fig. 23). The adoption of the Evangelist as the new patron saint marks the beginning of Venice's gradual breakaway from Byzantine domination.

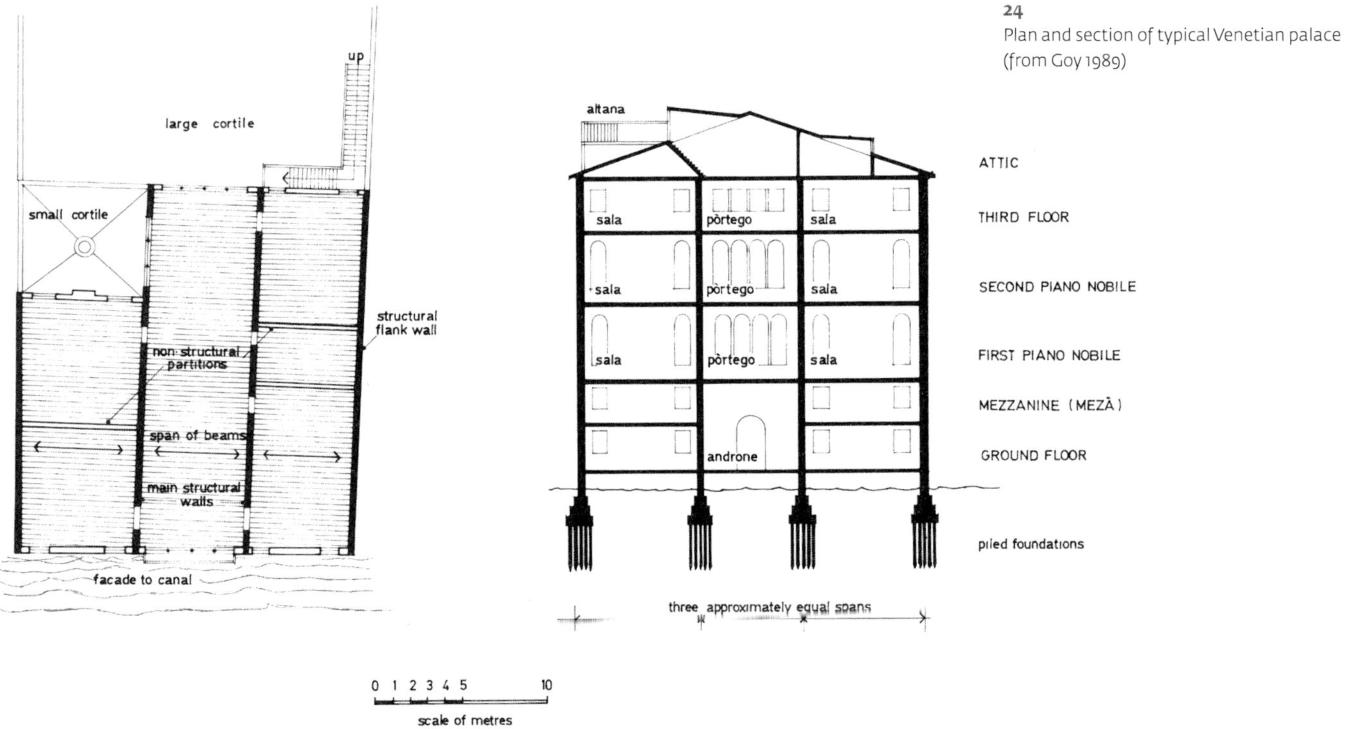

24
Plan and section of typical Venetian palace
(from Goy 1989)

By the end of the first millennium, a group of marshy islands, centred on Piazza San Marco and the Rialto, formed the core of the future city, but there were still extensive tracts of open water separating the settlements. Each of the islands became a parish of the city, its church facing an open grassy space or *campo*, literally a field. From this time on, land was wrested from the water by a long and arduous process of land reclamation. The fringes of each island were consolidated, filled in and built up, until the seventy parishes began to coalesce into a coherent land-mass surrounded by the brackish, tidal waters of the lagoon. As soon as the city acquired a more compact form, streets began to link the various islands to create a continuous network for pedestrians, while the waterways continued to carry heavy loads – as today.[7]

Although the Italian word for land reclamation, *bonìfica,* suggests a benign procedure, the process was in fact hard-earned and expensive. Each site had to be surrounded by a wooden retaining wall so that the water could be pumped out and the area filled with rubble and mud dredged from the canals to prepare the site for building. The Venetian state soon realised that the waterways and public throroughfares had to be protected from encroachment by private landowners, and insisted that all reclamation schemes had to gain official approval.[8] This is a crucial point, for it gave the Republic the power to determine the shape of the city as it grew. Reclamation could be encouraged in certain areas and prevented in others, not only to protect trade and water circulation, but also to enhance the layout of the city.

It needs to be stressed that the terrain is very poorly suited to building, and only through centuries of trial and error did the city's *proti* or building experts evolve a technology able to support large-scale masonry structures.[9] The subsoil is a mixture of poorly consolidated sand and mud, through which the tide rises and falls twice daily, creating constant movement in the foundations. The load-bearing walls of heavy buildings are supported on wooden piles, but there is no firm ground in which to root the foundations, so that, in effect, the structures 'float' on wet, mobile mud and sand (fig. 24). In consequence, the weight has to be very evenly balanced and the structures need a certain elasticity to withstand movement. To make matters worse, the materials have to resist the humid conditions and the incursions of exceptionally high tides.

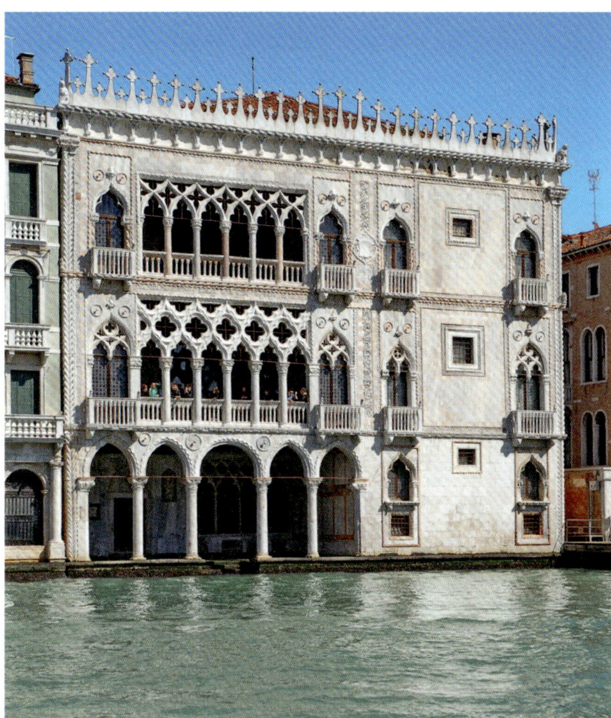

creating a negative version of their day-time appearance. The waterborne spectator, observing the townscape from a constantly moving viewpoint, easily submitted to reverie. As Dickens remarked of Piazza San Marco in a letter of 1844, "Enchantment couldn't shadow it forth in a vision".[10]

It is the subjectivity of perception that forms the central theme of this book. Each person views the city from the perspective of personal experience, tempered by the mood of the moment. Every detail is assimilated by analogy with comparable elements from the viewer's own geographical repertoire. Each spectator compiles an

In the face of such challenges, the magical face of the city conceals the phenomenal effort and ingenuity underlying its creation. This sense of insubstantiality is enhanced by the perforated wall surfaces. The well-defended site allowed a transparency in the façades of important buildings such as the Doge's Palace that would be unthinkable on the Italian mainland. Many early palace frontages are remarkable for their filigree lightness, made possible by the fact that the load-bearing walls run perpendicular to the façades (fig. 25). The crisp whiteness of the limestone, imported from nearby Istria, gives a lacy quality to the traceries, while the large windows are a measure of the plentiful supply of locally manufactured glass.

The shimmering quality of the amphibious townscape gives a further sense of impermanence to the mirage: reflections from the water ripple on the walls of buildings and on the undersides of bridges, and incrustations of glistening marbles intensify the luminosity. Inside, in earlier centuries, light was refracted through the small disc-like window panes, allowing sunlight to dapple the highly polished terrazzo floors. At night the Murano glass chandeliers lit up the palaces like magic lanterns,

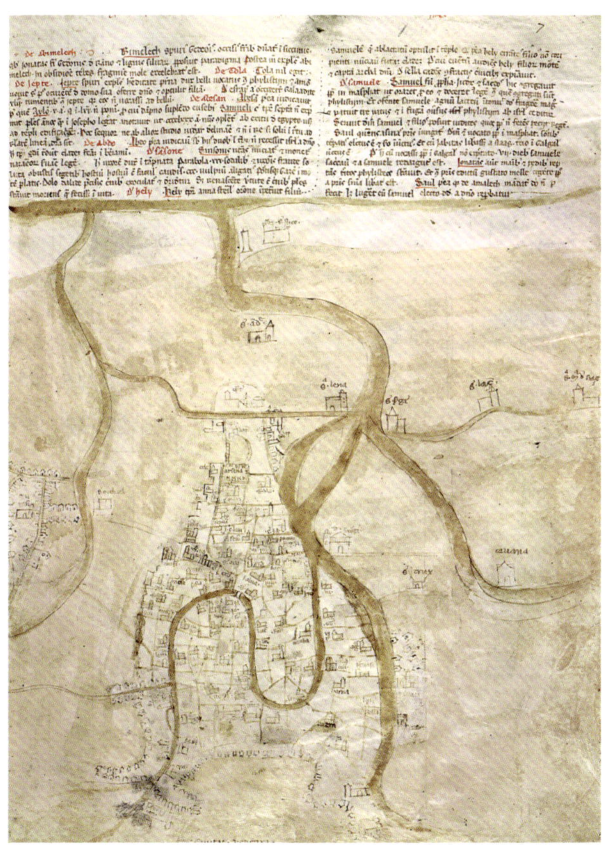

27
Alessandro Badoer, *Plan of Venice*, dated 1627,
reprinted 1667, engraving, 35.8 × 50.9 cm
Venice, Museo Correr, inv. no. M 36267

individual vision of the whole townscape, enlivened
by particular details that seem especially noteworthy.
Inserted into a personal jigsaw of memories, this
image is, of course, not stable but becomes transformed
over time: some features grow in significance, while
others fade into oblivion. Memories can be shared and
reinforced – or even deformed – by oral exchange among
communities, or dialogue within families, or through
written descriptions.

Words and images alike contribute to perceptions
of the townscape of Venice. From earliest times, the
inhabitants had to know the layout of islands and
waterways intimately to allow safe navigation. Early
maps show a remarkably accurate comprehension of the
shape of the site. A map drawn by Paolino da Venezia in
1340s, but probably copied from an eleventh-century
original, reflects quite closely the true shape of the site,
and reveals the cellular structure of the island-parishes
as they coalesced (fig. 26). This sheet is unusual in being
drawn from a viewpoint directly above, like a modern
map. Another map, dating from 1627, shows the later,
more regular land-reclamations in the north-west of the
city and at the western end, but the organic, cellular
structure of the older settlements is still evident (fig. 27).

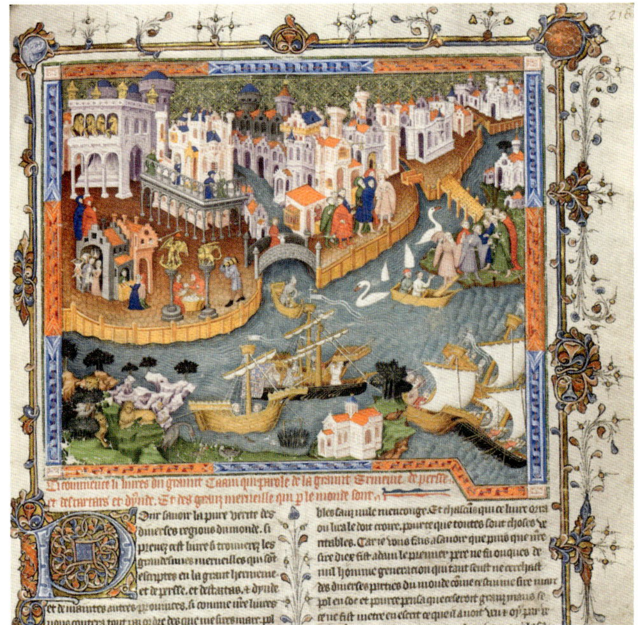

28
Johannes, *Marco Polo's Departure from Venice*, from
Marco Polo, *Li livres du Grant Caam*, England, c. 1400–10,
tempera and gold on parchment, 41.5 × 30 cm
Oxford, Bodleian Library, inv. Ms. Bodley 264, fol. 218r

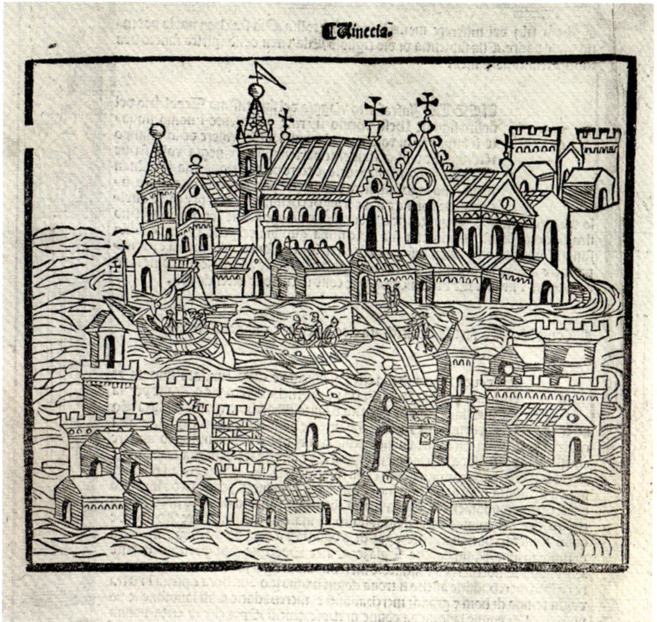

It is important to stress that the morphology of the city was well-known, at least by the city authorities, from the Middle Ages onwards. Yet artists adopted a wide variety of viewpoints and modified the shape to fit their own perceptions. Some were based purely on hearsay, like the beautiful illumination in a manuscript of Marco Polo's travels now in Oxford, painted by an English miniaturist named Johannes (fig. 28). With the development of printing in the late fifteenth century, images of the city became more widely diffused across Europe. A woodcut of 1500, in one of the first printed editions of Poggibonsi's fourteenth-century pilgrim narrative, shows the city of "Vinecia" with the buildings half-drowned in waves (fig. 29). German pilgrims from north of the Alps gave special prominence to the back-drop of mountains that they had crossed in order to reach Venice, as seen in Reuwich's view published in the chronicle of Bernhard von Breydenbach in 1486 (fig. 31). A similar view appears in the Nuremberg Chronicle of 1493. These are views from the south, that is, the perspective of the *departing* pilgrim, but this was always the primary viewpoint – as Thomas Mann remarked, "to come to Venice by the station [i.e. from the north] is like entering a palace by the back door".[11]

The rapid growth in printing and publishing in Early Modern Venice forms the context for one of the most remarkable views of Venice ever created, namely Jacopo de' Barbari's woodcut bird's-eye view, published in 1500 (fig. 30). As the publisher, Anton Kolb, asserted when he requested copyright privileges from the Venetian Senate, the work involved years of effort.[12] Extending over six A1 sheets, the map covers four square metres, and its unprecedented size necessitated innovations in paper manufacture as well as the manufacture of extra large presses. Even the provision of fine-grained woodblocks of sufficient size was a challenge. In consequence, Kolb argued that the costly preparation justified the high price of three ducats.

It has been convincingly shown by Juergen Schulz that the view was prepared using a collage of surveys made from the tops of the city's numerous *campanili*, with the draughtsman always looking towards the north.[13] The whole city is rendered as if seen from the top of the *campanile* of San Giorgio Maggiore, although the island of San Giorgio itself is shifted northwards to allow its inclusion near the bottom of the map. The two sides of the city have been pulled apart to emphasize the prominence of the Grand Canal, for its alignment is not, in fact, easily visible from the top of the *campanile* of San Giorgio – nor even from that of San Marco. Given Jacopo de' Barbari's expertise in mathematics and perspective, it is likely that the layout was constructed by tilting a base map to show the townscape from a bird's-eye perspective.[14] Most of the city fits this procedure rather closely, but there are significant areas of deformation near the join between the two left-hand sheets (fig. 32). This has the effect of squashing inwards a long projection to the west, and the resulting image gives the city the distinctive silhouette of a dolphin.

Given the positive associations of delphinic imagery at the time, this seems to have been an intentional choice, although it has also been argued that de' Barbari simply ran out of space and had to compress the western

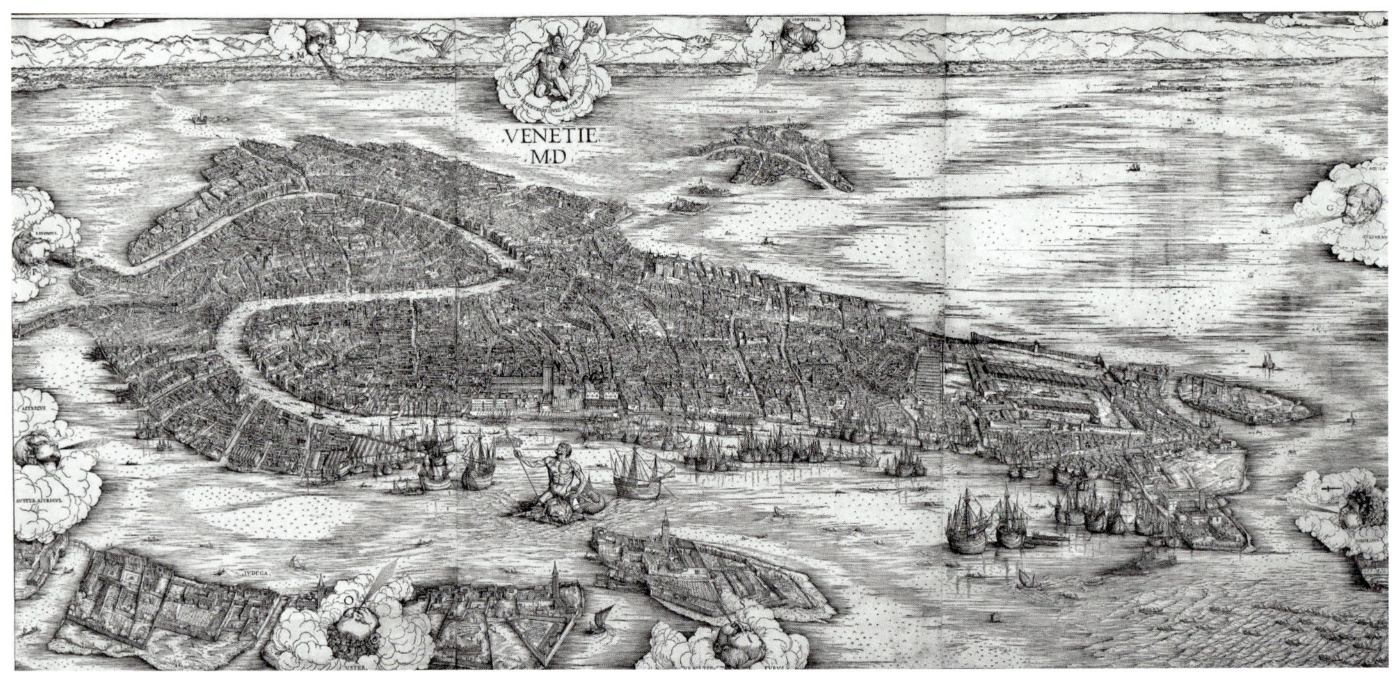

30
Jacopo de' Barbari, *Bird's-eye-view map of Venice*, woodcut
on six sheets, 134.0 x 280.8 cm, inscribed *VENETIE MD*
London, British Museum, inv. no. 1895, 0122.1192–1197

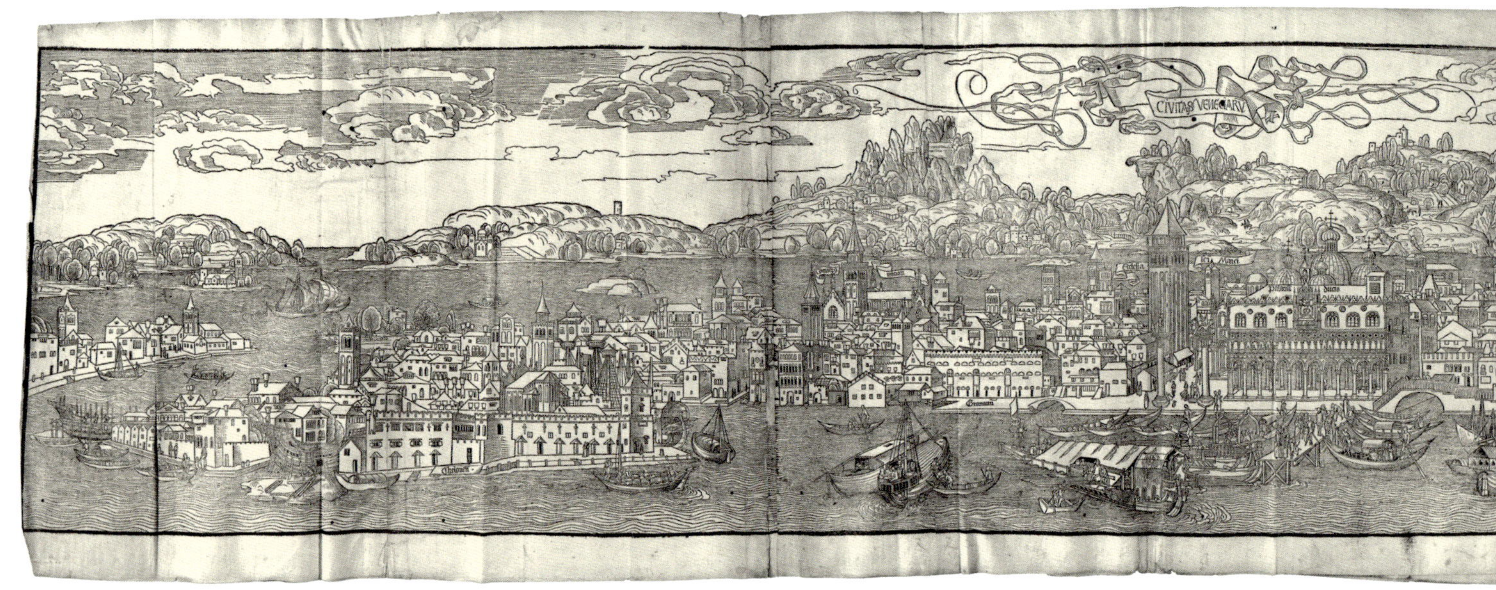

31
Erhard Reuwich, *View of Venice from the south*, woodcut,
265 x 1620 mm, from Bernhard von Breydenbach,
Peregrinationes in Terram Sanctam, Mainz, 1486
Trinity College, Cambridge (Grylls. 2.173)

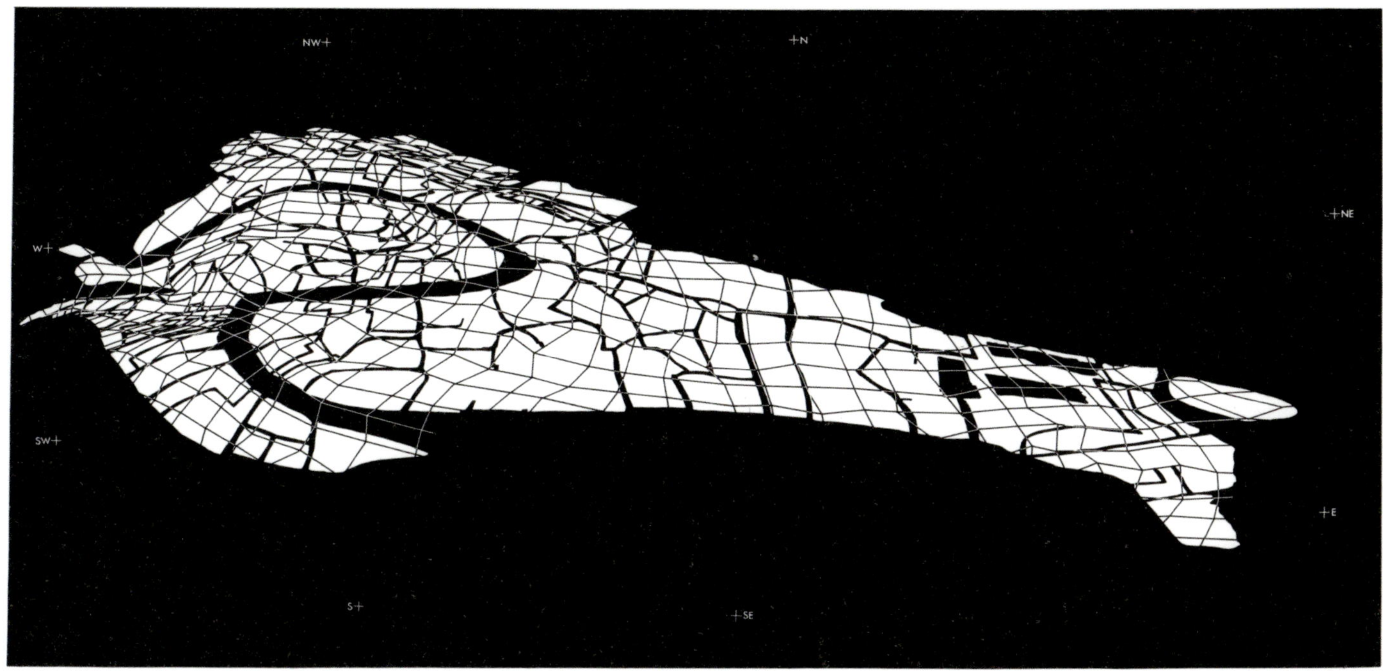

32
Jacopo de' Barbari, *Bird's-eye view map of Venice*,
with grid co-ordinates marked (after Schulz 1978)

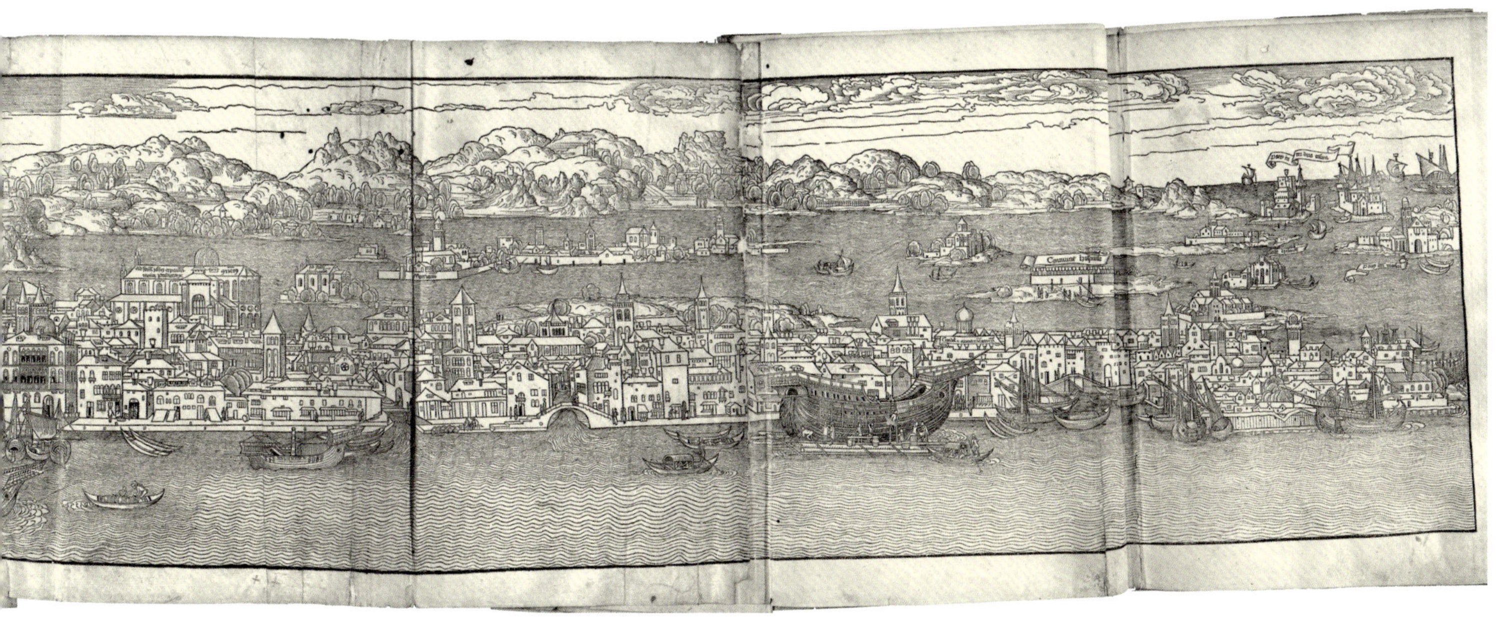

edge to fit on the paper.[15] Dolphins were associated with Christian redemption, good fortune and speed, not to mention both Venus and Neptune, all of which fitted the aspirations of this aquatic city. Venice's mercantile and maritime interests are highlighted by the depiction of Mercury and Neptune at either end of the vertical axis running through the city centre in de' Barbari's view (fig. 34). If radial lines are drawn between the eight winds distributed around the edge of the map, they converge on the top of the campanile of San Marco (fig. 33).[16] The inclusion of the winds, in imitation of world-maps of the time, confers a timeless, universal quality, enhanced by the almost complete absence of inhabitants. The city is represented as an empty stage, on which its future history can be played out.

At the same time, both spatial and temporal specificity are strongly emphasized. The quinquennial date of 1500 (MD) highlights the significance of the historical moment, while the individuality of the city is defined by the unprecedented density of meticulously observed visual detail. The fidelity of the depiction of the townscape and the virtuosity of the wood-carving make this one of the most exceptional printed images ever created. The collaboration between a German publisher and an Italian artist produced an image that appealed to Venetians and foreigners alike. Indeed, half of the surviving copies of the first edition are still in Venice, while the rest are in collections outside Italy.[17] The woodblocks were re-used for later editions, with minor changes, and may still be seen in the Museo Correr in Venice (fig. 35).

This fascination with the particularity of the city, rendered in minute detail, is revealed in other artistic representations of the time. Called the 'eye-witness style' by Patricia Fortini Brown, this intense realism proved a powerful propaganda instrument, for the inclusion of recognizable everyday details allowed artists to make miraculous events or political messages more believable and relevant.[18] A well-known example is the series of *Miracles of the True Cross* painted for the Scuola di San Giovanni Evangelista and now in the Accademia Gallery in Venice. These canvases include Carpaccio's *Miracle of the Possessed Boy* of 1494 (fig. 36) and Gentile Bellini's *Procession in Piazza San Marco* of 1496 (fig. 37). The power of the

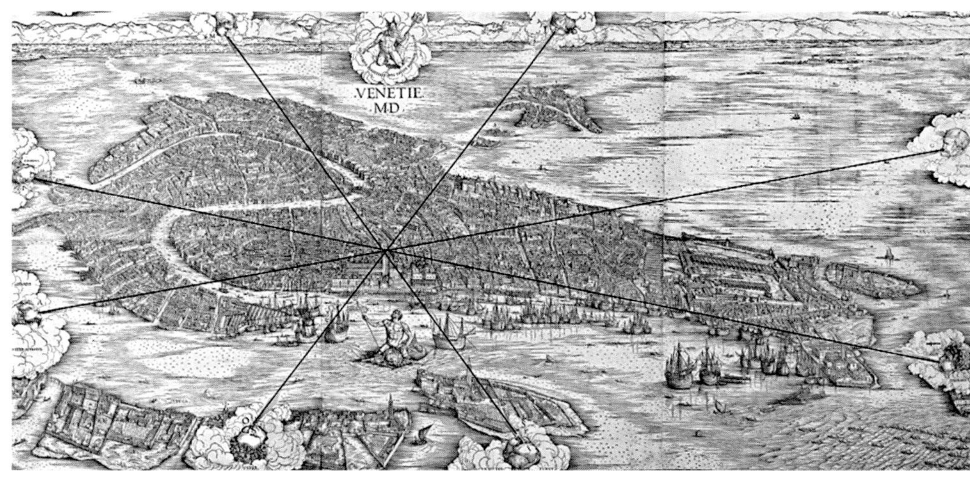

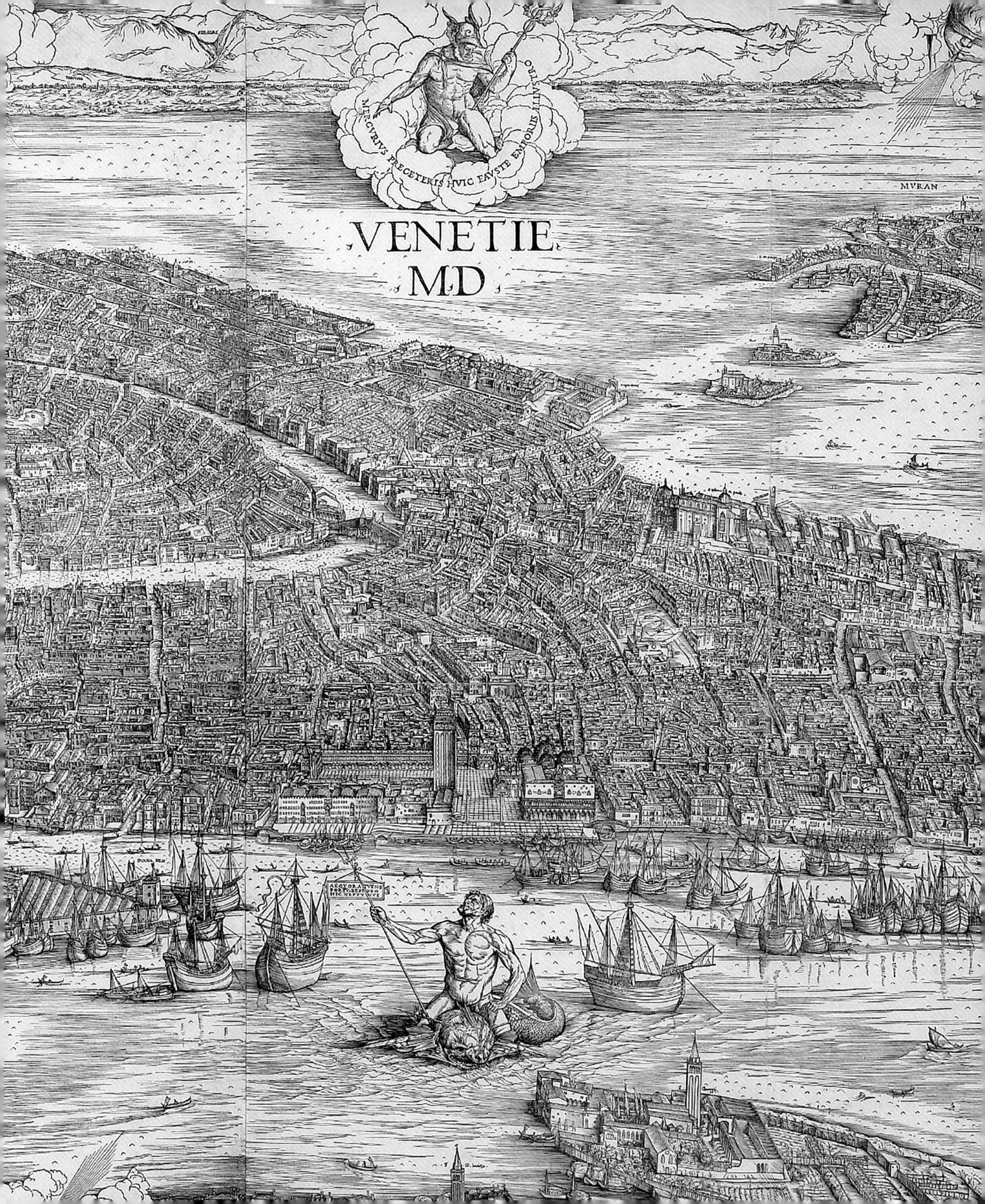

MERCVRIVS PRECETERIS HVIC FAVSTE EMPORIIS ILLVSTRO
VENETIE
MD
MVRAN
AEQVORA TVENS PORTV RESIDEO HIC NEPTVNVS

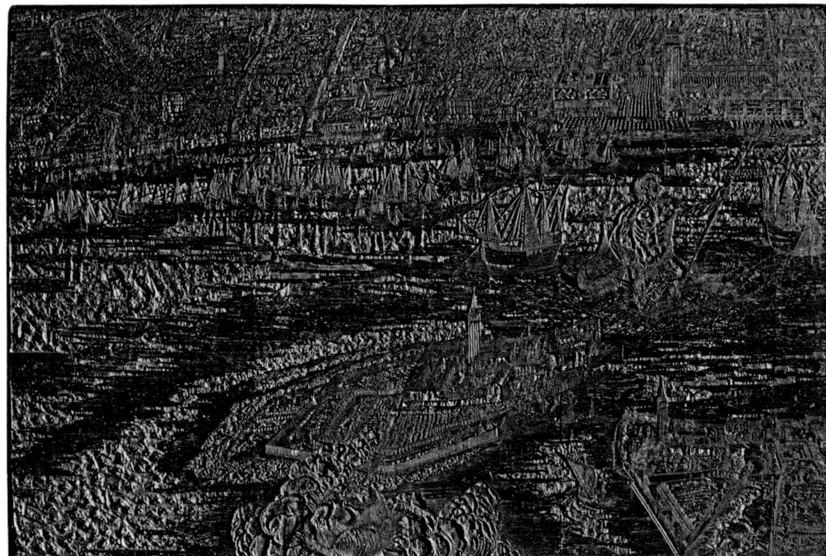

Scuola's treasured relic of the True Cross was made
manifest by miracles apparently taking place in the
familiar streets of Venice.[19]

A similar obsession for recording daily life in
meticulous detail pervades the writing of the time.
The most extraordinary example is the remarkable diary
kept by Marin Sanudo the Younger between 1498 and
1533.[20] Using the expressive vocabulary and cadences of
local dialect, Sanudo lurches back and forth between
world-shaking events of war and peace and the banal
accidents of Venetian daily life. He also compiled a
detailed description of the city.[21] A similarly detailed
description by Marcantonio Sabellico, *De Venetae urbis situ*,
was first published in Venice in 1490, and it has even
been suggested that it was intended as a companion
text to accompany Jacopo de' Barbari's view.[22]

At the turn of the sixteenth century the city's
uniqueness was compelling, for Venice was then at
the climax of its power and prosperity. The Republic
dominated trade between Europe and the Eastern
Mediterranean and controlled a *terraferma* empire from
Bergamo and Brescia in the west to Udine in the east,
as well as colonies in the Greek world, most notably the
strategically located islands of Crete and Cyprus. The
stato da terra e da mar must have seemed almost invincible.
In 1509, however, this dream was to be shattered when
the alliance of the League of Cambrai overran the Veneto
and almost eliminated the Serenissima. By 1517, after a
long and expensive military effort, most of the *terraferma*
territories had been recovered, but from that moment
on the supremacy of the city was sustained in text and
image rather than in reality. Jacopo de' Barbari's view
became a template for future reiterations of the so-called
'myth of Venice'.[23]

Because of its extraordinary virtuosity, de' Barbari's
bird's-eye format influenced representations of the city
for centuries to come. Many engravers and woodcutters
simply copied the map, with greater or lesser degrees of
fidelity, in a range of different sizes, updating buildings
at will.[24] At the same time, de' Barbari's beguiling
view encouraged the city authorities to plan future
land reclamations to enhance the dolphin-like profile.
The expansion of the city on the north side to create the
Fondamenta Nuove during the sixteenth century seems
to reflect this ambition, even if in the end the watery
incursion of the Sacca della Misericordia was never filled
in (fig. 38).

Although Jacopo de' Barbari depicted the island of
Giudecca around the southern margins of the city,
he did not include the *lidi*, and his map gives little
prominence to the smaller lagoon islands apart from
Murano. Even Burano and Torcello are mere slivers in the
far distance. A powerful alternative image of the lagoon
was produced by Benedetto Bordone in his *Tutte l'isole del*

36
Vittore Carpaccio, *The Miracles of the True Cross: The Healing of the Possessed Boy*, 1494, oil on canvas, 365 x 389 cm
Venice, Gallerie dell'Accademia

37
Gentile Bellini, *A Procession in Piazza San Marco*, signed and dated 1496, oil on canvas, 367 x 745 cm
Venice, Gallerie dell'Accademia

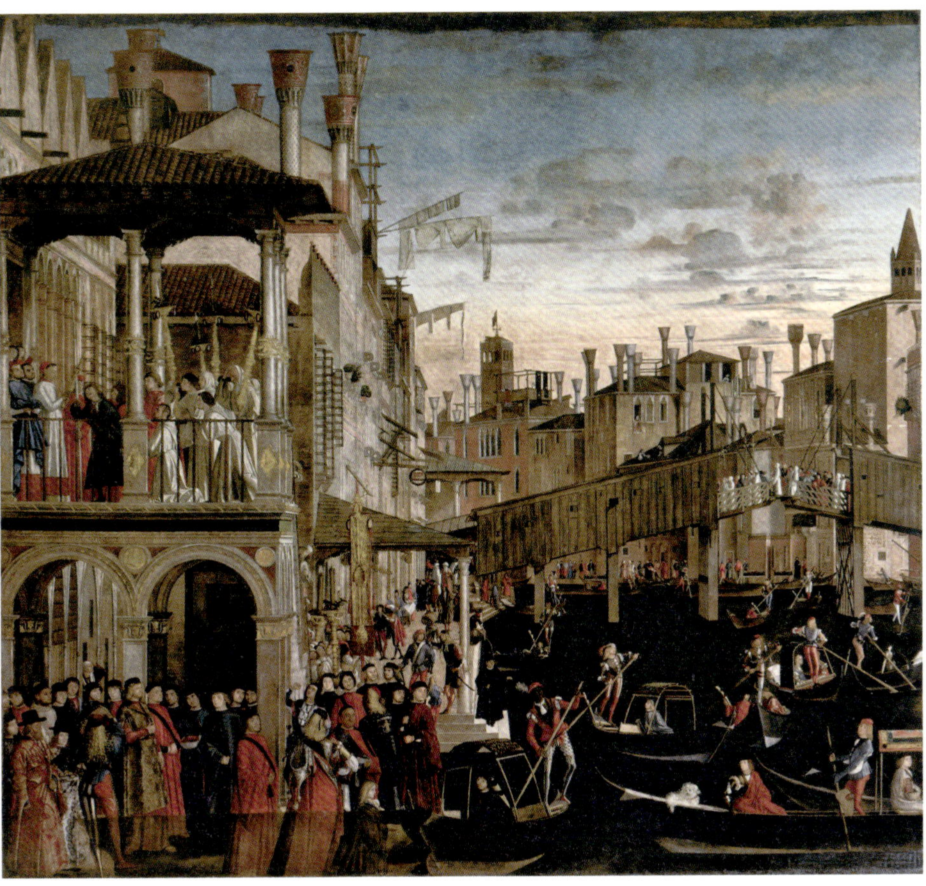

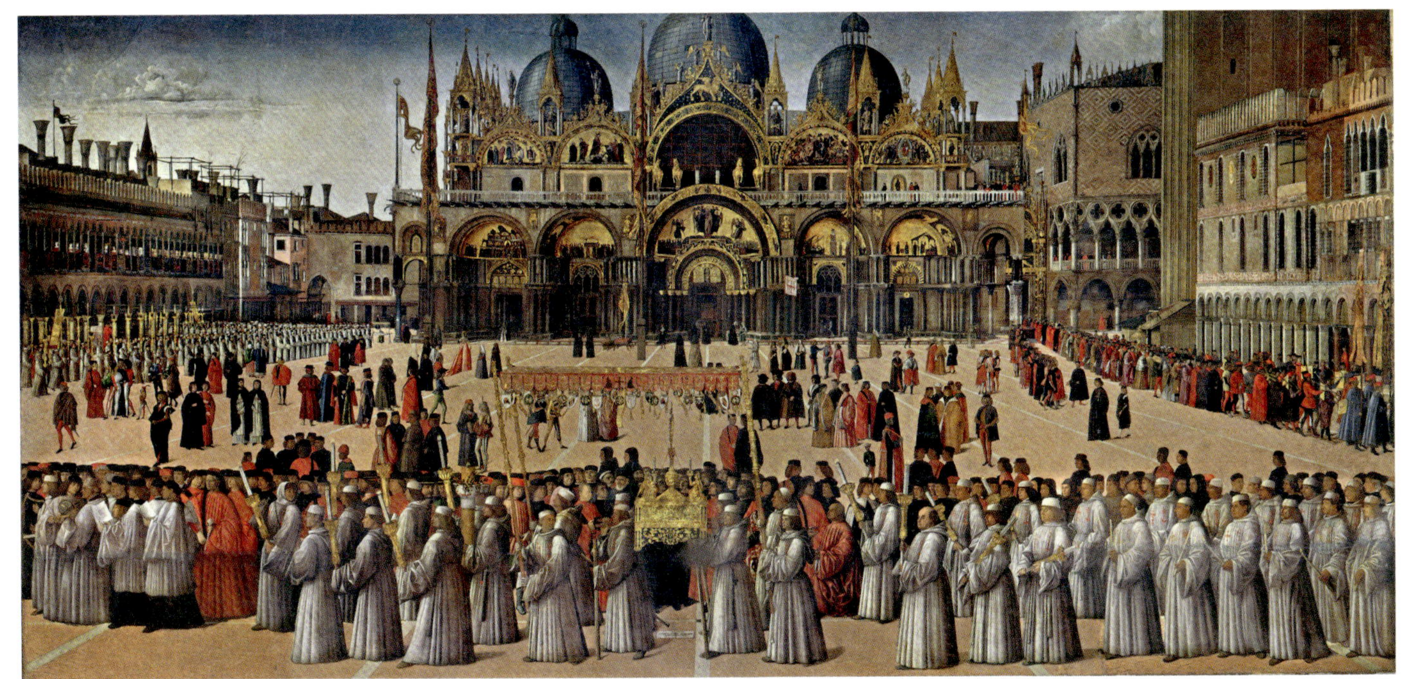

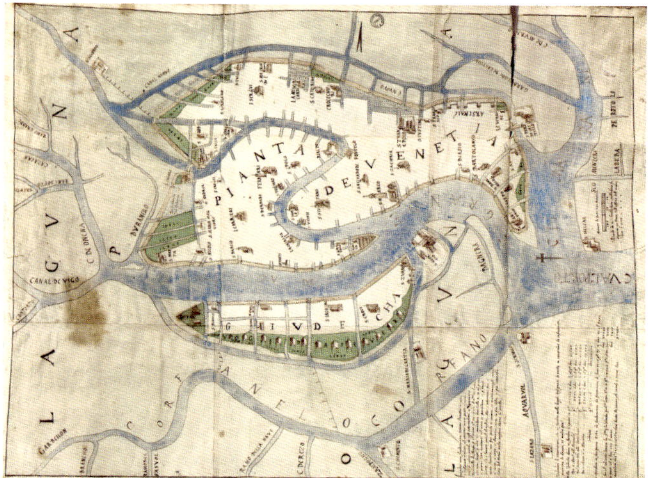

38
Cristoforo Sabbadino, *Plan of Venice*, showing
proposed reclamation on the north side of the city,
1557, pen and water-colour, 83.2 × 62.6 cm
Venice, Biblioteca Marciana, vol. 138.c.180, fol. XVIIb

mondo, published in Venice in 1528 (fig. 39).[25] A pioneer
in the genre of publication known as the *isolario*, this
volume placed stress on the phenomenon of the island
as a discrete entity. Venice's insular topography was
zealously maintained by the Republic to protect trade
and navigation: rivers laden with silt from the foothills
of the Alps were diverted to either side of the lagoon to

prevent the silting up of the waters. Bordone's woodcut
reconfigured the Venetian lagoon as an almost square
enclosure rimmed by *lidi* on the south and east and by
the *terraferma* on the other two sides. He filled the waters
with islands, each bearing a simplified representation
of the monastery sited there. Like that of Jacopo de'
Barbari, Bordone's image of Venice exerted a strong
influence, and some print-makers attempted to combine
aspects of both views.

By the end of the sixteenth century, the shape of
the city of Venice had become imprinted on the visual
consciousness of Europe through the two pioneering
woodcuts of Jacopo de' Barbari and Benedetto Bordone.
These celebrated images defined memorable urban
forms that would be imitated – separately or together –
for centuries to come.

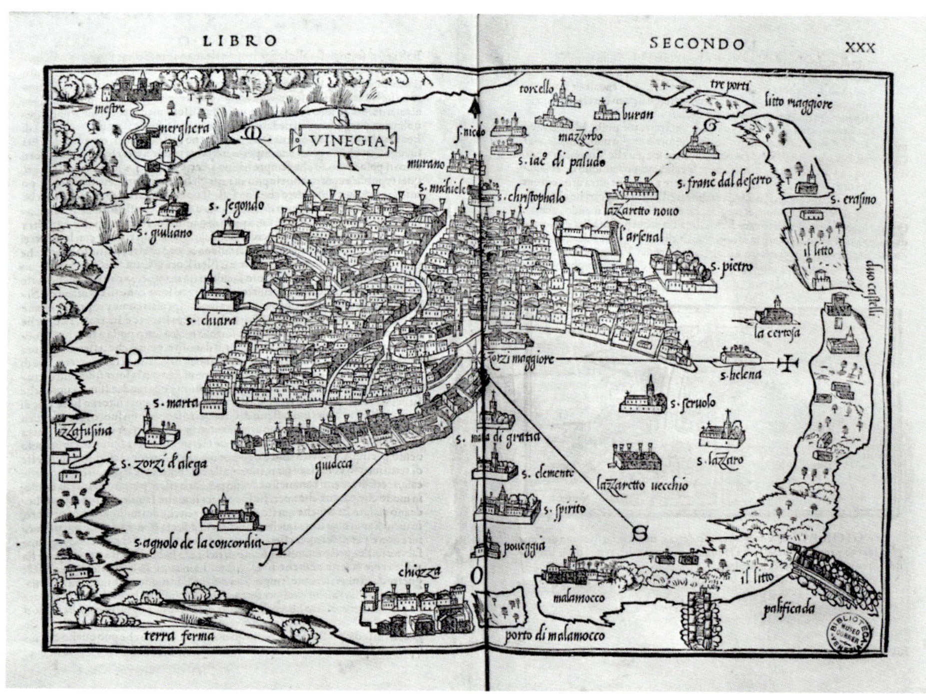

39
Benedetto Bordone, *Venice and the surrounding
islands*, woodcut from his *Isolario*, Venice, 1528
Venice, Museo Correr

NOTES

1 Felix Fabri (Faber), *The Wanderings of Felix Fabri*, transl. Aubrey Stewart, 2 vols., London, 1892, I, p. 79.

2 A.J. Ammerman and C. E. McClennen (eds.), *Venice before San Marco: Recent Studies on the Origins of the City*, Hamilton, NY, 2001; J. Schulz, 'The Origins of Venice: Urbanism on the Upper Adriatic Coast', *Studi Veneziani*, n.s. LXI, 2010, pp. 15–56.

3 See, for example, A. Carile and G. Fedalto, *Le origini di Venezia*, Bologna 1978, pp. 19–126.

4 D. Rosand, *Myths of Venice: The Figuration of a State*, Chapel Hill and London, 2001.

5 This translation is quoted from F.C. Lane, *Venice: A Maritime Republic*, Baltimore and London, 1973, pp. 3–4. For the full text of the letter, see T. Hodgkin (ed.), *The Letters of Cassiodorus*, London, 1886, pp. 515–18. The Latin text was well known in Venice and was published in Francesco Sansovino's guidebook *Venetia città nobilissima et singolare*, Venice 1581, fols. 207v–208r.

6 Lane, *Venice: A Maritime Republic*; Deborah Howard, *Venice and the East: The Impact of the Islamic World on Venetian Architecture*, New Haven and London, 2000.

7 D. Howard, *The Architectural History of Venice*, revised edn, New Haven and London, 2002, pp. 43–71, with further bibliography.

8 E. Crouzet-Pavan, *'Sopra le acque salse': Espaces, pouvoir et société à Venise à la fin du Moyen Âge*, 2 vols., Rome, 1992, especially I, pp. 265–89; S. Zaggia, '"Far la città": Il ruolo dei Provveditori di Comun nell'evoluzione dell'ambiente urbano di Venezia – Strade, ponti, pozzi, case', *Mélanges de l'École française de Rome. Italie et Méditerranée*, 116, 2004, pp. 665–81.

9 On traditional building methods, see R.J. Goy, *Venetian Vernacular Architecture: Traditional Housing in the Venetian Lagoon*, Cambridge, 1989; idem, *The House of Gold: Building a Palace in Medieval Venice*, Cambridge, 1992; idem, *Building Renaissance Venice: Patrons, architects and builders, c. 1430–1500*, New Haven and London, 2006. A brief introduction for non-specialists is G. Gianighian and P. Pavanini, *Venice: The Basics*, Venice 2010. E.R. Trincanato, *Venezia minore*, Venice, 1948, remains a classic study.

10 Charles Dickens, letter to John Forster, 12 November 1844, from K. Tillotson (ed.), *The Letters of Charles Dickens (1844–46)*, Oxford, vol. IV, 1977, p. 217.

11 Thomas Mann, *Death in Venice; Tristan; Tonio Kröger*, transl. H.T. Lowe-Porter, Harmondsworth, 1955, p. 24.

12 J. Schulz, 'Jacopo de' Barbari's View of Venice: Map Making, City Views, and Moralized Geography before the Year 1500', *The Art Bulletin*, 60, 1978, pp. 425–74; republished in idem, *La cartografia tra scienza e arte: Carte e cartografi nel Rinascimento italiano*, transl. T.D. De Zuliani, Modena, 1990, pp. 13–63; D. Howard, 'Venice as a Dolphin: Further Investigations into Jacopo de' Barbari's View', *Artibus et historiae*, 18/35, 1997, pp. 101–11; S. Biadene and C. Tonini (eds.), *A volo d'uccello: Jacopo de' Barbari e le rappresentazioni di città nell'Europa del Rinascimento*, Venice, 1999; C.B. Trincanato, E. Balistreri, A.M. Ghion and D. Zanverdiani, *Venezia città mirabile: Guida alla veduta prospettica di Jacopo de' Barbari*, Verona, 2009.

13 Schulz, 'Jacopo de' Barbari's View of Venice', pp. 436–41.

14 Howard, 'Venice as a Dolphin', pp. 104–06.

15 *Ibid.*, pp. 106–9; Schulz, 'Jacopo de' Barbari's View of Venice', p. 437–39.

16 Trincanato *et al.*, *Venezia città mirabile*, p. 300.

17 Schulz, 'Jacopo de' Barbari's View of Venice', p. 474.

18 Patricia Fortini Brown, *Venetian Narrative Painting in the Age of Carpaccio*, New Haven and London, 1988.

19 *Ibid.*, p. 4.

20 Marin Sanuto (Sanudo), *I diarii*, ed. R. Fulin *et al.*, 58 vols, Venice, 1879–1903.

21 Marin Sanudo il giovane, *De origine, situ et magistratibus urbis Venetae, ovvero La città di Venetia (1493–1530)*, ed. A. Caracciolo Aricò, enlarged and revised edn Venice, 2011.

22 This was suggested by D.S. Chambers, 'Bird's-eye View of Venice', in J. Martineau and C. Hope (eds.), *The Genius of Venice 1500–1600*, exh. cat., Royal Academy of Arts, London, 1983, no. H1, p. 392.

23 See, for example, James S. Grubb, 'When Myths Lose Power: Four Decades of Venetian Historiography', *Journal of Modern History*, 58, 1986, pp. 43–94; R. Finlay, 'The Immortal Republic: The Myth of Venice during the Italian Wars (1494–1530)', *Sixteenth Century Journal*, 30, 1999, pp. 931–44.

24 G. Cassini, *Piante e vedute prospettiche di Venezia 1479–1855*, Venice, 1982; S. Biadene and G. Romanelli (eds.), *Venezia: piante e vedute: catalogo del fondo cartografico a stampa*, Venice, 1982.

25 L. Armstrong, 'Benedetto Bordon, "Miniator", and Cartography in Early Sixteenth-Century Venice', in *Studies of Renaissance Miniaturists in Venice*, 2 vols., London, 2003, vol. 2, pp. 591–643 (first published in *Imago Mundi*, 48, 1966, pp. 65–92).

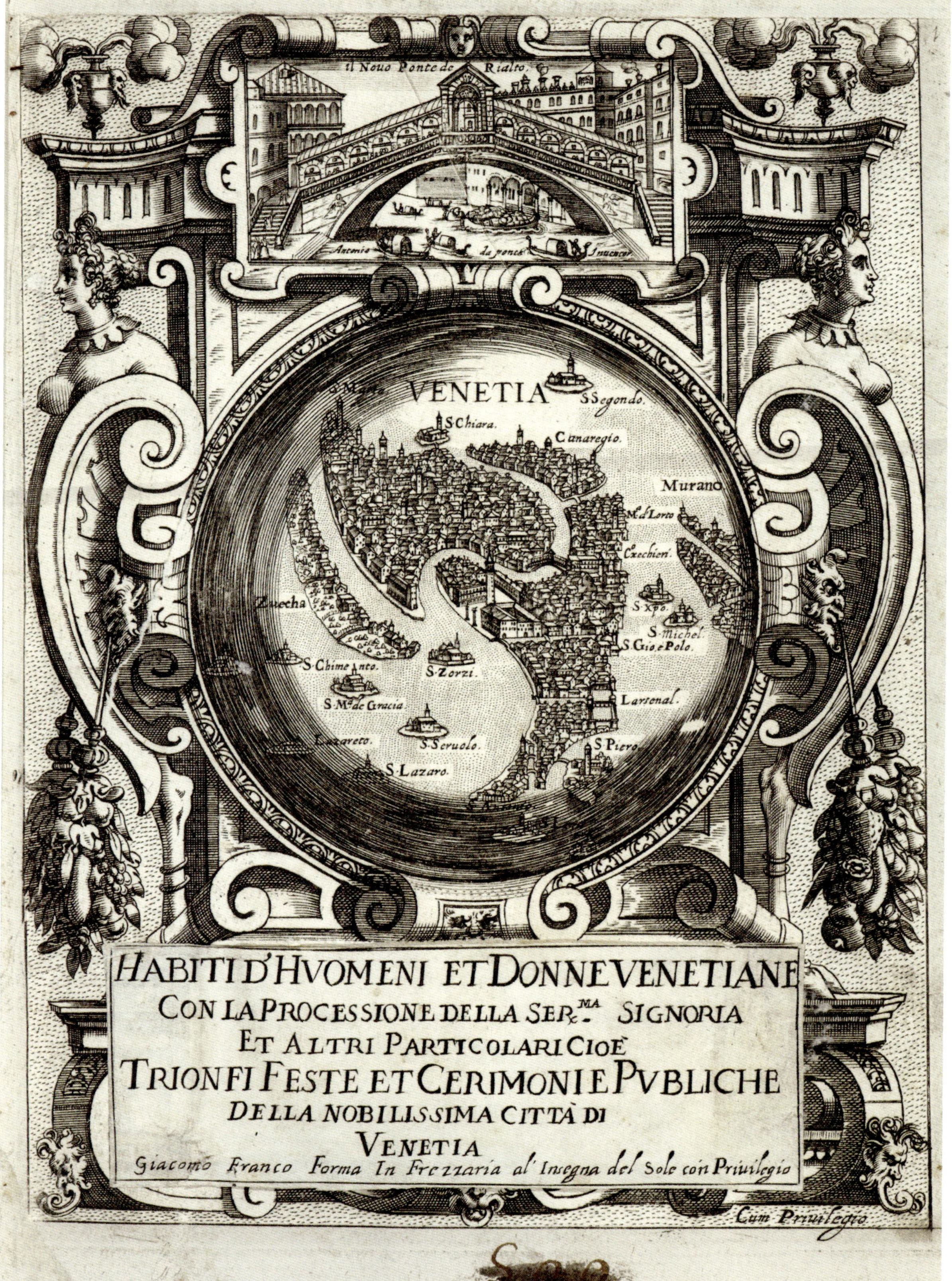

HABITI D'HVOMENI ET DONNE VENETIANE
CON LA PROCESSIONE DELLA SER.MA SIGNORIA
ET ALTRI PARTICOLARI, CIOE
TRIONFI FESTE ET CERIMONIE PVBLICHE
DELLA NOBILISSIMA CITTÀ DI
VENETIA
Giacomo Franco Forma In Frezzaria al'Insegna del Sole con Priuilegio
Cum Priuilegio

3. The Image of Venice in the Sixteenth Century

ALLISON SHERMAN

JACOPO DE' BARBARI'S WOODCUT bird's-eye-view of Venice of 1500 (fig. 30) and Odoardo Fialetti's painted rendition of the city in 1611 (fig. 1) serve as remarkable visual brackets to one of the most fascinating periods in Venetian history, and to the golden age of Venetian cartography.[1] In the century or so that separated their production, much had unfolded on the stage of de' Barbari's Venice. Less than a decade after the first impressions of the view had been issued, the Republic experienced a crisis of confidence. This crisis was precipitated by a combination of factors that had been mounting for decades – a precipitous decline in Venice's dominance as a military and economic power, signalled by bank crashes, losses to the Ottoman Turks, and its marginalization as a hub between east and west due to the development of alternative trade routes by the Portuguese. Perhaps most damaging was the Republic's sobering brush with the loss of its territorial supremacy in 1509, when the combined forces of the papacy, France, Spain and the Holy Roman Empire – the League of Cambrai – advanced dangerously close to the shores of the lagoon, as mentioned in the previous chapter. While Venice was ultimately successful in recovering its lost mainland holdings, the crisis shook the very foundations of its identity and compromised the carefully crafted and relatively recently codified 'myth of Venice', with its all its connotations of stability, longevity, serenity, wisdom, justice and divine protection.[2]

The dissemination of this utopian ideology was a crucial component of the Republic's attempt to reassure its citizens and repair its status on the international stage in the wake of the War of the League of Cambrai. A further catalyst for this campaign was the sack of papal Rome by the imperial troops of Charles V in 1527. Recently delivered from its own series of misfortunes, the Most Serene Republic was once again a bastion of security and order, proving the ideal haven for intellectuals displaced by this violence. Among the refugees from Rome was Jacopo Sansovino, a Florentine architect who was equipped with first-hand knowledge of antique remains and the contemporary revival of classical antiquity in Central Italy, a valuable background most Venetian architects did not possess. His arrival in the lagoon city proved enormously opportune, for it coincided with the ambitious plans of the shrewd Doge Andrea Gritti to mobilize the propagandistic power of art and architecture in an effort to repair the Republic's tarnished image, and to give the city a facelift on an unprecedented scale. The focus of this overhaul was on the major civic, commercial, industrial and religious spaces in the city, and the aesthetic it employed was deliberately Romanizing.[3] It channelled the power and imperial associations of the *all'antica* architectural vocabulary towards the promotion of the Venetian Republic as the New Rome. Venice's connection to its classical past – to its foundation by refugees of the crumbling Roman Empire – had already been delineated by 1493 in Bernardo Giustinian's *De origine urbis Venetiarum*.

This text initiated the genre of official (and non-official) state historiography that would continue to emphasize this heritage throughout the following century.[4]

Already the premier printing capital of Europe by the end of the fifteenth century, Venice made able use of its presses and capitalized on its well-established mercantile network to transmit this information at home and abroad in the form of text and printed image.[5] Written histories played an important role in the proliferation of Venice's utopian myth and the promotion of the Venetian republican system as model, but printed perspectival and panoramic views of the city also contributed to what William Bouwsma has called the "political education of Europe".[6] Indeed, these objects seem to have been geared primarily towards an international audience increasingly interested in map collecting.[7] Deborah Howard has already outlined how elegantly and deliberately Jacopo de' Barbari's bird's-eye view embodied the central tenets of this ideology in visual form, something that was not lost on the Republic that granted the copyright and export licence to the German merchant Anton Kolb. He claimed to have undertaken the ambitious enterprise "for the fame of this exceedingly noble city" and in order to inspire a vision of the place in the minds of people everywhere, but he is unlikely to have known the extent to which he would realise that ambition.[8] The view he published, whether by direct imitation or filtered through other derivative examples, would serve as the benchmark for virtually every topographical view of the city created in Venice and beyond in the century that followed.

Although the scale, medium and level of detail varied from plan to plan, the views frequently maintained the basic shape and perspective established by the de' Barbari precedent, emphasizing the timeless, eternal quality of the Republic. But they also perpetuated some of its distortions and its multivalent cues to larger ideas.[9]

Like the 'myth of Venice' itself, the view had some basis in reality, but was selectively manipulated to project a particular vision of the city, to convey meaning and metaphor, a phenomenon Juergen Schulz has labelled 'moralizing geography'.[10] The seemingly scientific accuracy with which details are rendered in the de' Barbari plan serves to convince us of the reality of the ideas it communicates, but the viewer must be conscious of the fact that there are major inaccuracies and omissions. Studies have revealed that the shape and layout of the city has been distorted for symbolic purposes, perhaps to suggest the silhouette of a dolphin and certainly to place emphasis on the religious, political and economic organs of the city.[11] This highlights a critical point: that these plans were not official surveys or navigational tools. Their function, then as now, was didactic. As Bronwen Wilson has argued, they gave the viewer an opportunity to compare their place in the world with others, an exercise that seems to have been in greater demand from a wider audience as the known world expanded.[12]

Even so, the fidelity with which many of the topographical details are rendered in the 1500 woodcut makes it an immensely useful document for historians, to say nothing of its entertainment value. It is full of intriguing particulars, from the views into long-lost gardens to the rather macabre vignette of the body hanging from the gallows propped up in the lagoon near the island of San Secondo. The view amounts to a snapshot of Venice on the brink of the major physical transformation it would undergo during the *renovatio urbis*. It provides a portrait of Mauro Codussi's recently completed Torre dell'Orologio, still awaiting its flanking wings and the construction of its impressive neighbour, Bartolomeo Bon's Procuratie Vecchie (begun 1513). The top of the famous bell tower of San Marco still betrays the damage it sustained from a lightning strike in 1483,

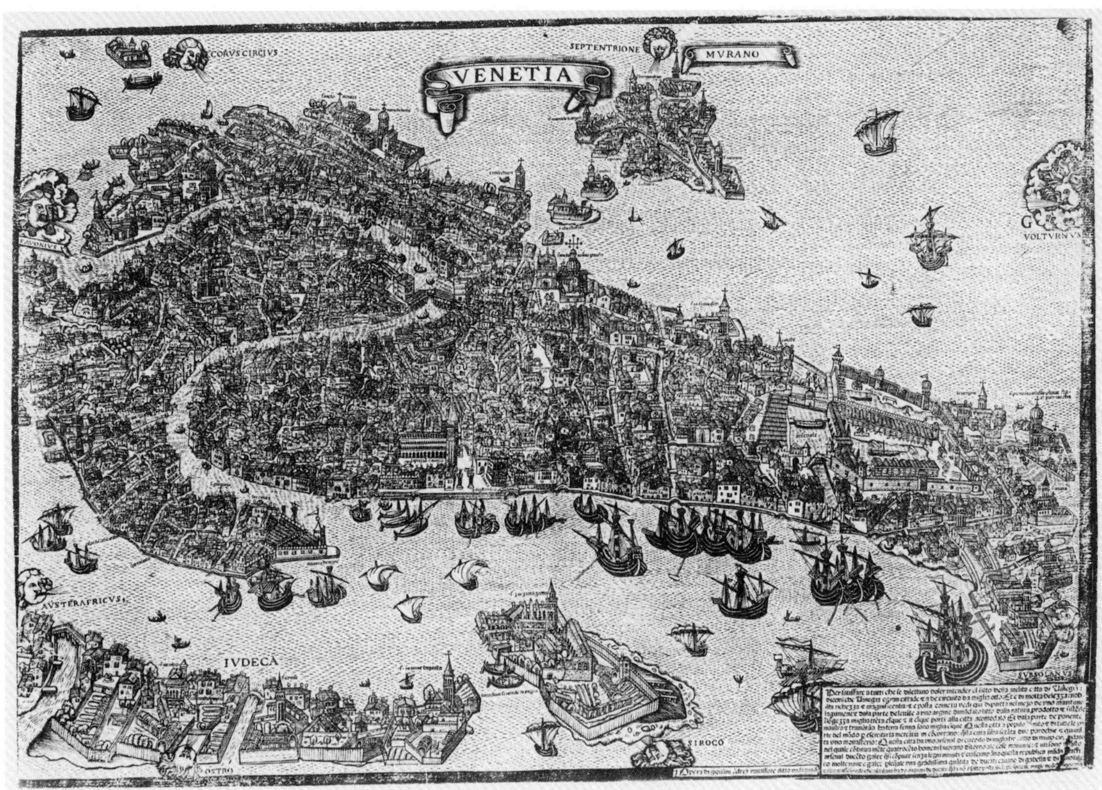

and lacks the handsome Sansovinian Loggetta (begun 1538) that would carry its own sculpted iconographical statement of the 'myth of Venice'. The sites of other famous products of the Grittian renewal, such as the Marciana Library (begun in 1537), were as yet hostels and the stalls of butchers and bakers, and Venice was still more than fifty years shy of receiving the indelible mark of the architect Andrea Palladio, who produced some its most majestic and memorable churches. The Rialto Bridge was then still made of wood and the view of the Grand Canal it spanned – a view that de'Barbari and others distorted their perspective to accommodate – lacks the impressive later Renaissance palaces that would eventually line its banks. If by chance or contrivance the city took on the shape of a dolphin, the jaw and dorsal of de' Barbari's Venice had yet to receive the smoothing enhancements of the addition of the promenade of the Zattere (1519) and the Fondamenta Nuove in (1589), and the Arsenale still awaited various sixteenth-century updates to its fabric, which was capable at its height of producing a galley in a single day.

It would be the task of subsequent views, Odoardo Fialetti's included, to enhance the image of Venice with these new features.[13] Until the middle of the century the bulk of these plans continued to be produced in woodcut, a technique eventually superseded by copperplate engraving, a more costly process, but one that afforded greater potential for detail.[14] Few of the subsequent views were the equal of the de' Barbari plan in precision, and its ambitious scale remained unmatched. Their formats ranged from the quarto size or smaller, used as illustrations to books or atlases, to the more ample folio size or larger. The latter would have been sold individually or bound into large compiled atlases.[15] Several detailed studies have focused on the abundance of plans of Venice produced in this period and their numerous variations:[16] the most remarkable views were those produced by Giovanni Andrea Vavassore (1525; fig. 41), Benedetto Bordone (1528; see fig. 39), and two anonymous woodcuts published in 1550 and 1552 by Sebastian Münster and Balthazar Arnoullet respectively (figs. 42, 43).[17] A woodcut plan by Master I.C.A. (1565;

42
Master C.S. (Cristoph Stimmer?), *View of Venice*, woodcut, 247 x 386 mm, published in Sebastian Münster, *Cosmographiae Universalis Lib. VI*, Basel: Heinrich Petri, 1550

43
View of Venice, woodcut, 160 x 255 mm, published in Guillaume Gueroult, *Premier livre des figures et poutraitz des villes plus illustres et renommes d'Europe*, Lyons: Balthazar Arnoullet, 1552

fig. 44) proved an important intermediate prototype between two innovative xilographs by Matteo Pagan, one large (1559), the other small (1562–65), and the copperplate engraving by Paolo Forlani (1566; figs. 45, 46, 47).[18] The Forlani view, along with those of Pagan, was much imitated, perhaps most imaginatively in Franz Hogenberg's plan published in Georg Braun's 1572 *Civitates orbis terrarum* (fig. 48), and in the multiple variations Giacomo Franco produced from 1580 to 1597 (fig. 49).[19]

Each of these plans innovated in one way or another, finding new ways to communicate the central tenets of the 'myth of Venice' and to promote the image of the Republic.

Beginning with Vavassore's 1525 woodcut (fig. 41), the plans increasingly incorporated some descriptive textual component. The practice of placing a small cartouche placed in the corner of the print with a brief expository passage gives way to the provision of even more detailed information through the placement of labels beside monuments, and eventually numbers that correspond to a detailed legend added to the bottom of the plan. The woodcut view that appeared in Guillaume Gueroult's *Premier livre des figures et pourtraitz des villes plus illustres et renommes d'Europe* in 1552 (fig. 43) was the first to provide such a legend. Subsequent plans such as those by Forlani and Franco became even more precise in elucidating the parishes, churches and notable civic or private spaces for viewers through the use of an extensive legend. This interest in more microscopic or microcosmic detail that is manifest in maps around the middle of the century corresponds, perhaps not by coincidence, with the publication of texts that provided a more vivid, encyclopedic sense of Venice, made accessible to a wider public through the use of the vernacular language. Indeed, the larger plan by Matteo Pagan (fig. 45) directs the reader of its cartouche to the twelve-page book *Tutte le cose notabili e belle che sono in Venetia* of 1556, written by Francesco Sansovino (published under the pseudonym Anselmo Guisconi). This author and publisher would revolutionize the new genre of the guidebook over the course of the second half of the century.[20] Francesco's architect father, who (we have some sense) may have been disappointed by his son's failure to pursue a successful career in law, did not live to witness the full impact that Francesco's literary works would have in promoting his own architectural legacy, as well as the image of the city he had spent half a century renovating.[21]

The 1556 effort proved only the first in a series of works by this author that glorified the city, its history, government, rituals, customs and visual culture. A lengthier work of 79 folios appeared under Sansovino's own name in 1561: *Delle cose notabili che sono in Venetia*, a dialogue between a Venetian and a foreigner whose own origins are not specified. The reader is therefore able to situate himself with ease in the place of Sansovino's visitor as he is conducted around the city by gondola and instructed in the particulars of Venetian dress, the city's most conspicuous buildings, victories, and illustrious citizens, the composition of the Republic's government and the treasures produced by its sculptors and painters. This book was reprinted a dozen times during the following four decades, and it was presumably the success of these first ventures that encouraged the author to produce his seminal 1581 guidebook, *Venetia città nobilissima et singolare*. This work expanded vastly on the scope of the original dialogue and moved to a more practical format the better to facilitate consultation.[22] The text is divided into fourteen books, the first six dedicated to descriptions of the contents of each of the city's districts, called *sestieri*. The other eight address Venice's major lay confraternities (Scuole Grandi), its buildings, both private and public, and elaborate on the

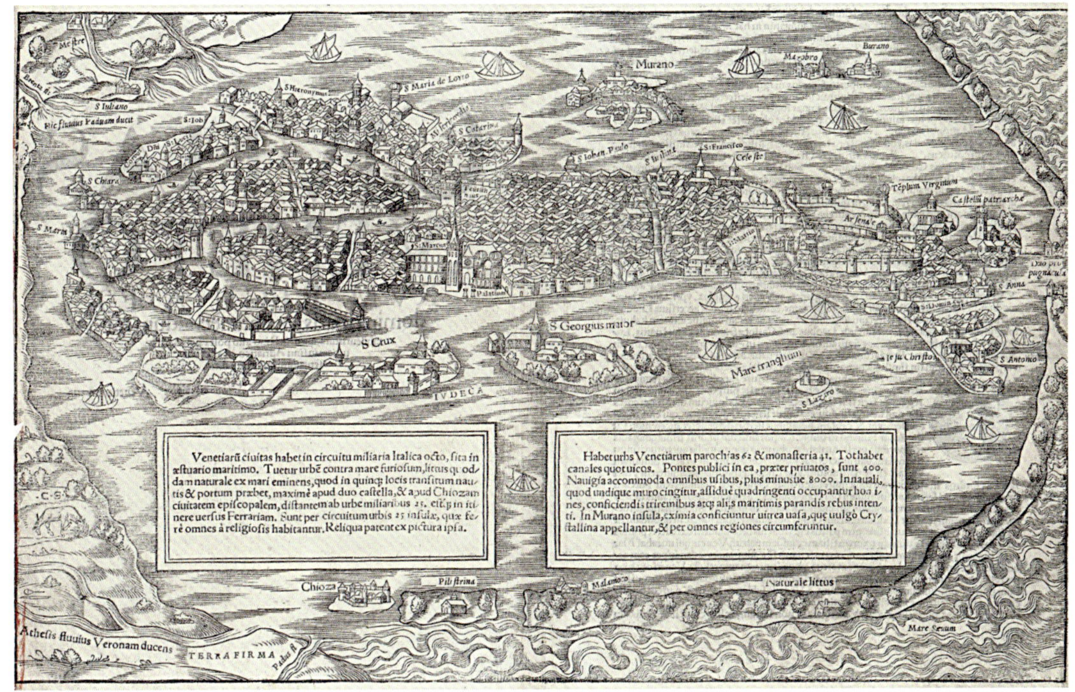

Venetiarū ciuitas habet in circuitu miliaria Italica octo, sita in æstuario maritimo. Tuetur urbē contra mare furiosum, littus quoddam naturale ex mari eminens, quod in quincʒ locis transitum nautis & portum præbet, maximè apud duo castella, & apud Chiozam ciuitatem episcopalem, distantem ab urbe miliaribus 25. estʒ in itinere uersus Ferrariam. Sunt per circuitum urbis 25 insulæ, quæ ferè omnes à religiosis habitantur. Reliqua patent ex pictura ipsa.

Haber urbs Venetiarum parochias 62 & monasteria 41. Tot habet canales quot uicos. Pontes publici in ea, præter priuatos, sunt 400. Nauigia accommoda omnibus usibus, plus minusûe 8000. In nauali, quod undique muro cingitur, assiduè quadringenti occupantur homines, conficiendis triremibus atʒ alijs maritimis parandis rebus intenti. In Murano insula, eximia conficiuntur uitrea uasa, quę uulgò Crystallina appellantur, & per omnes regiones circumferuntur.

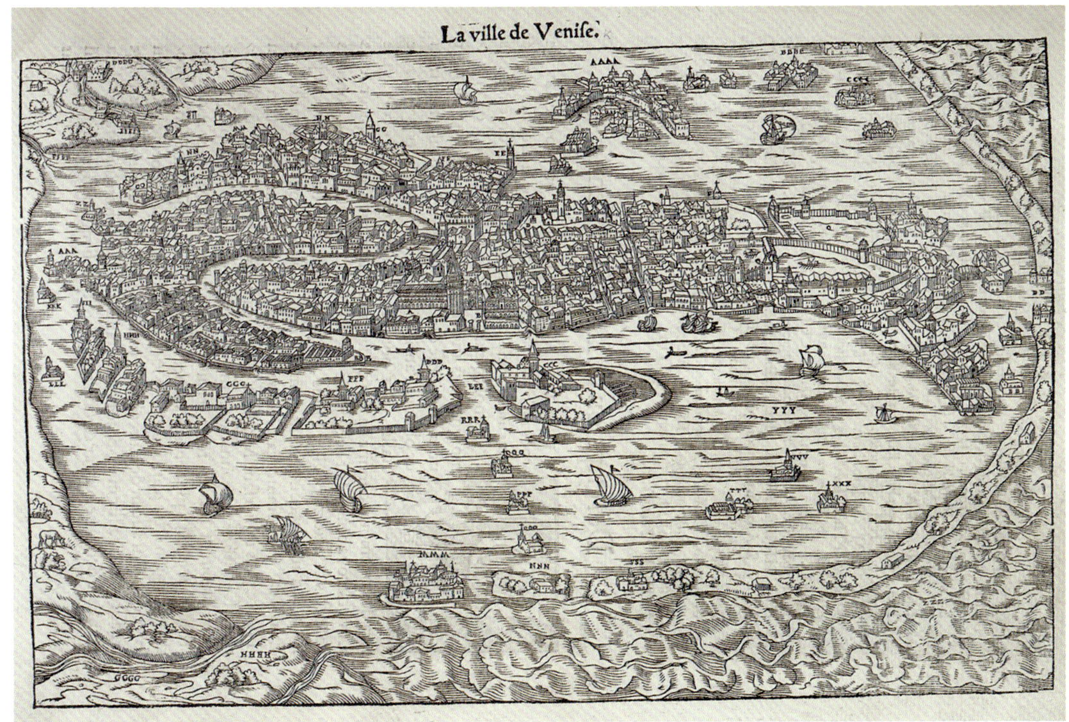

La ville de Venise.

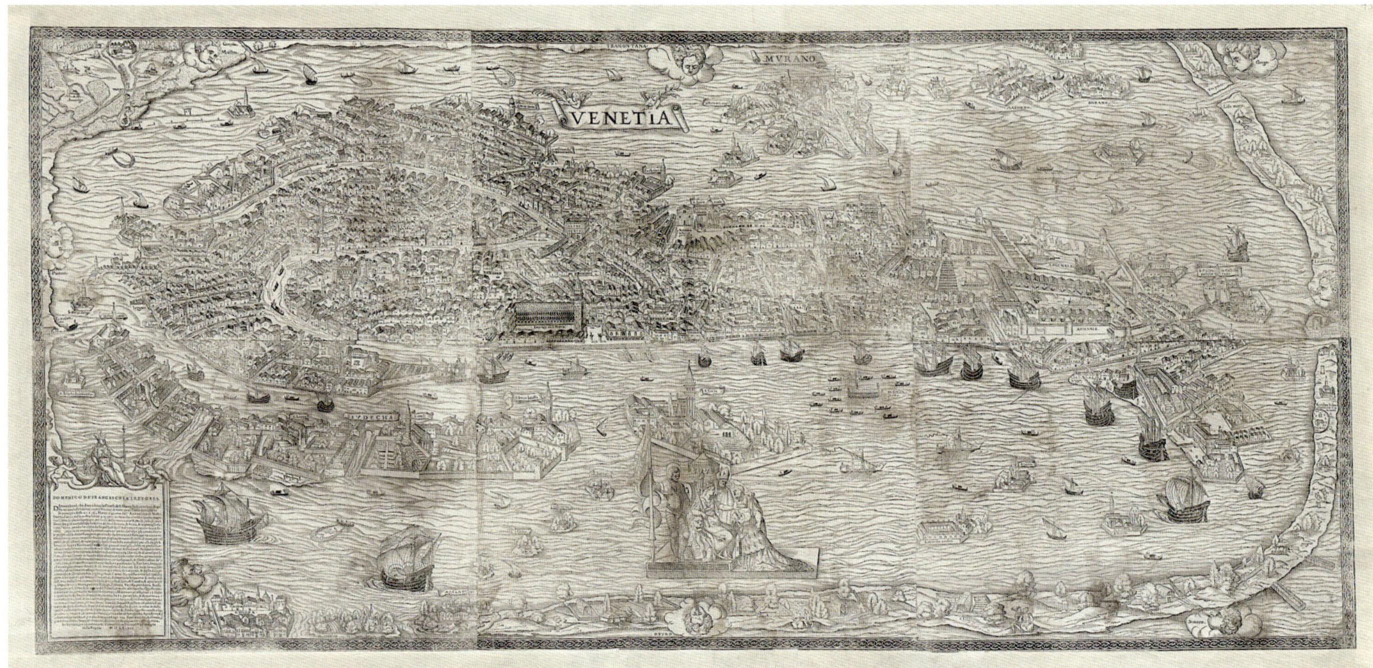

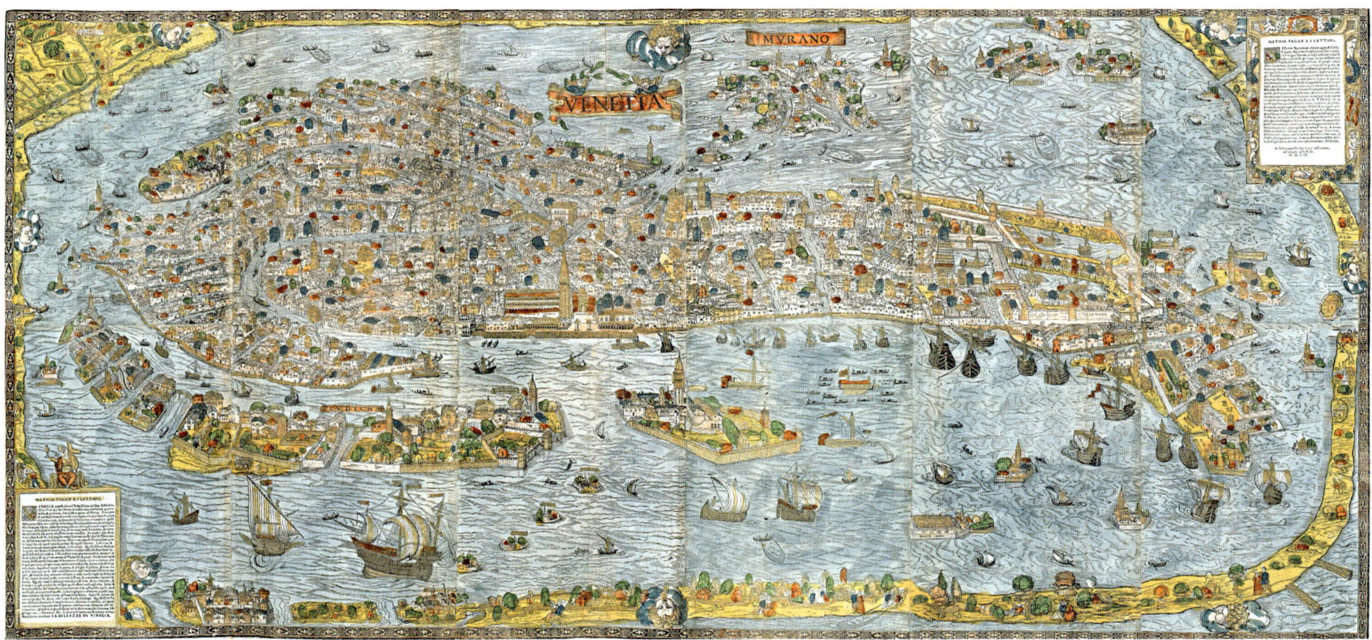

history, rituals and customs that had been treated more economically in the earlier permutations.

The endeavour was enormously well received, and, although Sansovino died before he could realise his plan to reprint the text, it was updated and republished several times during the following century.[23] The 1604 edition, revised by Giovanni Stringa, a canon at San Marco, featured a map of the city on its frontispiece, an indication of the close connection between the spirit of this text and the printed views of the city. In essence, Sansovino's guidebook addressed the same sort of interest in topographical detail that fuelled demand for visual depictions, but it provided something the plans, however detailed, could not offer – an amplified look at Venice from ground level. The text amounted to an early modern 'zoom' function, providing a view inside the buildings, and a glimpse of the people who inhabited them. It is easy to appreciate how rewarding such a handy interpretative aid would have made the experience of visiting the city as a foreigner, or of discovering it anew as a local. It supplied just the sort of information that would be useful for anyone, from the casual traveller to the merchant or statesman, and it is not difficult to imagine that Wotton and even Fialetti were familiar with its contents.[24] Nor is it a challenge to conceive how happily the Republic must have received such a panegyric text. The objective of the guidebook is not analysis. It aims to extol the author's chosen homeland, and in so doing it perpetuates the utopian ideal and mirrors in textual form the sorts of ideas propagated by published histories and perspectival plans.

An emphasis on the miraculous nature of Venice's existence, shaped by the combined forces of God, nature and the ingenuity of Venetians, remained a consistent theme across both written and visual descriptions of the city.[25] Sansovino was able to elaborate on Venice's most prized foundation legends, from its establishment on the feast of the Annunciation in the year 421 to the special connection it shared with Mark the Evangelist, in a way that the short descriptive texts included in views could not. The foreigner in the 1561 dialogue marvels at having witnessed "the impossible in the impossible", a miracle in stone shaped in the most unlikely and inhospitable of conditions.[26] In the 1581 guidebook Sansovino stressed the perfection of Venetian geography and its position in the middle of the sea, affording the convenience and protection of the water and the pleasure of land.[27] The geographical singularity

of the city also receives emphasis in the cartouches in woodcuts such as Pagan's and in the publications of Münster and Arnoullet (figs. 42, 43, 45, 46). The woodcuts also provide visual clues to its containment and emphasize the natural barrier the lagoon provided against invasion by external forces. The Dolomite mountain range, visible on the horizon in the de' Barbari map, affords a further sense of insulation and a measure of added protection from attacks from the North, but this feature was not to be repeated in subsequent printed views. The impression of impenetrability was communicated instead through the depiction of Venice's smaller outlying islands and *lidi*, an innovation that appears for the first time in Bordone's 1528 woodcut (see fig. 39). The strip of islands depicted on the left and top coalesces with the terra-ferma, shown as a band on the right and below, to form a sort of ring or cocoon that encircles a simplified profile of Venice at its core, with the city itself rendered on a different scale from the array of its smaller counterparts in the lagoon. The feature introduced by Bordone was repeated in all the subsequent plans named above, but was merged with the more complex form of the city from the de' Barbari model to form a hybrid of these two pioneering views. The importance of depicting the mainland would only intensify after the Republic's victories during the Cambrai wars, as the Venetian elite increasingly focused on the cultivation of agricultural holdings in the countryside, a shift that resulted in the building boom which kept Andrea Palladio busy designing villas during the second half of the century.[28]

While these views communicated a sense of Venice's insularity, they also conveyed a degree of openness, suggesting the freedom and confidence it enjoyed as a result of its geographical position, something no other city in the world could claim. Sixteenth-century views present the city as it was – relatively unfortified, with

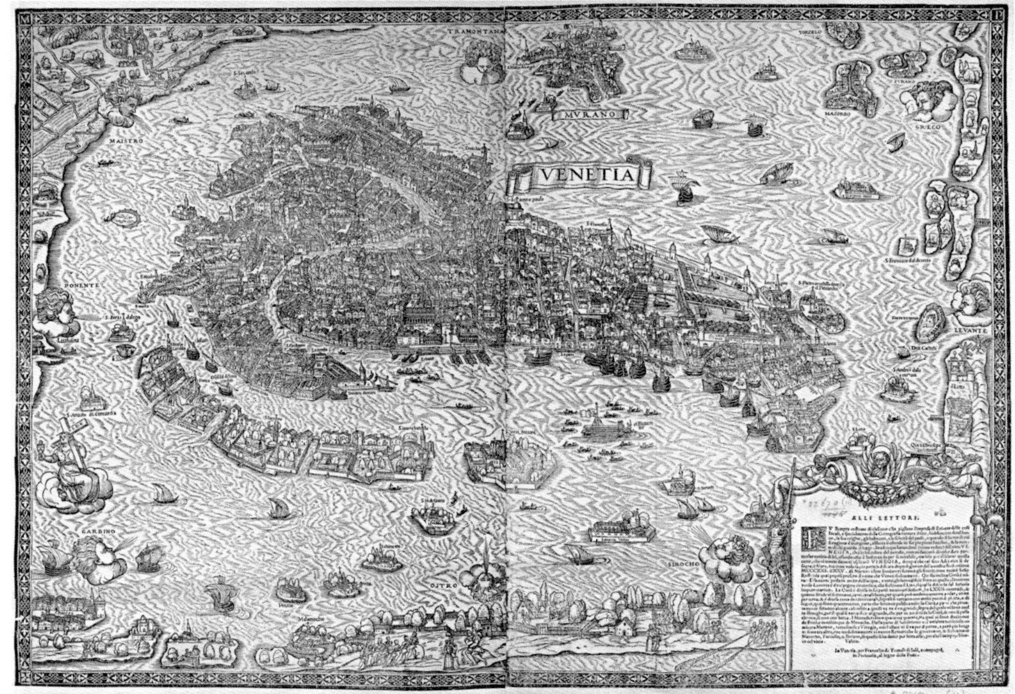

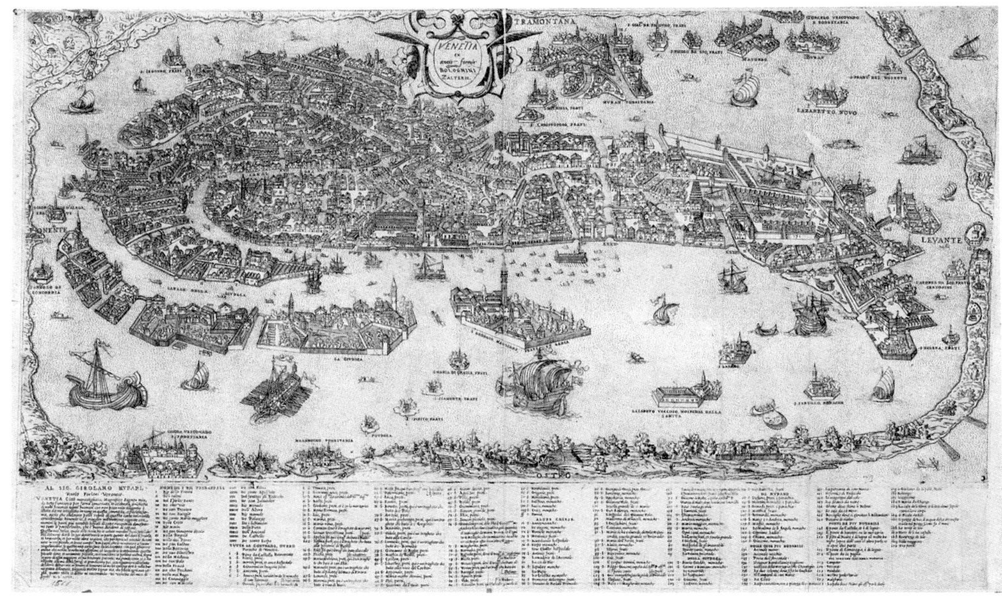

a few exceptions. The Fortezza di Sant'Andrea (begun 1543), built for the purposes of defense at the mouth of the lagoon, was added to Pagan's small plan (fig. 46), and to the views produced by Forlani and Franco (figs. 47, 49). The variety of ships produced within the confines of the Arsenale's three-metre-high walls was depicted with great precision across all the plans illustrated here, galleys dotting the lagoon as a less than subtle reminder of yet another reason Venetians had to be confident. The viewer of Jacopo de' Barbari's plan was prompted to recall the celestial arsenal that guarded Venice's interests as a maritime power through the depiction of the Roman deities Mercury, the patron of commerce, and Neptune, god of the sea (fig. 34). Their presence and inscribed declarations of protection served to emphasize Venice's industry and its Roman connections.[29] The way they were positioned to the north and south of the main island of the city also anchored the visual focus to the Piazza San Marco and the Rialto. These were the premier socio-economic spaces in the city, but they carried additional associations with the legends that formed the core of the 'myth of Venice' – the foundation of the church of San Giacomo di Rialto on the feast of the Annunciation in 421, and the translation of the body of their great patron St Mark in 828.

Although Mercury and Neptune did not appear in subsequent views, the Piazza, Piazzetta and Rialto continued to enjoy special emphasis. Here we see how the physical perfection of the arrangement of the city that was presented in these maps served as an indicator of the ways in which it was unique in political, social and historical terms – a uniqueness that was reinforced in their legends and cartouches, as well as Sansovino's dialogues and guidebook. Not only was Venice naturally insulated from threatening forces in the world beyond the lagoon, it was also described as impervious to internal strife thanks to its wise and stable constitution. For Sansovino, the recipe for the Republic's success in this regard was reflected in the topography of the Piazza San Marco, where the most important religious space in the city, the ducal chapel, stood adjacent to the seat of government and the courts. In the Venetian system, church and state worked symbiotically to ensure justice and liberty for its citizens. This interrelationship is communicated in the plan by Master I.C.A. of 1565 (fig. 44) through the depiction (just below the island of San Giorgio Maggiore) of a genuflecting doge presented by St Mark to a female figure, crowned and seated upon the wise King Solomon's throne of lions, and flanked

by a bishop and Venice's first patron, the warrior saint Theodore. The iconography would have been familiar from imagery that proliferated throughout the city, and the deliberately polyvalent female figure of Venetia would have been instantly recognisable as alluding simultaneously to the Virgin *and* to a personification of Justice.[30] The doge, regarded by Venetians as the earthly proxy of St Mark, therefore kneels humbly before two ideals at once – the faith he is bound to protect (the Virgin) and the law he is required to enforce (Justice), buttressed by the support of the bishop, representative of the pope, and the militant St Theodore. Here Pagan aims to deliver a visual message about the spirit behind the egalitarian governance of the Republic and, once again, the divine protection it enjoyed.

In his guidebook Sansovino offered a description of the astonishingly complex system of balloting used to protect against corruption in the election of a new doge as evidence of the ongoing concern with that maintenance of the democracy on which the earliest settlement was founded.[31] The sixth-century Roman prefect Cassiodorus testified that the first Venetians lived without the blight of envy, for their homes, diets and occupations remained virtually identical, preventing one from standing out amongst the others.[32] Later, even the doge was considered to be no more than the first among equals. Observance of this communal spirit and an ethos of moderation remained critical to the maintenance of social order in Venice. Cassiodorus's text was well-known in later sixteenth century Venice and was cited in Sansovino's guidebook.[33] Although Sansovino described the lavish banquets and dress of the Venetians, he also praised the Republic for its wisdom in the creation of sumptuary laws that attempted to discourage these behaviours and promote modesty. Unity was further reinforced by the exceptional communal piety of the Venetians, exemplified by the city's many lavishly decorated churches and the public displays of religious devotion by its confraternities. Venetian spirituality was treated in printed maps in a variety of ways. Matteo Pagan highlighted the importance of religion in the maintenance of harmony in both his plans through the inclusion of a female personification of Faith holding a cross and chalice. In the large plan of 1559 (fig. 45) she is placed atop the descriptive cartouche in the lower left corner, glancing in the direction of the city. In the smaller plan of 1562–65 (fig. 46) she is shifted to the left margin of the woodcut, floating on a cloud and dynamically poised to chart a course across the length of the city she governs, perhaps upon the breeze generated by the heads of the winds blowing furiously from around the periphery, a design element lifted from Jacopo de' Barbari's precedent (fig. 30). The authors of most sixteenth-century views made a special effort to represent each of Venice's many churches, some in almost archaeological detail. From Vavassore's pioneering cartouche onwards, the descriptive texts that accompanied these maps make a habit of listing the more than seventy parishes and forty monasteries, and Forlani's innovative addition of a numbered legend in 1566 allowed viewers to identify each of the shrines by name (fig. 47). Sansovino's guidebook provided the added bonus of descriptions of the architects of these churches and the contents of their interiors, paintings, sculpture, memorials and an astonishing array of relics.

By 1581, the multitude of artistic treasures to be seen in the city had vastly multiplied. The shimmering mosaics and exotic marbles of San Marco (fig. 23) and the delicate traceries and fenestrations of Venice's Gothic buildings (fig. 25) now commingled with classically inspired monuments of Istrian stone. Sansovino claimed that Venice's interiors were filled with more paintings than in the rest of Italy, including the works of its great Renaissance artists – Giovanni Bellini, Giorgione, Titian,

Tintoretto and Veronese.[34] But these marvels were only one component of the spectacle that was Venice. The texts and legends in maps increasingly cited specific curiosities, like the number of bridges and boats, the laudable costume of the Venetians, and the pageantry of their ubiquitous public processions and ceremonies. It is difficult not to associate the mounting interest in the minutiae of the living city with Matteo Pagan's decision to depart from the tradition of depicting the city as an empty stage and to populate his sizeable 1559 view with vignettes of life throughout the city (fig. 45). Gondolas ply the grand canal, boats of every variety dot the lagoon or are constructed in the Arsenale by tiny labourers, Venetians recline, fish and promenade on the *lido* in the foreground, while smaller figures frolic on the mainland in the distance.[35] A year later Pagan produced an impressive woodcut of a ducal procession in Piazza San Marco in profile, revelling in the opportunity to depict and label Venetians of every rank in their processional attire, making use of a second tier of space above to depict turbanned spectators and women leaning out of balconies in their finery (fig. 50). Like Sansovino's written descriptions, such images brought the curious viewer to ground level and provided them with an opportunity to observe Venetian daily life. By 1572 Franz Hogenberg had moved beyond the borders of the printed plan to incorporate the highest-ranking slice of a procession just like the one shown in the Pagan woodcut, placing it between the two parts of the legend at the bottom of the plan (fig. 48). Viewers of the map of the city were now provided with a means of forming a more vivid image of the processions that so frequently wended their way through the veins of the city. Giacomo Franco and Bernardo Salvioni elaborated on this motif in their 1597 views (figs. 49, 51). Franco included a vastly expanded two-tiered procession and a variety of maritime festivities in honour of the coronation of the

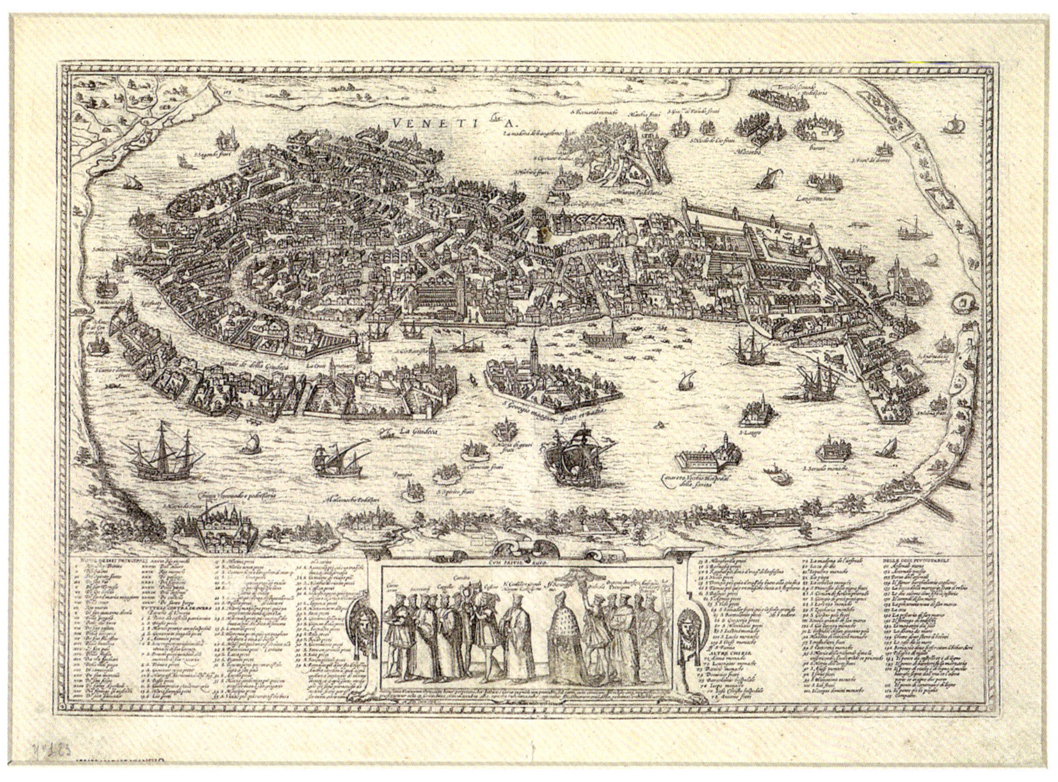

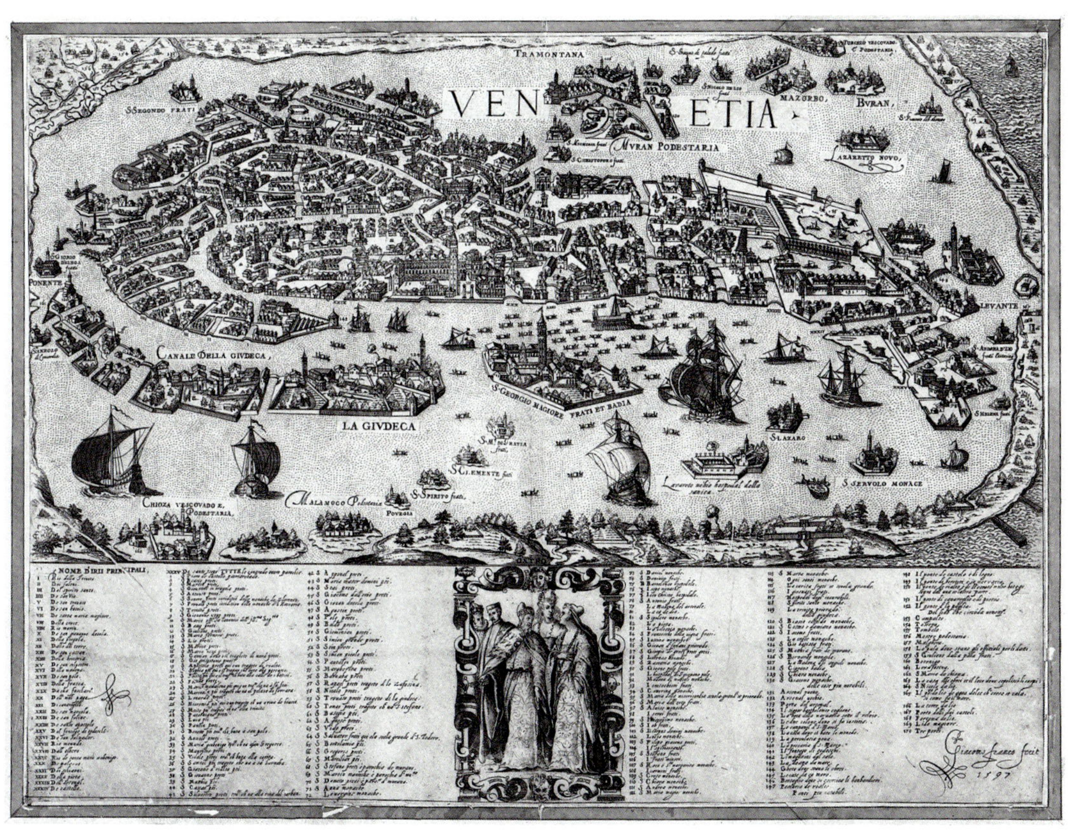

TRAMONTANA
VENETIA
MAZORBO, BVRAN,
SEGONDO PRATI
MVRAN PODESTARIA
PONENTE
LEVANTE
CANALE DELLA GIVDECA,
LA GIVDECA
S. GEORGIO MAGIORE PRATI ET BADIA
S. LAZARO
S. CLEMENTE
CHIOZA VESCOVADO E PODESTARIA,
MALAMOCO Podesteria
S. SPIRITO
S. SERVOLO MONACE

Dogaressa Morosina Morosini Grimani. Salvioni's variation maintained the procession, but paired it with flanking images of the Piazza San Marco and the newly rebuilt Rialto Bridge. In 1610, Franco included one of his views in his treatise on the costume of Venetian women, a book whose very existence depended on the desire of the international community to put Venetian life under the microscope.[36] Indeed, the frontispiece of an expanded version of Franco's treatise, published the same year, featured a simplified aerial view of Venice, not unlike Bordone's, but rendered as if viewed through a convex lens.[37]

The evolution of techniques, both in science and in the graphic arts, that permitted increasing realism in the rendering of topographical details coincided with the remarkable prosperity of the Venetian print industry. At the same time, this was a period in which the slowly declining Republic was exceptionally focused on disseminating a particular image of itself to an international community that grew ever more curious about the nature of the city and its inhabitants.

Although more map titles were published in Venice in 1566 than in any other city at any other time, in the late 1570s its dominance in the production of maps, and in publishing in general, began to wane.[38] The plague of 1574–76 wiped out nearly fifty thousand people and sent multitudes of others fleeing, including printers and graphic artists, who ended up in the more thriving centres of production in the Low Countries.[39] The city views of the following century were far more imitative of their sixteenth-century predecessors, especially Pagan, Forlani and Franco – plans that may also have been models for Fialetti.

In the context of a book about a view of Venice made by a non-Venetian and acquired by a foreigner it is interesting to reflect upon the sheer quantity of the material, both literary and visual, that was produced to promote the image of Venice in the sixteenth century by and for those who were not Venetian. As their petitions for privileges record, Anton Kolb, Francesco Sansovino, and a good number of the authors and publishers of the views discussed here worked tirelessly at their tributes to

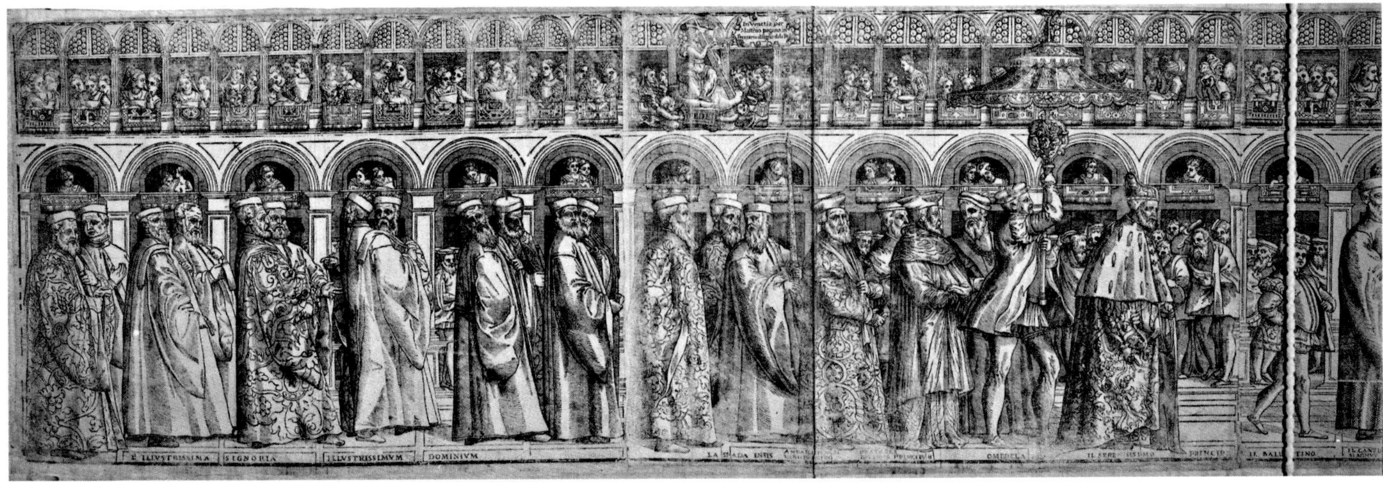

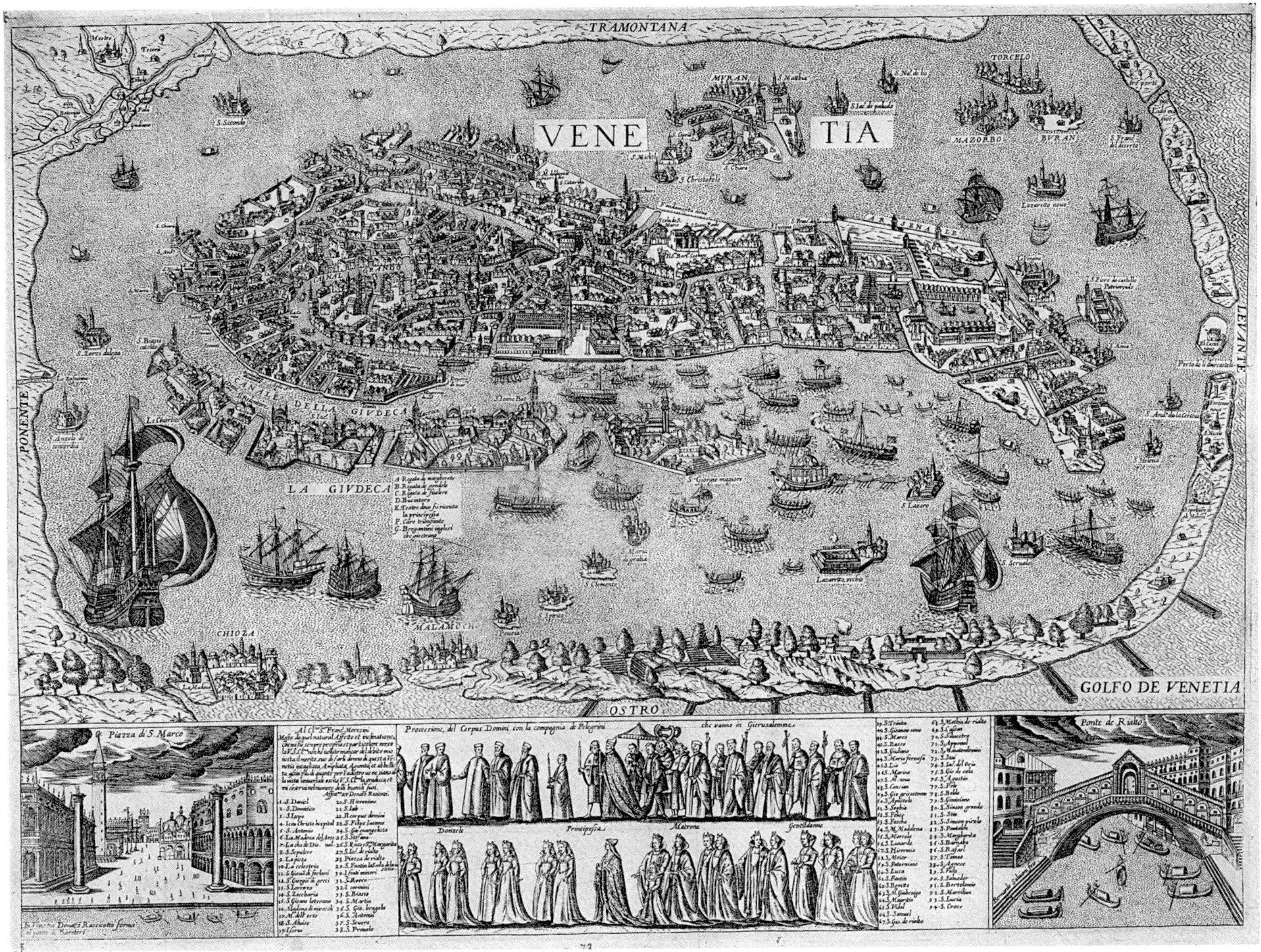

a city that was not their own, in works that have ultimately proved formative in shaping the historical image of Venice.[40] We can imagine that, like Fialetti and Wotton, each had their own motivations and biases in producing these objects, but in a way the admiring descriptions they provided – whether genuine or contrived, accurate or flawed – are rendered all the more convincing and instructive exactly because they represent the testimony of foreigners addressed to other outsiders.

Francesco Sansovino reported that the word 'Venetia' was thought by some to have derived from '*Veni etiam*', that is, come again and again, for, "however oft you come, you will always see new things, and new beauties".[41] There is reason enough to be dubious about these etymological origins, but the sentiment is beguiling, and anyone familiar with Venice will know that there is more than a bit of truth to the statement. A first trip is unlikely to be the last, and each visit brings some new revelation of place and space. So, too, the maps and views discussed here encourage repeat encounters for the viewer to seek out new details within the endlessly rich and descriptive pictorial space. Then, as now, they serve to trigger memories of visits past, or to conjure in the imagination the image of a place still waiting to be discovered, a city where, after more than a thousand years, the impossible continues to exist within the impossible.

NOTES

1 G. Cassini, *Piante e vedute prospettiche di Venezia: 1479–1855*, Venice, 1971, p. 27; D. Woodward, *Maps as Prints in the Italian Renaissance: Makers, Distributors and Consumers*, London, 1996, pp. 2–5. Venice and Rome became the major centres for the publishing of maps in the early sixteenth century, eclipsing Florence, where the trade had been first established, and remained dominant until the late 1560s. An estimated five to six hundred copper plates for maps were in active use in Venice in the sixteenth century.

2 R. Finlay, 'The Immortal Republic: The Myth of Venice during the Italian Wars (1494–1530)', *Sixteenth Century Journal*, xxx, 1999, pp. 931–44; D. Rosand, *Myths of Venice: The Figuration of a State*, Chapel Hill, 2001; E. Crouzet-Pavan, *Venice Triumphant: The Horizons of a Myth*, Baltimore, 2002.

3 D. Cosgrove, 'The myth and the stones of Venice: an historical geography of a symbolic landscape', *Journal of Historical Geography*, viii, 1982, p. 149; M. Tafuri, *Venezia nell'età di Andrea Gritti (1523–1538)*, Rome, 1984; D. Howard, *Jacopo Sansovino: Architecture and Patronage in Renaissance Venice*, New Haven and London, 1987; M. Tafuri, *Venice and the Renaissance*, transl. Jessica Levine, Cambridge, 1989, pp. 103–38.

4 Other influential texts of the late fifteenth and sixteenth centuries included Domenico Morosini's *De bene instituta republica Venetiarum* (1497–1509), Marcantonio Sabellico's *De Venetae urbis situ* (1490), Marin Sanudo's *De origine, situ et magistratibus urbis venetae, ovvero La Città di Venetia* (1493), Donato Gianotti's *Libro dela Republica de' Vinitiani* (1540), Gasparo Contarini's *De Magistratibus et Republica Venetorum* (1543), Pietro Bembo's *Historiae Venetae* (1551), and Paolo Paruta's *Della perfettione della vita politica* (1579).

5 Woodward, *Maps as prints*, p. 69. There were about 450 printers, publishers and booksellers in sixteenth-century Venice. On the print industry in Venice see: H.F. Brown, *The Venetian Printing Press*, London, 1891; D. Landau and P. Parshall, *The Renaissance Print*, 1470–1550, New Haven and London, 1994; G.J. van der Sman, 'Print Publishing in Venice in the Second Half of the Sixteenth-Century', *Print Quarterly*, xvi, 2000, pp. 235–47; M. Bury, *The Print in Italy*, 1550–1620, London, 2001.

6 W. Bouwsma, 'Venice and the political education of Europe', in J.R. Hale (ed.), *Renaissance Venice*, London, 1974, pp. 445–66.

7 B. Wilson, *The World in Venice: Print, the City, and Early Modern Identity*, Toronto, 2005, p. 3; Woodward, *Maps as prints*, pp. 39, 83. The lack of record of these maps and views in Venetian inventories suggests that the local audience was not the primary target of this industry, although the relatively low survival rate for many of these objects is an added obstacle to determining who exactly possessed them and precisely how they were used or displayed.

8 J. Schulz, 'Jacopo de' Barbari's View of Venice: Map Making, City Views, and Moralized Geography before the Year 1500', *Art Bulletin*, lx, 1978, p. 427.

9 G. Mazzi, 'La cartografia per il mito: le immagini di Venezia nel Cinquecento', in *Architettura e utopia nella Venezia del Cinquecento*, Milan, 1980, pp. 50–58; D. Howard, 'Venice as a Dolphin: Further Investigations into Jacopo de' Barbari's View', *Artibus et Historiae*, xviii, 1997, pp. 101–11.

10 Schulz, 'Jacopo de' Barbari's View', pp. 425–74.

11 *Ibid.*, pp. 431–41; Howard, 'Venice as a Dolphin', pp. 105–07.

12 J. Schulz, 'The Printed Plans and Panoramic Views of Venice (1486–1797)', *Saggi e memorie di storia dell'arte*, vii, 1970, p. 21; Schulz, 'Jacopo de' Barbari's View', p. 442; Wilson, *The World in Venice*, p. 4. Subsequent plans were not the result of the process of surveying undertaken by Kolb and Jacopo de' Barbari, although they may well have been informed by the regular surveys executed for the government.

13 Giovanni Andrea Vavassore updated his 1525 plan with buildings such as the Palazzo dei Camerlenghi at the Rialto, the Procuratie Vecchie, the completed Torre dell'Orologio, and the rebuilt Fondaco dei Tedeschi. Matteo Pagan's large plan of 1559 was the next to update the view in any remarkable way, adding the recently constructed buildings of the Scuola Grande di San Rocco, the Zecca (the Mint), the first portion of the Marciana Library, and the extension to the Arsenale. The view by Master I.C.A. of 1565 was the first to depict Sansovino's Loggetta and his church of San Geminiano.

14 Woodward, *Maps as prints*, p. 45.

15 Schulz, 'The Printed Plans', p. 22.

16 Schulz, 'The Printed Plans'; Cassini, *Piante e vedute*; S. Biadene and G. Romanelli (eds.), *Venezia: piante e vedute. Catalogo del fondo cartografico a stampa*, Venice, 1982; G. Moretto (ed.), *Venetia. Le immagini delle Repubblica. Piante e vedute prospettiche della citta' dal 1479–1797*, Piazzola sul Brenta, 2001.

17 Giovanni Andrea Vavassore, woodcut, 371 x 527 mm, Venice: Vavassore, 1525; see Schulz, 'The Printed Plans', no. 5; Cassini, *Piante e vedute*, no. 7; Moretto, *Venetia. Le immagini*, no. 10. Bordone, woodcut, 225 x 328 mm, in the *Libro di Benedetto Bordone nel quale si ragiona di tutte l'Isole del mondo*, Venice: Nicolò Zoppino, 1528; see Schulz, 'The Printed Plans', no. 8; Cassini, *Piante e vedute*, no. 8; Biadene and Romanelli, *Venezia: piante e vedute*, no. 7; Moretto, *Venetia. Le immagini*, no. 11. Master C.S (Cristoph Stimmer?), woodcut, 247 x 386 mm, in *Cosmographiae Universalis Lib. VI. Autore Seb. Mustero*, Basle: Heinrich Petri, 1550; see Schulz, 'The Printed Plans', no. 14; Cassini, *Piante e vedute*, no. 11; Biadene and Romanelli, *Venezia: piante e vedute*, no. 8; Moretto, *Venetia. Le immagini*, no. 13. Anonymous, woodcut, 160 x 255 mm, in Guillaume Gueroult, *Premier livre des figures et poutraitz des villes plus illustres et renommes d'Europe*, Lyons: Balthazar Arnoullet, 1552; see Schulz, 'The Printed Plans', no. 8; Cassini, *Piante e vedute*, no. 21; Moretto, *Venetia. Le immagini*, no. 14.

18 Matteo Pagan, large perspectival plan of Venice, woodcut, 770 x 1652 mm (in 12 sheets), 1559; see Schulz, 'The Printed Plans', no. 34;

Cassini, *Piante e vedute*, no. 12; Moretto, *Venetia. Le immagini*, no. 16. Matteo Pagan, small perspective plan of Venice, woodcut, 410 x 585 mm (in two sheets), Venice: Francesco de Tomaso da Salò, 1562–65; see Schulz, 'The Printed Plans', no. 35; Cassini, *Piante e vedute*, no. 10; Moretto, *Venetia. Le immagini*, no. 18. Master I.C.A., woodcut, 573 x 1200 mm (in six sheets), Venice: Domenico de' Franceschi, 1565; see Schulz, 'The Printed Plans', no. 36; Moretto, *Venetia. Le immagini*, no. 19. Paolo Forlani, copperplate engraving, 437 x 744 mm, Venice: Bolognino Zaltiero, 1566; see Schulz, 'The Printed Plans', no. 39; Cassini, *Piante e vedute*, no. 13; Biadene and Romanelli, *Venezia: piante e vedute*, no. 9.

19 Franz Hogenberg's perspective plan of Venice, copperplate engraving, 337 x 484 mm, in Georg Braun, *Civitates orbis terrarum*, Cologne: Godefridus von Kempensis, 1572; see Schulz, 'The Printed Plans', no. 42; Cassini, *Piante e vedute*, no. 18; Biadene and Romanelli, *Venezia: piante e vedute*, no. 13; Moretto, *Venetia. Le immagini*, no. 26. Giacomo Franco, copperplate engraving, 375 x 545 mm, Rome: Claudio Duchet, 1580; see Schulz, 'The Printed Plans', no. 49; Cassini, *Piante e vedute*, no. 23; Biadene and Romanelli, *Venezia: piante e vedute*, no. 15. Two variations on the plan by Giacomo Franco, published in Venice by Giacomo Franco in 1597 and *c.* 1598, both copperplate engravings, 407 x 530 mm; see Schulz, 'The Printed Plans', no. 58; Cassini, *Piante e vedute*, no. 25; Biadene and Romanelli, *Venezia: piante e vedute*, no. 19; Moretto, *Venetia. Le immagini*, nos. 37, 38.

20 Francesco Sansovino [A. Guisconi], *Dialogo di tutte le cose notabili che sono in Venetia*, Venice, 1556. See also P. Grendler, 'Francesco Sansovino and Italian Popular History 1560–1600', *Studies in the Renaissance*, xvi, 1969, pp. 139–80; A. Moz, *Francesco Sansovino, a Polygraph in Cinquecento Venice. His Life and Works*, PhD diss., University of Carolina at Chapel Hill, 1985; E. Bonora, *Ricerche su Francesco Sansovino: imprenditore, libraio e letterato*, Venice, 1994, pp. 163–94; A.

Casper, 'A taxonomy of images: Francesco Sansovino and the San Rocco *Christ Carrying the Cross*', *Word and Image*, xxvi, 2009, pp. 100–14.

21 Moz, *Francesco Sansovino*, pp. 20, 31.

22 *Ibid.*, p. 233.

23 *Ibid.*, p. 172; Casper, 'A taxonomy', p. 102. *Venetia, città nobilissima et singolare* was updated by Giovanni Stringa in 1604 and Giustiniano Martinioni in 1663.

24 Grendler, 'Francesco Sansovino', p. 167.

25 E. Crouzet-Pavan, '*Sopra le acque salse*': *Espaces, pouvoir et société à Venise à la fin du Moyen Age*, Rome, 1992, pp. 294–95.

26 F. Sansovino, *Delle cose notabili che sono in Venetia*, Venice, 1561, fol. 1v.

27 Francesco Sansovino, *Venetia, città nobilissima et singolare*, Venice, 1581, fol. 3r: "*Ma questa [i] sola posta nel mezzo dell'acque, non ha cosa in terra alla quale si possa paragonare. Conciosia che l'unico sito suo è di modo congiunto con le sue parti, che si gode in un tempo medesimo, la commodità dell'acqua, & il piacere della terra.*"

28 D. Cosgrove, 'Mapping New Worlds: Culture and Cartography in Sixteenth-Century Venice', *Imago Mundi*, xliv, 1992, pp. 76–79.

29 'I Mercury shine favorably on this above all other emporia' (MERCVRIVS PRE CETERIS HVIC FAVSTE EMPORIIS ILLVSTRO), and 'I Neptune reside here, watching over the waters at this port' (AEQVORA TVENS PORTV RESIDEO HIC NEPTVNVS).

30 An identical figure is represented on both the southern and the western façades of the Ducal Palace, in a wealth of painted decoration inside, and on Jacopo Sansovino's Loggetta. See D. Rosand, 'Venetia Figurata: the iconography of a myth', in D. Rosand (ed.), *Interpretazioni veneziane: studi di storia dell'arte in onore di Michelangelo Muraro*, Venice, 1984, pp. 177–96.

31 Sansovino, *Venetia, città nobilissima et singolare*, fol. 180v.

32 Crouzet-Pavan, *Venice Triumphant*, pp. 4–6.

33 Sansovino, *Venetia, città nobilissima et singolare*, fols. 207v–208r.

34 *Ibid.*, fol. 35: "*In Venetia son più pitture, ch'in tutto il resto d'Italia*".

35 Some of these figures were repeated in Pagan's small plan of 1562–65, as well as that of Master I.C.A. in 1565.

36 Giacomo Franco, *Habiti delle donne intagliate in rame nuovamente*, Venice, 1610.

37 Giacomo Franco, *Habiti d'huomeni et donne venetiane con la processione della ser.ma Signoria et altri particolari cioè trionfi feste et ceremonie publiche della nobilissima città di Venetia*, Venice, 1610. On costume books see Wilson, *The World in Venice*, pp. 70–132, and on Franco's views of Venice of 1597, *ibid.*, pp. 174–80.

38 Woodward, *Maps as prints*, p. 45.

39 Cassini, *Piante e vedute*, p. 29.

40 Bonora, *Ricerche su Francesco Sansovino*, p. 164; Woodward, *Maps as prints*, p. 69. Sansovino's petition to the Council of Ten for a privilege for *Venetia, città nobilissima et singolare* emphasizes that he worked for nearly a decade to compile his guidebook. Likewise, Paolo Forlani stressed the hardship he endured in producing his view of Venice, just as Kolb had before him.

41 Sansovino, *Venetia, città nobilissima et singolare*, fol. 4r: "*Onde però fu interpretato da alcuni, che questa voce VENETIA, voglia dire Veni etiam, cioè vieni ancora, & ancora, percioche quante volte verrai, sempre vedrai nuove cose, & nuove bellezze*".

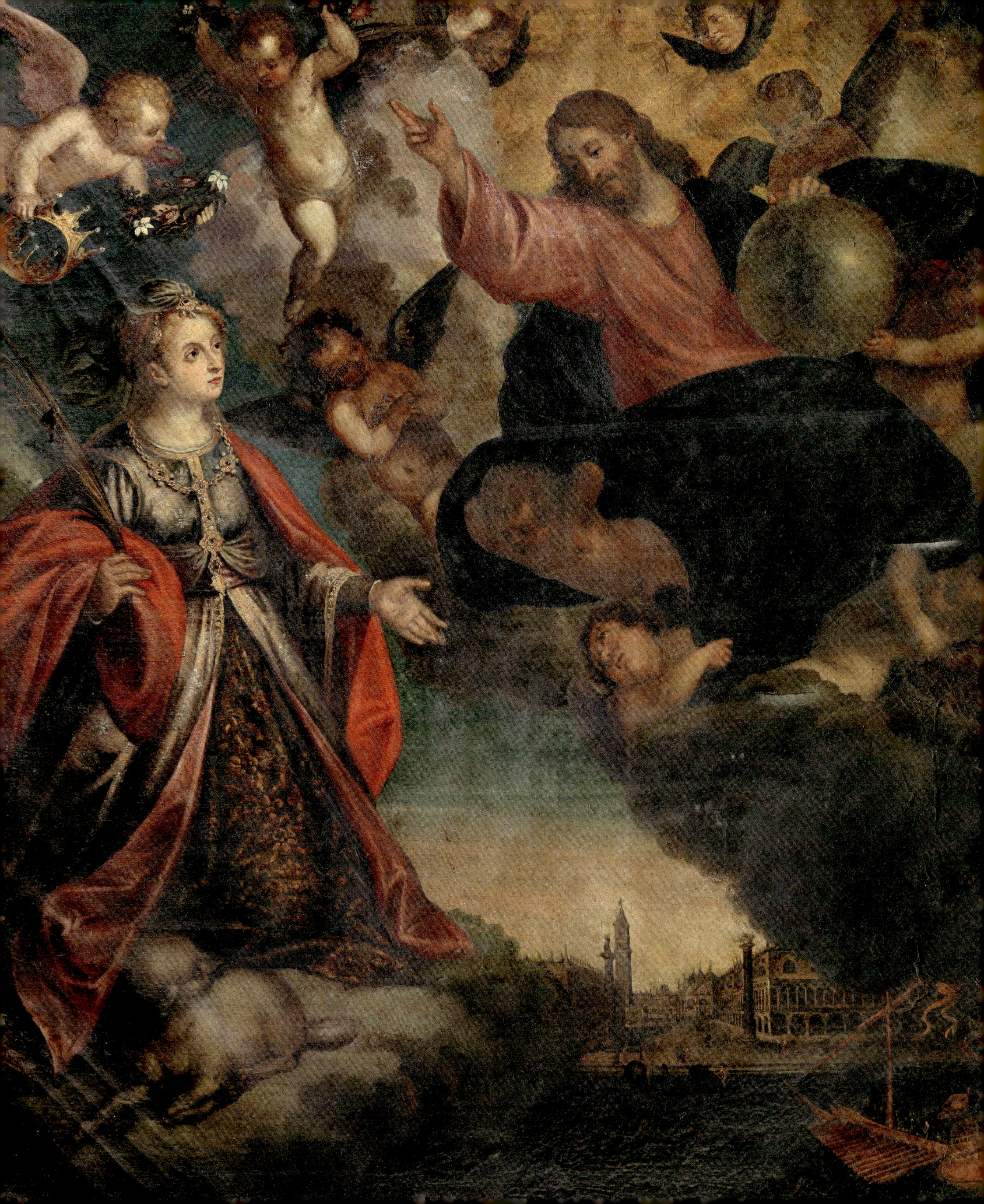

4. Odoardo Fialetti: Painter and Printmaker

LAURA WALTERS

ODOARDO FIALETTI occupies a very different place historically from the great Venetian painters who preceded him. While the importance of artists such as Titian, Veronese and Tintoretto is clear, thanks to their prolific output and enduring influence, the significance of a number of early Seicento artists active in the city, including Fialetti, who worked in a variety of media, is less obvious.[1] Fialetti exemplifies the changing role of the artist at the turn of the seventeenth century, in the context of the divide in Venetian painting between *disegno* and *colorito*, and the new interest placed in the academic tradition of drawing.

Fialetti's oeuvre is extraordinarily varied, encompassing paintings, prints, books on drawing and ornament, illustrations of city defences and anatomical treatises.[2] His subjects, produced for a wide range of patrons, spanned religious works, portraits, city views, sport, hunting, allegory and literary and mythological themes. His influence on artists in France, Northern Europe and England, in the vanguard of the increasing importance placed on *disegno* and academic practice in art in Venice and Northern Italy, was wide-reaching.[3]

Biography

Odoardo Fialetti (1573–*c*.1638) was the posthumous son of a 'Dottore Odoardo'.[4] The family, originally from Beaufort-sur-Dozon in Savoy, had settled in Bologna before Odoardo's birth.[5] He was apprenticed to Giovanni Battista Cremonini (a disciple of the Carracci), learning the foundations of good *disegno*, before moving to Padua with his brother, and then to Venice. Before settling in Venice he travelled to Rome, passing through several other studios and workshops, including Ludovico Carracci's in Bologna, Guercino's academy in Cento, and that of Guido Reni in Rome.[6] These travels and associations also probably played a large part in his artistic practice. A number of biographers claim that Fialetti left Bologna to avoid competition with the Carracci and, given the similarities in their practice and output, this seems a strong possibility.[7]

When he arrived in Venice, Fialetti became associated with Tintoretto's studio, probably during the last years of the master's life.[8] Masini calls Fialetti one of the best disciples of Tintoretto, and Ridolfi, in his life of Tintoretto, states that he gave instructions to the young artist "to draw, and then draw again, reasoning that it was *disegno* that gave grace and perfection to painting".[9] Beyond this, there exist only a few pieces of hearsay concerning the relationship between Fialetti and Tintoretto, including a recurring note in modern biographies stating that he was an executor of Tintoretto's will.[10] Fialetti's particular skill in the depiction of human anatomy (as first learned under the tutelage of his anatomist brother, Tiberio) may have been to his advantage in attracting Tintoretto's attention and then maintaining a place within his studio; it was not uncommon to have apprentices with artistic specialities.[11]

Odoardo Fialetti, *St Agnes intercedes with the Redeemer on behalf of Venice*, c. 1602–10, oil on canvas
Venice, San Niccolò da Tolentino

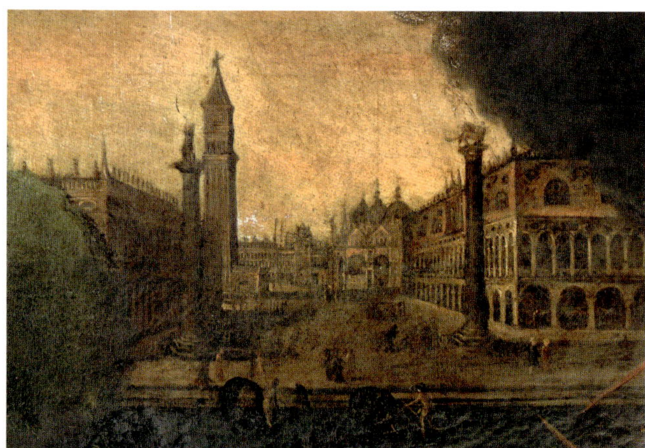

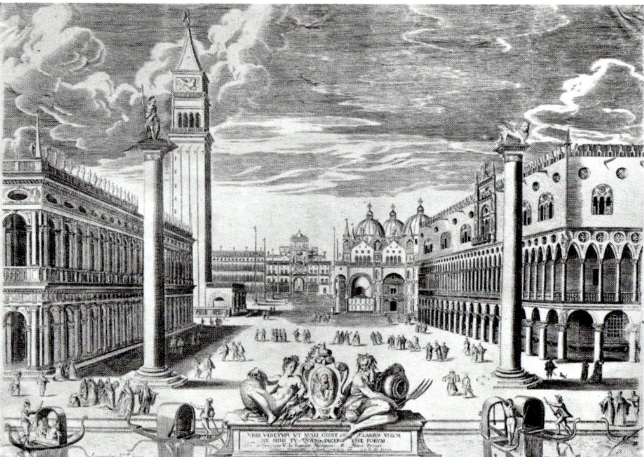

Two years after the death of Tintoretto, Odoardo reached artistic maturity when he was first listed as a printmaker in 1596, and then as a painter in 1604. Beyond his memberships of both the painters' and the printmakers' guilds, he was a member of the Scuola Grande di San Teodoro between the years 1620 and 1622.[12]

Fialetti as painter

The reputation of Odoardo Fialetti as a painter is eclipsed not only by those of his predecessors but also by his own printed works, which outnumber his paintings by ten to one. There are fewer than fifty paintings by him recorded – and of those, fewer than ten Italian paintings that can be firmly attributed have survived – yet they are discussed extensively in early biographies and guides to Venice from the seventeenth to the early twentieth centuries. Fialetti's paintings, comprising scenes from the lives of Old Testament figures, of Christ and of the saints for churches and confraternities, and a small number of portraits for private patrons, are more traditionally Venetian than his prints.[13] They are, or attempt to be, Venetian in their use of colour, but are more highly finished than the works of other artists of the late sixteenth and early seventeenth centuries in Venice. Original in terms of their composition, colour and variety of visual influences, they are stylistically distinct from those which were produced in the Tintoretto studio at the end of the sixteenth century. Two notable paintings of his, *St Agnes interceding with the Redeemer on behalf of Venice* for the new church of the Tolentini, and *The Miraculous Payment of the Boatmen* for the Dominican church of Santi Giovanni e Paolo, are typical of the artist's style, and are important for understanding the later *View of Venice* now at Eton.

The church of San Niccolò da Tolentino was founded in 1591 and consecrated in 1602.[14] Fialetti's picture of *St Agnes* was probably painted soon afterwards, perhaps before 1610.[15] The painting hangs on the entrance wall of the church and is dominated by the figures of St Agnes and Christ, surrounded by putti (fig. 52). The artist pays particular attention to the variety of textures, for example in the robes of the saint and the lamb at her feet (acting to identify her, along with her martyr's palm), but the detail is largely lost in the work's ill-lit position. Here Fialetti moves away from the depictions of St Agnes by Tintoretto, exerting his artistic independence instead of simply producing a copy or studio piece. More interesting than the saint in the present context, however, is the background view of the Piazzetta San Marco at sunset in the lower right of the painting (fig. 53). This vignette is Fialetti's only known view of Venice besides the Eton *View*. It seems to have been based on Justus Sadeler's 1585 engraving of the Piazzetta after the Flemish artist Lodewijk Toeput,

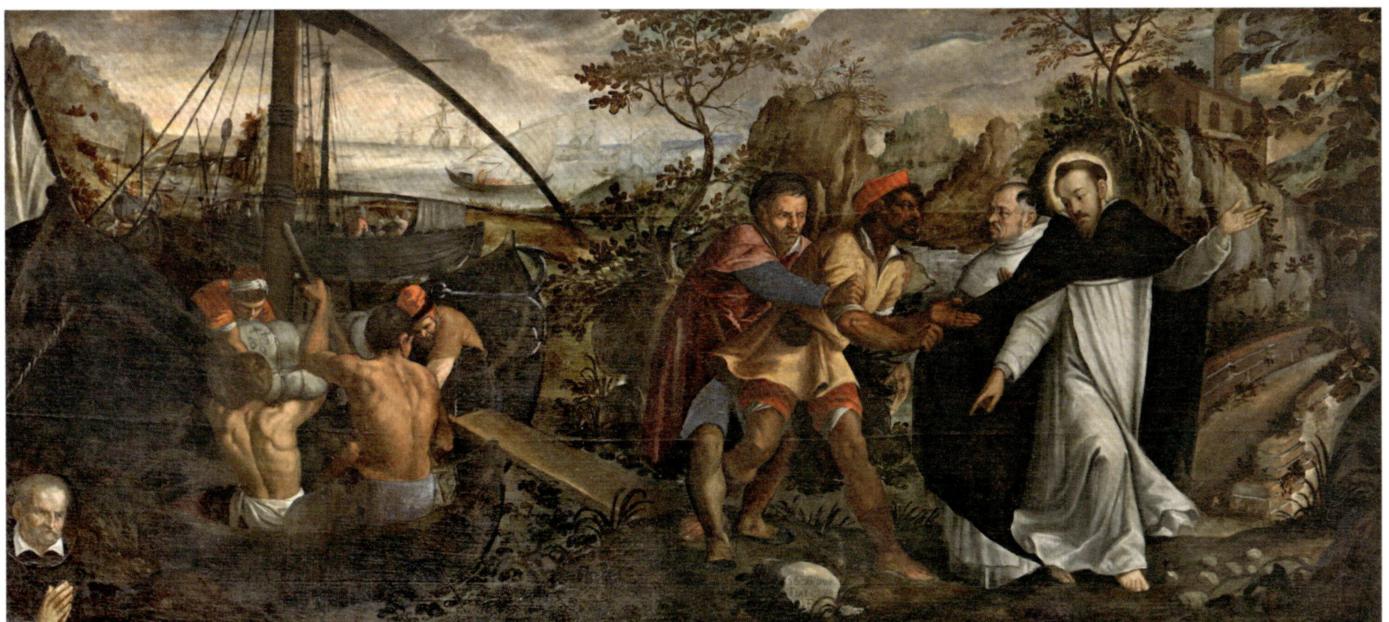

known as il Pozzoserrato (fig. 54), transformed in his painting into an atmospheric townscape by the introduction of warm colours and a soft evening light.[16] As again in the Eton *View*, here Fialetti shows his ability to transform black-and-white prints into evocative full-colour painted views.

The *Miraculous Payment of the Boatmen* (fig. 55) in the sacristy of Santi Giovanni e Paolo, painted in about 1606, is a representative example of the mixture of influences that Fialetti's work shows. His painting style was formed on the cusp of a general artistic change – the shift between the Renaissance and Baroque, the divide between *disegno* and *colorito*, and the debate between idealism and naturalism. Zava Boccazzi stresses Fialetti's interest in naturalistic detail and landscape in this picture, calling it "minutely depicted, with an almost Northern sensibility".[17] There are echoes of his printed oeuvre throughout, from the musculature of the boatmen at the left of the painting – which seem to foreshadow certain plates for his 1608 book on the art of drawing, *Il vero modo et ordine*, probably being prepared by him at the time, and others again for an anatomical atlas to which he contributed – to the detailed boats in the background, seen again later in similar arrangements in his plates for Tensini's treatise on fortification of 1624. The main protagonist,

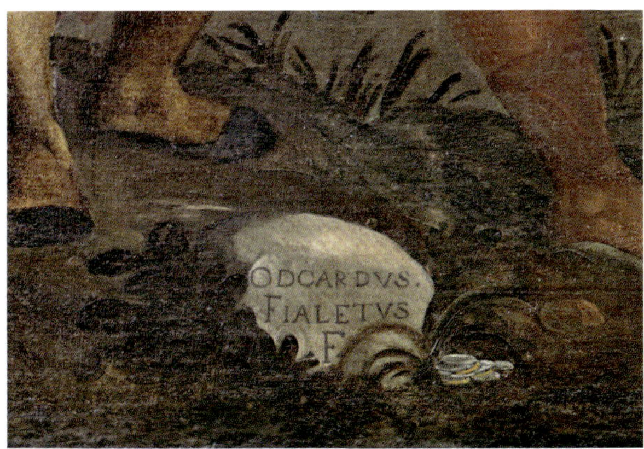

55
Odoardo Fialetti, *The Miraculous Payment of the Boatman*, oil on canvas, *c.* 1606 (with detail showing the artist's signature)
Venice, Santi Giovanni e Paolo, Sacristy

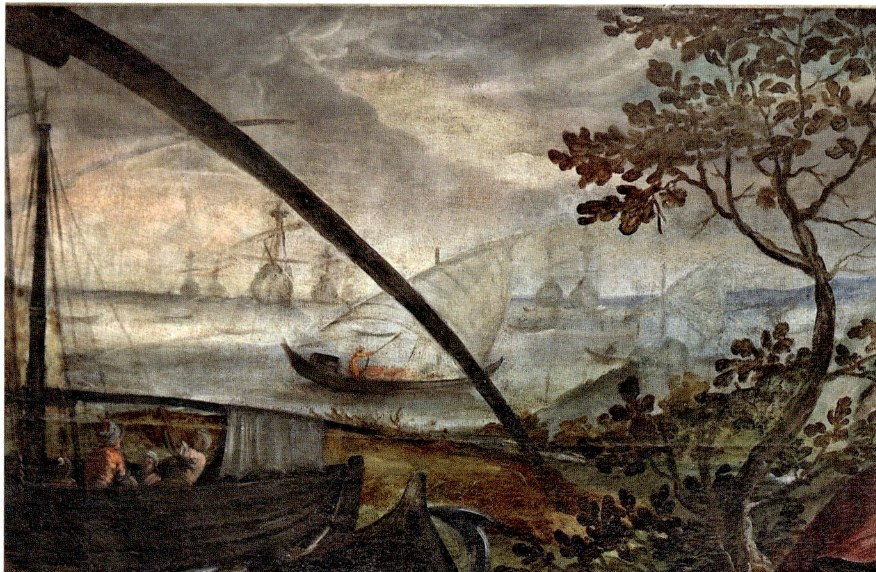

56
Fialetti, *The Miraculous Payment of the Boatman*,
detail of fig. 55 showing the harbour scene

St Dominic, points emphatically towards a white stone in the centre foreground, inscribed with the artist's name, beside which a small pile of coins has miraculously appeared (fig. 55). Although the patron, Fra Antonio Serafino, is depicted in a vignette in the lower left of the picture, it is Fialetti himself who has seized the opportunity for self-promotion.

The setting is a non-specific harbour with a town and bridge (supposedly Toulouse according to the legend); the composition actively draws the eye into the background, inviting the viewer to engage with it (fig. 56). The atmospheric pinkish sky reflected in the water, the fantastical jagged rocks and the robust trees signal Fialetti's interest in landscape as a genre, while the careful attention to the different types of boats displays a lively nautical interest, evident again in the Eton *View*. Because this painting resonates so closely with his future printed works, one can deduce that he was already trying to propagate his idea of good *disegno* (and thus good art) in public commissions, challenging earlier Venetian artists. Here as elsewhere, pictorial ideas pass freely back and forth between canvas and print.

Fialetti's printed work
While his painted style might be described as based on that of the Carracci but informed by Tintoretto,[18]

Fialetti's printed style is fluent and expressive, his landscapes and figures often characterized by what has been described as a "free sketchiness".[19] Whereas discussion of his paintings eclipses his prints in early sources, it is the prints which today overshadow the paintings as the more accomplished artistic expression. And although it is likely that the changing artistic climate necessitated his shift toward the printed medium, at least in part, it is imperative to remember that the number of artists capable of creating such a large and diverse portfolio is very small, and the number who did so successfully is even smaller. Fialetti's extant prints number between 425 and 450, covering both individual etchings and series of prints and books. His early prints include a number of copies by Venetian masters, including works after Tintoretto's *St Sebastian* and his *Wedding at Cana* for the Crociferi, which possibly contributed to his unfair reputation as a mere copyist.[20]

After he matured as a printmaker, Fialetti diversified into other genres and formats, including a number of portraits for book dedications, religious and mythological figures and scenes, and fully illustrated series of plates for books. His etchings of the habits of the religious orders (figs. 57–58) not only reveal his refined graphic skills but also attest to a lively interest in habits (in the sense of both customs and costumes). In the context of the Eton *View*'s apparently pro-Jesuit bias, it may be noted

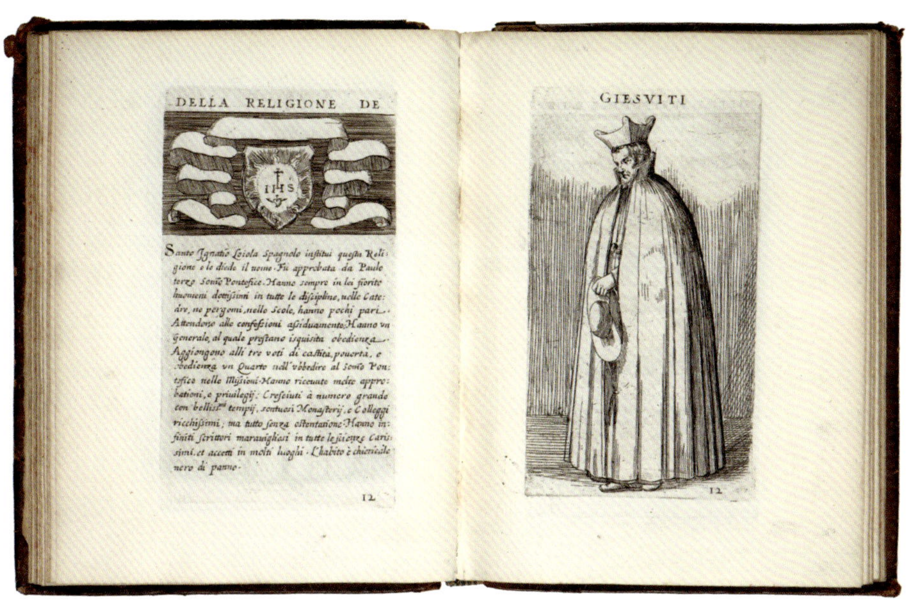

57

Odoardo Fialetti, *Jesuiti*, etching from *De gli habiti delle religioni*, Venice:
Marcus Sadeler, 1626 (reproduced from the French edition, *Briefve histoire
de l'institution des ordres religieux*, Paris: A. Menier, 1658), plate 12
University Library Cambridge, classmark F165.c.4.1

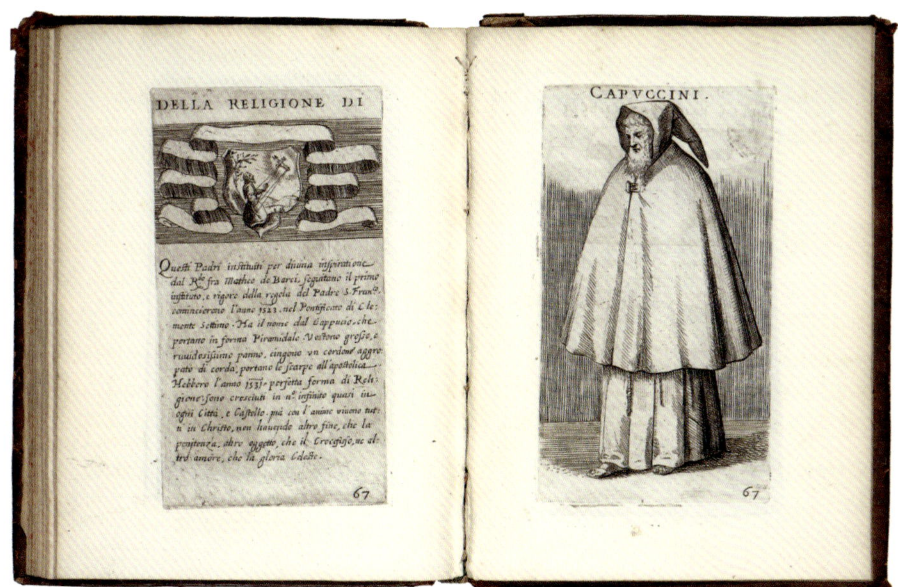

58

Odoardo Fialetti, *Cappuccini*, etching from *De gli habiti delle religioni*,
Venice: Marcus Sadeler, 1626 (reproduced from the French edition, *Briefve
histoire de l'institution des ordres religieux*, Paris: A. Menier, 1658), plate 67
University Library Cambridge, classmark F165.c.4.1

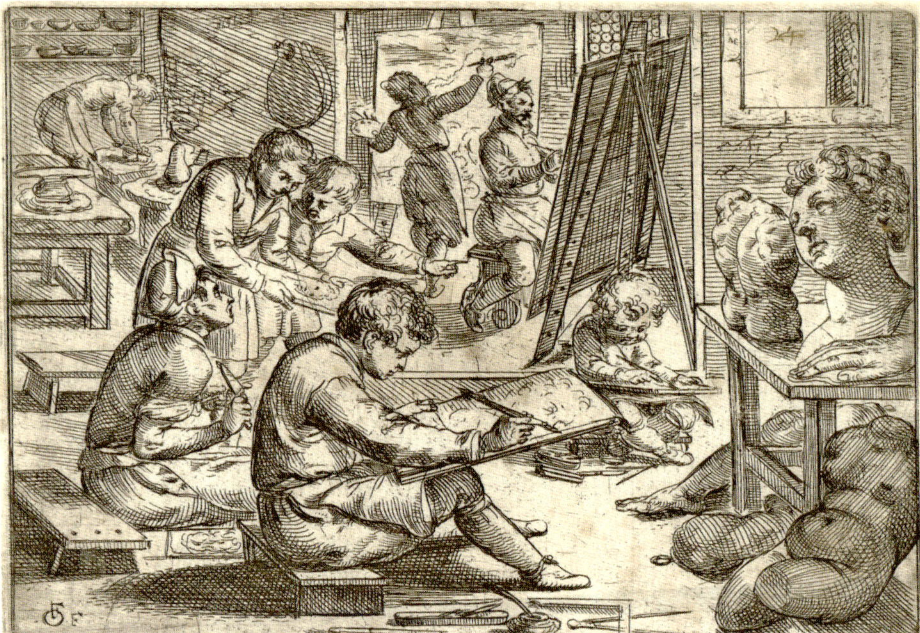

that Fialetti is entirely even-handed in his treatment of the different orders in this book. His work on books demonstrates his contacts with leading publishers and thus his wide influence in varied intellectual and social spheres. Through his relationships with publishers and other printmakers in Venice he could gain access to a range of printed imagery, which, as noted elsewhere in this book, he incorporated liberally into his paintings. As is clear from the dedications of his books, he addressed various different audiences – aristocratic for his books on sport, love and allegory; artistic for his drawing manuals; and scientific and medical in his anatomies.

Odoardo Fialetti was first listed as a printmaker in 1596, only two years after the death of Tintoretto, which suggests that he was probably experimenting with the medium while he was still a member of Tintoretto's studio. According to Ridolfi, Tintoretto's advice to the young artist also included the note that "*disegno* was that which gives grace and perfection to pictures",[21] clearly reinforcing the ideas that Fialetti had already begun to develop in his travels around other studios in North Italy. Gert Jan van der Sman has noted that "selling prints was a sideline" for publishers,[22] subordinate to books, a reputation that would have also reflected on the artist who designed and engraved the prints. However, the

arrival of the Sadeler printing family in Venice around 1596 helped to elevate the profile of this kind of enterprise. Most of Fialetti's early prints are single plates or short series; then, as he grew in artistic stature, his printed production shifted towards longer series for books, which were more prestigious.

Fialetti is probably best known for his drawing book, *Il vero modo et ordine per dissegnar tutte le parti et membra del corpo humano*, published in Venice by Justus Sadeler, for Signor Don Cesare d'Este, Duke of Modena and Reggio in 1608.[23] This appears to have been the earliest drawing book of its kind to come out of Venice.[24] It is a fully illustrated manual of over thirty pages detailing the way in which one should build up the face and body of individual figures from line drawings, and also containing studies of parts of the human body, including arms, legs, sculptural torsos and grotesque heads. Again, there is no evidence to support any link between Fialetti and Agostino Carracci, but the similarity of these plates and extant Carracci studies is striking, suggesting that the two artists were aware of each other.[25]

The volume includes a depiction of an *Artist's studio*, (fig. 59), which is a very clear representation both of the method that he advocates and, probably, of Fialetti's own training. The plate depicts apprentices of several

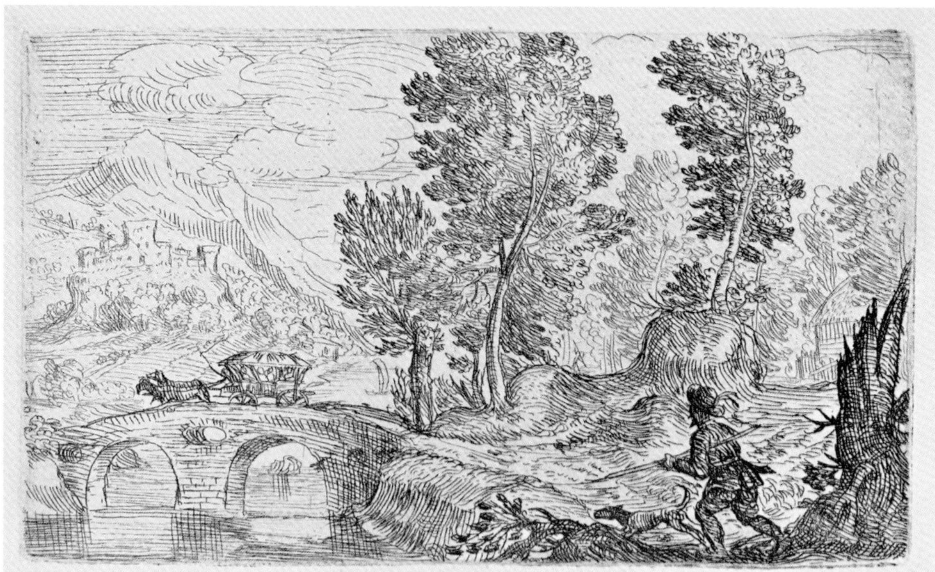

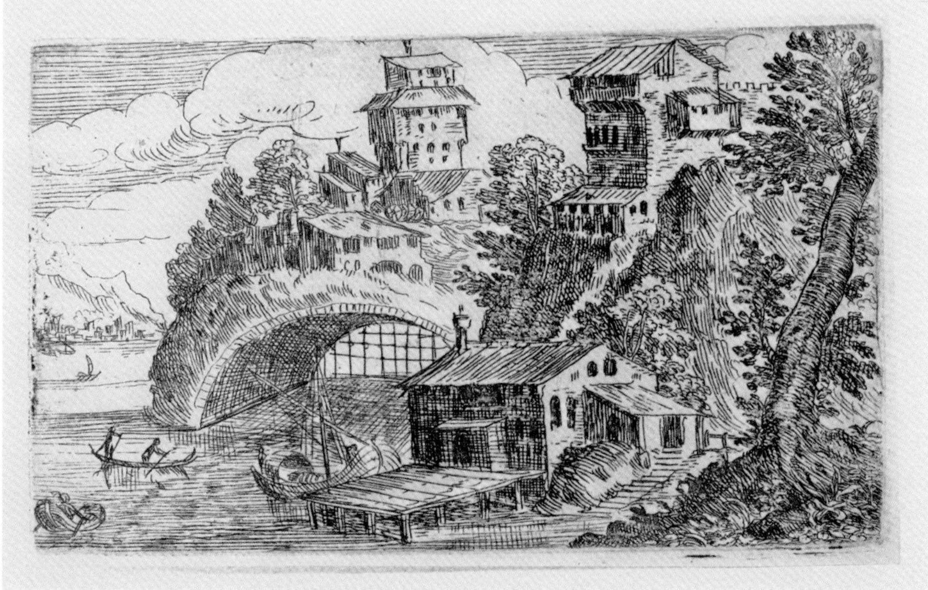

ages drawing after casts of antique sculpture (including one torso and a bust that later appear in *Il vero modo*), and more experienced members of the studio in the background working on canvases.[26] Various disciplines necessary for the art of painting are indicated: geometry is represented by a pair of compasses, and sculptural casts seem to denote the need to study both antique sculpture and anatomy.

Though for a slightly different audience, the book of *Landscapes* dedicated to Alvise Priuli in 1610 was the second of Fialetti's instructional books (figs. 60–61). Here the similarity to the technique of the Carracci is again notable, as is the probable influence of Pozzoserrato, who was active in the Tintoretto studio.[27] The scenes take place in hilly, forested settings, often with rivers, lakes and bridges, in addition to small

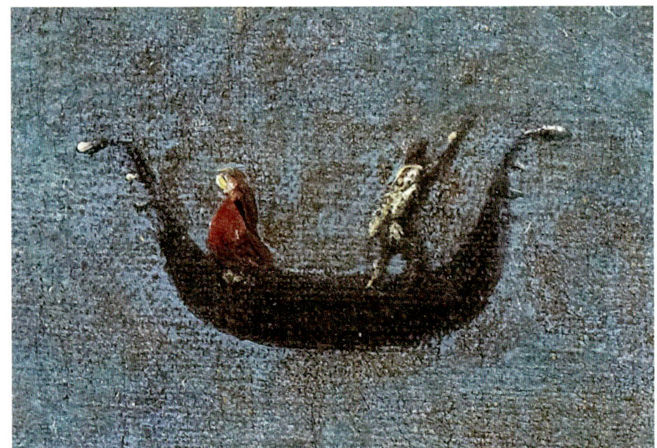

farmhouses and towers, which are remarkably varied in design. The landscapes are almost 'legitimized' as small genre pictures by the addition of figures, farmers engaged in manual labour, and peasants fishing, boating or hunting. The small river boat, the round-bottomed sailing boat and the spidery figures rowing a gondola in the *View of a river* resemble some of the boats in the Eton *View*, painted in the following year (figs. 61 and 62).

Fialetti's contact with Wotton
As far as we know, Fialetti never left Italy; however, his ideas concerning *disegno* played an important part in the formation of a taste for Italian art in England. Printed material and several paintings, brought back to Britain by Henry Wotton, by Thomas Howard, Earl of Arundel, and his wife Aletheia Talbot, and by William Cecil, Baron Roos, provided examples of ideas laid out and popularized in earlier Italian treatises on art, including Gian Paolo Lomazzo's, and underlined the importance of the new emphasis on academic art for the enthusiast, gentleman scholar and artist alike. In addition to the aristocratic and political figures who would later form the key group of Fialetti's foreign patrons, a number of artists passed through English circles in Venice and probably had contact with Fialetti. These included Edward Norgate, Inigo Jones and Anthony van Dyck, who responded in their own work to the newly orientated Venetian (Bolognese-influenced) ideals of composition.[28]

Just as Venetian art was in crisis, so, too, was the Venetian economy, and it became a buyer's market as collections were dispersed. Henry Wotton's insatiable interest in collecting dated back to the early years of the seventeenth century, and in the 1610s many of the paintings that the English had commissioned and purchased were being displayed in London and Westminster where they could be seen by the court and 'persons of quality'.[29] In his *Panegyrick of King Charles* Wotton praised the Venetian art with which the king was surrounded: while figures are said to breathe in Raphael's paintings, they speak in Titian's and move in those works of Tintoretto.[30] At the same time Wotton characterized the Venetian style in a letter of 1608 as "done truly and naturally but roughly": he was describing a portrait of Doge Leonardo Donà, probably painted by Fialetti, which he had sent to the Earl of Salisbury in 1608.[31] Wotton's phrase sums up in a remarkably concise manner the 'impressionistic' style trypical of the late Titian and of Tintoretto, in which the forms may appear unfinished when seen at close quarters and the brushstrokes make better sense when the painting is, as he stipulates, "set at a good distance from the sight".

Though we have no record of the meeting between Wotton and Fialetti, it probably took place during Wotton's first embassy. Wotton seems to have admired Fialetti's "exacting understanding" of earlier works of art and his ability to translate them into a graphic expression.[32] Interestingly, in the Eton view he reverses the process, transforming into paint printed images by others.

Views of Venice by Fialetti, Arzenti and Heintz
It is in this context, firmly situated in English collecting and connoisseurship circles in Venice, that Fialetti painted the *View of Venice*, dated 1611. Like many of his

other works, Fialetti's *View* is rooted in an earlier pictorial tradition and embraces his academic tendency to create a whole out of composite parts (as in *Il vero modo*, for example), with a strong reliance on earlier printed images. The bird's-eye view and lively details distinguish the Eton *View*, and other painted views of the seventeenth century such as those by Arzenti and Heintz (figs. 4, 5), from functional maps, turning them into reminders of a visit, residence or event. They are, in essence, seventeenth-century souvenirs.

By the late fifteenth and sixteenth centuries illustrated town views were increasingly prized for being lifelike, true and accurate representations of the location they depicted.[33] As Allison Sherman's chapter has shown, there was also a concurrent rise in the popularity of geography and cartography among learned audiences in Venice, peaking in the late sixteenth century.[34] As a Bolognese, Fialetti would have been struck by the huge bird's-eye view of his native city in fresco painted by Lorenzo Sabatini in 1575 on the wall of the Sala Bologna in the Vatican. The challenge for the artist was to overcome the inherent difficulties in a topographical view, by creating both an aesthetically pleasing image and one which depicted the city or landscape convincingly.[35] Floriano dal Buono in 1636 inscribed his view of the city

of Bologna with a similar thought: "The image that captures the essence of a city is not, except for someone who wants to attack it with mines or build another just like it, its plan, but one that represents it just as the eye sees it from a specific viewpoint".[36]

Though smaller in scale than the large topographical views of the seventeenth century, the tradition of Venetian view painting continued under eighteenth-century artists, including, most notably, Canaletto.[40] Fialetti, Arzenti and Heintz can be seen as early proponents of this tradition of *vedutisti*, removing the realities of Venice from both the demands of cartography and topographical accuracy, and presenting them instead as views of the power, the fortune, the piety, and the cultural and intellectual dominion of the Republic of Venice.

The sum total of Fialetti's influence, in Italy and England, suggests an artist whose position has been historically rather neglected, and who, because of the variety and breadth of his oeuvre and patronage base, deserves a higher status, thus acknowledging both his importance to contemporary Seicento concerns and aesthetics and his later influence on the tradition of *disegno* in both the painted and printed media.

NOTES

1 For a full examination of Fialetti's life and works, see my doctoral thesis (from which the research for this paper was drawn): L.M. Walters, 'Odoardo Fialetti: The Interrelation of Venetian Art and Anatomy, and his Importance in England (1573 – c. 1638)', PhD thesis, University of St Andrews, 2009. On Venetian Seicento art at the turn of the seventeenth century, see M. Loh, *Titian Remade: Repetition and the Transformation of Early Modern Italian Art*, Los Angeles, 2007.

2 See, for example, A. Spieghel, *De Humani Corporis Fabrica Libri Decem*, Venice, 1627, and F. Tensini, *La fortificatione guardia difesa*, Venice, 1624. He produced nearly 500 known prints, and between 40 and 50 paintings.

3 H. Potterton, "Aspects of Venetian Seicento Painting", *Apollo* 110, 1979, p. 408.

4 C.C. Malvasia, *Felsina Pittrice*, Bologna, 1678. The *Felsina Pittrice* is much in the vein of Vasari's *Lives of the Artists*, and details and up-to-date account of artists, their lives and works (including prints, in Fialetti's case). Like Vasari's, some of the biographical details are, however, questionable. Later biographies suggest that his father was a doctor of Llaw at Padua, and Benezit specifies that Fialetti was born into a noble family of lawyers, and in addition to being a professor at Padua, was also dean and rector: Benezit, 'Fialetti, Odoardo', *Dictionary of Artists*, vol. 5, Paris, 2006, p. 669.

5 Malvasia, *Felsina Pittrice*, p. 301. Several modern biographies of Fialetti exist, though these are generally cursory. They usually accept the timeline as outlined by the seventeenth-century biographers, but omit much of the detail. See F. Benvenuti, 'Fialetti, Odoardo', *Grove Dictionary of Art*, London, 2008; V. Maugeri, 'Fialetti, Odoardo', *Dizionario biografico degli italiani*, vol. 47, 1997, pp. 322–24; C. Galetti, 'Fialetti, Odoardo', *Enciclopedia della Pittura*, vol. A-G, p. 930.

6 There is not much available information concerning Fialetti's travels or associations with other studios and workshops. Though it is thought that he passed through the workshop of Lodovico Carracci, there is no evidence (despite the similarities in later instructional drawings and engravings) that he had any contact with Agostino Carracci.

7 F. de Boni, *Biografia degli artisti*, Venice, 1840, p. 356.

8 Miguel Falomir supposes that "Tintoretto's long career as a painter was fundamentally over by 1590": M. Falomir (ed.), *Tintoretto*, exh. cat., Museo Nacional del Prado, Madrid 2007, p. 59. We must then consider how much contact the young artist actually had with Tintoretto before his death.

9 Carlo Ridolfi, *Le Maraviglie dell'Arte* (1648), Bologna, 2000, p. 248.

10 Benezit, p. 669. Tintoretto's will was filed on 30 May 1594 by Antonio Brinis, and the text of the will itself does not mention Fialetti. I have been unable to consult the original copy of the will, or the *busta* in which it is held, and therefore I cannot say whether the artist is mentioned on the outer sheath of the will or in supporting documentation from the same period: Archivio di Stato di Venezia, Archivio Notarile, 30 May 1594, 'Jacopo Tintoretto', Atti Notaio Brinis, *busta* 157, no. 483.

11 Lodewijk Toeput (il Pozzoserrato), for example, was a specialist in landscapes. Tintoretto's skill, or lack thereof, in drawing and painting the human body is widely known, and instead of understanding the body as a whole made of component parts he utilized a kind of "anatomical shorthand" to create an intermediary between real bodies in nature and the ideal; see Falomir, *Tintoretto*, p. 28.

12 Archivio di Stato di Venezia, Mariegole, Scuola Grande di S. Teodoro, Scuole Grandi, reg. 3, 'Odoardo Fioletti Pitor. 1620 / 1621'; Registro delli Confratelli, b. 21, 1622, 'Odoardo Fioletti pittor, 1622'.

13 See Malvasia, *Felsina Pittrice*, pp. 309–11, where all his paintings are listed. For a full discussion of Fialetti's paintings, both extant and lost, and of early accounts of them, see Walters, 'Odoardo Fialetti', pp. 16–55.

14 U. Franzoi and D. di Stefano, *Le Chiese di Venezia*, Venice, 1976, p. 80.

15 This date is likely, given that Fialetti is only listed as a painter until 1612.

16 D. Howard, *Venice Disputed: Marc' Antonio Barbaro and Venetian Architecture 1550–1600*, New Haven and London, 2012, p. 181, and fig. 220 on p. 184.

17 F. Zava Boccazzi, *La Basilica dei Santi Giovanni e Paolo in Venezia*, Venice, 1965, p. 243. See also M. Hochmann, *Peintres et commanditaires à Venise (1540–1628)*, Rome, 1992, p. 299.

18 D.M. Federici, *Memorie trevigiane sulle opere di disegno dal mille e cento al mille ottocento, per servire alla Storia delle Belle Arti d'Italia*, Venice, 1803, p. 54

19 S.W. Reed and R. Wallace, *Italian Etchers of the Renaissance and Baroque*, exh. cat., Boston, 1989, pp. 248–51; M. Bury, *The Print in Italy, 1550–1620*, exh. cat., British Museum, London, 2001, p. 226; K. Sloan, *A Noble Art: Amateur Artists and Drawing Masters, c. 1600–1800*, exh. cat., British Museum, London, 2000, pp. 55–56.

20 His work, especially the instructional and pattern books, lends itself to, and encourages, copying by young artists; however, his own practice is firmly rooted in Bolognese naturalism and drawing after life and learning based on studio models. Copying was an accepted form of training and artistic output at the time; see Loh, *Titian remade*.

21 Ridolfi, *Le maraviglie dell'arte*, II, p. 248.

22 G. van der Sman, 'Print Publishing in Venice in the Second Half of the Sixteenth Century', *Print Quarterly*, xvii, 2000, p. 233.

23 There are numerous copies of this book still in existence, and in individual plates that have been cut down. A rare copy of the book with Fialetti's text printed on the versos of the plates has been identified in the Rijksmuseum (see A.A. Greist, 'A rediscovered text for a drawing book by Odoardo Fialetti', *Burlington Magazine*, clvi, January 2014, pp. 12–18). The drawing book exists in two editions, a small and a large edition, which is a misnomer, given that both books are the same

physical size, but the latter contains one extra plate of an artist measuring human proportion. The large edition is much rarer than the small, and comparatively few copies of this additional plate survive as single prints. Of additional significance is the fact that Fialetti is one of two Italian etchers for whom Sadeler published work, the other being Paolo Farinati, a single etching in 1567. See P. Sénéchal, 'Justus Sadeler Print Publisher and Art Dealer in Early Seicento Venice', *Print Quarterly*, 7, 1990, p. 29.

24 Pattern and model books had been in long use, of course; however, the concept of a drawing book for novice artists is new in this context. For further reading on model books, see F. Ames-Lewis, 'Model books and drawing books', *Apollo*, 144, 1996, pp. 59ff.

25 For examples of similar studies by Agostino Carracci, see R. Wittkower, *The Drawings of the Carracci in the Collection of Her Majesty the Queen at Windsor Castle*, London, 1952, nos. 130–33.

26 It has been suggested that this is in fact an illustration of Tintoretto's studio.

27 W. Wegner, 'Drawings by Pozzoserrato', *Master Drawings*, 1, 1963, pp. 27–32 and 82–86.

28 For a more complete discussion of academic practice in the Seicento, see Walters, 'Odoardo Fialetti', I, pp. 68–79.

29 T. Wilks, 'Art Collecting at the English Court from the Death of Henry, Prince of Wales to the Death of Anne of Denmark', *Journal of the History of Collections*, 9, 1997, p. 32.

30 H. Wotton, *A Panegyrick of King Charles*, London, 1649, pp. 103–07.

31 See Ch. 1, p. 23; also E. Chaney, *The Evolution of the Grand Tour: Anglo-Italian Cultural Relations since the Renaissance*, London, 1998, p. 207.

32 Giorgio Vasari, *Lives of the Artists*, transl. and ed. G. Bull, London 1965, I, p. 455.

33 L. Nuti, 'The Perspective Plan in the Sixteenth Century: The Invention of a Representational Language', *Art Bulletin*, 76/1, March 1994, pp. 107–08.

34 D. Cosgrove, 'Mapping New Worlds: Culture and Cartography in Sixteenth-Century Venice', *Imago Mundi*, xliv, 1992, pp. 65–89, at p. 81. Venice was also noted for its school of cartography: see A. Zorzi, *Venice: the Golden Age 697 – 1797*, New York, 1980, p. 131.

35 Nuti, 'The Perspective Plan', p. 117.

36 See D. Woodward, *The History of Cartography*, vol. 3, part I, Chicago and London, 2007, p. 687.

40 "The view pictures of Canaletto and many others, which are so often thought typical, were chiefly produced for tourists, not natives. What continued to be a fundamental need within the city was for pictures consciously removed, in subject as in style, from mundane reality: scenes of mythology … and (to a lesser extent) of history": M. Levey, *Painting in Eighteenth-Century Venice*, New Haven and London, 1994, pp. 96–97.

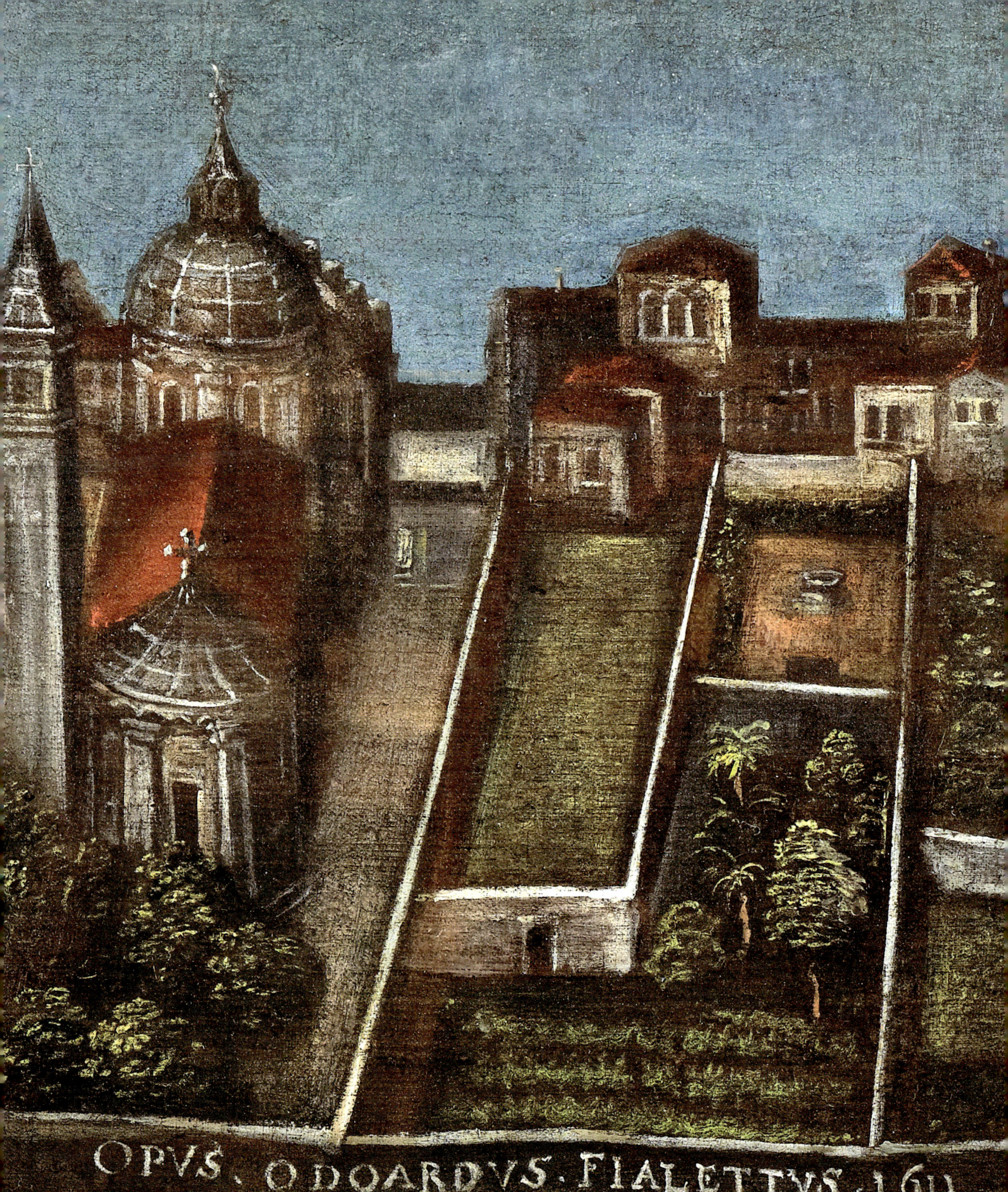

OPVS . ODOARDVS FIALETTVS . 1611

5. Odoardo Fialetti's *View of Venice* Restored

RUTH BUBB

THIS CHAPTER reflects on the interplay between technical and visual aspects in Fialetti's *View of Venice*. The picture's restoration in 2009–10 (described in full in the Technical Appendix, pp. 148–58) revealed copious new information about its conception and execution, and cast new light on its relationship to earlier maps and the townscape of Venice.

Fialetti's View and its debt to other map views
It is generally accepted that Jacopo de' Barbari's woodcut of 1500 (fig. 30) was the starting point for Fialetti's painting. Indeed, it was impossible for that not to be the case. De' Barbari's masterpiece, three years in the making, was a feat not emulated for another two centuries in Venice, for here "plan makers … preferred to copy one another".[1] Impressions of de' Barbari's work were dispersed among collectors throughout Europe, but a significant number remained in Venice.[2] It is not known who might have given Fialetti access to one, as local maps were not recorded in the inventories of Venetian households.[3] It was probably too expensive for him to have owned, selling for at least three ducats, equivalent to the monthly salary of artists working in the Ducal Palace at the time of its production.[4] However, the smaller, later maps derived from de' Barbari were more widely disseminated, and maps generally were common in Venetian collections by the second half of the seventeenth century.[5] Moreover, Fialetti's connections with publishers and printmakers, described in Chapter 3 above, gave him access to collections of maps and prints.

As Allison Sherman has shown, Benedetto Bordone, in his woodcut of 1528, is credited with the innovation of surrounding the city with the mainland to the west and the barrier islands to complete the ring (fig. 39). Although not topographically accurate, Bordone's convention of an encircling rim of land was adopted by almost every imitator and became part of the standard image of Venice. It is this view that seems to be approximated by the unknown Northern European painter of ambassador Sir Henry Unton's memorial picture of *c.* 1596, now in the National Portrait Gallery, which features a vignette of Venice in the background.[6] Fialetti preserves the visual tradition with a fragment of the Lido, improbably shown to the north-east of Venice.

In 1525 Andrea Vavassore produced a smaller, simplified version of de' Barbari's bird's-eye view, in which some important buildings were updated (fig. 41). These include the cupola of the church of the Madonna dell'Orto, completed in 1503; he also altered the outlines of the gardens on the Giudecca and introduced different details within the gardens. Fialetti's view is closer to his than to de' Barbari's in those parts of the Giudecca obscured in the woodcut by the heads of Winds. Elsewhere, however, he copies the Giudecca gardens from de' Barbari rather precisely (figs. 9, 10). Vavassore omits any encircling land-forms and closes in on Venice to the extent that its eastern end touches the right hand border of the sheet. The western end of the city and part of the Giudecca are cut off at the left. Although Fialetti includes the whole of the Giudecca by moving it closer to

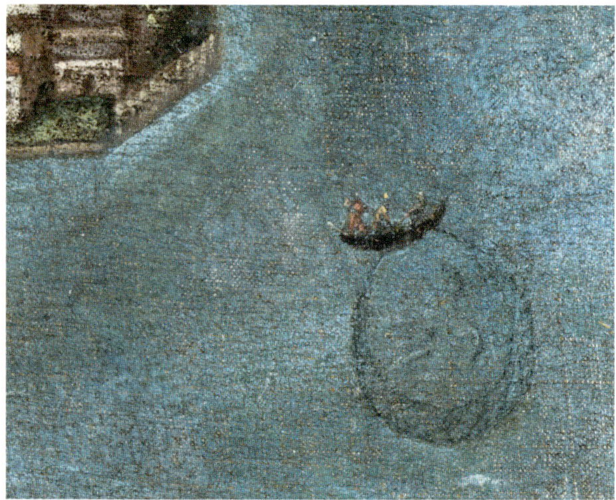

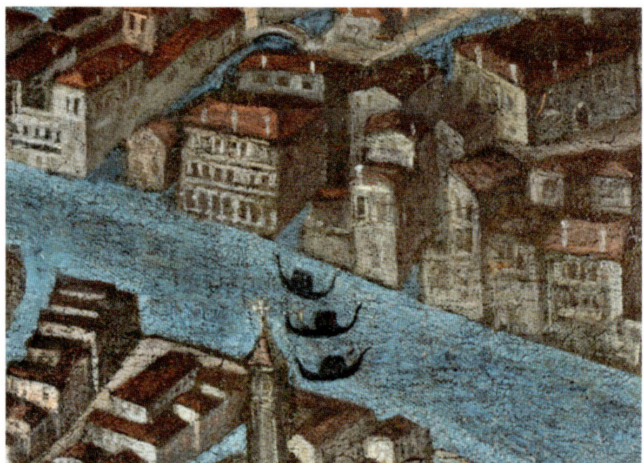

maps, such as those by Forlani (1565) and Salvioni (*c.* 1597; figs. 47 and 51). To represent the ferry routes from Venice to Murano and the mainland, Pagan depicted a line of identical gondolas. Fialetti adopts a similar device to show the location of *traghetti* on the Grand Canal (fig. 65).

Paolo Forlani's plan of 1565 was derived from Pagan. It was the most widely diffused of the sixteenth-century plan-views and is still the most commonly found in collections.[7] It gave rise to many more imitations, including Braun and Hogenberg in *Civitates orbis terrarum* (1572), Giacomo Franco (before 1580) and one engraved by Bernardo Salvioni and published by Donato Rascicotto (*c.* 1597; figs. 48, 49 and 51). Francesco Valegio, with whom Fialetti collaborated on engraved illustrations for an edition of Andreas Vesalius's *De humani corporis fabrica*,[8] also published a variant of Forlani's map, almost exactly contemporary with Fialetti's painting.[9]

Forlani had made the innovation of substituting text labels on the plan with letters and numbers for the principal sites, and including a key to them on the same page (fig. 47). Salvioni took this further, embellishing the area below the map with detailed views of St Mark's and the new Rialto Bridge (fig. 51). Fialetti depicts the *campanile* of San Marco and the Rialto Bridge similarly out of scale. Astonishingly, he painted the *campanile* of the Madonna dell'Orto, which, having worked in the same *sestiere,* he must have known well, with a pointed spire instead of its characteristic bun-shaped cupola, by then over a century old. This error also appears on Salvioni's engraving (figs. 66–68). There are a number of other instances where Fialetti ignored significant contemporary changes to the landscape and architecture – such as the Palladian re-working of San Giorgio Maggiore, which was completed in 1610, the church of the Redentore, consecrated in 1592, and buildings on land reclaimed behind Santi Giovanni e Paolo.[10]

its real position, he uses the same cropping device at the extreme ends of the city. This increases the sense of immersion in the scene. At the distance required to appreciate the detail, the edges of the image are invisible and the viewer must physically move around the expanse of canvas.

In 1559, Matteo Pagan's *Large View* was published (fig. 45). This incorporated the design of Bordone's view and details, such as the gardens on the Giudecca, from the related work of Guillaume Gueroult (1551) and from Vavassore (figs. 41, 43). Pagan's plan was very successful and was reprinted in 1567. A smaller version, with updated details, was also published at some time between 1559 and 1562 (fig. 46). Fialetti adopted several innovations found in Pagan's work and not in de' Barbari's, including fishing boats with nets full of fish (fig. 64). These are also found in smaller numbers on later

As Andrew Hopkins will show below, his interest lay
not in architectural accuracy, but rather in depicting
a recognisable and memorable image.

Fialetti's painting materials and techniques

CANVAS PREPARATION

The huge painting is executed on five pieces of linen
canvas stitched together, measuring approximately
2 × 4.25 m (figs. 122, 123). Giorgio Vasari specifically
associated the use of canvas as a painting support with
large works "such as are seen in the halls of the palace
of San Marco at Venice".[11] A connection between the
use of canvas as a painting support and the sailmaking
industry in Venice is sometimes assumed, but specialist
suppliers of artists' canvas existed there by the sixteenth
century.[12] It made sense to use a relatively lightweight
and economical material for painting large images,
including decorative maps and city views.[13]

The preparation of canvas for painting was described
by Giovanni Battista Armenini in 1586. After stretching
the canvas on a frame, two or three coats of soft glue
were applied to the side to be painted, and one on the
reverse. "The effect is to close the interstices well and
make the canvas surface even." Then slubs and knots
in the cloth were cut off and the surface smoothed
with pumice.[14]

Armenini stated that some practitioners mixed wet
gesso with the glue, but advised against this because
it might provoke flaking if the canvas were to be bent
when carried from one place to another. For Vasari,
the principal advantage of painting on canvas was that
it was "of little weight and when rolled up is easy to
transport".[15] When Henry Wotton sent a Titian and a
Palma to the Marquess of Buckingham in 1622 he wrote
that "they both come distended on their frames, for
I durst not hazard them in rolls, the youngest being

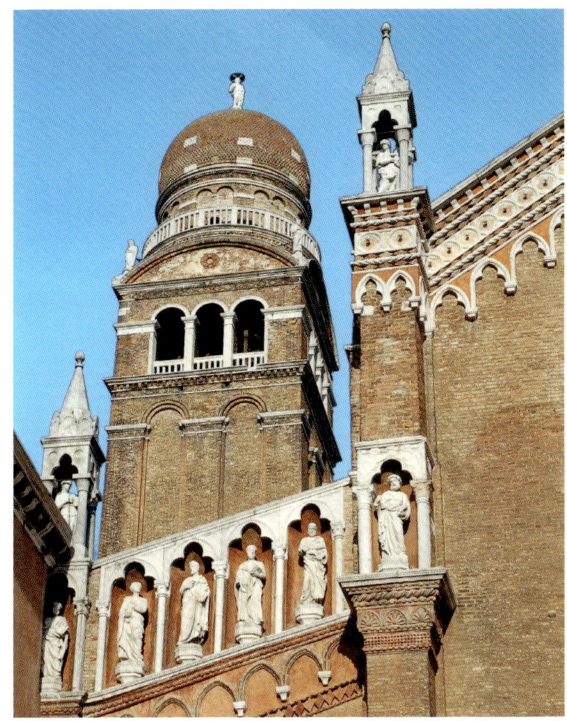

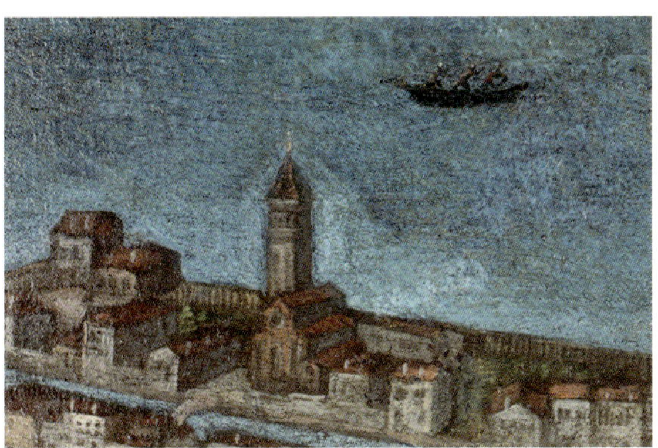

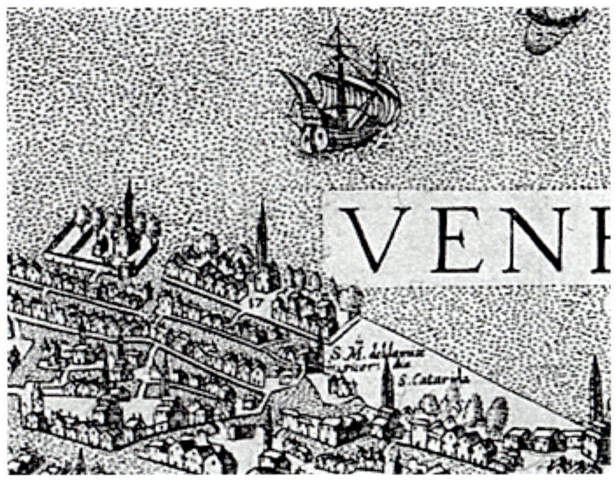

twenty-five years old, and therefore no longer supple or pliant".[16] On removal of the lining canvas from Fialetti's *View* during treatment, vertical creases were visible on the reverse of the original canvas, suggesting that at some point relatively early in its history it had been removed from its stretcher and rolled. Correspondence by Wotton and his successor ambassadors Dudley Carleton[17] and Lord Feilding[18] concerning the transport of paintings indicates that it was safer, but also more expensive, to ship works crated and framed. Since Fialetti's *View* was unusually large, the cost of transporting it on its stretcher would have been prohibitive in relation to its value. But, as discussed in Chapter 7, we do not know at what point during the twenty-five years between its execution and its arrival at Eton it travelled to England.

The glue size locks the canvas weave to form a stiff substrate for painting. Cusping, that is distortion of the weave between the tacks attaching the canvas to the stretching frame, is present along all edges of the five canvases that make up the whole, except along the central horizontal seam. This indicates that the canvas pieces were stretched and at least sized separately before being joined, except for the two largest in the centre, which appear to have been stitched together before stretching (fig. 122). Examination of the paint layers in cross-section provided evidence that painting had started on the central canvas before the sides were extended,[19] changing the format from 1:1.5 to 1:2.

The presence of cusping and selvages around the edges of the painting confirms that it has not been cut down since it was painted, so the cropping of the extreme ends of the city must be intentional. Vavassore's plan offers a precedent for this. Margherita Azzi Visentini, in her examination of the relationship between painted map-views and their printed antecedents, also found it to be the case that the layout of the city could be distorted or cropped to fit the canvas format, and the perspective

manipulated to make selected features more visible.[20]

The first canvas format is consistent with single-sheet maps by Bordone and Vavassore and the smaller two-sheet edition of Pagan.[21] The alteration to the more panoramic proportions of de' Barbari and Pagan's large-scale multi-sheet productions suggests that Fialetti may have had access to more than one source, and could have switched from one to another. It also suggests that the painting may not have been an entirely routine production.

The canvas is prepared with a fairly dark brown ground layer containing a mixture of charcoal black and earth pigments.[22] Ground layers made from earth colours bound in linseed oil are discussed as normal Venetian practice in the Volpato manuscript.[23] Similar dark grounds were used by Fialetti's master in Venice, Jacopo Tintoretto.[24]

Armenini advised that once the *imprimatura* or tinted ground was dry it should be scraped down to a smooth finish, on which "one then draws with delight whatever one wishes to paint".[25] Vasari described Tintoretto as "working haphazardly and without [a preliminary] design",[26] but research has shown the assumption that the Venetians did not draw to be false. Preliminary drawings on paper by Tintoretto, some squared up for transfer, exist.[27] However, technical examination of his paintings shows that drawing was a dynamic process which continued in paint on canvas after the preliminary sketch on paper. Although he mentions the option of transferring a design on to canvas mechanically by means of a perforated cartoon or a grid, Armenini does not distinguish very clearly between drawing on the prepared canvas in the rough, expressive media of chalk or charcoal, for instance, and beginning to paint.[28] Five surviving drawings attributed to Fialetti, all figure studies, four in ink and one in chalk, were examined by Laura Walters but she found no evidence of squaring for transfer.[29] In some ways this is curious, because Fialetti was best known, in England at least, for his graphic work and for his drawing manual *Il vero modo et ordine per dissegnar tutte le parte et membra del corpo humano*, which was intended to rectify the view that the Venetians were lacking in draughtsmanship. Although Edward Norgate's book *Miniatura or the Art of Limning* is subtitled 'The Names Order and use of the Colours', it has a section 'Of Designe' in which he advises beginners to practise copying from prints, especially those of "Edwardo Phialetti, my old acquaintance in Venice".[30]

No drawing as such was found on the painting by x-radiography or infra-red reflectography. It seems unlikely that an image so demanding of reasonably accurate organization of information could have been made without any preliminary drawing at all, but whatever materials were used to make these marks were not visible to the analytical techniques available.

By overlaying digital images of Fialetti's painting on to de' Barbari's map or later derivatives, it can be seen that the outlines and proportions of the painted islands are not an exact match for any of them. This seems to indicate that Fialetti did not use a mechanical method of transferring the design on to the canvas but sketched it freehand. In fact, the added canvas pieces suggest that the format of the painting was not even finalized before the artist began laying out the image on the support.

Working freehand without a grid would seem to make distortions of the final image inevitable. Juergen Schulz showed, by superimposing a modern projection of Venice on to the corresponding points on de' Barbari's map, that the image becomes increasingly compressed at the upper left (figs. 30, 32). He attributed this to the artist running out of space as the drawing progressed, although he also acknowledged that 'kinks'

in the perspective grid had been introduced intentionally to avoid placing landmarks on the junction of separate woodblocks.[31] Deborah Howard, on the other hand, considers that this compression was a "deliberate manipulation … to give Venice the visual imagery of the dolphin".[32] By comparison with the printed maps, Fialetti's Venice is compressed at the right-hand end, which might be attributed to the progression of a right-handed painter from left to right across the canvas.

It should be noted that this image could only be derived from other works of art: the view could by no means be observed in physical reality at the time, unlike other Italian cities such as Florence or Bologna with conveniently placed high ground. But artifice did not devalue the work in contemporary eyes: in Henry Wotton's opinion, "an excellent Piece of Painting is … the more admirable Object, because it comes neere an Artificial Miracle …. The uttermost value and virtue of a Painter lay in creating the illusion of three dimensions."[33] He was impressed by Kepler's demonstration of a landscape panorama made by the use of a camera obscura,[34] but wrote that "to make landscapes by it were illiberal", [35] that is, mechanical or slavish work. [36]

PAINTING THE COMPOSITION

The artist began painting by applying a very broad lay-in of warm white and blue over the brown ground in the centre of the painting, covering Piazza San Marco and environs. Tintoretto had used lead white to establish outlines and highlights, or just to indicate the positions of compositional elements.[37] X-radiography provides some evidence for the evolution of the image during the painting process: the radiograph shows the presence of a pentiment consisting of a canal, south of the Grand Canal, running diagonally behind the Campanile and forming a T junction with the rio di San Salvador (figs. 69–71). The painting of this canal was abandoned

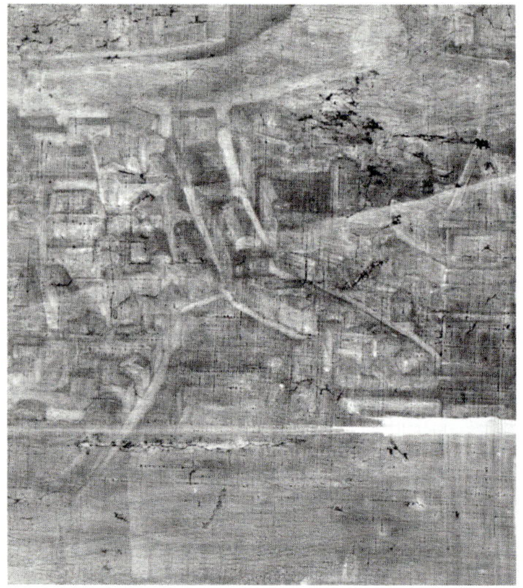

69
X-radiograph of Fialetti's *View* showing
pentiment to canal

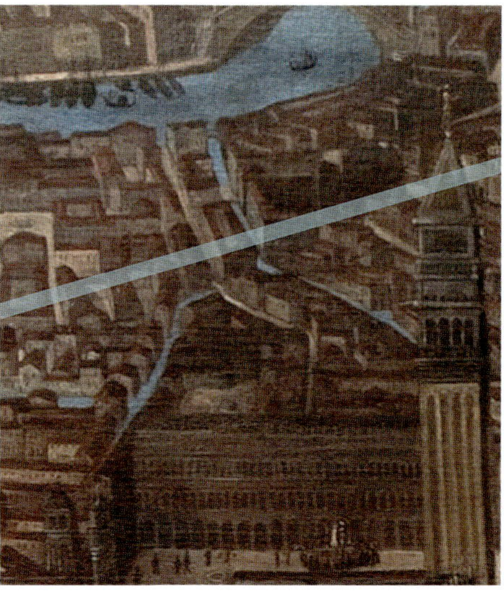

70
Fialetti's *View*, detail reconstructing pentiment

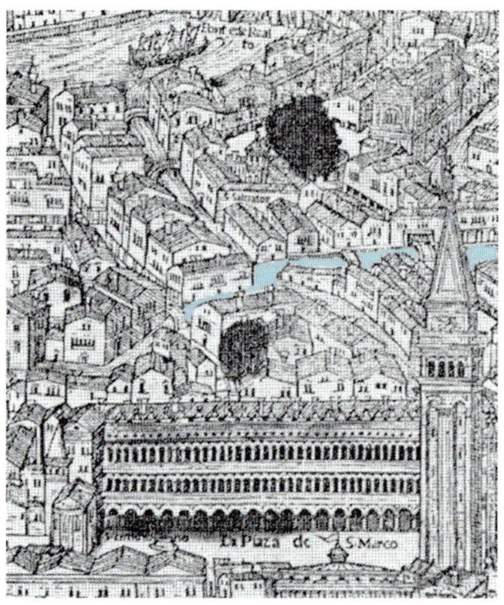

71
Pagan's larger *View* (fig. 45), detail
showing canal south of the Grand Canal

and replaced with buildings. The canal exists and is
visible in both the smaller and the larger versions of
Pagan's print (fig. 71), and also in the smaller prints
by Forlani and Salvioni (figs. 45, 46, 47, 51). It is not
apparent in de' Barbari's view (fig. 30) because his chosen
perspective conceals the canal between buildings at that
angle. This may be further evidence for Fialetti shifting
his attention between sources. Adjustments have also
been made to the position of the inlet at the Western end
of the Molo and the bridge over the rio di San Vio.

After the land forms and architecture, blue water was
filled in and the outline of the buildings reinforced with
a thicker application of blue. This method of, as it were,
carving out forms from the dark ground by surrounding
them with a thick, luminous contour is characteristic
of Tintoretto's work. Wotton aptly compared the use
of "*contorni taglienti*" to "when Taylors cut out a Sute".[38]
Finally the boats were added over the water and figures
indicated by economical dashes of paint that at their
best anticipate the facility of Canaletto (fig. 21). The
miniature representations of the statue of St Theodore,
the angel on the Campanile and the Doge on the Torre
dell'Orologio recall the flame-like shapes of the draperies

in Fialetti's *Doge Leonardo Donà giving Audience to Sir Henry
Wotton* (fig. 96) and also Tintoretto's *Cardinal Virtues* in the
apse of the church of the Madonna dell'Orto.

One of the main goals of the conservation treatment
was to remove uniform blue overpaint from the water
(see fig. 72).[39] The original blue paint, although badly
damaged in some areas, shows variations of tone from
a lighter blue in shallow water and canals to a darker
shade for deep water channels. The roughness of open
water is suggested by previously invisible wispy strokes
of very light blue paint, analogous to some of the marks
in Fialetti's varied vocabulary for representing texture in
his etchings.

The shifting navigable channels of Venice, revealed by
removal of the uniform overpaint, are visible in reality
from the Campanile at low tide. Marin Sanudo recounted
that in 1517 the Turkish ambassador had made a request
to climb the tower and asked leading questions about the
approaches to Venice by sea, provoking security concerns
about sharing this view.[40] There is evidence from the
seventeenth century that access to decorative schemes
incorporating maps in the Doge's Palace was carefully
controlled.[41]

Fialetti's paints

Fialetti's paint and ground layers were bound in oil.[42] According to Armenini, "any important works on panels or canvas are now done in oil".[43] Pigments were ground with oil to make paint in the artist's studio. In Fialetti's etching (fig. 59), three grinding slabs are visible in the background with an assistant working at one of them. Small saucers containing ground colours can be seen on shelves at the back of the studio, as described in the Volpato manuscript.[44] Armenini describes the way the paints were used on "delicate boards of boxwood, which are held in one's hand while working".[45] The painter at the back of Fialetti's studio has a wooden palette in his hand and more are hanging on the wall. The paints would be set out on the palettes by the apprentice and the palettes stored under water to prevent the paint drying out overnight.[46]

Fialetti used two blue pigments for the all-important areas of water. In the canals and shallow water, he used only indigo, mixed with lead white and carbon black. At this time Venice was the main port of arrival for the dyestuff indigo, imported from India.[47] It was used by many Italian artists, including Tintoretto, whose father, of course, was a dyer or *tintore*.[48] In other areas, such as the open water at the lower right, the indigo has been glazed with smalt, "a cobalt containing potash glass".[49] Smalt was known to Venetian glass-makers as early as the fifteenth century. Painting treatises recommended glazing with smalt to improve the light-fastness of indigo in an oil medium.[50]

Elsewhere, at the entrance to the Grand Canal, for instance, the layer structure was reversed and smalt was found underneath indigo. It would therefore appear that for the shallow water Fialetti ignored contemporary advice to protect the indigo from light-induced fading by glazing with another pigment. The possibility cannot be ruled out, however, that thin final glazes have been lost

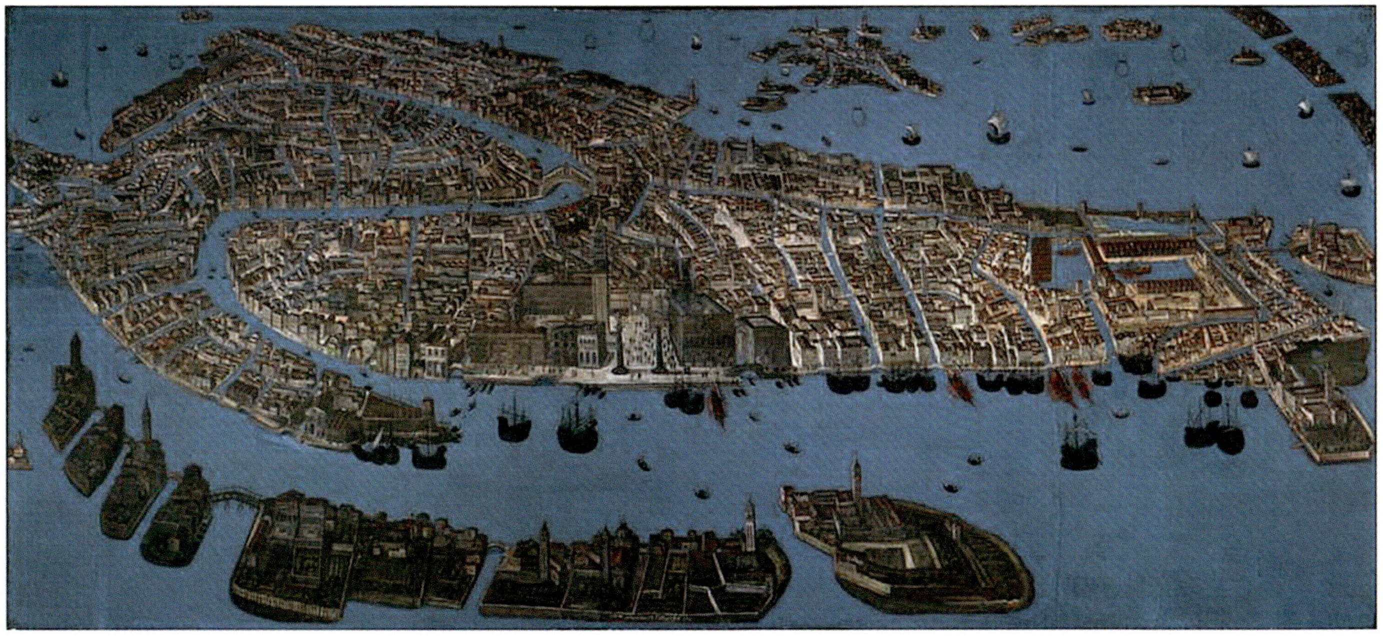

through previous treatment (fig. 130). Nevertheless,
 the indigo blue has retained its colour remarkably well
even where it has been exposed. Where smalt forms
the final glaze, on the other hand, it now appears
completely discoloured, which probably accounts for the
comprehensive overpainting of the water in later times.

The value of the painting
Fialetti used cheaper blue pigments for the large
expanses of sea, at a time when Venice was the principal
importer of the most precious blue, ultramarine from
Afghanistan.[51] In 1542, ⅔ ounce of ultramarine sold in
Venice for 6 *lire* but in 1534 Francesco and Jacopo Bassano
had paid half that sum for four pounds of smalt and a
pound of bristles for brushes.[52] Indigo could be more
expensive than smalt, but its high tinctorial power
meant that it could be used economically when mixed
with lead white, as recommended in the seventeenth-
century Paduan manuscript.[53] Both blues were in the
middle range of prices.[54] A mixed brown containing
red lead and a small amount of cinnabar with black
was found on some of the boats,[55] when it would have
been cheaper to use an earth brown. The red galleys are
painted with cinnabar, worth approximately 1 *lira* 10 *soldi*
per pound in 1541,[56] although it was cut with cheaper
red lead.[57] So the materials used are neither the most
expensive nor the cheapest.

In her study of Fialetti's commissions by Italian
patrons, Walters notes that one Agostino Correggio
owned two paintings by Fialetti, which are listed, along
with their valuations, in an inventory of his family
house made in 1646.[58] The paintings, described as "very
good", of the *Children in the Furnace* and *Daniel in the Lion's Den*,
are each valued at 10 ducats, the same value accorded
each of four paintings by Palma and Tintoretto of *The Ages
of Man*, and a painting of *Christ* by Tintoretto, and higher
than *An old man and a young man with a lily* by Bronzino,

valued at 8 ducats. On the basis that a portrait by Carracci
of *Giovanna Correggio* is valued at 150 ducats, and a half-
length portrait in armour by Giorgione at 200 ducats,
Walters concludes that "it is safe to say that 10 ducats is
at the lower end of the valuations for paintings in the
inventory", recognising, however, that we do not know
the sizes or materials used for any of the paintings listed.
Cecchini describes how painters in Venice, generally not
employed individually by grand households, maintained
a stock of ready-made, commercially viable work,
which might not be in the top rank of quality, for sale at
reasonable prices.[59] The Agostino Correggio valuations
indicate that in 1646 a good-quality Fialetti was worth
about ten ducats. In 1627, "a large painting of Venice"
in the Mantua collection was similarly valued at
90 Mantuan *lire*, that is, nine ducats or approximately
£2 five shillings in English currency of the time.[60]
A painting of the city of Mantua was valued at the same
price, but this is the upper end of the scale for both maps
and landscapes. Fialetti's *View* is likely to have have
commanded value both for its size and on account of its
curiosity and the skill involved in its making. Wotton's
"five Dukes", or portraits of Doges, were valued at £5
each in 1649, having acquired an attribution to Tintoretto
(Chapter 10). While it is difficult to assess what Fialetti
might have charged for his *View*, these comparisons
suggest that it may have been a more affordable painting
than, for instance, the Palma *Prometheus* that Wotton
purchased for the Earl of Salisbury, which was valued at
£25 in 1650 (see p. 103, fig. 94).[61]

Although Wotton had advised connoisseurs, when
assessing the quality of a painting, to ignore the name
of the artist,[62] Fialetti added to the value of his work by
signing and dating it (in ungrammatical Latin; fig. 63).
This confirmed it as his own work and not a copy.
His name is written on the wall in the foreground,
reinforcing the fiction that he has painted an actual

view as he witnessed it, just as Ludovico degli Uberti
depicted himself drawing his 1472 view of Florence.[63]
From the mid fifteenth century, Venetian painters'
workshops had used standardized signatures on
works intended for export, as a form of branding.[64]
When Fialetti signed works in Venetian churches,[65]
or when providing the Venetian Nicoletti Giganti with
illustrations for 'The Book of Fencing',[66] he often used
the epithet *Bononense* to advertise his Bolognese birth
and training (though not in fig. 55). This was omitted
in works marketed to foreigners looking for authentic
Venetian paintings.

The meaning and purpose of the painting
In the technical examination carried out by the
Hamilton Kerr Institute in 1990, attention was focused
on the apparently empty area of sea at the lower
right. It seemed reasonable to suppose, from printed
antecedents, that there might be an emblematic device
or explanatory text beneath the overpaint. The area was
examined by infra-red reflectography and x-radiography,
but, with the exception of a single overpainted ship, no
hidden features were revealed either by these techniques
or by the eventual removal of the overpaint. So, if the
painting was made for a specific occasion or patron,
the artist did not announce it overtly.

De' Barbari represented a regatta in the lower right-
hand corner. These took place annually on 25 January
and intermittently on special state occasions.[67] Salvioni's
map shows an even more specific event, the progress
of the Dogaressa to the Ducal Palace. The later painted
views of Arzenti and Heintz also depict the city *en fête*
for the Feast of the Ascension.[68] Fialetti chose not to
do this, perhaps out of the wish to present a timeless
image, underscored by the inconsistent updating of
the architecture, just as later updates to de' Barbari's
woodblocks were subsequently undone.[69]

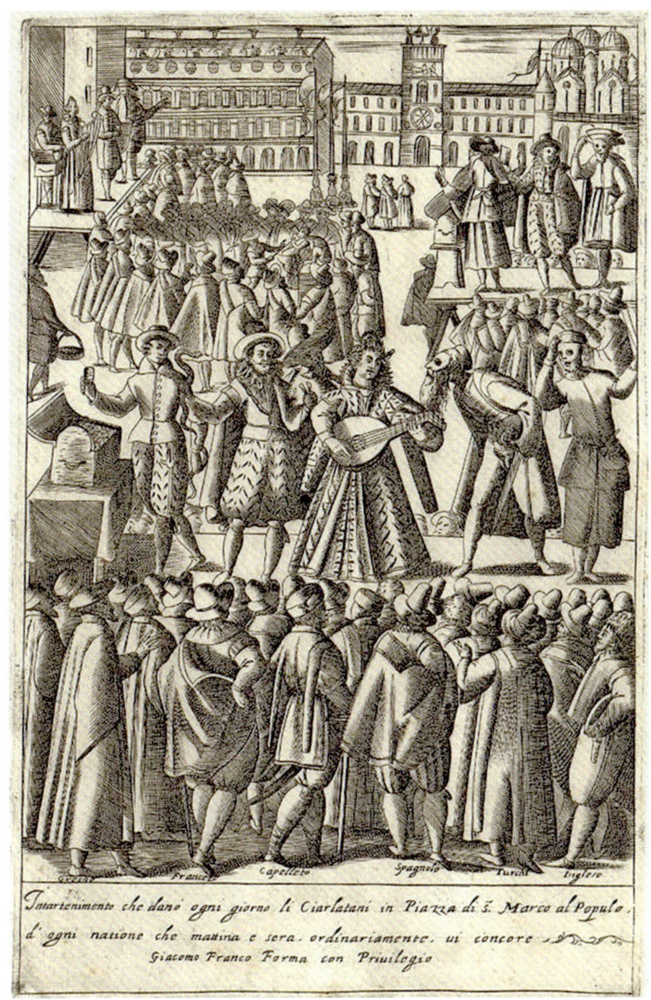

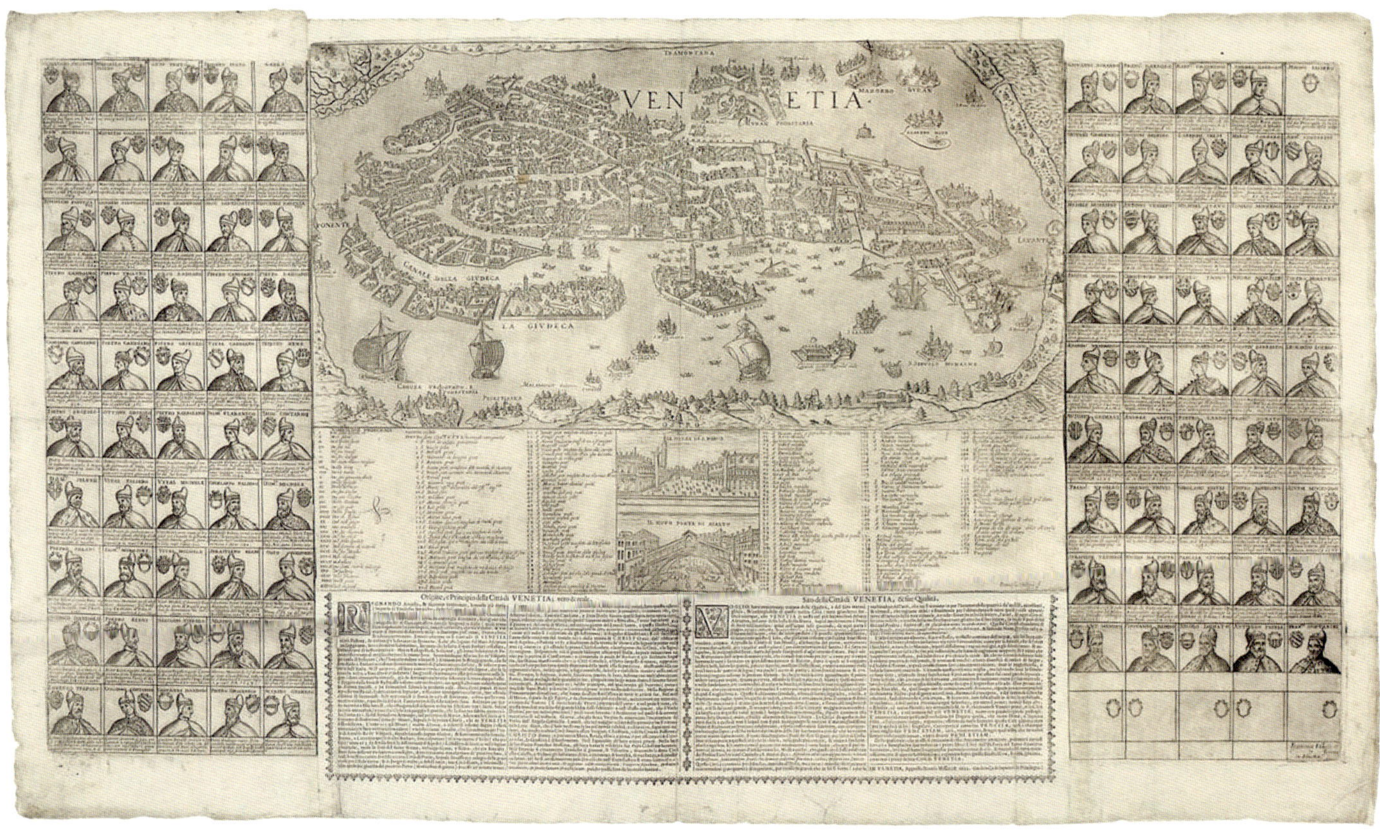

Performers on a raised stage surrounded by spectators in front of the Procuratie Vecchie (fig. 82) are found at the geometrical centre of the painting in its first format (fig. 122), so some interpretation of this detail seems to be required. Fialetti's inclusion of this group, or any figures at all in this part of the city, seems to be a departure from earlier printed map views. Wotton's contemporary in Venice, Thomas Coryate, described twice daily performances by mountebanks or charlatans exactly where Fialetti has painted them.[70] There is an image of such a performance in Giacomo Franco's book, *Habiti d'huomini et donne venetiane,* of 1610 (fig. 73), and the caption to the plate states that the charlatans performed in the Piazza every day to people of all nations. The nationalities of the spectators, distinguished by their dress, are inscribed under their figures. Costume books formed part of the mass of printed material produced for visitors to Venice, to which Fialetti made his own contribution in 1626 with the reference work *De gli habiti delle religioni* (figs. 57, 58).[71]

Marin Sanudo described *mommarie* performed on a raised platform in semi-public spaces such as the smaller city squares to celebrate betrothals between important families.[72] Shakespeare's *A Midsummer Night's Dream* (*c.* 1590–96) was created in this tradition. The plot of the *commedia* is typically resolved when the right couples are matched up, reinforcing the hint that the painting could originally have been intended to play a role in the wooing of a royal bride. In 1561, Francesco Sansovino called Venice "the theatre of the world and the eye of Italy".[73] Describing the focal point of the painting in her article, Azzi Visentini knowingly uses the vocabulary of the stage: the paved quay is the proscenium, the two giant columns the *frons scenae*, the opening through which the actors appear, and so on.[74] The god-like overview provided by the map offers the spectator the visual equivalent of Shakespeare's remark that "all the world's a stage".[75]

As the gold standard of de' Barbari's image became debased by repeated copying and loss of detail, the credibility of later versions was reinforced with additional material.[76] In Francesco Valegio's version of Forlani's view of Venice, the map was accompanied by descriptive text and flanked by the portraits of 94 Doges (fig. 74). This makes clearer the connection between the *View* and the portraits of doges that Wotton also purchased from Fialetti. As mentioned in chapter 1, De' Barbari's map may have been designed to accompany Marcantonio Sabellico's written description of Venice of 1490.[77] The lengthy inscription inserted into the large Pagan plan specifically refers the reader to "our booklet entitled Le Bellezze di Vinegia" for more detailed information.[78] Azzi Visentini writes that, given its date, Fialetti's painting ought to represent the visual counterpart to Giovanni Stringa's 1604 updated edition of Sansovino but that there are too many omissions in the painting for the correspondence to be convincing.[79]

The close connections between verbal and visual description and between memories or souvenirs of travel are underlined by Norgate. In his fable of the origins of landscape painting, a traveller visits his friend, "an ingenious Painter", and recounts "the adventures of his long Journey, and with all, what Cities he saw", while the artist "begins to paint, what the other spake,

describing his description in a more legible and lasting Character".[80] And indeed there was a text to accompany the painting, the "monument made of Sir H. Wotton's giving of it to the College",[81] displayed underneath on a separate panel (fig. 113).

Fialetti's *View*, almost certainly designed to be exported, reflects a divergence between the accurate and therefore sensitive topographical information of the earlier images and later decorative views more concerned with nature and landscape for its own sake. When Armenini praised the decoration of the wall of the Terza Loggia in the Vatican "whereon are shown things of cosmography, painted here with the distances of places realised through exact measures", he stated that "one sees with delight almost all the parts of the world, with all its boundaries and colours".[82] The purpose, then, was not just to convey exact information, but also to give delight, to enable the owners of these landscape decorations to visit in their imagination the places depicted, or, as Wotton's friend Izaak Walton put it, "the college being to his mind as a quiet harbour to a seafaring man after a tempestuous voyage … he might sit in a calm, and, looking down behold the busy multitude".[83]

ACKNOWLEDGMENTS

The restoration project was funded by the Friends of Eton College Collections. It would also not have been possible without Henrietta Ryan and Justin Nolan of Eton College. The Hamilton Kerr Institute generously shared documentation of the previous treatment and examination of the painting. Laura Walters kindly supplied a copy of her PhD thesis on Fialetti. The following people collaborated on the restoration, documentation and technical analysis of the painting: Lucia Brzozowska, Sophie Brummitt, Trevor Cumine, Helen Davis, Irina Dolgikh, Brian Singer and Chantal Thür.

NOTES

1　J. Schulz, 'The printed plans and panoramic views of Venice (1486–1797)', *Saggi e memorie di storia dell'arte*, 7, 1970, p. 13.

2　E. Balistreri (ed.), *Venezia città mirabile. Guida alla veduta prospettica di Jacopo de' Barbari*, Verona, 2009, p. 19.

3　B. Wilson, *The World in Venice: Print, the City and Early Modern Identity*, Toronto, Buffalo, and London, 2005, p. 45.

4　J. Schulz, 'Jacopo de' Barbari's View of Venice: Map Making, City Views, and Moralized Geography before the Year 1500', *Art Bulletin*, 60/3, 1978, pp. 425–74, at p. 441 n. 44.

5　I. Cecchini, *Quadri e commercio a Venezia durante il Seicento*, Venice, 2000, p. 36.

6　National Portrait Gallery, London, NPG 710.

7　Schulz, 'The printed plans', p. 25.

8　L.M. Walters, 'Odoardo Fialetti: The Interrelation of Venetian Art and Anatomy, and his Importance in England (1573 – c. 1638)', unpublished PhD thesis, University of St Andrews, 2009, pp. 117–136, 200.

9　Schulz, 'The printed plans', p. 61.

10　M. Azzi Visentini, 'Ancora un'inedita pianta prospettica di Venezia in un dipinto di Odoardo Fialetti per Sir Henry Wotton', *Bollettino dei musei civici veneziani*, 35/1, 1980, pp. 19–25, at pp. 19–21.

11　Giorgio Vasari, *Vasari on Technique*, transl. L.S. Maclehose, ed. G. Baldwin Brown, New York, 1960, p. 237.

12　L.C. Matthew, '"Vendecolori a Venezia": the Reconstruction of a Profession', *Burlington Magazine*, cxliv, 2002, pp. 680–86, at pp. 681, 685, nn. 52–53.

13　Earlier examples on canvas include the copy of Francesco Roselli's *View of Rome*, after 1538, Palazzo Ducale, Mantua. See also T. de Wesselow, 'Ambrogio Lorenzetti's *Mappamondo*: A Fourteenth-Century Picture of the World Painted on Cloth', in C. Villers (ed.), *The Fabric of Images*, London, 2000, pp. 55–65, at pp. 56, 57, 63 n. 10.

14　G.B. Armenini, *On the True Precepts of the Art of Painting*, ed. and transl. E.J. Olszewski, New York, 1977, p. 188.

15　*Vasari on Technique*, p. 236.

16　L. Pearsall Smith, *The Life and Letters of Sir Henry Wotton*, 2 vols., Oxford, 1907, II, p. 257.

17　F. Portier, 'Prices paid for Italian Pictures in the Later Stuart Age', *Journal of the History of Collections*, 8/1, 1996, p. 56.

18　P. Shakeshaft, '"To Much Bewiched with Thoes Intysing Things": The Letters of James, Third Marquis of Hamilton and Basil, Viscount Feilding, concerning Collecting in Venice 1635–1639', *Burlington Magazine*, cxxviii, 1986, pp. 114–134, Appendix I, xi, p. 123.

19　See Technical Appendix, pp. 149–50.

20　M. Azzi Visentini, 'Venezia in una sconosciuta veduta a volo d'uccello del seicento', *Antichità viva*, 17/4, 1979, pp. 31–38.

21　The format of the single sheet Furlani and Salvioni/Rascicotto plans is 1:1.5, but the proportions of the de' Barbari image are retained by filling the lower portion of the sheet with additional text and illustration.

22　See Technical Appendix, p. 150.

23　M.P. Merrifield, *Medieval and Renaissance Treatises on the Arts of Painting*, New York, 1999, pp. 721–24, 728–32. Volpato was writing at the beginning of the eighteenth century but refers back to Armenini and to his own master, said to have been a pupil of Tintoretto.

24　J. Dunkerton, 'Tintoretto's Painting Technique', in M. Falomir (ed.), *Tintoretto*, exh. cat., Museo del Prado, Madrid, pp. 139–58, at pp. 152–54;

A. Wallert and C. van Oosterhout, *From Tempera to Oil Paint – Changes in Venetian Painting, 1460–1560*, Amsterdam, 1998, pp. 56, 58, 63.

25　Armenini, *On the True Precepts*, pp. 192–93.

26　*"a caso e senza disegno"; Vasari on Technique*, p. 509.

27　See J. Plesters, 'Tintoretto's Paintings in the National Gallery', *National Gallery Technical Bulletin*, 4, 1980, pp. 32–48; Dunkerton, 'Tintoretto's Painting Technique'; A.G. Mozo, 'El concepto de dibujo en Jacopo Tintoretto Análisis de los recursos técnicos utilizados en algunos cuadros del Museo Nacioanl del Prado', in M. Falomir (ed.), *Jacopo Tintoretto: Proceedings of the International Symposium*, Madrid, 2009, pp. 165–77.

28　Armenini, *On the True Precepts*, p. 188. The production and use of cartoons is discussed in Book 2, Chapter VI, pp. 170–74.

29　Walters, 'Odoardo Fialetti', pp. 17–23.

30　J.M. Muller and J. Murrell (eds.), *Edward Norgate: Miniatura or the Art of Limning*, New Haven and London, 1997, p. 106.

31　Schulz, 'Jacopo de' Barbari's View of Venice, pp. 438–39.

32　D. Howard, 'Venice as a Dolphin: Further Investigations into Jacopo de' Barbari's View', *Artibus et historiae*, 18/35, 1997, pp. 101–11, at pp. 104–06.

33　Henry Wotton, *The Elements of Architecture*, London, 1624, p. 66.

34　Kepler's equipment consisted of a portable black tent with a small hole and lenses that projected an image of the landscape outside on to a piece of paper, where he traced the outlines in ink.

35　Pearsall Smith, *Life and Letters*, II, pp. 205–06.

36　"not befitting or of the nature of a free man; not pertaining to or acquainted with the liberal arts": Oxford English Dictionary, Second Edition on CD-ROM (v. 4.0), Oxford, 2009.

37　Wallert and Oosterhout, *From Tempera to Oil Paint*, pp. 58, 63.

38　Wotton, *Elements*, p. 69.

39 See further pp. 143–44.

40 Marin Sanudo, *Venice Città Excelentissima: Selections from the Renaissance Diaries of Marin Sanudo*, ed. H. Labalme and L.S. White, transl. L.L. Carroll, Baltimore, 2008, p. 215.

41 M. Bourne, 'Francesco II Gonzaga and Maps as Palace Decoration in Renaissance Mantua', *Imago Mundi*, 51, 1999, pp. 51–82; J. Schulz, 'Cristoforo Sorte and the Ducal Palace of Venice', *Mitteilungen des Kunsthistorischen Institutes in Florenz*, 10/3, 1962, pp. 193–208, at pp. 202–05.

42 See Technical Appendix.

43 Armenini, *On the True Precepts*, p. 187.

44 Merrifield, *Medieval and Renaissance Treatises*, pp. 739–40.

45 Armenini, *On the True Precepts*, p. 191.

46 Merrifield, *Medieval and Renaissance Treatises*, p. 740.

47 M. van Eikema Hommes, 'Indigo as a Pigment in Oil Painting and its Fading Problems', in *Changing Pictures, Discolouration in C15th-C17th Oil Paintings*, London, 2004, pp. 99–156, at p. 104.

48 Dunkerton, 'Tintoretto's Painting Technique', p. 149.

49 M. Spring *et al.*, 'Investigation of Pigment-Medium Interaction Process in Oil Paint containing Degraded Smalt', *National Gallery Technical Bulletin*, 26, 2005, pp. 56–70, at p. 56.

50 Eikema Hommes, 'Indigo', pp. 133–34, 137–38, 165 n. 183. On the use of smalt in Venetian painting, see N. Hammond, 'Bellini's birds: avifauna in the Frick "St. Francis", *Burlington Magazine*, cxlix, 2007, pp. 36–38.

51 R.D. Harley, *Artists' Pigments c. 1600–1835*, 2nd edn, London, 1982, p. 43.

52 J. Kirby, 'The Price of Quality: Factors influencing the cost of pigments during the Renaissance', in G. Neher and R. Shepherd (eds.), *Revaluing Renaissance Art*, Aldershot, 2000, pp. 19–39, at p. 35. See also Cecchini, *Quadri e commercio*, p. 170.

53 'Paduan Manuscript', in Merrifield, *Medieval and Renaissance Treatises*, p. 676.

54 Kirby, 'The Price of Quality', p. 25.

55 Identified in dispersion by polarized light microscopy.

56 Kirby, 'The Price of Quality', p. 36.

57 Identified in dispersion by polarized light microscopy.

58 Walters, 'Odoardo Fialetti', pp. 39–40.

59 Cecchini, *Quadri e commercio*, p. 134.

60 A. Luzio, *La Galleria dei Gonzaga venduta all'Inghilterra nel 1627–28*, Milan 1913, pp. 71ff.

61 J. Shearman, *The Pictures in the Collection of Her Majesty the Queen: The Early Italian Pictures*, Cambridge, 1983, pp. 172–73.

62 Wotton, *Elements*, pp. 67–68.

63 Kupferstichkabinett, Berlin.

64 Matthew, '"Vendecolori a Venezia"', p. 627.

65 *St Dominic saves a Book from the Flames* in the Sacristy of Ss. Giovanni e Paolo and *The Ecstasy of St James* in San Giuliano, Venice, are signed fairly conspicuously on rocks *Odoardus Bonon. F* and *Odoardus Fialetus Bononense pinxit* respectively. The tomb of St Dominic is in Bologna.

66 Walters, 'Odoardo Fialetti', pp. 62–63.

67 Balistreri, *Venezia città mirabile*, pp. 341–42.

68 Both Museo Correr, Venice.

69 Schulz, 'Jacopo de' Barbari's View of Venice', pp. 473–74; D.S.Chambers, in J. Martineau and C. Hope (eds.), *The Genius of Venice 1500–1600*, exh. cat., Royal Academy of Arts, London, 1983, pp. 392 –93.

70 Thomas Coryate, *Coryat's Crudities: Hastily Gobled up in Five Moneths Travells* (1611), online at http://www.archive.org/details/ coryatscruditieso1coryuoft, accessed 27 May 2010, p. 410.

71 Walters, 'Odoardo Fialetti', pp. 107–10, Appendix III, figs. 98–103, pp. 294–96, 305–07 nn. 167–69.

72 Sanudo, *Venice Città Excelentissima*, pp. 490–91.

73 Francesco Sansovino, *Delle cose notabili che sono in Venetia*, Venice, 1556, dedication, quoted in Wilson, *The World in Venice*, pp. 4, 268 n. 4.

74 Azzi Visentini, 'Ancora un'inedita pianta', p. 19.

75 *As You Like It*, II, 7, line 140. The same idea is found in Sonnet 15 and in the name of the Globe Theatre.

76 D. Woodward, *The History of Cartography*, vol. III, *Cartography in the European Renaissance*, Chicago and London, 2007, p. 691.

77 Chambers, in Martineau and Hope, *The Genius of Venice*, pp. 392–93.

78 Schulz takes the book to be Francesco Sansovino's *Tutte le cose notabili e belle che sono in Venezia* of 1556: Schulz, 'The printed plans', p. 106 n. 10.

79 Azzi Visentini, 'Ancora un'inedita pianta', p. 24 n. 7.

80 Muller and Murrell, *Edward Norgate*, pp. 83–84.

81 http://www.pepysdiary.com/ archive/1666/02/26, accessed 17 May 2010.

82 Armenini, *On the True Precepts*, p. 248.

83 I. Walton, *The Lives of Dr John Donne, Sir Henry Wotton, Mr Richard Hooker, Mr George Herbert and Dr Robert Sanderson*, 1685, reprinted London, 1857, p. 99.

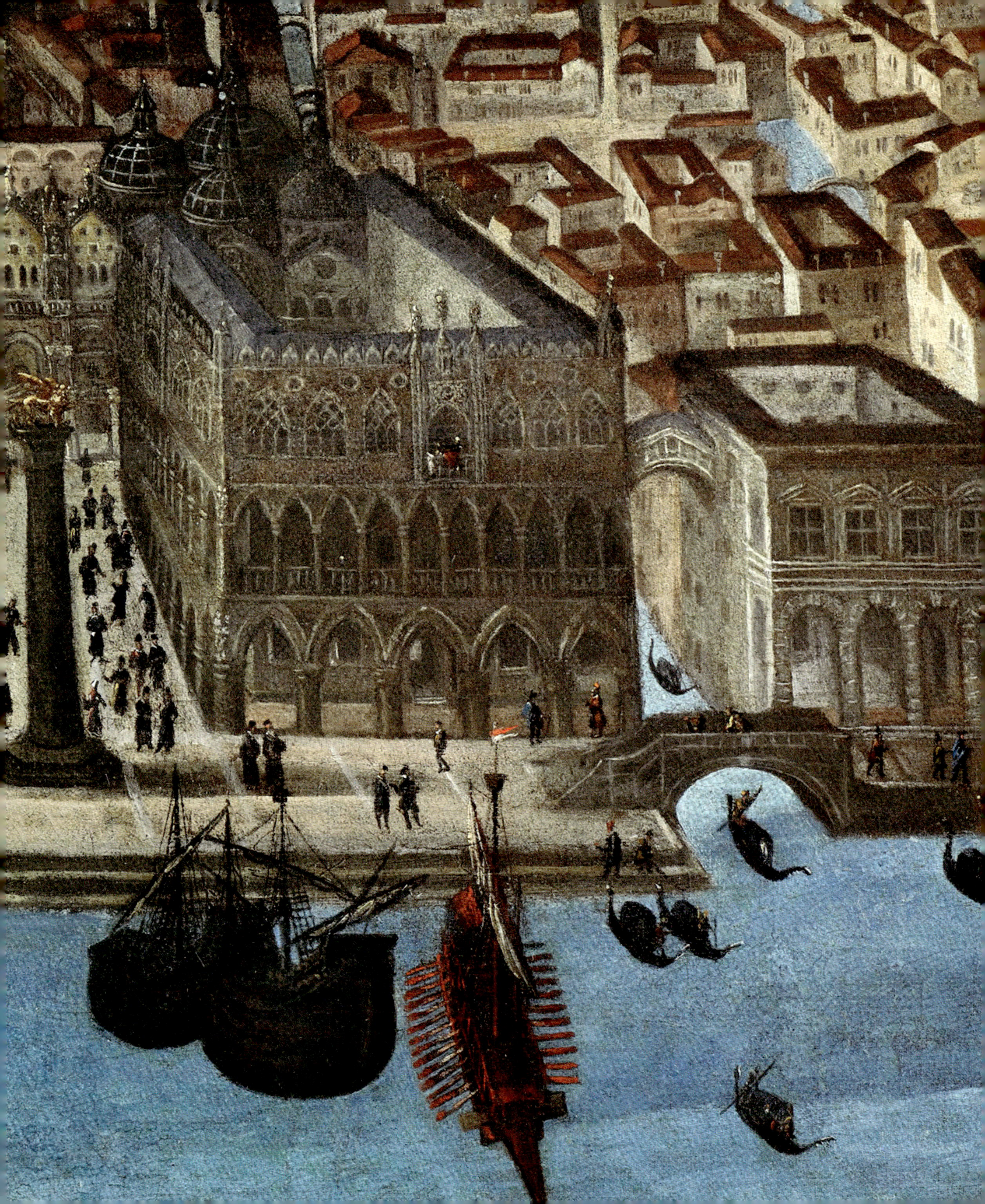

6. Sights and Sighs in the Serenissima *c.* 1610: Built Architecture and its Depiction

ANDREW HOPKINS

Introduction: Fialetti and the forma urbis

Filling the gap between built architecture and its depiction has long been the quest for anyone working on architecture and urbanism in the Early Modern period.[1] The challenge is to work out how reliable or not a map or city view might be. But as one seeks out the discrepancies between built architecture and its depiction it is also useful to consider what other conventions for image-making might apply. There is a world of difference, for example, between Odoardo Fialetti's work of 1611 (fig. 1) and Jacopo de' Barbari's celebrated bird's-eye view of Venice of 1500 (fig. 30), which scholars use to probe such issues as the 'missing' dome of the church of San Giobbe, precisely because his topography and architectural rendering are so accurate.[2]

Any painter who, like Fialetti, chose to depict the Doge's Palace both obviously oversized and having just five ground-floor arches rather than seventeen along its Bacino front clearly had different artistic aims (figs. 75 and 76). His approach is reminiscent of those earlier painters, both Italian and Byzantine, whose more important saints were literally depicted on a bigger scale than those of lesser figures in the celestial hierarchy. So too, with Fialetti, his principal focus on St Mark's Square and its surrounding buildings, set at the heart of Venice's urban geography, together with Rialto, the Arsenale and a few other buildings thrown in for good measure, loom larger than life in his city view, but are

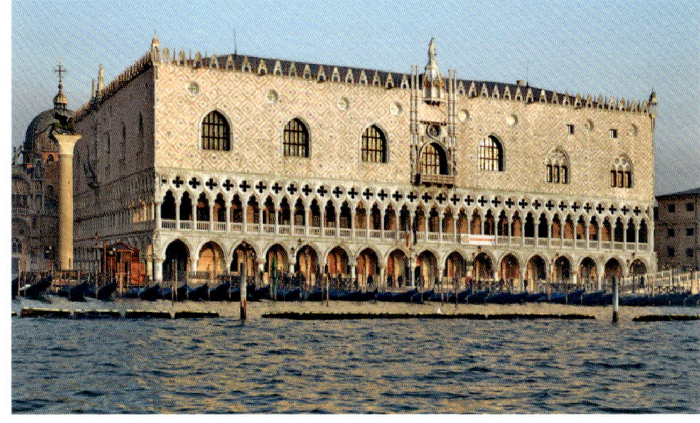

76
Venice, Doge's Palace, south wing, begun 1341

simplified to create a bolder effect.[3] He even significantly shifted the location of the Giudecca islands and that of San Giorgio Maggiore to the east, probably to provide a weighty visual anchor at the bottom of the picture plane. Thus the gardens of the Giudecca are closest to the viewer, and had the church of the Redentore been represented rather than omitted it would have appeared opposite the Dogana da Mar rather than in its correct location on the Zattere opposite the small Renaissance church of the Spirito Santo.[4]

"No one enters Venice as a stranger"

Like countless architects, artists and visitors to Venice,
Fialetti came to the task with his own 'idea of Venice' to
hand, but this was quite conservative and traditional.[5]
Unlike architects in the seventeenth century, who had
an eye for new buildings and did measured drawings
of them to get to grips with what was innovative in
their architectural design, Fialetti appears to have been
content to depict the major monuments but 'not to
notice' the completion, for example, of the façade of
Palladio's church of San Giorgio Maggiore built by
Simon Sorella in exactly these years, despite the island's
location at the bottom front of the picture plane (figs. 77
and 78).[6] Here it would have been possible to depict more
detail, and offer a more up-to-date rendering. Foreign
architects, especially, took advantage of the opportunity
to record new buildings, for example Erik Dahlberg and
David Ehrenstrahl, who in 1655–56 drew the interior of
the church of Santa Maria della Salute, then still under
construction.[7] Thus they countered the experience of
entering the city forearmed with knowledge of the
townscape and its principal architectural sights by
drawing recent and ongoing construction, celebrating
the modernity of the city and disseminating beyond
the confines of the lagoon up-to-date knowledge
about Venice.[8]

Fialetti, by contrast, provides little new detail,
despite the fact that, had he so wished, he could have
produced what might have become one of the most
valuable and informative of views of the Serenissima.
His relative disinterest in precise architectural rendering
reveals the traditional bias of the artist as painter
towards his mainstay of the human figure. This lack
of cultural curiosity in architectural terms can be
contrasted with an insider's updating of Venice in the
figure of Giovanni Stringa, Canon of the Ducal Chapel
of St Mark's, who in 1604 published a revised edition of
Francesco Sansovino's classic guide to the city, originally

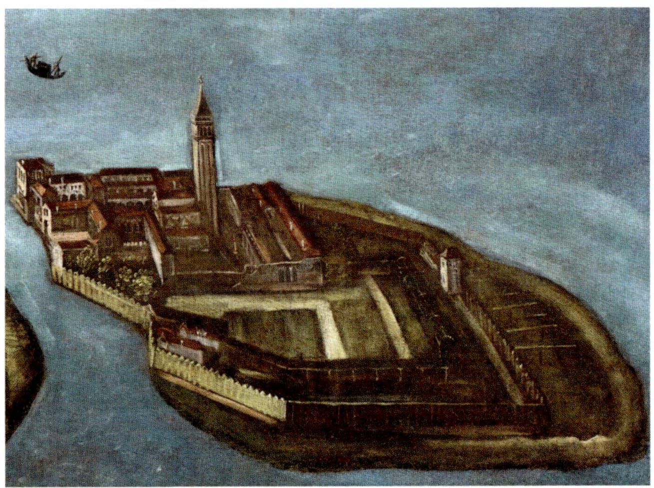

77
Fialetti's *View*, detail showing the
island of San Giorgio Maggiore

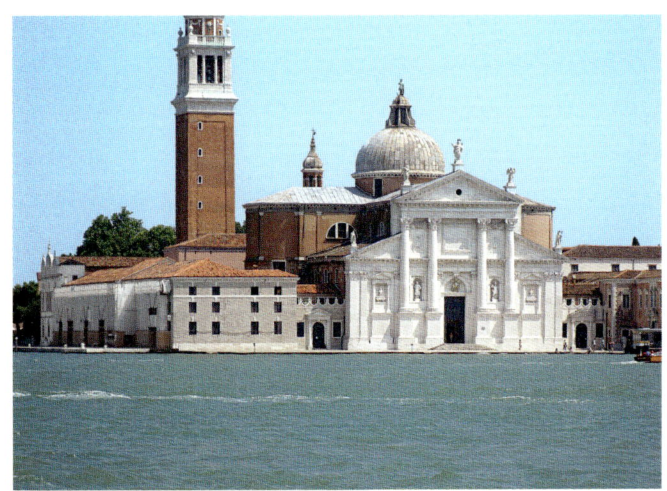

78
Venice, San Giorgio Maggiore, façade built 1607–10

published in 1581. This underlines Ruth Bubb's view, expressed in the previous chapter, that Fialetti's view and Stringa's edition cannot be companion pieces. Stringa added a plethora of new information about recently completed churches such as Andrea Palladio's Il Redentore, Antonio Da Ponte's Rialto Bridge and even a thirteen-page addendum – almost certainly ghost-written by Vincenzo Scamozzi – full of informative detail about recent developments, including the projected completion of the Procuratie Nuove.[9] As we shall see later in this chapter, one of Fialetti's few exceptions is his inclusion of the New Prisons, designed in 1563 but finished only in 1614, and the adjoining Bridge of Sighs, built in 1600 by Tommaso Contin (figs. 75 and 83). This fascinating bridge, without external beginning or end, was evidently a far more interesting and noteworthy item for Fialetti – perhaps pinpointing its future fame as a celebrated tourist attraction – than the addition of yet another church in this city already overloaded with ecclesiastical complexes.[10]

Forum Marcianum

The best place to consider the peculiar characteristics of Fialetti's view is the Forum Marcianum, the buildings in and around Piazza San Marco (frontispiece and fig. 82). This had been the site of considerable polemic precisely in the period leading up to Fialetti's view, as Manfredo Tafuri was at pains to point out in 1985, and as Deborah Howard has recently demonstrated with particular regard to the involvement of the Venetian patrician Marc'Antonio Barbaro.[11] Following Doge Andrea Gritti's *renovatio urbis* between 1523 and 1538, which saw Jacopo Sansovino design and begin execution of the Mint, the Loggetta and what became the Marciana Library, as well as the internal renovation of the liturgical spaces of San Marco, in the late 1550s work came to a halt on the Library and the projected ideas for the Procuratie Nuove.

In theory, the shops and apartments of the latter were to extend from the bell tower all the way to the western end of the square and the church of San Geminiano. This church, for which Sansovino designed and built the façade in the 1550s, was recorded by Fialetti but demolished following Napoleon's invasion of the Republic.[12]

The southern end bays of Sansovino's Library are correctly represented in the view with three ground-floor arches but incorrectly with four first-floor arched windows when there are in fact only three (figs. 81, 82).[13] This appears to be a painter's rather than an architect's way of thinking about window openings, one that was probably motivated, once again, by wanting to distinguish larger and smaller apertures rather than to represent the relationship between the various floors. Fialetti also commits heresy according to architectural theory by placing solids over voids, as the arches of the ground floor do not correspond vertically to those of the first floor. Evidently he was aiming for a bold, simplified rendering, but cared little for architectural accuracy or structural logic. Yet he does record the Library as complete and of twenty-one bays in length, terminating towards the Bacino of St Mark's where it is perfectly aligned with the adjacent Mint, a state of affairs achieved only after 1582 when the contract for the final five bays of the Library was awarded.[14] Earlier execution of these had been halted after just sixteen bays because of the obstructive presence of the Beccaria or meat market, shown in most prints and paintings until the 1580s.[15] The adjacent Mint is depicted by Fialetti as being only as wide as the contiguous end bays of the Library and as having only three instead of nine bays on all three floors. But conversely he was one of the first to record the additional third storey of the Mint, executed from 1558 but not part of Sansovino's original design (figs. 81, 82).[16]

While Scamozzi's controversial proposal for three storeys was rejected for the Library it was accepted for

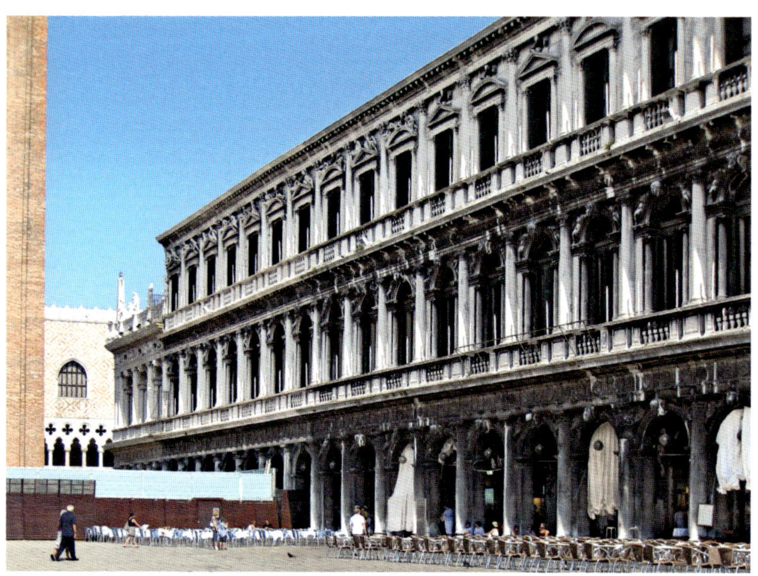

79
Venice, Procuratie Nuove, begun 1588 to designs by
Vincenzo Scamozzi

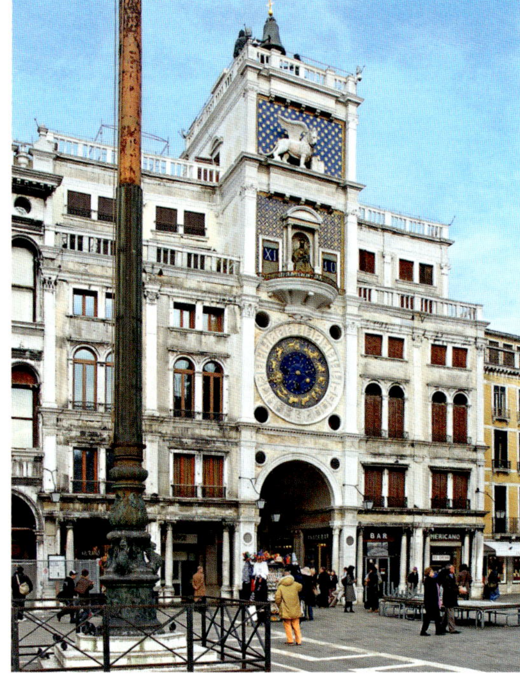

80
Venice, Torre dell'Orologio (Clock Tower), 1496–1500,
attributed to Mauro Codussi

the Procuratie Nuove and allowed him to realise his
design for duplex apartments of considerable grandeur
for the procurators' residences over the ground-floor
shops.[17] It is undeniable, however, that their much
greater height considerably altered the proportions
and perceptions of the square (fig. 79). Is this the new,
regular building Fialetti appears to have represented as
progressing halfway along the square to the left before
abruptly stopping? One cannot be certain, given the
loose approach he adopted, evident in the architectural
representation of the opposite side of the square,
where the Procuratie Vecchie are incorrectly shown
as terminating behind the Campanile, and the Torre
dell'Orologio (fig. 80) is shown flanked by anomalous
elevations (fig. 82).[18] Yet the red-roofed building here
could well be the new construction work by Scamozzi,
and probably indicates Fialetti's attempt to be up-to-date
with respect to the major monuments in and around the
Piazza San Marco.[19]

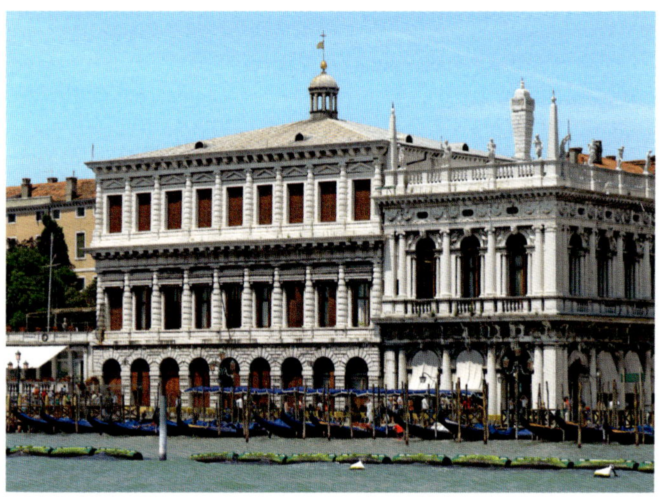

81
Venice, Zecca (Mint), begun 1536, and Library, begun 1537,
completed 1590, both designed by Jacopo Sansovino

82
Fialetti's *View*, detail showing Piazza San Marco
and the Mint and Library

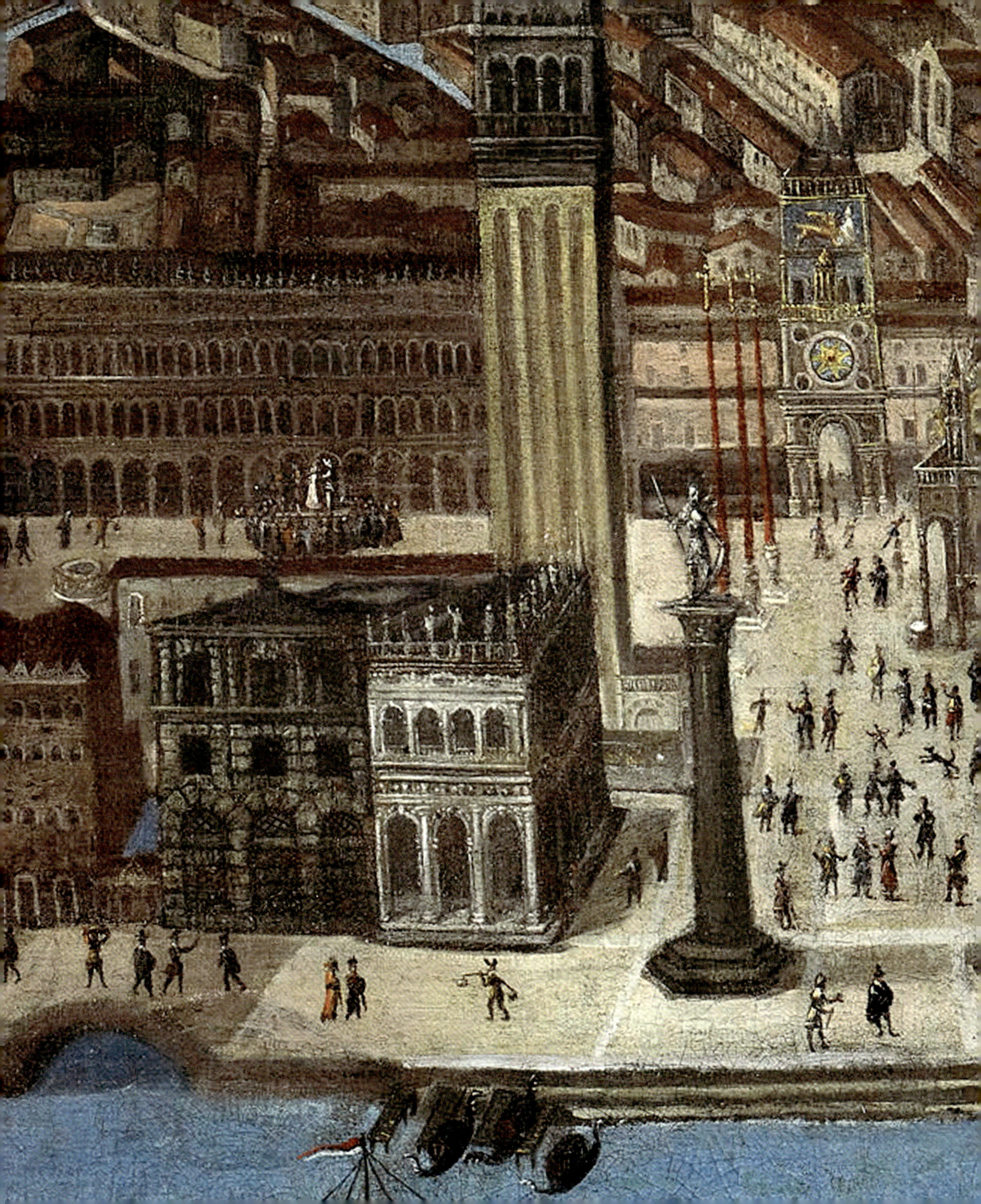

Sights and sighs: The Ponte dei Sospiri and the Prigioni Nuove
Fialetti records the recent new additions to the govern-
mental area of St Mark's – the Prigioni Nuove (New
Prisons), designed by Giovanni Antonio Rusconi with
Antonio da Ponte in 1563 but only completed in 1614, and
the 'Ponte dei Sospiri' or Bridge of Sighs by Tommaso
Contin of 1600 (figs. 75, 82, 83).[20] The building of the
Prisons was done in tandem with the repairs to the
Doge's Palace following the fire of 1577 and Fialetti
operates with less compression here than with the
adjacent Palace, as the ground-floor width of the Prisons
is shown as of five arches rather than seven as built.[21]

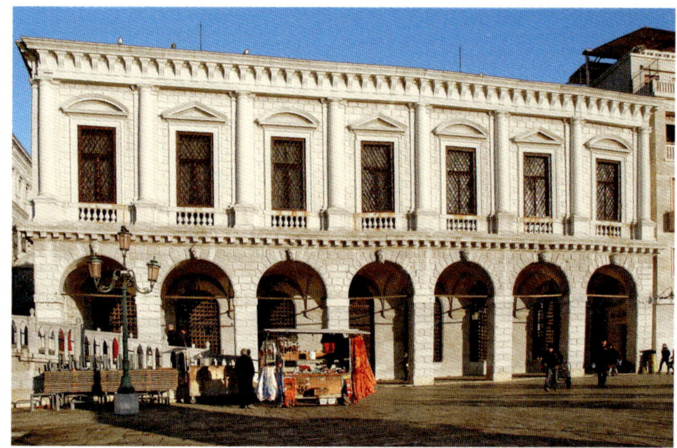

What the project for the New Prisons represents,
and what Fialetti depicts, is the increasing stratification
and specialization of spatial function that characterized
architecture for public institutions of the Early Modern
period.[22] In this case the existing prison spaces within
the Doge's Palace were no longer considered adequate
not only because they were located in parts of the ground
and mezzanine of the south wing of the Doge's Palace
and regularly filled with water at high tide, but also
because they were overcrowded. Prisoners kept
in such poor conditions inevitably became sick and
diseased, and infection spread to other inmates. Those
cells that were located under the lead-covered roof
were extremely hot in the summer because of their low
ceilings, under which prisoners could not even stand up,
and were rat-infested because of the squalid conditions,
despite being located directly above the magistrates
working in the rooms below.[23] Thus one of Antonio
da Ponte's first jobs in 1563 after being appointed
proto, or architectural superintendent, was to overhaul
the existing prisons and to plan with Rusconi the
construction of a new prison building in response
to the idea that prisoners ought to be specifically
accommodated in a purpose-built structure.[24]
The Bridge of Sighs was the link between the new
edifice with its bespoke spaces for prisoners and the

existing spaces of magistrates and other government
officials in the Doge's Palace (fig. 83).[25] Although the
transformation of the interior of the Doge's Palace
could not be seen externally, the new interior spatial
solutions achieved through rebuilding the principal
seat of government were just as important as the
creation of the New Prisons that now represented more
explicitly the stern face of justice to the citizens of the
Serenissima.[26]

After proceeding in fits and starts, with one phase in
1563, a second from 1569, and a third in 1581, it was only
in 1591 that Antonio Da Ponte presented three models of
his project,[27] this time together with Zaccaria Briani,
a prisoner in the palace who was given a partial
remittance of his sentence in exchange for his expert
advice. This project proposal reveals a more complex
awareness of the social needs and requirements of
this newly developing independent building-type. To
represent the prison as a public institution, Da Ponte
employed the traditional architectural language of
robustness in the form of rustication, as Sansovino
had done for the Mint. Perhaps because of its location
adjacent to the Doge's Palace, or perhaps because it

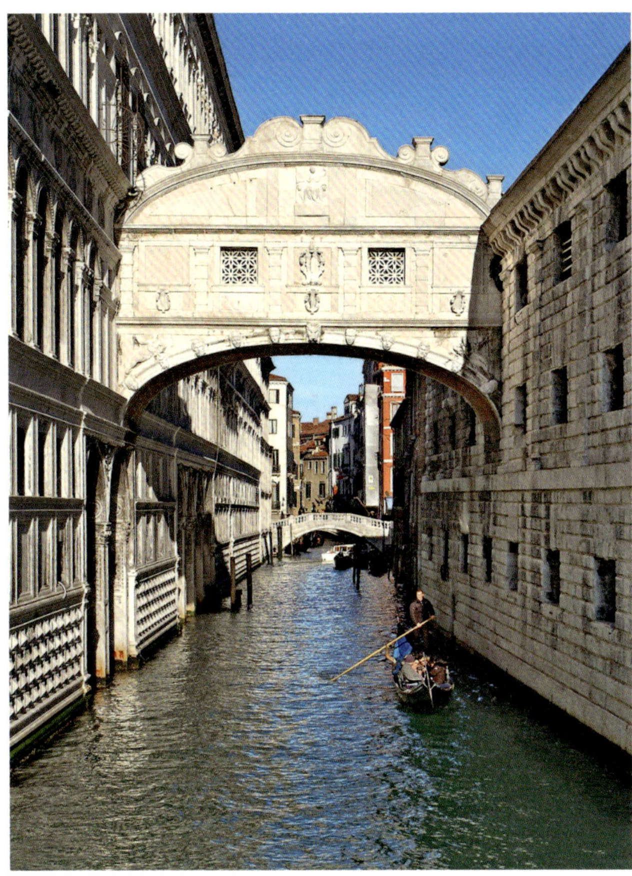

was also a new sight in Venice and Fialetti had to come up with his own depiction of it rather than relying on an earlier representation done by someone else. Despite the incorrect number of bays, he clearly represents the double storey 'palace' façade and its side bay on the canal and distinguishes this section from the plethora of smaller windows extending back along the canal.

Fialetti also clearly depicts the Bridge of Sighs, which represented the solution to the problem of the lack of a link between the new building and the Doge's Palace – remedied in 1600 (frontispiece). The bridge served the practical function of providing a connecting passageway, not for prisoners passing to and from their cells, as is usually assumed, but connecting the Room of the Censors and the Rooms of the Avogadori with the cells on the second floor where the prisoners of the Council of Ten were housed. Those arrested were in fact taken directly into the New Prisons and only brought across into the Doge's Palace as required by the magistrates in order to be interrogated in the torture room, although a second torture room also had been set up in the New Prisons, again indicating spatial specialization.

The bridge provided the various functionaries such as gaolers with a efficient means of access to the prisoners, and it was in order to provide light and fresh air to what would otherwise be a dark and airless corridor that the ornamental grilles were designed, rather than supposedly giving condemned prisoners a last glimpse of the outside world before incarceration – a Romantic invention. Apart from providing a unique and efficient means of communication, the bridge with its twin, parallel, corridors also served the purpose of making clear the connection between both buildings, thereby legitimizing the role of the New Prisons – which provided systematic incarceration without undermining the public role of the Doge's Palace's as the palace of justice.

was one of the most recently constructed buildings, largely terminated probably in 1601, but only properly complete in 1614, Fialetti depicts it as being taller and wider than both the Mint and the end bays of the Library together.[28]

Fialetti depicts the New Prisons as being of a uniform height (frontispiece), whereas Da Ponte grafted a taller 'palace' section on to the front of the prison block. This set of rooms for the magistrates of the Signori della Notte Criminale expressed architecturally their role in administering Venetian justice. The newly built site

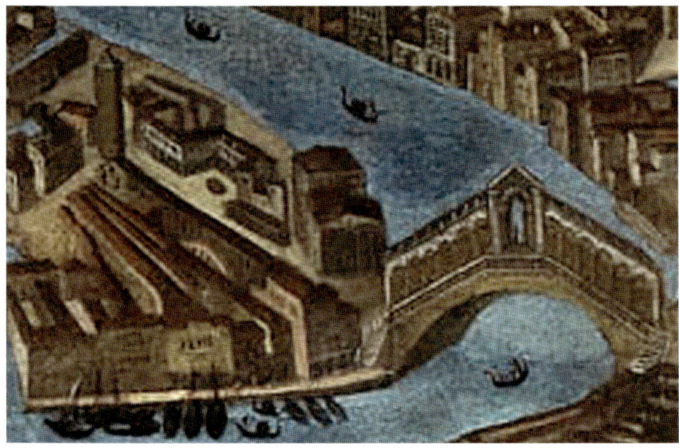

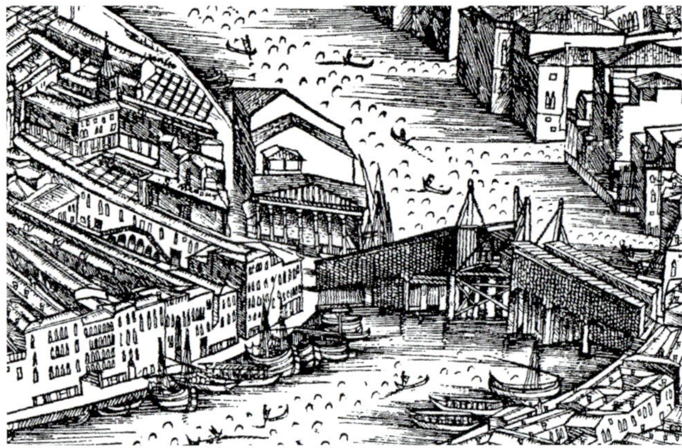

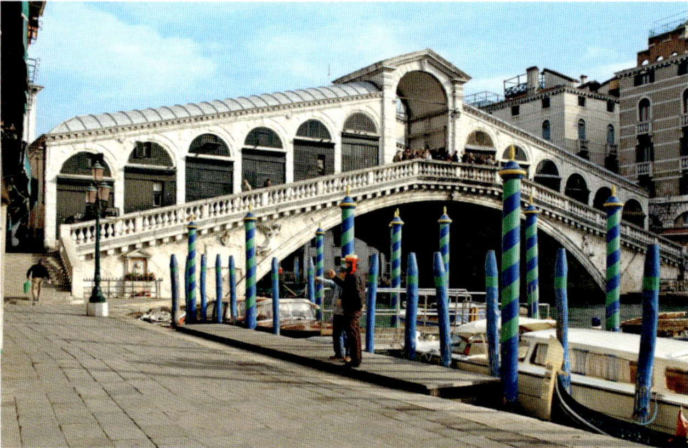

85
Fialetti's *View*, detail showing the Rialto Market and Bridge

86
Jacopo de' Barbari, *Map of Venice*, detail of fig. 30 showing Rialto area

87
Venice, Rialto Bridge, by Antonio da Ponte, 1588–91

Rialto rebuilt: Da Ponte's ponte

Besides Contin's diminutive but highly symbolic work, emblematic of the myriad bridges spanning canals in this city built on water, Fialetti made a feature of another bridge, that recently rebuilt at Rialto (figs. 85, 87). A crucial piece of urban infrastructure, it was a triumph of engineering and construction on a watery site, proclaiming the modernity and expertise of the technicians who worked for the Republic. Eventually the bridge was built by the appropriately named and accomplished engineer Antonio da Ponte, although the outline of his design was influenced by the proposals of Vincenzo Scamozzi.[29] This impressive new construction already appears in the bird's-eye-view plan engraved by Bernardo Salvioni and published by Donato Rascicotto in about 1597 (fig. 51). There it was singled out in one of the two accompanying vignette views at the bottom of the map (the other being St Mark's Square), thus flagging up its importance as a vital urban node and, in this case, its contemporaneity as one of the most recent additions to the cityscape.[30] These surrounding views set into maps became a key strategy for highlighting what was new or important, just as in tapestries the main scene was surrounded with a series of vignettes.[31] Here Fialetti carefully follows Salvioni and accurately depicts the bridge with six arched shops on either side of the main, Serlio-inspired, central arch. Unlike Salvioni, by 1611 Fialetti was no longer breaching copyright, for Da Ponte had been awarded a patent in 1590 forbidding the sale of any views of the new Rialto Bridge for 20 years.[32] While the bridge is carefully and accurately shown, the Rialto market buildings are depicted in their state before the 1514 fire, following de' Barbari's bird's-eye view (fig. 86), and do not include Sansovino's interventions, for example. This is all the more surprising since every other printed map of the sixteenth century tried, with varying degrees of success, to show the market area in its post-fire state. This underlines the extent to which Fialetti used Jacopo de' Barbari as his principal point of departure.

The Arsenale

The third key zone in the city along with St Mark's and Rialto was the Arsenale, the celebrated ship-building zone of the Maritime Republic (fig. 88).[33] In the 1560s this area had undergone recent rebuilding and expansion to the north-west, on the Campo della Tana, and 1385 m² (4544 square feet) of land owned by the nuns of the Celestia was expropriated and developed. As a consequence of a powder tower exploding and causing a massive conflagration in the Arsenale on the night between 13 and 14 September 1569, large-scale repair and restructuring works in the 1570s included rebuilding the Corderie in 1579–90, and this 664 m long rope-works designed by Antonio da Ponte was carefully detailed by Fialetti.[34] Yet none of the hustle and bustle, chaos and confusion of what was still the largest ship-building site in Early Modern Europe appears. In fact its spaces are curiously lacking the thousands of workers – the

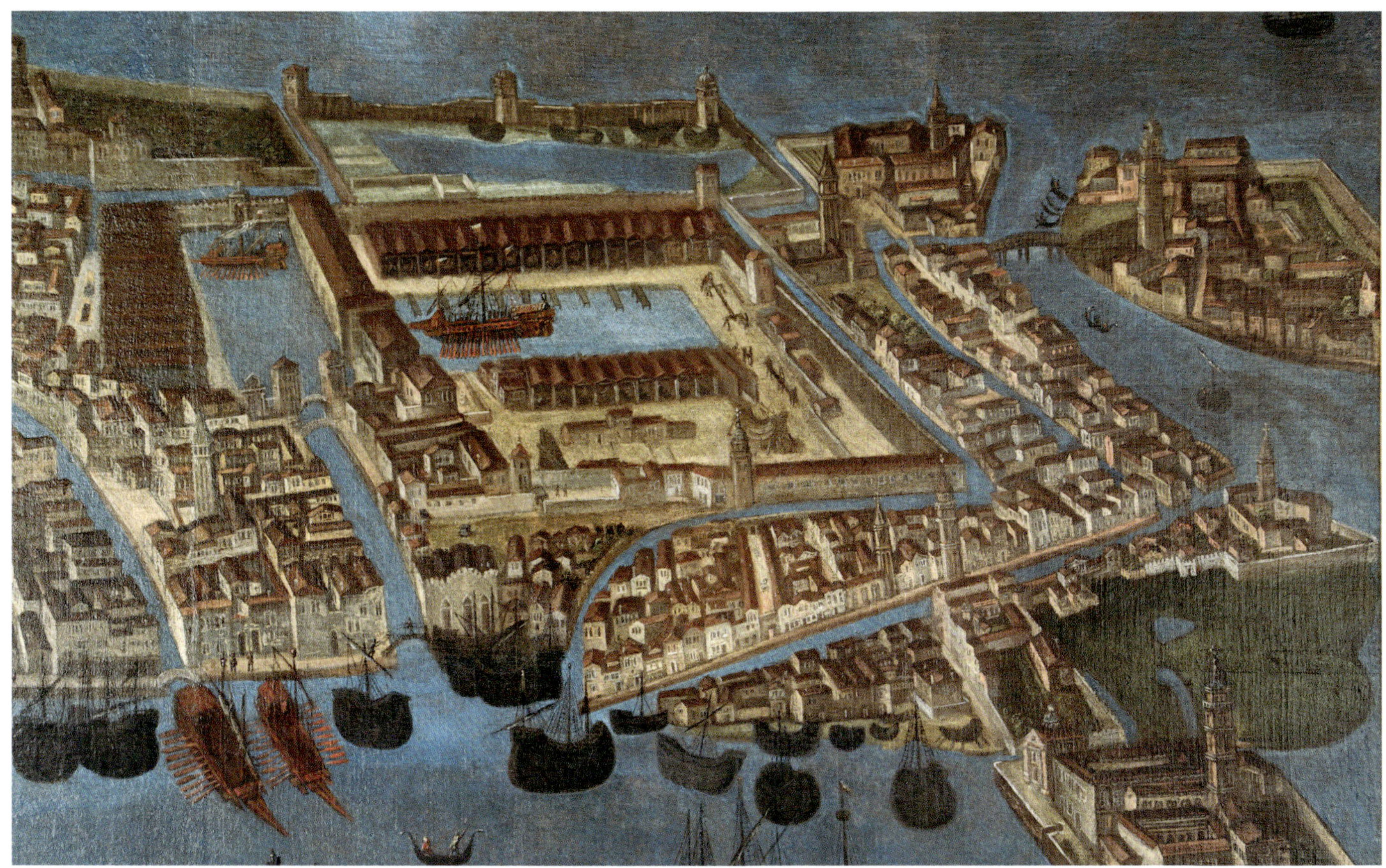

Castellani – who defined the adjacent residential zone and populated the Arsenale every day, just as only a few token ships are represented.

One notable aspect of Fialetti's view is the series of wide canals in Castello that proceed more or less vertically from the Bacino through to the Biria canal (fig. 89, and see fig. 1). While they perhaps appear to be too wide, this is partially a result of the Arsenale being depicted on an additional piece of canvas where Fialetti had to operate considerable visual 'compression'

in comparison to the luxurious spatial layout afforded Castello. Yet certainly these broad canals existed or exist, although some of them were interred and transformed in the Napoleonic era into a series of *rii terra*. This is also true for the Biria canal, which traversed in an almost straight line the northern part of the city from Santi Apostoli near Rialto all the way to the canal of San Pietro di Castello, debouching between San Daniele and Santa Maria delle Vergini. It has recently been suggested that this 'short-cut' must have been the major acquatic

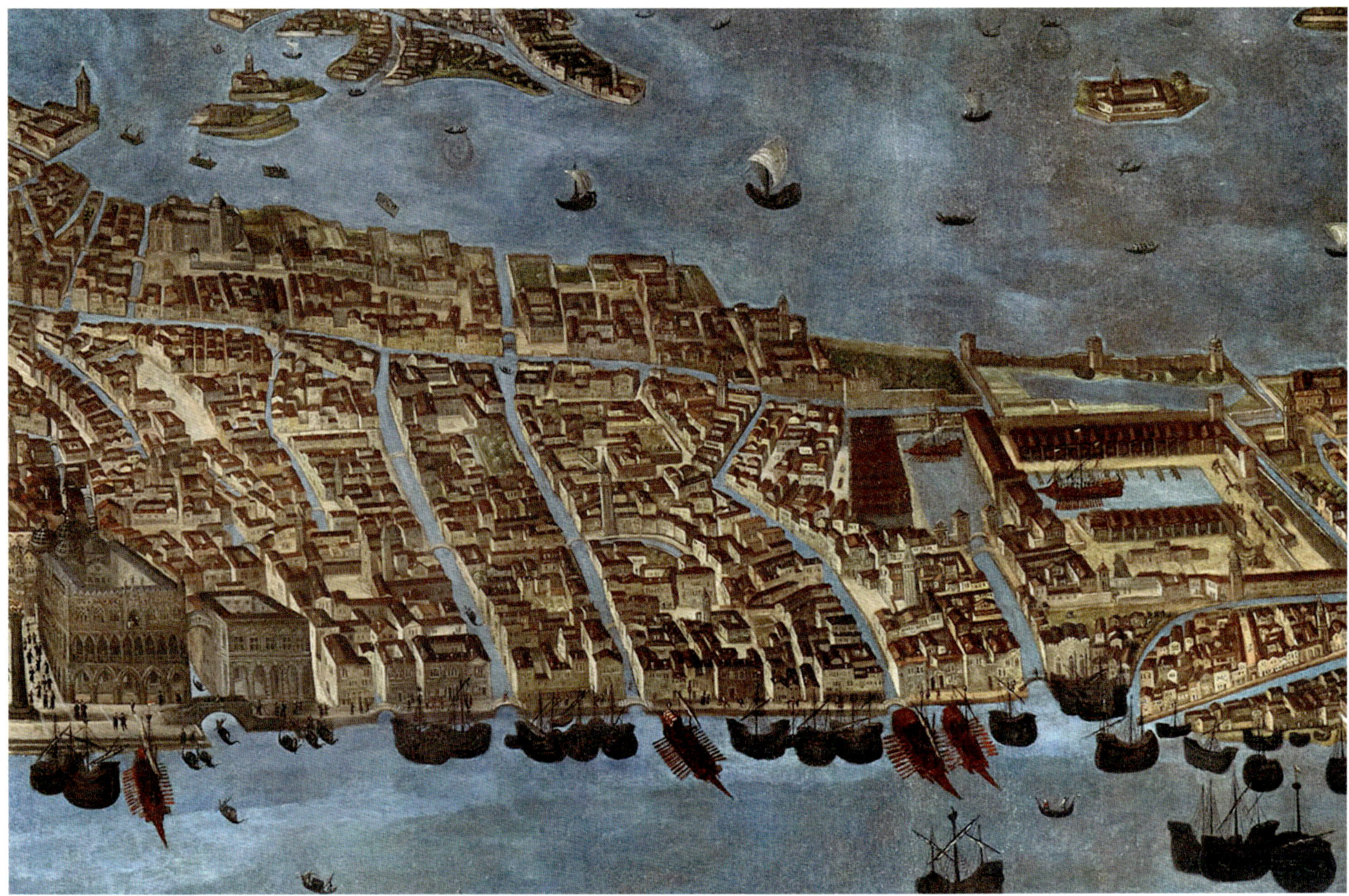

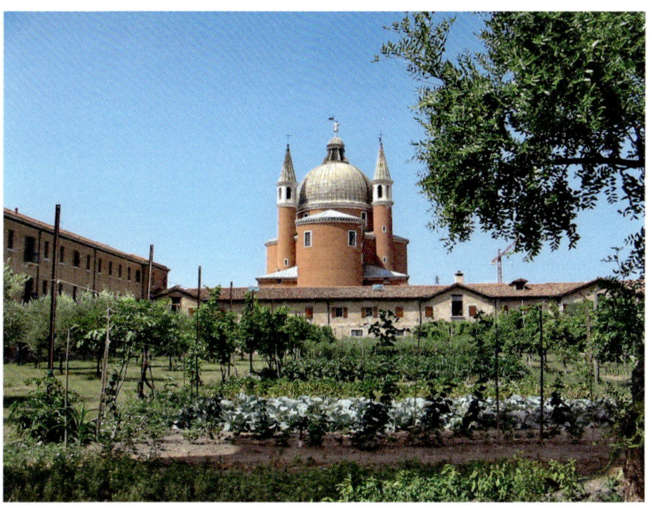

thoroughfare through the city in its early history before the Grand Canal came to dominate.[35]

One indication that this may have been the case is the presence along the Biria canal and around the southern, eastern and western confines of the Arsenale of a series of important churches officiated by distinguished and wealthy orders. Most of these were demolished in the Napoleonic era but Fialetti records them – Santa Maria della Celestia and Santa Ternità just to the east of San Francesco della Vigna; San Domenico on the rio Sant'Anna, and San Daniele and Santa Maria delle Vergini to the east between the Arsenale and the cathedral of Venice, San Pietro di Castello.[36] The Arsenale gateway is shown with its triangular pediment but it is hard to discern Girolamo Campagna's statue of Santa Giustina placed on the pediment in the 1570s following victory at the Battle of Lepanto.[37]

Absence makes the heart grow fonder: ciò che non c'è
One of the most fascinating aspects of Fialetti's work, as with so many views of cities, is what it does not represent. The massive construction work to create the Fondamenta Nuove on the northern edge of the city in Cannaregio, begun in 1588, is absent despite its radically changing the perimeter outline of that part of the townscape.[38] Palladio's new church of San Giorgio Maggiore is missing and Fialetti still shows the houses sited in front of the medieval church that blocked the Benedictines' view of the Doge's Palace (fig. 77). It is hard to understand how one could have overlooked this spectacular church with its gleaming white Istrian stone façade completed in 1610 (fig. 78), although, as Salvioni's map makes the same omission (fig. 51), it illustrates just how far both Salvioni and Fialetti were dependent on the precedent of Jacopo de' Barbari.[39] Among the palaces of recent construction lining the Grand Canal omitted by Fialetti was the Balbi palace of the 1580s,

traditionally attributed to Alessandro Vittoria, despite its highly visible position '*in volta al canal*'. Other palaces were impossible to represent as they faced the 'wrong way' on the Grand Canal, a good example being the Contarini degli Scrigni palace of *c*. 1609, traditionally attributed to Scamozzi.[40] The Scuola Grande della Misericordia is not recorded despite its being one of the largest buildings on the Venetian horizon, its meeting hall the same dimensions as the Sala del Maggiore Consiglio of the Ducal Palace, on which it was modelled.[41]

Perhaps the most surprising omission, however, is Palladio's church of the Redentore (figs. 1 and 90).[42] This is even odder given that Fialetti does include the nearby Palladian church of the Zitelle, basing himself on Salvioni's strange view with its single bell-tower and long retrochoir, so that the main drum and dome appear in front of the back of the façade of the church, somewhat like the halo behind the head of a saint in a primitive painting (fig. 63).[43] While the Zitelle was an important religious institution for unmarried women, it cannot compare in actual architectural size or historical importance with the major state-commissioned votive church of the Redentore designed by Andrea Palladio.[44] Given that Salvioni depicts it in his 1597 map, one is forced to hypothesize that Fialetti chose deliberately not to include it.

Unexpected presences: cio che c'è

In contrast, one of the oddest and most surprising new buildings among those that Fialetti decided to represent in oversize mode is the large and highly visible church of Santa Maria dell'Umiltà on the Zattere, just beyond the Punta della Dogana and the Magazzini del Sal which had belonged to the Jesuits since 1549 (fig. 91). It was rebuilt around 1580 and reconsecrated in 1589. The church was occupied by the Jesuits until their unceremonious expulsion from Venice in 1606, just five years before Fialetti painted his view.[45] After the departure of the Jesuits, it remained empty until 1615, but continued to be known as the 'Jesuit church' until in that year it was granted to a group of Benedictine nuns from the Isola di San Servolo.[46] It is hard to judge whether Fialetti recorded it at a larger scale because of its visual vicinity to St Mark's, although the adjacent Dogana da Mar is relatively small by comparison. No previous printed map gives such prominence to the (empty) but still 'Jesuit' church, so it seems it must have been a deliberate choice, especially given Fialetti's tendency to copy almost everything from prints.

Does this prominent representation have some political or religious significance? The fact is that the Jesuits who officiated the Umiltà were expelled in 1606 while the Capuchins who officiated the Redentore remained. Was the still-present order to be represented

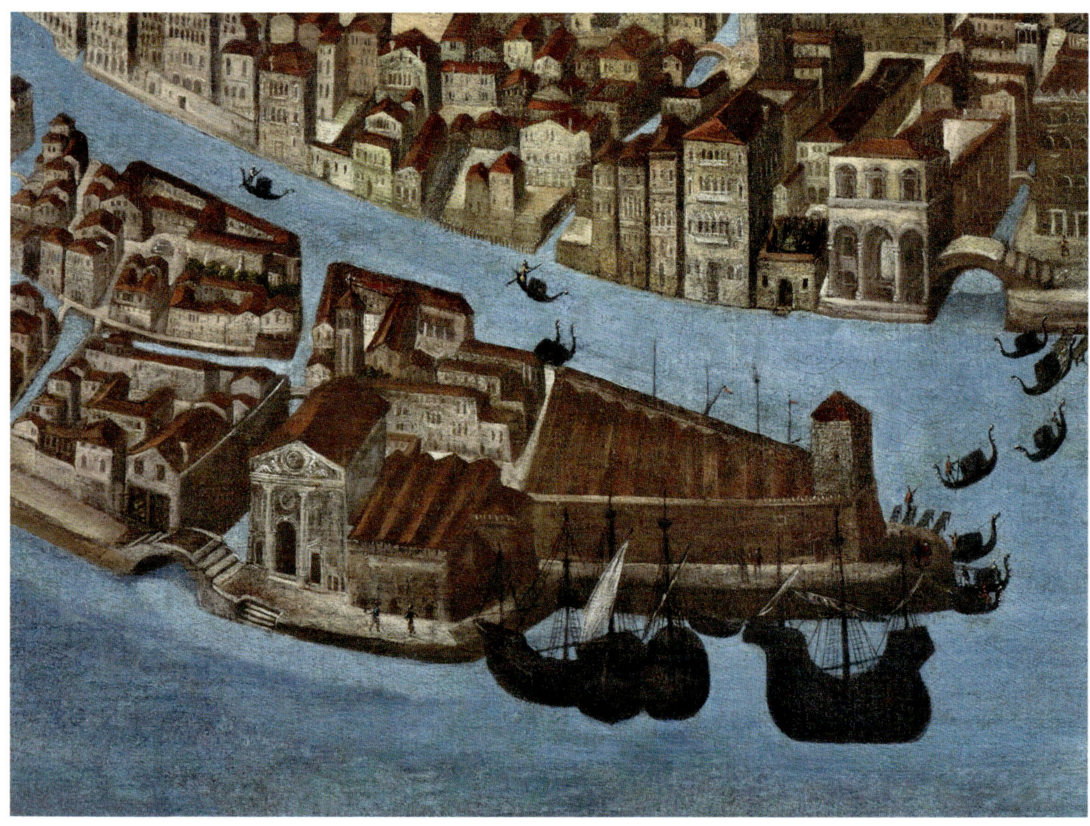

by the glaring absence of their celebrated building, and
the absent order by the oversized presence of their small
church?[47] Indeed, there had been competition between
the Jesuits and the Capuchins to obtain the officiation
of the church of the Redentore, and so one might
wonder whether the patron of the map could have been
pro-Jesuit and annoyed about their failure to win the
competition for the state-sponsored votive church and
their subsequent expulsion from the Serenissima.[48]

On another note, one might wonder whether Fialetti
paid special attention in his view to the churches in
which his own painted altarpieces were conserved.
Certainly Santi Giovanni e Paolo is highly accurate and
detailed, which is notable given its location in the urban
fabric, far away from the front of the picture plane. On
the other hand the matching mendicant church of the
Frari is equally well depicted, while nearby San Nicolò
dei Tolentini, where another Fialetti painting resided,
is difficult to distinguish among the mass of indeter-
minable buildings in that area (presumably because this
area was highly compressed in Jacopo de' Barbari's *View*).

Conclusion: city and ceremony

The buildings depicted in Fialetti's *View* seem to be a
combination of images borrowed from earlier views
(primarily Jacopo de' Barbari) and details copied from
life. The *View*'s details include vignettes of daily life
and festivities as well as features of the townscape.
Fialetti's depiction of some sort of ceremony in Piazza
San Marco (fig. 11) is unusual in that clearly it is not a
ducal procession but a civic or secular rite that resembles
something like a Punch and Judy show.[49]

Perhaps the best way to understand the significance
of the Piazza San Marco in this period is to compare
it with the creation at this precise moment of 'Places
Royales' in Europe, in Paris for Henri IV, in Madrid for
Philip. Of course Venice had had its own extended Place

Royale for centuries, set in front of the Ducal Chapel
and Ducal (Doge's) Palace, the focus of a century-long
programme of completion, renovation and extension
from the 1530s to the 1640s, and parallel issues of
urbanism and spatial use emerge.

In the Baroque age ceremony had become the
principal means through which the ruler expressed
his power in the capitals of Europe. Etiquette and
court hierarchy were deployed to manifest a ruling
house's power to their citizens and the world; such
representations were directed from one prince to another
as well as to visitors, giving rise to internal documents
such as the registers of the masters of ceremonies that
codified practice, as well as the plethora of engravings
publicizing and recording events enacted in the spaces
of the city.[50] Private ceremonial moved into the public
sphere as squares were transformed into theatres of
persuasion for superlative urban manifestations, and
numerous religious feasts were recorded in pamphlets
and publications, confirming both David Cannadine's
formulation, "pomp is itself a visible form of power",
and José Antonio Maravall's complex thesis considering
the culture of the Baroque as residing in the powerful
institutions of church and state together, using
elaborate visual means to reinforce their dominant
status and convince, persuade and manage the masses.
Certainly the constant, almost frenetic activity enacted
on the main squares of Early Modern Europe influenced
the urban design and architecture that enclosed them.

Squares such as Piazza San Marco that had originally
served pragmatic and utilitarian functions, such as
hosting daily markets, rapidly, or over longer periods
of time, became focused on providing residential
accommodation and royal boxes or their equivalent, as
industry and commerce were minimized and aristocratic
demeanour enhanced. From the Largo before the Palazzo
Reale in Spanish Naples in 1600, to Bernini's Piazza San

Pietro for the popes of the 1660s, to the French monarch's Place Vendôme in Paris of 1702, such spaces exemplified what had been noted around 1550 in an architectural treatise dedicated to Philip II of Spain: "squares are of foremost importance in the city given that they are the most frequented places for residents and foreign visitors who tend to report about these cities in their homelands". They represented a city's reputation and with unmatched intensity in the seventeenth century most of the major European courts chose to express their status and power through ceremonial performed there. Despite its proudly defended Republican rule, Piazza San Marco had fulfilled this purpose for centuries.

Doing so created conflict with the traditional presence of ground-floor shops which, like city walls, had an ambiguous and changing status: for centuries these had lined the squares of Europe and their inclusion in most new projects is an index of the utilitarian approach of the Early Modern city. On the other hand, as ceremonial became the primary focus, there was a desire to remove them, especially the food shops, in order to create a dignified spatial setting: the meat-market and brothel sited on the corner opposite the Ducal Palace in Venice – long considered both undignified and inappropriate – were finally removed from Piazza San Marco in 1580, in order to complete the Marciana Library, and Fialetti in fact is one of the first to show this area complete.

All the evidence points to Fialetti generally relying on earlier images for the generation of his painting, but including personally observed if rather schematically represented buildings where there were no extant images, as in the case of the Prisons and the Bridge of Sighs, Library and Mint, suggesting his focus on the easily accessible buildings on and around the Forum Marcianum. The decision to emphasize the former Jesuit church, which looms large in the painting while the Redentore is conspicuously absent, implies that he was making a deliberate political point, probably at the request of the map's patron.

Rather than simply consider Fialetti's 'cut and paste' clumsy, one could see it in other terms, and here music might help. A century later Antonio Vivaldi's eclectic drama *Bajazet*, composed in 1735 and first performed in the Philharmonic Theatre at Verona, deliberately featured a *pasticcio* or pastiche of Carnevale and openly combined the popular arias of other composers into an overall narrative composition by the maestro. This was a way for him to introduce the newer and more popular styles of his contemporaries and thus keep his music up-to-date and attractive to audiences. So too, Fialetti creates an artful *pasticcio* based heavily on Jacopo de' Barbari's woodcut of 1500 and Salvioni's view of 1597, adds a few new tunes of his own, and creates a perfect pastiche of old and new, accurate and mistaken, observed and overlooked. Neverthless this enormous painted view from the beginning of the seventeenth century remains unmistakably the city of the Serenissima.

NOTES

1 See the classic study of dissimulation by travellers, P. Adams, *Travelers and travel liars 1660–1800*, Berkeley, 1962. See also Z. von Martels (ed.), *Travel fact and travel fiction: Studies on fiction, literary tradition, scholarly discovery and observation in travel writing*, Leiden, 1994.

2 J. McAndrew, *Venetian Architecture of the Early Renaissance*, Cambridge, Mass., and London, 1980, p. 135: "The retrochoir behind the chancel is a late addition made by the friars when they became so numerous that they had to have more space". That the first retrochoir in Venice belonged to the church of San Francesco della Vigna, built in 1534, was suggested by the author in A. Hopkins, 'The Influence of Ducal Ceremony on Church Design in Venice', *Architectural History*, 41, 1998, pp. 38 and 48n. 18. Now see J. Allen, "Radical innovation or conventional afterthought? Dating the San Giobbe retrochoir', in N. Avcioglu and E. Jones (eds.), *Architecture, Art and Identity in Venice and its Territories 1450–1750*, Aldershot, 2013, pp. 171–84.

3 J. Schulz, 'Jacopo de' Barbari's view of Venice: Map Making, City Views, and Moralized Geography before the Year 1500", *Art Bulletin*, 60, 1978, pp. 425–72; D. Howard, 'Venice as a dolphin: Further investigations into Jacopo de' Barbari's view', *Artibus et historiae*, 18/35, 1997, pp. 101–11. Also see the late Denis Cosgrove's classic study, 'The myth and the stones of Venice: an historical geography of a symbolic landscape', *Journal of Historical Geography*, 8, 1982, pp. 145–69. For Cosgrove see V. della Dora, 'Denis Cosgrove (1948–2008)', *Imago Mundi*, 61/1, 2009, pp. 97–100.

4 This shift was first formulated by de' Barbari presumably to provide a horizontal-base visual anchor corresponding to the confines of the lagoon and the Dolomites represented above. This representational tradition was taken up and continued by Matteo Pagan in his map of 1559 and by Bernardo Salvioni in 1597. See J. Schulz, 'The printed plans and panoramic views of Venice (1486–1797)', *Saggi e memorie di storia dell'arte*, 7, 1970. Without the additional canvas on which the Arsenale is depicted, the visual role of the Giudecca islands filling the base of the picture would have been even more accentuated.

5 The quote is from M. Plant, *Venice: Fragile City 1797–1997*, New Haven and London, 2002, pp. 124–31. Fialetti's work was first discussed at length by M. Azzi Visentini, 'Ancora un'inedita pianta prospettica di Venezia in un dipinto di Odoardo Fialetti per Sir Henry Wotton', *Bollettino dei musei civici veneziani d'arte e di storia*, 25, 1980, pp. 19–25. Also see J. Fletcher, 'The Arundels in the Veneto', *Apollo*, 144/414, 1996, pp. 63–69; F. Panzarin, 'Il collezionismo inglese a Venezia nel Seicento: Henry Wotton letterato, agente, collezionista, mecenate e il suo rapporto con Odoardo Fialetti', *Arte in Friuli, arte a Trieste*, 20, 2000, pp. 37–60. For Fialetti see V. Maugeri, 'Fialetti. Odoardo', in *Dizionario biografico degli italiani*, vol. 47, Rome, 1997, pp. 322–24.

6 For the completion of the façade see D. Howard, *Venice Disputed: Marc'Antonio Barbaro and Venetian Architecture, 1550–1600*, New Haven and London, 2011, pp. 116–22; J. Ackerman, 'Palladio, Michelangelo and publica magnificentia', *Annali di Architettura*, 22, 2010, pp. 63–78; S. Sciamberg, 'Palladio's lost, rejected, and found porticos: façade projects for San Giorgio, the Redentore, and San Petronio', *Annali di Architettura*, 22, 2010, pp. 79–88.

7 A. Hopkins, *Baldassare Longhena*, New Haven and London, 2012, pls. 17, 19, 20.

8 A. Hopkins, *Santa Maria della Salute: Architecture and Ceremony in Baroque Venice*, Cambridge, 2000, pp. 211–12, 217–21.

9 Vincenzo Scamozzi(?), 'Descrittione di alcune fabriche moderne', in Giovanni Stringa, *Venetia città nobilissima, et singolare … ampliata dal M. R.D. Giovanni Stringa*, Venice, 1604, fols. 426v–432v. For Stringa see J. Bettley, 'The Office of Holy Week at St Mark's, Venice, in the late 16th century, and the musical contributions of Giovanni Croce', *Early Music*, 22/1, 1994, pp. 45–62, at p.45.

10 L. Orsini, 'Gli architetti Contin da Lugano: dal ponte dei Sospiri alla chiesa di S. Maria del Pianto', *Arte e storia*, 8/40, 2008, pp. 150–55, is merely a summary whereas L. Tessarin, 'I Contin: una dinastia di proti nel '500 veneziano', tesi di laurea IUAV University, Venice, 1985, with its archival research, remains unpublished.

11 M. Tafuri, *Venezia e il Rinascimento: Religione, scienza, architettura*, Turin, 1985 (Eng. edn Cambridge, Mass., 1989); Howard, *Venice Disputed*,

12 D. Howard, *Jacopo Sansovino: Architecture and patronage in Renaissance Venice*, New Haven and London, 1975 (2nd edn 1987); M. Tafuri (ed.), *Renovatio Urbis: Venezia nell'età di Andrea Gritti*, Rome, 1984; A. Hopkins, 'Architecture and Infirmitas: Doge Andrea Gritti and the chancel of San Marco, Venice', *Journal of the Society of Architectural Historians*, 57, 1998, pp. 182–97. For the demolitions see A. Zorzi, *Venezia scomparsa*, 2nd edn, Milan, 1984, pp. 223–27.

13 These differences in the architecture of the Piazza were first noted by M. Azzi Visentini, 'Ancora un'inedita pianta prospettica di Venezia in un dipinto di Odoardo Fialetti per Sir Henry Wotton', *Bollettino dei musei civici veneziani*, 35/1, 1980, pp. 19–25, at p. 19.

14 For recent research see E.J. Johnson, 'A window in the Venetian mint and the Libreria di San Marco 2010', *Journal of the Society of Architectural Historians*, 69/2, 2010, pp. 190–205, at p. 196, citing Vincenzo Scamozzi, *L'Idea dell'architettura universale*, 6 vols., Venice, 1615, I, 6: 171; Howard, *Venice Disputed*, p. 181.

15 A. Hopkins, 'Longhena proto e architetto: disegni e documenti per le aree attorno alla Piazza', *Arte veneta*, 60, 2003, pp. 199–206.

16 For the third storey see Howard, *Venice Disputed*, pp. 180–89. For their completion by Longhena from the 1640s see Hopkins, *Baldassare Longhena*, pp. 21–24.

17 Howard, *Venice Disputed*, pp. 171–91. Earlier discussions of this issue are Tafuri, *Venezia e il*

Rinascimento, pp. 252–71; A. Hopkins, 'Completamento delle libreria sansoviniana (1581–1588)', and 'Procuratie Nuove in piazza San Marco (1581)', in F. Barbieri and G. Beltramini (eds.), *Vincenzo Scamozzi 1548–1616*, exh. cat., Museo Palladio, Vicenza, 2003, pp. 202–20, nos. 11–12; P. Placentino, 'Politica ed economia nella riconfigurazione tardocinquecentesca di piazza San Marco: il cantiere delle Procuratie Nuove', *Mélanges de l'École Française de Rome. Italie et Méditerranée*, 119/2, 2007, pp. 321–40.

18 A. Viggiano, *Le procuratie vecchie in Piazza San Marco*, Rome, 1994.

19 G. Morolli, *Le procuratie nuove in Piazza San Marco*, Rome, 1994.

20 U. Franzoi, *Le prigioni di Palazzo Ducale a Venezia*, Milan, 1997, pp.42–56; Howard, *Venice Disputed*, pp. 136–44. For Rusconi, see L. Cellauro, 'La biblioteca di un architetto del Rinascimento: la raccolta di libri di Giovanni Antonio Rusconi', *Arte veneta*, 58, 2001, pp. 224–37.

21 Oddly enough, given the matching number of apertures on ground and first floors, Fialetti nevertheless does not manage to make the vertical axes of the Prison façade coincide and the lateral arched ground floor aperture at the right is squashed as a consequence presumably of Fialetti beginning his painting of the arches from the left and making the first two too big and hence having progressively to reduce their width, culminating in the feeble arch at the right.

22 Now see K. Ottenheym *et al.* (eds.), *Public Buildings in Early Modern Europe (Architectura Moderna* 9), Turnhout, 2010.

23 See the engraved cross-section by Angelo Gambini in U. Franzoi, *Le prigioni di Palazzo Ducale a Venezia*, Milan, 1997, p. 17.

24 See Franzoi, 'Le prigioni oltre il rio', in *Le prigioni*, pp. 42–49, .

25 *Ibid.*, 'Antonio Contin e il ponte dei Sospiri', pp. 66–69.

26 Howard, *Venice Disputed*, pp. 137–38, 143–44, with further bibliography.

27 Tafuri, *Venezia e il Rinascimento*, p. 276; Franzoi, 'Seconda fase della costruzione', in *Le prigioni*, pp. 49–52, and 'Antonio da Ponte e Zamaria de Piombi', pp. 52–56.

28 Franzoi, *Le prigioni*, pp. 198–212 (documentary appendix).

29 Deborah Howard has recently shed much light on Marc'Antonio's involvement in the architectural competitions for this project, including the celebrated proposals by Andrea Palladio: see Howard, *Venice Disputed*, pp. 151–69. An earlier discussion is in D. Calabi and A. Hopkins, 'Progetto per il ponte di Rialto a Venezia (1588)', in Barbieri and Beltramini, *Vincenzo Scamozzi*, pp.285–88.

30 Schulz, 'The printed plans', no. 53, pp. 26, 59, fig. 29.

31 See the two splendid exhibition catalogues, T. Campbell (ed.), *Tapestry in the Renaissance: Art and Magnificence*, exh. cat., Metropolitan Museum of Art, New York, 2002; *idem*, *Tapestry in the Baroque: Threads of Splendor*, New Haven, 2007.

32 Howard, *Venice Disputed*, p. 167.

33 E. Concina, *L'Arsenale della Repubblica di Venezia*, Milan, 2006, pp. 143–65, 'Espansione e declino: gli anni di Lepanto e gli anni dei corsari 1570–1620'.

34 *Ibid.*, p. 161, who notes that the rebuilt and remodelled Arsenale of Venice was used as the basis for the description of the ideal Arsenale by Vincenzo Scamozzi in his treatise of 1615 (see note 12), p. 173; Howard, *Venice Disputed*, pp. 146–50.

35 A. Ammerman, 'Venice before the Grand Canal', *Memoirs of the American Academy in Rome*, 48, 2003, pp. 141–58, at p. 150, fig.4.

36 E. Bassi, *Tracce di chiese veneziane distrutte: Ricostruzioni dai disegni di Antonio Visentini*, Venice, 1997. For the cathedral see now G. Guidarelli, 'Venice's Cathedral of San Pietro di Castello, 1451–1630', in Avcioglu and Jones 2013, pp. 185–201.

37 R. Lieberman, 'Real architecture imaginary history: the Arsenale gate as Venetian mythology', *Journal of the Warburg and Courtauld Institutes*, LIV, 1991, pp. 117–26, at p.124.

38 Azzi Visentini, 'Ancora un'inedita pianta', p. 21; Tafuri, *Venezia e il Rinascimento*, pp. 244–97.

39 For the façade of San Giorgio see T.E. Cooper, *Palladio's Venice: Architecture and Society in a Renaissance Republic*, New Haven and London, 2005, pp. 109–45, with further bibliography; Ackerman, 'Palladio, Michelangelo', pp. 63–78. So, too, the new façade of the cathedral of Venice, San Pietro di Castello, cannot be seen. A. Marina, 'From the myths to the margins: the Patriarch's piazza at San Pietro di Castello in Venice', *Renaissance Quarterly*, 64, 2011, pp. 353–429.

40 E. Bassi, *Tre palazzi veneziani della Regione Veneto: Balbi, Flangini-Morosini, Molin*, Venice, 1982, pp. 39–124; M. Dal Mas, 'Contributo alla conoscenza dell'opera architettonica di Alessandro Vittoria', in *Atti del XXIII Congresso di storia dell'architettura* (Conference proceedings Rome 1988), 2 vols., Rome, 1989, II, pp. 255–63; L. Finocchi Ghersi, *Alessandro Vittoria: architettura, scultura e decorazione nella Venezia del tardo Rinascimento*, Udine, 1998, pp.170–79. J.-C. Rößler, 'Da Andrea Palladio a Francesco Contin: i palazzi Mocenigo a San Samuele e Contarini degli Scrigni', *Arte veneta*, 66, 2009, pp. 53–63, questions the traditional attribution of the Contarini degli Scrigni palace to Scamozzi but the logic of his reasoning is faulty. For this period also see A. Roca de Amicis, 'Il primo Seicento e l'architettura dei proti', in *idem* (ed.), *Storia dell'architettura nel Veneto: il Seicento*, Venice, 2008, pp. 20–35.

41 D. Howard, 'The Scuola Grande della Misericordia di Venezia', in G. Fabbri (ed.), *La Scuola Grande della Misericordia di Venezia: storia e progetto*, Milan, 1999, pp. 13–58.

42 Azzi Visentini, 'Ancora un'inedita pianta', p. 21.

43 Schulz, 'The printed plans', no. 53, p. 59, fig. 29. For the Zitelle see L. Puppi (ed.), *Le Zitelle: Architettura, arte e storia di un'istituzione veneziana*, Venice, 1992.

44 See V. Pizzigoni, 'I tre progetti di Palladio per il Redentore', *Annali di Architettura*, 14, 2003, pp. 165–78; Howard, *Venice Disputed*, pp. 98–109;

Ackerman, 'Palladio, Michelangelo'; Sciamberg, 'Palladio's lost, rejected, and found porticos'. See also A. Hopkins, 'Combating the plague: devotional paintings, architectural programs and votive processions in early modern Venice', in G. Bailey *et al.* (eds.), *Hope and Healing: Painting in Italy in a time of plague*, exh. cat., Worcester Art Museum, 2005, pp. 137–52.

45 Francesco Sansovino, *Venetia Citta Nobilissima et Singolare, descritta in XIIII Libri*, Venice, 1581 (reprint 1998), fol. 98r–v; Flaminio Corner, *Notizie storiche delle chiese e monasteri di Venezia, e di Torcello tratte dalle chiese veneziane, e Torcellane*, Padua, 1758 (reprint Bologna, 1990), pp. 524–25. See S. Mason Rinaldi, 'Il Tabernacolo della chiesa dei "Giesuiti" alla Dogana di mare', *Arte Veneta*, 36, 1982, pp. 211–16; S. Tramontin, 'Le nuove congregazioni religiose', in G. Gullino (ed.), *La chiesa di Venezia tra riforma protestante e riforma cattolica*, Venice, 1990, pp. 77–112, at p. 97; M. Zanardi, *I gesuiti e Venezia: momenti e problemi di storia veneziana della Compagnia di Gesù* (conference proceedings, Venice 1990), Padua, 1994; Hopkins, *Santa Maria della Salute*, p. 13; N. Locatelli, 'Ancora sul tabernacolo della chiesa dell'Umiltà a Venezia', *Arte veneta*, 62, 2005,

pp. 102–10. Howard, *Venice Disputed*, pp. 109–10, has the best account of the development of the site and the Jesuit expansion there.

46 Mason Rinaldi, 'Il Tabernacolo della chiesa dei "Giesuiti"', pp. 211–16, especially pp. 211 and 214 n.2.

47 'Their church newly rebuilt in a commodious and beautiful way, is continuously visited by the major part of the city' ("*La chiesa loro restaurata di nuovo in comoda e bella forma, è visitata di continouo dalla maggior parte della città*"): Sansovino, *Venetia città nobilissima*, fol. 98r–v, cited in Howard, *Venice Disputed*, p. 239, n. 137.

48 *Ibid.*, pp. 109–10.

49 I. Fenlon, *Music, Ceremony and Identity in Renaissance Venice*, New Haven and London, 2006.

50 P. Fortini Brown, 'Measured Friendship, calculated pomp the ceremonial welcomes of the Venetian Republic', in B. Wisch and S. Munshower (eds.), *"All the world's a stage ...." Art and pageantry in the Renaissance and Baroque*, University Park, 1990, pp. 136–86; D. Howard, 'Ritual space in Renaissance Venice', *Scroope* 5, 1993–94, pp. 4–11.

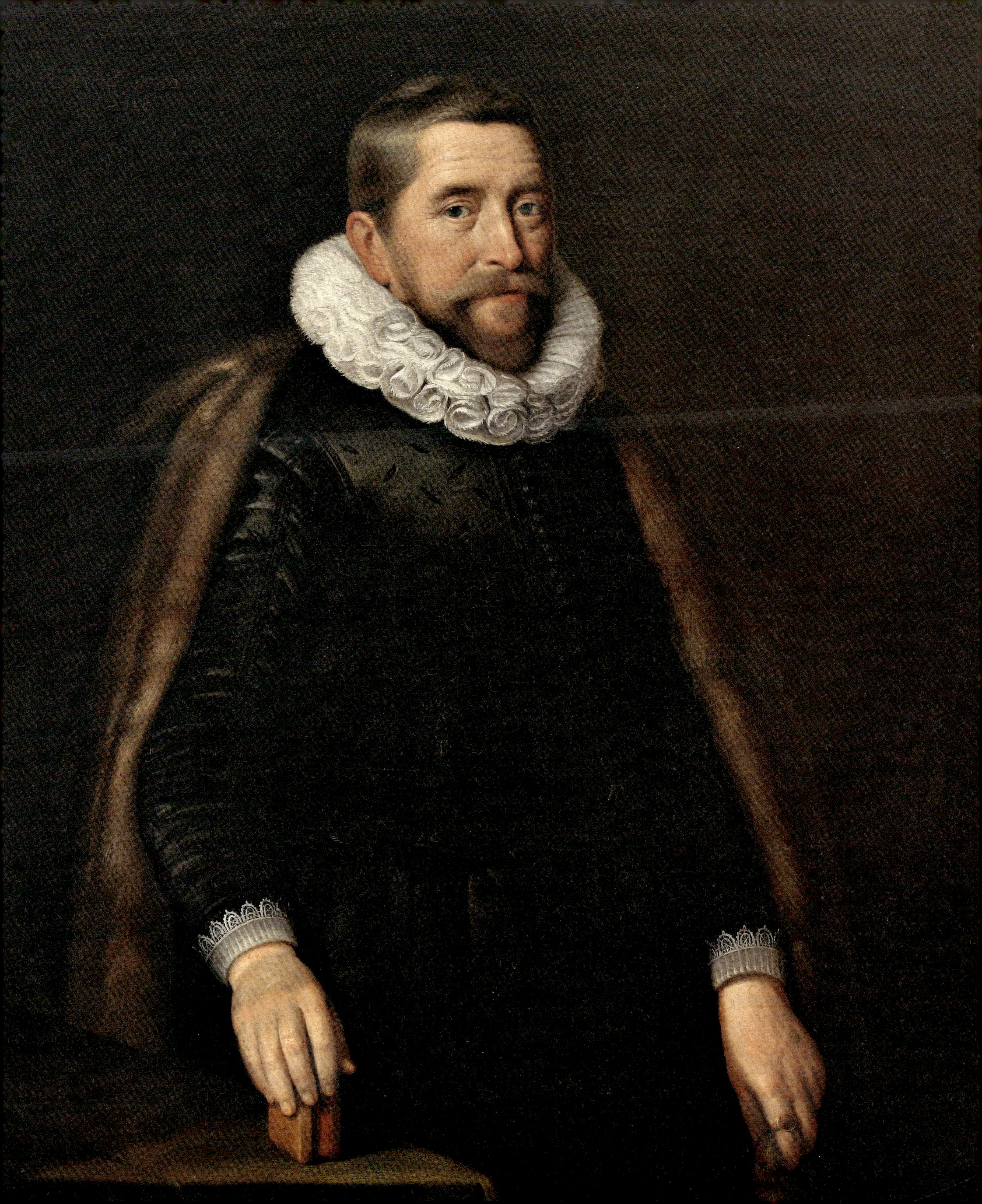

7. Sir Henry Wotton: Collector and Patron

HENRIETTA MCBURNEY

Henry Wotton (1568–1639) was born into an old gentry family in Kent.[1] Educated at Winchester and Oxford, he spent the next five years of his life travelling on the Continent, where he studied law in Heidelberg and Vienna, immersed himself in the study of classical authors and in the art and architecture of major cities of the Italian Renaissance, became proficient in German, Italian and French, and built up a network of contacts, cultural and political. His acquisition of what Henry Peacham was later to describe as the necessary prerequisites for a true gentleman – familiarity with the cities of Europe and fluency in languages – was no doubt intended as a preparation for public life.[2] Here Wotton had the example and indeed shared the ambition and some of the talents of his older half-brother, Edward, 1st Baron Wotton, a diplomat and ambassador, also skilled in languages. However, Henry did not have the natural statesman-like character of his half-brother, who was to be appointed to senior court positions; instead his erratic political judgement, his unpredictable character and his over-zealous attachment to Protestant causes led to a chequered diplomatic career, and he never achieved the high state offices he coveted. Nonetheless, Henry Wotton's undoubted talents and engaging personality meant that he survived disgrace and salvaged his reputation on several occasions when others might not have done.[3]

Wotton's first public appointment after his tour of the Continent was as a secretary to the Earl of Essex, during which time he travelled with him on expeditions to Cadiz, the Azores and Dublin. Wisely ceasing his employment at the first sign of Essex's fall from royal favour, Wotton left for the Continent again in 1600, this time with his nephew; while they were in Florence Wotton was sent on a mission to Scotland by the Medici Grand Duke Ferdinand I to warn James VI of a plot to poison him, a mission he undertook successfully, disguised as an Italian merchant. After returning to Italy, Wotton wrote from Venice in 1603 offering his services to Essex's successor, the Earl of Salisbury. This led to the appointments of the middle part of his life as ambassador to Venice and Savoy (1604–12), The Hague (1614–15), Venice (1616–19) and lastly for a third spell in Venice (1621–23). On his final recall to London, out of the running for any of the public posts for which he had had ambitions, Wotton gained – after some bargaining – the Provostship of Eton, a position which he held for the last fifteen years of his life. Removed from the centre of politics, Wotton spent this last phase of his career encouraging Eton not merely as a school but as "a centre of liberal learning",[4] and according to the inscription he composed himself to hang beneath Fialetti's *View*, "grew old in the happy bosom of Eton College … in most agreeable amity with the Fellows".[5]

Attributed to Jans van Miereveld, *Sir Henry Wotton*, 1620, oil on canvas, 99.1 x 82.6 cm
University of Oxford, Bodleian Library

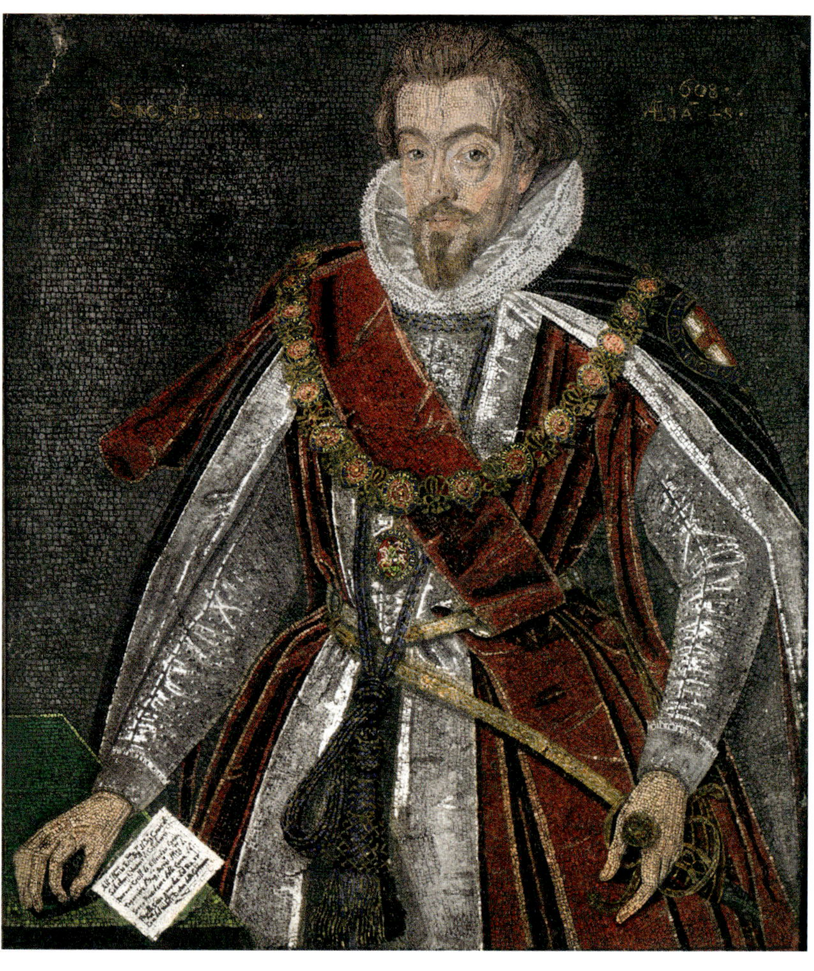

Wotton as collector

Despite Wotton's lack of success in his diplomatic posts (including his failed strategy to persuade Venice to join a Protestant alliance in the aftermath of the Interdict of 1606 – for which see Chapter 8), his knowledge accumulated over two decades in Italy, together with his natural taste and appreciation of Venetian art and architecture, allowed him to play a prominent role as a cultural mediator, advising and acquiring works of art for English art collectors. The formation of collections of fine art amongst the greatest men at court was emerging as an essential mark of their status, and Wotton was not only ideally connected and placed but also had the skills and cultivated eye to make the most of this situation. Timothy Wilks describes him as "the arch-procurer and giver of pictures" and observes how readily Wotton "bought art to ingratiate himself"

with the powerful figures at court; and Robert Hill emphasizes similarly the extent to which Wotton used works of art to pander to the desires of his patrons in order to further his political career.[6]

During his first embassy to Venice Wotton was actively involved in procuring and commissioning paintings for such high-profile English patrons as Robert Cecil, 1st Earl of Salisbury (Lord Treasurer), the Prince of Wales and the Duke of Hamilton;[7] the Earl of Northampton (Lord Privy Seal) and Queen Anne of Denmark may well also have been patrons.[8] King James I had no interest in art, but Wotton found other objects of interest to send him (see below). However, Wotton commissioned a portrait of Fra Paolo Sarpi, the key figure in Venice's split from the papacy, which he intended Salisbury to deliver to James I (fig. 102),

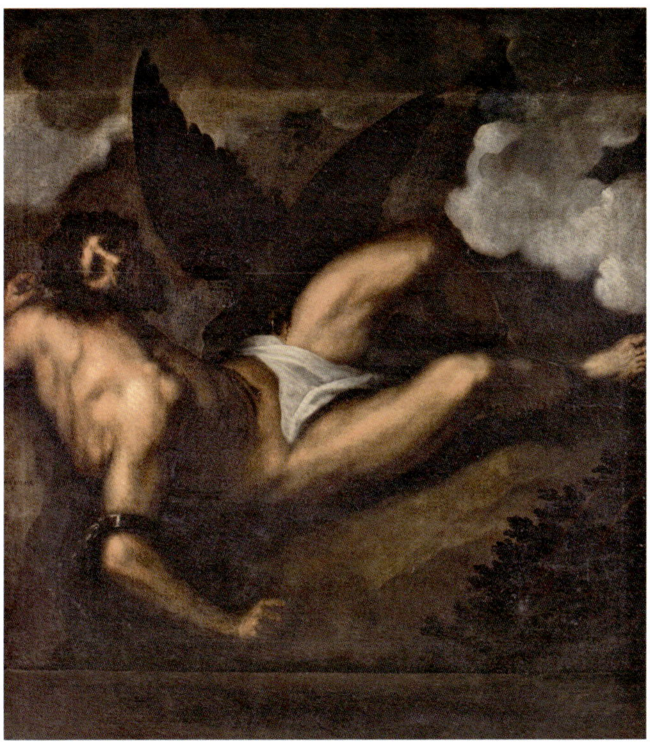

hoping that it would provide "some pleasure to his Ma[jes]tie to beholde a sound Protestant, as yet in the habit of a Friar".[9] A consignment of art works for Salisbury sent in 1608 which Wotton trusted would "be worthy of a corner in one of your Lordship's galleries", included, in addition to a portrait of Doge Donà "done truly and naturally but roughly, *alla Venetiana*", very probably by Fialetti (see pp. 23 and 64), paintings by Titian, Palma Il Giovane – including his *Prometheus chained to the Caucasus* (fig. 94) – and "a map of Italy (the country where by your favour I have received my first credit)".[10] He had also promised him "some draughts of architecture", and was apologetic that these were not yet ready.[11] A year later he sent him a Venetian novelty – a portrait of the earl in mosaic (made after an oil original by John de Critz the Elder in 1606 which he had requested Salisbury to send him for this purpose) "made precisely according to the draught … as near as the natural colours of stone can approach to artificial" (fig. 93). Cecil's titles are painted in Italian on the letter he is shown holding in his right hand.[12] Wotton was careful to pass on the advice of the craftsman about how the mosaic should be displayed, noting, "It is the workman's special suit and remembrance that it may be set in his true light, and at a little more height from the eye than a coloured picture would require".[13]

Thanks to Salisbury, Wotton was in a prime position to encourage an interest in Venetian art in Prince Henry. In March 1610 when a selection of Salisbury's Venetian paintings were shown to Henry as an incentive for him to begin his own collection, Henry chose to keep for himself the Palma *Prometheus* (fig. 94) which Wotton had given to Salisbury two years earlier. Wilks observes that it was this painting that "helped to stimulate Henry's liking for [the Venetian] school".[14] Wotton was then, it seems, responsible for the large shipment of paintings sent from Venice to the Prince of Wales at the end of

1610: numbering probably between twenty and fifty large canvases, the cargo cost the huge sum of £408 17s 6d.[15] It is not known precisely what the paintings were, although it seems they included classical and Old Testament subjects of "extreme violence" (*Cain and Abel, Judith and Holofernes, The Sacrifice of Isaac*), and more sensuous subjects such as a *Mary Magdalene* attributed to Titian and a *Ceres, Bacchus and Venus* from the studio of Tintoretto.[16] The portrait of Prince Henry which Wotton hung in his study in the ambassador's residence in Venice no doubt advertised this royal patronage.[17]

After Prince Henry's death, it is likely that Wotton had hopes of advising the young Prince Charles on artistic matters. We know of two items he gave Charles, while still prince, which were recorded by Van der Doort as hanging in the Cabinet Room at Whitehall; the works, one most improbably "said to be painted by Rafael d'Urbino … a Little peece in oyle Cullors of .2. mise", the other equally curious, a small wood carving "of a farmers house wherein a little dog is running, and a barking at a Countrey-fellow passing by", are also of interest for being small-scale, highly wrought works typical of curiosity

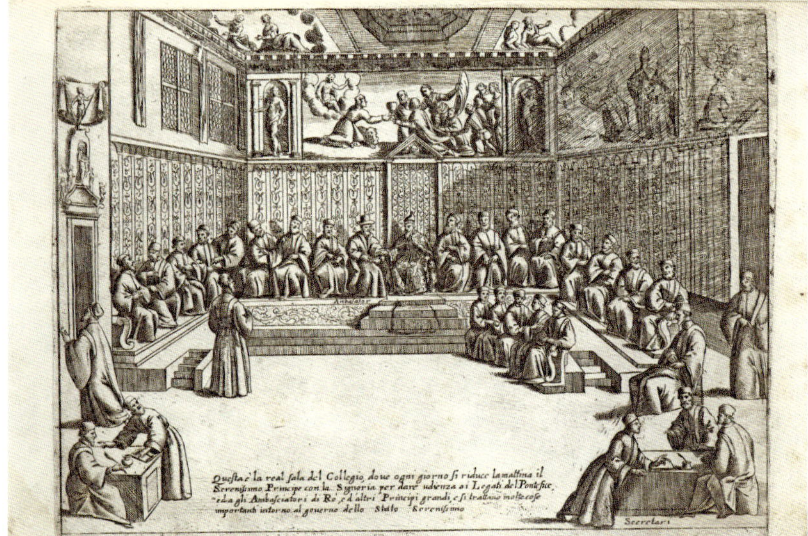

95
Giacomo Franco, *Questo è la real Sala del Collegio*, from
Habiti d'huomini et donne venetiane, etching, Venice, 1610
Cambridge, University Library

cabinets, in contrast to the spectacular canvases Wotton
had procured for his earlier patrons.[18] Arthur MacGregor
notes that it was in this Cabinet Room at Whitehall that
Charles "came closest to creating an installation in the
manner of a *tribuna* or of a European *Kunstkammer* such as
that of Rudolf II".[19] The fact that Wotton left six paintings
from his own collection to Charles I in his will suggests
that contact continued between Wotton and Charles I
over artistic matters (see Chapter 10). Indeed in 1631,
Wotton was summoned to Whitehall by the king to give
his judgement on some newly arrived pictures.[20]

By the time of his third and last embassy to Venice
Wotton was also collecting works for the new favourite,
the Duke of Buckingham. A shipment described in his
letter to Buckingham of 13 December 1622 included two
paintings "distended in their frames", one by Titian of
The Virgin and Child and the other by Palma il Giovane of
King David in his Old Age.[21] The cargo also included an Italian
still life of "a dish of grapes" for Buckingham's sister,
the Countess of Denbigh.[22] Wotton further took the
opportunity of this shipment to send a parcel of
"the choicest melon seeds of all kinds" for the king.[23]

Meanwhile, Wotton's deep and long-lasting interest
in architecture led him to compose the first modern
architectural treatise in the English language, *The
Elements of Architecture* (1624), the publication of which
coincided with his appointment as Provost of Eton
(see Chapters 9 and 10 below).[24]

Ridolfi tells us that Wotton commissioned portraits
of himself by two of the most accomplished Venetian
portrait-painters of the time – by Leandro Bassano, who
showed him "standing dressed in red", and Domenico
Tintoretto.[25] These portraits, probably made between 1616
and 1619 during Wotton's second embassy, are no longer
known. Two other portraits have survived: one in the
Bodleian attributed to Jans van Miereveld shows Wotton
aged fifty-two, wearing a heavy fur-lined overcoat
possibly referring to his ambassadorial status, with a
book in his right hand evoking his literary pursuits
(fig. 92); the portrait at Eton (fig. 2) may have been
commissioned for the College by Wotton. It shows him
seated in a Venetian chair with a red curtain behind,
leaning, in the pose of melancholia, on a table mantled
in red silk, a deliberate demonstration of his high-
ranking status as an ex-ambassador, and his crown
appointment as Eton Provost. The portrait conjures
up vividly Wotton's engaging personality: gazing out
with witty eyes he invites the viewer to 'philosophize'
with him.[27]

Wotton and Fialetti

As a respected and successful artist in Venice, Fialetti
would have known the art collections in the city well
and was certainly considered an authority on Venetian
masters.[28] As such he acted in the capacity of an art
adviser to foreign dealers, agents and ambassadors.[29]

Although we have details of Wotton's dealings with the Flemish art dealer Daniel Nijs (whose sumptuous collection in his residence in the parish of Santa Marina included drawings by Fialetti), there are few references to Wotton's contact with Fialetti.[30] It is likely, however, that Wotton encountered the artist soon after his arrival in Venice in 1604. His mention of Fialetti by name occurs in only one surviving letter, written to the Duke of Mantua on 22 April 1606. There he notes that the portraits he was sending the Duke were being delivered belatedly because of a long illness suffered by the artist Fialetti,

suggesting the commission had been made some time before.[31] That same year Wotton commissioned for himself a scene of his presentation in the Sala del Collegio to Doge Leonardo Donà (Doge 1606–12); the painting, attributed to Fialetti by Wotton in his will of 1636, was left to Charles I and is now in the Royal Collection (fig. 96).[32]

Four portraits of doges ("in whose time I worked"), also left by Wotton to the king in his will were likewise attributed by him to Fialetti.[33] While the portrait of Doge Grimani (fig. 97) bears the hallmarks of Fialetti's style,

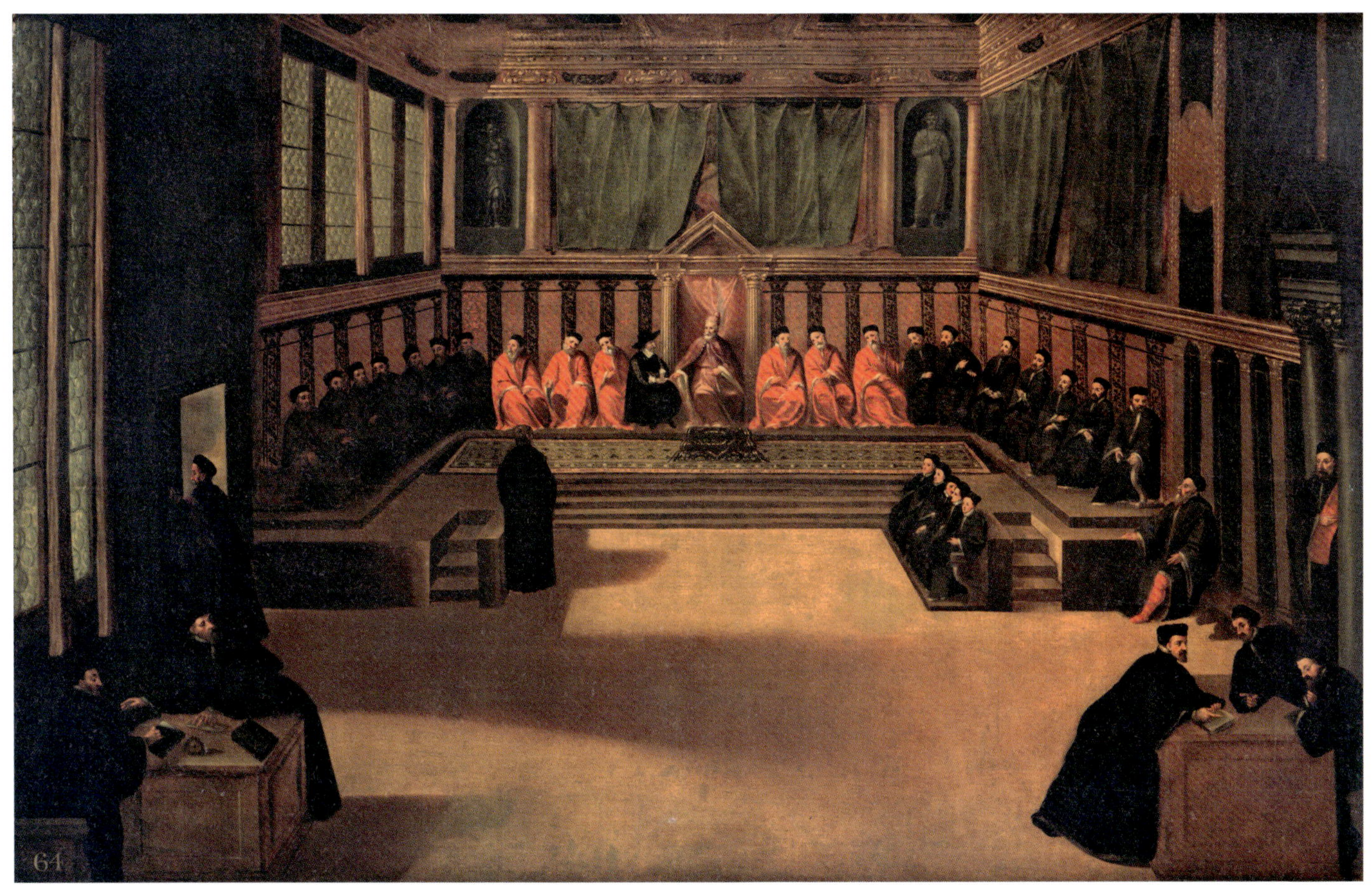

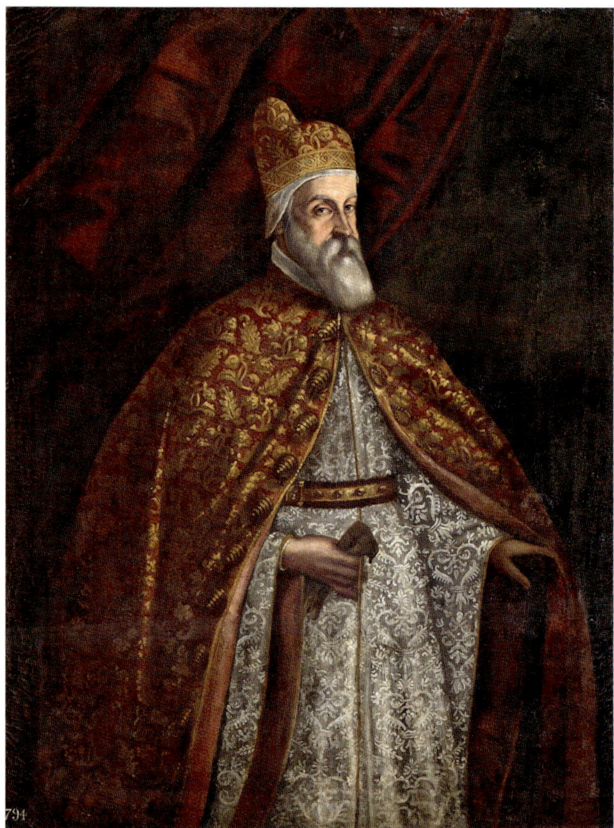

97
Odoardo Fialetti, *Doge Marino Grimani*,
c. 1604–05, oil on canvas, 164.5 x 123.3 cm
Royal Collection

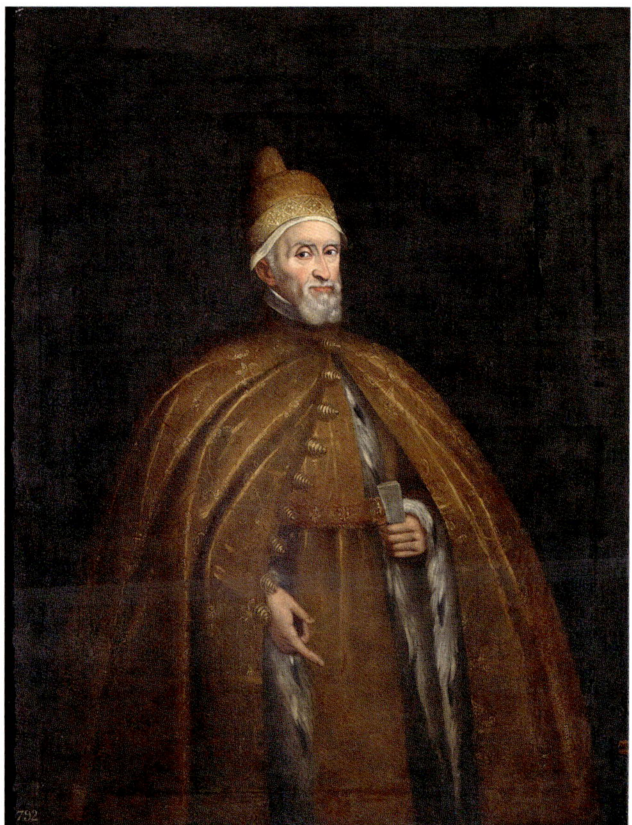

98
Unknown, early 17th century, *Doge Niccolò Donà*
(*Donato*), *c.* 1606–12, oil on canvas, 165 x 124.9 cm
Royal Collection

the other three (of Doges Donà, Bembo and Priuli) are
clearly by a different hand (figs. 98–100). Levey, who
was doubtful of the attribution to Fialetti, observed
that Wotton may have "associated [Fialetti] with their
execution without bothering overmuch about that
aspect". It may well have been the case in fact that
Fialetti was the agent in acquiring the other three
portraits of doges rather than their painter.[34] We know
that Wotton, like others in his position, employed
artists as agents to acquire works of art on his behalf,
and Fialetti would have been ideally placed to do this.
In a postscript to his letter of 13 December 1622 to
Buckingham concerning his shipment of art, Wotton
mentioned that he had dispatched "a servant of mine by
profession a painter to make a search of the best towns
through Italie for some principle pieces".[35] Whether

Fialetti might have been this painter-servant must
remain conjecture; Wotton's statement, however, is
indicative of his practice of using artists as art agents in
such a way.[36]

The patron of Fialetti's View
Although it has been assumed by virtue of Wotton's later
ownership of Fialetti's *View* that he was the patron of the
work, there is no documentation for this.[37] It is notable
that there is no record of the painting at all between
the date of its completion in 1611 and its appearance at
Eton in 1636. A number of factors make it intrinsically
unlikely that Wotton would have commissioned it for
himself, not least the absence of Palladio's Redentore
and San Giorgio Maggiore from the *View*. Wotton's
interest in Palladio's architecture, demonstrated in his

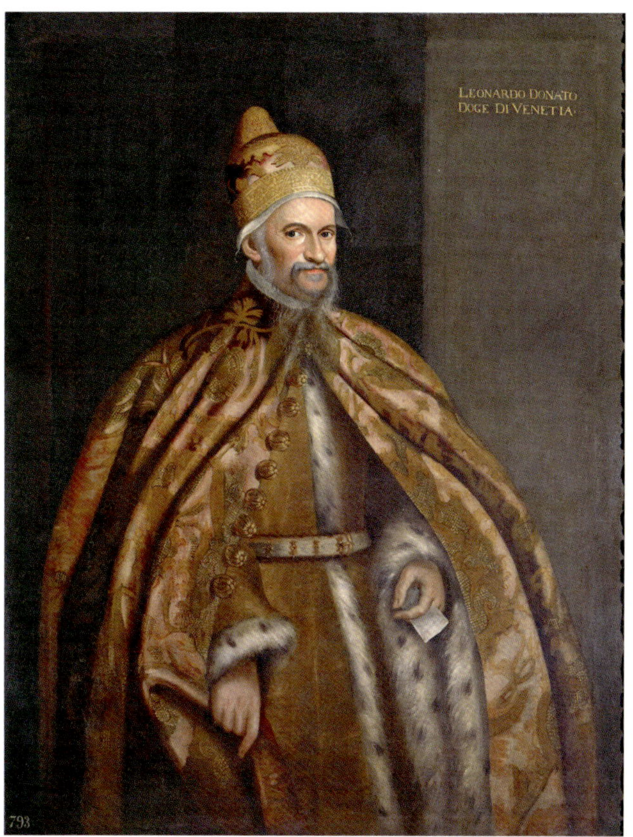

99
Unknown, early 17th century, *Doge Giovanni Bembo*,
c. 1615–18, oil on canvas, 165.0 x 123.7 cm
Royal Collection

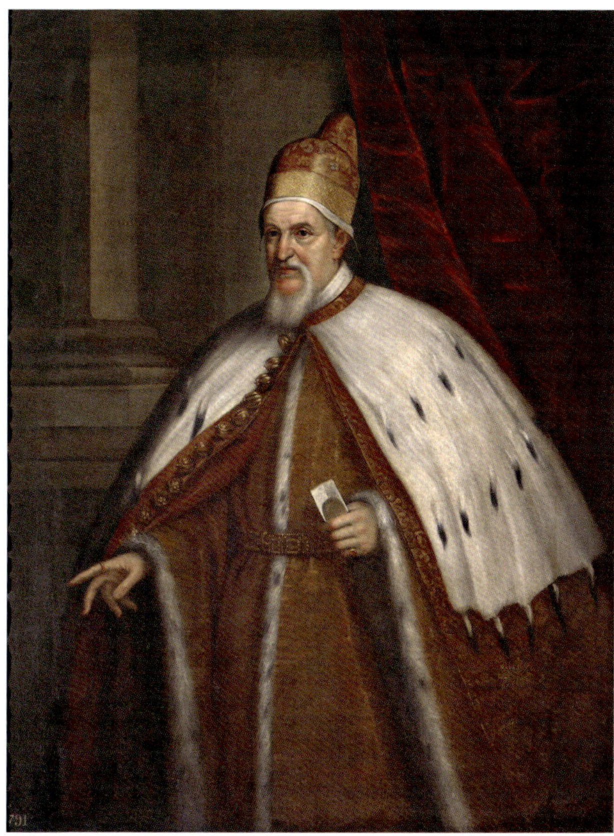

100
Unknown, early 17th century, *Doge Antonio Priuli*,
c. 1618–23, oil on canvas,165.2 x 125.1 cm
Royal Collection

ownership of drawings by Palladio as well as a copy of his *Quattro Libri dell' Architettura*, make it unlikely that he would have commissioned for his own record a view that ignored two of Palladio's greatest masterpieces.[38] It is also likely that the cost of such a huge painting would have been beyond Wotton's means; throughout his career he seems to have been short of money, not helped by the fact that ambassadors were always paid in arrears.[39]

A curious feature of the *View* is the prominence given to the former Jesuit church of Santa Maria dell'Umiltà facing the Giudecca canal (see fig. 8), a feature which does not appear so conspicuously in any of the earlier views which provided models for Fialetti. After the expulsion of the Jesuits in the Interdict of 1606, the church was vacant until 1615. However, Hopkins notes that the church "and the area around it were always seen as a Jesuit stronghold for their comeback" (see p. 94). As Wotton was strongly anti-Jesuit – as many of his letters show – it would have been strange if the church had been highlighted in this way for him.[40]

But, as already noted, Wotton spent much of his time during his first embassy to Venice acting as an artistic agent for high-profile patrons, and it is possible that he commissioned Fialetti's *View* on behalf of another party. If this was the case, the negotiations for its purchase must have collapsed, for the painting did not end up with its planned owner, but at some stage was subsumed into Wotton's own collection. Here another of the features in the *View* might perhaps give us a clue. The vignette showing players on a stage in the middle of the Piazza San Marco was, as Ruth Bubb shows in Chapter 5, at the centre of the original canvas (fig. 122, p. 149). The two figures standing side by side on the stage are a woman dressed in white and a man wearing a tall hat, which suggests he is a foreigner; two male figures, identically dressed and apparently wearing masks, advance towards the couple from the left. It is possible that this scene depicts a masque or *mommaria* in celebration of a wedding, and that the painting was commissioned in connection with marriage negotiations. If this was the case, and if Wotton was indeed the agent, the nuptial alliance in which he was involved precisely at this time was that between the English court and the House of Savoy.[41] At the end of his embassy in December 1610 he had travelled to Turin to discuss the proposal of a double marriage between Princess Maria of Savoy and Prince Henry and the Duke of Savoy's son, the Prince of Piedmont, and Henry's sister Princess Elizabeth; and in May 1611 he was sent again to Turin to further the arrangements, although by this time they involved only Prince Henry's marriage to the Savoy princess (the negotiations for Elizabeth now being for a marriage with Frederick V, the Elector Palatine).[42] Although Henry himself was against a Catholic bride, the king believed in religious conciliation through mixed marriages, and Wotton encouraged the Savoy alliance, hoping it would be a means whereby Protestantism could be introduced to Italy.[43] Wotton returned from Savoy in August the following year bearing portraits of members of the Savoy family.[44] By October negotiations seemed to be nearing completion but within weeks came to an abrupt end with Prince Henry's death from typhoid on 6 November.[45]

Could a possible explanation for the commissioning of the *View* – with its nuptial celebration in the Piazza San Marco and its nod to Catholicism in the prominent former Jesuit church – have been that it was painted through Wotton's agency in anticipation of Prince Henry's marriage to his Catholic bride? In Wotton's eyes, an image of Venice – containing within it a marriage scene in miniature – might have been not only an ideal symbolic scene but a desirable object in itself for Prince Henry, with his love of Venetian art.[46] If so, the painting, if Wotton had already had it shipped to England, would have had no obvious home after Prince Henry's death. There are indeed signs that the picture was transported relatively soon after it was painted. In her account of the recent restoration Ruth Bubb notes that the huge canvas suffered damage in the form of vertical creases, apparently from having been rolled up. Wotton was fully aware of the damage that could be caused to paintings by rolling, noting when he sent two paintings in frames to the Duke of Buckingham in 1622 that he "durst not hazard them in rolls: the youngest being 25 years old and therefore no longer supple and pliant".[47]

On his return from the Savoy embassy Wotton is described as having "gon toward the king with his pictures and his projects".[48] Amongst these pictures it seems were the portraits, noted above, of the Duke of Savoy, his father ("the old duke") and his two eldest daughters.[49] If the *View* had already been shipped to England, Wotton might have been waiting to present it to Prince Henry until the marriage negotiations were far enough advanced. On the other hand, it may not yet have arrived in England. Wotton wrote to his successor in Venice, Sir Dudley Carleton, on 25 February 1612/13, thanking him "for the care it pleased you to take about those pictures, which I have received by your means in very good condition".[50] Might the *View* have arrived only in that cargo? Wherever the painting was stored when it arrived, it may well have remained rolled up. The fact that such an enormous and eye-catching painting it is not mentioned in any of the accounts of visitors to London collections, or in any of the inventories of other

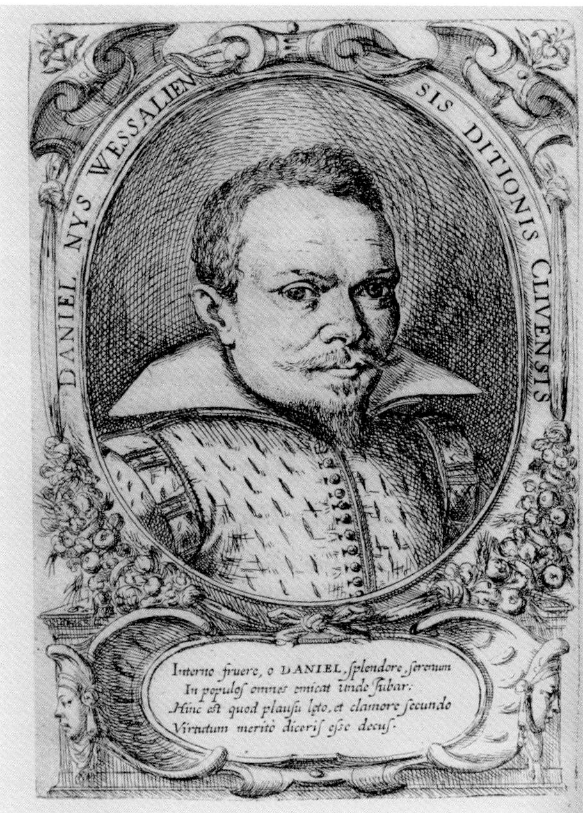

101
Odoardo Fialetti, *Portrait of Daniel Nijs*, etching
from frontispiece of Giulio Cesare Gigli, *La pittura
trionfante*, Venice: Giovanni Alberti, 1615

possible owners by whom it might have been purchased,
or who might, indeed, have simply given it wall space,
seems to imply that it was not hung at all.[51]

Amongst other figures to be considered as possible
patrons of Fialetti's *View* is the Netherlandish merchant
and art agent Daniel Nijs (1572–1647), resident in Venice
from the late 1590s. Nijs was a formidable connoisseur of
painting: his personal art collection, including around
eighty paintings as well as forty statues and eighty
portrait reliefs and a cabinet of precious miniatures
and gems said to be worth 10,000 *scudi*, was singled out
for praise by the architect Scamozzi in his treatise *L'Idea
dell'architettura universale* (1615).[52] For over two decades
Nijs was involved in procuring works of art for English
collectors, culminating in his acquisition of the Gonzaga
collection for Charles I in 1627. On his return to the city
in 1611 from a visit to the Netherlands, Nijs took a house
in the parish of Santa Marina – a plausible motive for the
acquisition of a very large picture.[53] It is clear from his
portrait by Fialetti, which appears as the frontispiece
to the poem *La Pittura Trionfante* by Giulio Cesare Gigli,

published in 1615 (fig. 101), that Nijs knew Fialetti by this
date, and in his dedication Gigli acknowledges Fialetti's
having introduced him to Nijs, in whose house "painting
itself triumphs".[54] However, as Robert Hill has pointed
out, Nijs does not appear to have been active as an agent
until around 1613.[55] Moreover, while we know from the
biographer Malvasia that Nijs commissioned a set of
ink drawings from Fialetti, there is no evidence that
he acquired anything else from the artist;[56] if the *View*
had indeed been in his collection it is likely to have been
mentioned. In addition, both Nijs's friendship with
Scamozzi, heir to Palladio's position as the most learned
classical architect in Venice, and his Protestantism seem
to weigh against some of the stranger characteristics of
the Eton *View* outlined above.

Other possible patrons to consider are dedicatees of
Fialetti's books of engravings (for Fialetti's work as a
printmaker see Chapter 4). However, again, many of
these collections of prints postdate 1611, the year of the
completion of the *View*. Among earlier names, Fialetti's
first drawing manual of 1608 was dedicated to Cesare
d'Este, Duke of Modena, while other early patrons
include Alvise Priuli, son of Gieronimo, and Giovanni
Grimani, dedicatee of a revised version of the manual.[57]
None of the three churches in Venice which still contain
works by Fialetti – San Giuliano (Zulian), Santi Giovanni
e Paolo and San Nicolò da Tolentino – provides any
obvious clues as to the patronage of the Eton *View* (see
Chapter 4).

Amongst possible Catholic patrons, the most obvious
would be the Earl of Arundel and his wife Aletheia
Talbot. Lady Arundel certainly knew Fialetti during the
Arundels' second stay in Venice in the 1620s, when she
took drawing lessons from him while her sons were
receiving a Catholic education at Padua University.
Arundel may have been acquiring works of art on his
earlier visit to Venice in 1613, during the embassy of Sir

Dudley Carleton, but this again is too late for a possible involvement with the *View*.[58] Significantly, there is no record of the painting in the Arundel collection, making its possible entry to that collection at a later date somewhat implausible; equally unlikely is that it could have passed from there to Wotton, whose relationship with the Arundels was strained.[59]

Another Catholic patron might be Henry Howard, Earl of Northampton. A keen collector, he hung paintings throughout his residences of Northampton House in the Strand and his park lodge at Greenwich.[60] It was in the gallery of his Greenwich residence that fourteen Venetian pictures were hung; although the provenance of these paintings is not known, Wilks suggests that they may well have been acquired for the Earl by Wotton at the end of 1610.[61] Hill further suggests that Northampton's great nephew, Henry Howard, may have "arrived in Venice [in the company of Viscount Cranborne in November 1610] with a commission to acquire Venetian paintings for his great uncle, and that he made use of the artistic experience of Wotton to purchase pictures on Northampton's behalf". [62] As, however, Northampton's Venetian paintings were described as all being of a similar size, the huge landscape-format *View* could surely not have been among them; nor is it mentioned in any of the collections amongst which Northampton's assets were divided after his death.

Although we know little about the collecting activities of Anne of Denmark, the inventories made of the contents of her different palaces – Oatlands, Denmark House and Greenwich – indicate that she, too, was a serious collector of fine art. While her early interests were in portraits and miniatures, her later acquisitions included landscapes, still lifes, histories and devotional pieces, with a bias towards Dutch and Flemish works.[63] Her inventories also list a number of Italian pictures, including some views of Venice which were hung in the Great Gallery in Denmark House.[64] But if the Fialetti *View* had been amongst them it would, presumably, have remained in the royal collection.

Might a different supposition be that the *View* was a commission by a prominent Venetian family to mark the occasion of a family wedding at the former Jesuit church in 1610/11, which perhaps then did not take place, leaving Fialetti without a purchaser? Such a theory might also account for the creases in the canvas resulting from the artist's rolling the painting up to store in his studio because of the lack of a buyer.[65] The argument against this suggestion, however, is that (as several chapters in this book note) the *View* bears the hallmarks of a painting done for export, not least in the artist's signature, which, unlike most of his Venetian commissions, does not include the adjective '*Bononense*' (of Bologna) after his name. Another theory to account for the prominent depiction of the former Jesuit church is that the artist himself, rather than his patron, had a particular affiliation to the building because of a painting he made for it. However, although Malvasia mentions a Jesuit church containing a work by him, this was the present Chiesa dei Padri Gesuiti (i.e. Santa Maria Assunta in Cannaregio), the church occupied by the Jesuits after their return to Venice, not Santa Maria dell'Umiltà.[66] And, as Hopkins points out, other churches for which Fialetti had produced paintings are not highlighted in this way.

Fialetti's *View* poses several riddles which we may never be able to solve. Their presence, nonetheless, continues to intrigue the painting's different audiences while drawing us into the fascinating world of art collecting and patronage in Early Stuart Britain.

ACKNOWLEDGMENTS
This chapter has involved the collaborative effort of several people whose input and suggestions have been crucial: Deborah Howard (who began as co-author), Christina Anderson, Robert Hill, Andrew Hopkins, Catherine MacLeod, Christopher Rowell and Timothy Wilks.

NOTES

1   L. Pearsall Smith, *The Life and Letters of Sir Henry Wotton*, 2 vols., Oxford, 1907, I, pp. 1–194; A.J. Loomie, 'Wotton, Henry', in *Oxford Dictionary of National Biography* (hereafter ODNB), ed. H.C.G. Matthew and B. Harrison, vol. 60, Oxford, 2004, pp. 377–82, gives an account of Wotton as a "diplomat and writer"; his artistic activities, however, are barely touched upon. G. Curzon, *Wotton and his Worlds: Spying, Science and Venetian Intrigues*, Bloomington, 2003, concentrates on Wotton as a diplomat/ intelligencer. T. Wilks, 'Art Collecting at the English Court from the Death of Henry, Prince of Wales to the Death of Anne of Denmark', *Journal of the History of Collections*, 9/1, 1997, pp. 31–48, and R. Hill, 'Art and Patronage: Sir Henry Wotton and the Venetian Embassy 1604–1624', in M. Keblusek and B.V. Noldus (eds.), *Double Agents: Cultural and Political Brokerage in Early Modern Europe*, Leiden and Boston, 2011, pp. 27–58, make important contributions to the study of Wotton's artistic activities.

2   Henry Peacham, *The Compleat Gentleman*, London, 1622. Pearsall Smith notes that "for young Englishmen of birth the main object of travel was almost always political": *Life and Letters*, I, p. 8.

3   Pearsall Smith describes him as "brilliant and unconventional": *Life and Letters*, I, p. 69. Sir Dudley Carleton, who took over from Wotton as ambassador to Venice in 1611, described him as "an elegant and incompetent dilettante"; Wotton was also referred to as 'Fabritio', the fabricator of lies, in correspondence between Carleton and his friend John Chamberlain, who stayed with Wotton in December 1610 (Hill, 'Art and Patronage', pp. 38–39).

4   C. Hollis, *Eton, a History*, London, 1960, pp. 81–84. David Howarth's comment that "justice has yet to be done to the educative influence of Wotton" was made in the context of his influence on the young Englishmen who travelled to Venice during his embassies (Howarth, *Images of Rule. Art and Politics in the English Renaissance, 1485–1649*, Berkeley, 1997, p. 235); the comment could, however, be extended to this last period of Wotton's life at Eton. See Chapter 10.

5   Izaak Walton in his idealized portrait of Wotton wrote of "the College being to his mind as a quiet harbour to a seafaring man after a tempestuous voyage" ('The Life of Sir Henry Wotton', in Walton, *Reliquiae Wottonianae: Or a collection of lives, letters, poems: with characters of sundry personages: and other incomparable pieces of language and art*, London, 1651, unpaginated).

6   Wilks, 'Art Collecting', pp. 34ff.; Hill, 'Art and Patronage', comments that "Wotton's *raison d'être* for presenting pictures to his patrons had been to advance his career" (p. 58).

7   Wotton laments in his letter (25 February 1612/13) to his successor at Venice, Sir Dudley Carleton, that he has "lost this fatal year two great patrons" (Prince Henry and Lord Salisbury): Pearsall Smith, *Life and Letters*, II, p. 14.

8   For the 2nd Duke of Hamilton's collection and his bias towards Venetian paintings, see Paul Shakeshaft, '"To Much Bewiched with Thoes Intysing Things": The Letters of James, Third Marquis of Hamilton and Basil, Viscount Feilding, concerning Collecting in Venice 1635–1639', *Burlington Magazine*, cxxvii, 1986, pp. 78, 114–34. The likely patronage of Wotton by Northampton and Queen Anne of Denmark is discussed by Wilks, 'Art Collecting', pp. 37–39, and Hill, 'Art and Patronage', pp. 37–38 and 42–43.

9   Poole and Garlick, *Catalogue of Portraits in the Bodleian Library*, Oxford, 2004, p. 272; Pearsall Smith, *Life and Letters*, I, pp. 398–400, 407–08, 431; Hill, 'Art and Patronage', pp. 28–29. The inscription, *Paulus Sarpius Venetus Concilii Tridentini Eviscerator*, was composed by Wotton. He later gave another portrait of Sarpi to Samuel Collins, Provost of King's in 1637, asking Collins to "allow it a favourable place" in his "luminous Parlour" (A. Austen-Leigh, *King's College*, London, 1899, p. 99). This portrait subsequently disappeared.

10   Pearsall Smith, *Life and Letters*, I, p. 419–20. The *Prometheus* was later given by Salisbury to Prince Henry: J. Shearman, *The Early Italian Pictures in the Collection of Her Majesty the Queen*, Cambridge, 1985, no. 173. Wilks notes that this picture "seems to have acted as a remarkable spur to the collecting of Venetian art" ('The Picture Collection of Robert Carr, Earl of Somerset (c. 1587–1645), reconsidered', *Journal of the History of Collections*, i/2, 1989, pp. 167–77, at p. 168). Salisbury, like his father, William Burghley, had a particular interest in maps. The inventories show that they were frequently used for decoration (for instance in the Lobby between the Great Chamber and Gallery in Salisbury House, hung "1 picture of England at large, in a frame") and in the earliest inventory of the contents of Hatfield House (30 September 1611) maps are mentioned several times, including "4 old maps of divers countries", and a "map of the world" in the dining room: see E. Auerbach and C.K. Adams, *Paintings and Sculpture at Hatfield House*, London, 1971, pp. 17, 20–21.

11   Robert Cecil was interested in the latest trends in architecture, employing Inigo Jones to advise on the design of the south front of Hatfield House in 1609–10 (see G. Worsley, *Inigo Jones and the European Classicist Tradition*, New Haven and London, 2007, pp. 10–11).

12   The inscription reads: *All Illmo et Eccmo Il Signore Conte de Salisburgo e Viconte de Cranburgo Barone Croll de Essendon Gran Tesoriere d'Inghilterra Maggiore di* [illegible]*Presidente della Corte di* ...[illegible].

13   Auerbach and Adams, *Paintings and Sculpture*, no. 67, where all Wotton's letters in connection with the mosaic portrait are published.

Charles Avery has suggested that the "workman" may have been a member of the Zuccati family (Hill, 'Art and Patronage', p. 30 n. 13).

14 Wilks, 'Art Collecting', p. 35.

15 It is described as "a quantity of Venetian paintings in a single purchase", by the Venetian ambassador in London, Marcantonio Correr, to the Doge and Senate (*Calendar of State Papers Venetian*, XII, p. 106, quoted by Wilks, 'Art Collecting', p. 28). Correr also noted on 14 January 1611 that Prince Henry "is paying special attention to the adorning of a most beautiful gallery of very fine pictures ancient and modern, the larger part brought out of Venice" (quoted in Wilks, 'The Picture Collection', p. 169).

16 See T. Wilks, 'Princely Collecting', in C. MacLeod (ed.), *The Lost Prince: The Life and Death of Henry Stuart*, exh. cat. (National Portrait Gallery), London 2012, p. 119.

17 Pearsall Smith, *Life and Letters*, I, p. 57.

18 Lucy Whitaker kindly pointed out the miniature painting of mice "wch Sr Henry Wootton gave to yor Matie when you were Prince ... Of 2 ¾ – of 3 ½ [inches]"; see O. Millar, *Abraham van der Doort's Catalogue of the Collections of Charles I*, Walpole Society 37, 1958–60, p. 82, no. 31; the painting subsequently belonged to the Duchess of Portland, by whom it was bequeathed to Mrs Delaney (H. Walpole, *The Duchess of Portland's Museum*, New York, 1936, p. 9). The carving which "was brought from Venice by Sr Henry Wootton. Given to yor Matie when you were Prince by Sr Hen: Wootton. Of 5 ½ x 7 1/2" appears as no. 60 on p. 87 of the van der Doort inventory.

19 A. MacGregor, 'King Charles I: a Renaissance Collector?', *Royal Stuart Papers*, Paper LVIII, 2001, p. 11.

20 PRO, S.P. Dom. Chas I, clxxxv, no. 5. See Chapter 10 for a discussion of Wotton's will.

21 Pearsall Smith, *Life and Letters*, II, pp. 211, 256–58. Hill notes the Palma II Giovane *King David* is listed in the Buckingham inventories

of 1635 and 1648 ('Art and Patronage', p. 51 n. 116).

22 Pearsall Smith, *Life and Letters*, II, p. 257, n. 3, writes in 1907 that the painting had "been found and identified at Newnham Paddox". It is possible that this was by the Milanese artist Fede Galizia (1578–1630), one of whose still-life paintings of a dish of fruit was acquired by Charles I from the Netherlandish art agent Daniel Nijs (M. Levey, *The Later Italian Pictures in the Collection of Her Majesty The Queen*, Cambridge, 1991, no. 490A).

23 Pearsall Smith, *Life and Letters*, II, pp. 253, 258.

24 T. Mowl and F. Earnshaw, *Architecture without Kings: The rise of puritan classicism under Cromwell*, Manchester and New York, 1995, p. 79, comment that the book was "published hurriedly in 1624, in a successful attempt to draw attention to his scholarly standing when the Provostship of Eton was vacant".

25 Carlo Ridolfi, *Le maraviglie dell'arte: ovvero Le vite de gl' illustri pittori veneti* (Venice 1648), ed. D. Von Hadeln, 2 vols., Berlin 1914–24, II, p. 158; Hill, 'Art and Patronage', p. 45.

26 It is inscribed and dated *Aetatis Suae 52. A° 1620*. Poole and Garlick, *Catalogue of Portraits in the Bodleian Library*, Oxford, 2004, p. 342. It has been variously attributed in the past; Karen Hearn notes that it is another version of a portrait (on panel) that was with the Weiss Gallery *c.* 2008–09, which is inscribed lower right, *M. Miereveld* and *Aetatis Suae 52. A° 1620*. She writes, "Miereveld is an extremely plausible attribution for [the Bodleian portrait]", noting that the artist was a popular choice for English visitors to the Netherlands who wanted their portraits painted (letter 12 November 2013).

27 Probably derivative of a lost original, the painting was described in the past as "in the style of Miereveld". A less good version is in the National Portrait Gallery, inv. no. 1482.

28 Edward Norgate wrote of "that excellent booke in folio of Jacomo Palma and graved by Odoardo Fialetti, my old acquaintance in Venice": see J. Muller and J. Murrell, *Edward Norgate. Miniatura and the Art of Limning*, New

Haven and London, 1997, pp. 106, 206 n. 295, where they describe Fialetti as "painter, printmaker, virtuoso draughtsman and connoisseur".

29 See M. van Gelder, 'Acquiring Artistic Expertise: Daniel Nijs and his contacts with artists in Venice', in Keblusek and Noldus, *Double Agents*, pp. 111–24, especially pp. 120–22. For Fialetti's career see Chapter 4.

30 For Wotton's contact with Nijs see Hill, 'Art and Patronage', p. 49.

31 Edward Chaney, *The Evolution of the Grand Tour: Anglo-Italian cultural relations since the Renaissance*, London, 1998, pp. 162–66: "*La cagione di non haverne udito prima alli suoi commendamenti è stata in vero una lunga infirmità dell'Odoardo Fialetti pittore qua di che mi soglio servire non volendo commetter la cosa a persona incognita che ne potesse forse haver fatto una copia per se*".

32 Now in Hampton Court Palace: Levey, *Later Italian Pictures*, no. 484, pp. 80–81, where a number of other versions of this type are listed. Despite Levey's doubts about its authorship, the painting is here given to Fialetti on the basis of a number of characteristics it shares with the *View* (see Chapter 10, pp. 138–39).

33 Now in Kensington Palace: *ibid.*, nos. 485–88, pp. 81–83.

34 *Ibid*, p. 81.

35 Pearsall Smith, *Life and Letters*, II, p. 258; Hill, 'Art and Patronage', p. 51 n. 119.

36 See Hill, 'Art and Patronage', p. 51: he favours Shakeshaft's proposal of Mark Bilford, an artist who had worked for Prince Henry.

37 M. Azzi Visentini, 'Ancora un'inedita pianta prospettica di Venezia in un dipinto di Odoardo Fialetti per Sir Henry Wotton', *Bollettino dei civici musei veneziani*, 25, 1980, pp. 19–25, at pp. 19, 22–24, makes this assumption and others have followed suit (for example, T. Card (ed.), *Eton 1440–1990: Portrait, Programme and Catalogue*, Eton, 1990, no. 4, p. 102).

38 Inigo Jones noted in his own copy of Palladio that he had seen some of the architect's

preparatory drawings for the plates in the *Quattro Libri* in Wotton's ownership: see B. Boucher, H. Burns and L. Fairbairn, *Andrea Palladio 1508–80: The Portico and the Farmyard*, exh. cat., Arts Council of Great Britain, London, 1975, no. 204, p. 108 (the drawings are now in the RIBA, nos. VI/10, VI/11 and X/6). For Wotton's copy of Palladio, see F. Panzarin, 'Il collezionismo inglese a Venezia nel Seicento: Henry Wotton letterato, agente, collezionista, mecenate e il suo rapporto con Odoardo Fialetti', *Arte in Friuli, arte a Trieste*, 20, 2000, pp. 37–60, at pp. 43 and 51. Mowl and Earnshaw observe, however, that Wotton "gives Palladio only occasional mention on technical matters [in his *Elements of Architecture*], as for instance his use of brick" (*Architecture without Kings*, p. 68).

39 For Wotton's debts from the expenses of his diplomatic posts, see ODNB, pp. 380–81.

40 Pearsall Smith writes that Wotton "saw Jesuits at the bottom of every wicked scheme", describing them as "this viperous brood" and "these caterpillars of Christianity" (Pearsall Smith, *Life and Letters*, I, pp. 65–66).

41 Strong notes that Wotton was "the key figure in all the negotiations for marriages with the House of Savoy": see R.C. Strong, *Henry Prince of Wales, and England's Lost Renaissance*, London, 1986, p. 75; see also Hill, 'Art and Patronage', p. 40.

42 Hill, 'Art and Patronage', pp. 38 and 40; Strong, *Henry Prince of Wales*, pp. 57–63.

43 Strong, *Henry Prince of Wales*, p. 59.

44 Hill, 'Art and Patronage', p. 40 n. 71.

45 See M. Smuts, 'Prince Henry and his World', in MacLeod, *The Lost Prince*, pp. 19–29, who takes a more optimistic view than previous writers of the Savoy wedding going ahead had it not been for Henry's unexpected death.

46 For Prince Henry's enthusiasm for Venetian art, see MacLeod, *The Lost Prince*, and Hill, 'Art and Patronage', p. 35.

47 Pearsall Smith, *Life and Letters*, II, p. 257; Hill, 'Art and Patronage', pp. 50–51. See Bubb, above, p. 72.

48 Hill, 'Art and Patronage', p. 40 n. 71, quoting John Chamberlain to Sir Dudley Carleton.

49 *Ibid.*; O. Millar, *Abraham van der Doort's Catalogue of the Collections of Charles I*, Walpole Society 38, 1958–60, items 63, 64, 71 and 73, pp. 33–34,.

50 Pearsall Smith, *Life and Letters*, II, p. 15.

51 It is notable by its absence, for example, in the accounts of the collections visited by various foreign dignitaries published by W. Rye, *England as seen by Foreigners in the days of Elizabeth and James I*, London, 1865. Wilks makes the point that pictures "were accessible to those who were interested in seeing them not only in princely or aristocratic collections but also in those of the wealthier gentry" (Wilks, 'Art Collecting', 1997, p. 31).

52 Vincenzo Scamozzi, *L'idea della architettura universale*, 2 vols., Venice, 1615, I, p. 306; cited in English in C.M. Anderson, 'Daniel Nijs's cabinet and its sale to Lord Arundel', *Burlington Magazine*, cliv, 2012, pp. 172–76, at p. 172. See also M. van Gelder, *Trading Places: The Netherlandish Merchants in Early Modern Venice*, Leiden and Boston, 2009, p. 177. The cabinet of smaller works in Nijs's study was also described by Gigli (see note 54).

53 Van Gelder, 'Daniel Nijs', p. 118. Nijs also had a home in Murano and a rural retreat, a *palazzo* on the lagoon island of Cavallino (Van Gelder, *Trading Places*, p. 184 n. 56).

54 Giulio Cesare Gigli, *La pittura trionfante* (Venice, 1615), ed. Barbara Agosti and Silvia Ginzburg, Porretta Terme, 1996. Here the editors state (on p. 18) that the portrait frontispiece was based on a drawing by Palma il Giovane.

55 R. Hill, 'Works of Art as Commodities', unpublished PhD thesis, Nottingham Trent University, 1999, p. 47 n. 21; *idem*, 'Ambassadors and art collecting in Early Stuart Britain', *Journal of the History of Collections*, 2003, pp. 211–88, at p. 225 n. 33; in 'Art and Patronage', p. 37, he notes: "The first mention of Nys in the State Papers Venetian does not appear until a letter written to Carleton by his secretary, Isaac Wake, in September 1613".

56 C.C. Malvasia, *Felsina pittrice*, 2 vols., Bologna, 1678, II, p. 312.

57 M. Bury, *The Print in Italy 1550–1620*, exh. cat., British Museum, London, 2001, nos. 141–46, pp. 198–200 (Bartsch XVII, 297, 208–09).

58 D. Howarth, *Lord Arundel and His Circle*, New Haven and London, 1985, pp. 36–38.

59 *Ibid.*, pp. 198–99.

60 Wilks, 'Art Collecting', pp. 37–40; he cites the inventory of paintings made at Northampton's death in 1614 (n. 54).

61 *Ibid.*, p. 39.

62 Hill, 'Art and Patronage', pp. 37–38.

63 For an account of Anne of Denmark's collections see Wilks, 'Art Collecting', pp. 41–45.

64 *Ibid.*, p. 45.

65 A suggestion made by Robert Hill.

67 Malvasia, *Felsina pittrice*, II, p. 310.

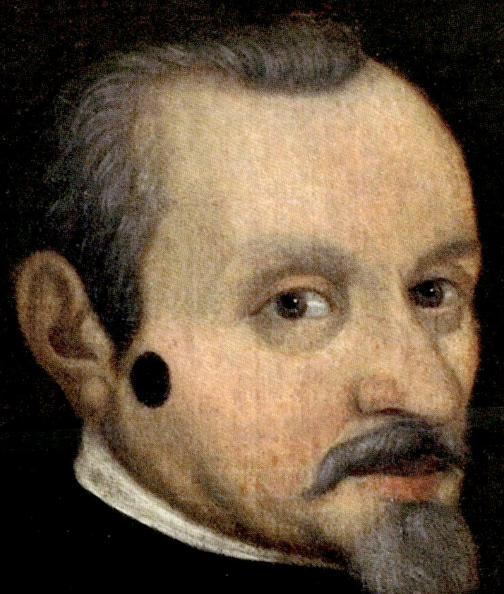

PAVLVS SARPIVS VENETVS
CONCILII TRIDENTINI
EVISCERATOR

8. Lying Abroad for the Good of His Country: Sir Henry Wotton and Venice in the Age of the Interdict

DANIEL MCREYNOLDS

WHEN HE FIRST SAW HIS WORDS IN PRINT, Sir Henry Wotton must have been mortified.[1] Certainly, when he had inscribed his cleverly ambiguous definition of an ambassador as "an honest man sent abroad to lie for the good of his country" in a friend's album in 1604, he had not the slightest clue that his words would come back to haunt him. Although he had intended the definition in jest, Gaspar Scioppius's publication of it in his *Ecclesiasticus* of 1611 transformed the witty remark into an incriminating admission that impugned not only Wotton's integrity but that of his sovereign James I as well.[2] Although the degree to which Wotton's actions as ambassador to Venice truly merit the accusation of outright duplicity remains open to debate, it is clear that there was more than a degree of truth to what he had written. Indeed, his unsuccessful machinations during and after the great diplomatic crisis of the Venetian Interdict reveal not only his capacity to operate independently of explicit instructions from the court of James I but also his zeal as a devout Protestant who would do everything within his power to separate Venice from the Roman Catholic Church.

Despite its status as a Catholic state, Venice staunchly defended its independence in all secular matters from Rome. In Wotton's eyes, this independence extended to the religious sphere as well, for he noted in a letter to Robert Cecil written the year before his appointment as ambassador that Venice had "almost slipped into a neutrality of religion".[3] Wotton's assessment proved prescient, for shortly after his arrival in Venice as ambassador in 1604, a long festering dispute between Venice and Rome regarding the prerogatives of the Church within Venetian territory escalated into an international diplomatic conflict that would culminate in 1606 in the papacy's placement of Venice under interdict, an action that officially barred the performance of all religious services and thereby effectively served to excommunicate the entire city's population.

Within this turbulent atmosphere Wotton zealously struggled to bring Venice into an alliance of Protestant states that could collectively provide a bulwark against the might of Catholic powers led by Rome and the Habsburgs. Although Wotton's grand plan to separate Venice from Rome would ultimately end in failure, it was paradoxically this pursuit of an unattainable and ultimately misguided union between the two states that provided for the strengthening of the cultural ties between them. It is for this reason that Wotton's actions during the age of the Interdict merit reconsideration. Indeed, as ambassador to Venice Wotton not only did much to establish friendly relations between the two states but moreover helped to inform the representation of Venice at home. Through the dispatches he penned, the art he procured, and the architectural treatise he would later write, Wotton cultivated an image of Venice that would continue to endure and fascinate long after his final departure from the city in 1623.

Given Elizabeth I's severing of permanent diplomatic relations with all European states, the task fell to James I to reconstitute an institutional structure for foreign

Unknown artist, *Portrait of Pietro Paolo Sarpi*, c. 1610,
oil on canvas, 76.2 x 63.5 cm
University of Oxford, Bodleian Library

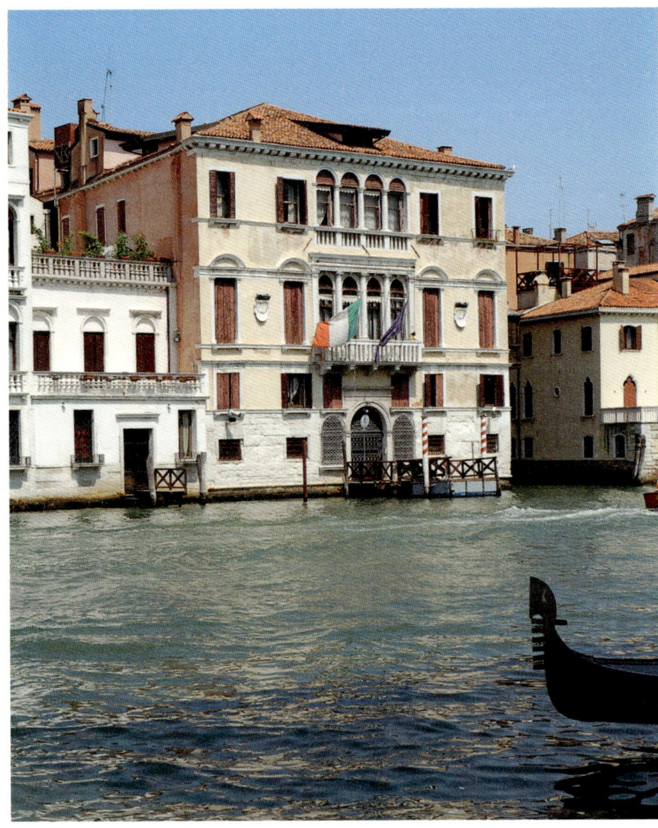

affairs through the establishment of embassies in Paris, The Hague, Madrid and Venice. Although it remained the least prestigious of these diplomatic posts, the Venetian embassy was still critical for the representation of James I's interests abroad. As a pan-European clearing-house for foreign intelligence Venice figured as one of the most important centres of international espionage in Europe. In Venice ambassadors as well as bankers, merchants, and sundry other agents actively gathered and exchanged sensitive information while representing the interests of their respective states. Well prepared for this environment of subterfuge and intrigue as a result of his extensive travels and mastery of several foreign tongues, Wotton received his appointment as ambassador shortly after his successful completion of a mission undertaken in 1601 on behalf of the Grand Duke of Tuscany to warn James VI of a plot to poison him and to provide him with a parcel containing Italian antidotes.[4] Upon his accession to the English throne in 1603, a grateful James I bestowed upon Wotton his first appointment as resident ambassador to Venice.

Soon after his arrival in the city in September 1604, Wotton enjoyed his formal reception as ambassador in a grand two-day-long ceremony that culminated in his meeting with Doge Marino Grimani in the Sala del Collegio of the Palazzo Ducale. The grandeur of the occasion reflected England's status as the most powerful Protestant state in Europe and the diplomatic equal of her rivals Spain and France.[5] Despite the pomp of his formal reception as ambassador, Wotton occupied a modest residence that belied his ostensibly elevated status. Although he would briefly occupy the stately Palazzo Gussoni Grimani della Vida on the Grand Canal (fig. 103) during his second term as ambassador to Venice in 1616, Wotton's financial condition required that the embassy be housed in less grandiose quarters.[6] Rented by Wotton from the Venetian Jew Isaac Luzzati, the

embassy during his first term as ambassador was located in the *sestiere* of Cannaregio, most likely in the Palazzo Silva at the Ponte degli Ormesini (fig. 104), and consisted of fifteen modestly furnished rooms that housed Wotton and his entourage as well as their domestic servants.[7] As an extraterritorial extension of England, the embassy occupied an ambivalent space that was in many ways characteristic of early modern embassies in general. As Wotton's residence and place of professional activity, the embassy frequently blurred the line between the private and public realms.[8] Certainly Wotton's embassy bears little resemblance to the professionalized bureaucratic space of its modern counterpart. More akin to a college than an institution of state, Wotton's embassy constituted an informal space in which intimacy and professionalism intermingled. Here, and in the villa he rented at Noventa near Padua, Wotton oversaw official foreign affairs while engaging in other tasks such as the entertaining of guests, informers and liberally minded Venetians, and the active acquisition of works of art for various clients and officials in England.[9] The embassy's ambivalent status as both a private and a public space proved fortuitous for the furthering of Wotton's diplomatic objectives, for in the battle of ideas he waged against Catholic orthodoxy and political power Wotton sought to further James I's foreign policy agenda by establishing political ties to Venice through the cultivation of social rather than purely professional relationships.

Despite Venice's laws barring social interaction with representatives of foreign powers, Wotton appears to have used his embassy as a space for hosting prominent Venetians whom he presumably thought of as Protestant sympathizers and potential allies.[10] Through these intermediaries, Wotton allegedly engaged in illicit activities such as the distribution of Protestant literature and the cultivation of Protestant converts while voci-ferously advocating Venice's separation from the Roman Catholic Church. Outraged at Wotton's surreptitious flaunting of Venetian law, the papal nuncio protested to the Doge and Collegio in 1604 that Wotton had even gone so far as to celebrate Protestant services in the embassy's chapel in the company of several Venetians. In response to Rome's unwelcome intrusion into the Republic's political affairs, Venetian officials defended Wotton against the accusation.[11] The Republic's claim that Wotton led a blameless life in the city, however, could not have been more disingenuous, for Venice actively monitored the foreign communities in the Republic's territory through a complex web of informers and spies, and was well aware of the English ambassador's activities in the city.[12] An examination of Venice's increasingly strained diplomatic relations with Rome does much to explain the Republic's tolerance of Wotton's transgressions.

Notwithstanding its adherence to Catholicism, Venice had jealously guarded its political independence from Rome. Events, however, conspired to transform

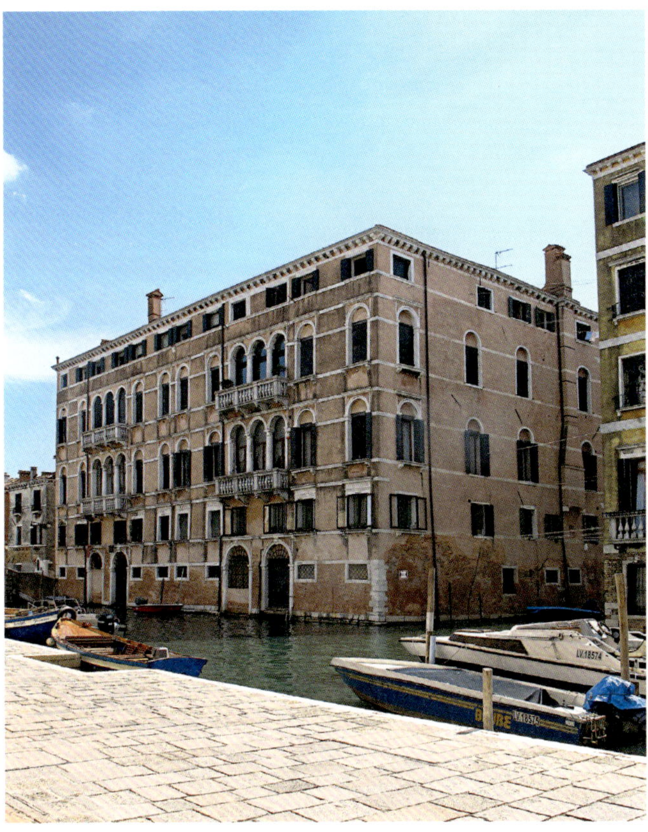

what was often a tense relationship between the two states into open conflict in the first decade of the seventeenth century. During the pontificate of Clement VIII Aldobrandini (1592–1605) disputes with Rome arose with increasing frequency as a result of a lack of agreement concerning the limits of ecclesiastical power within a secular state. Relations between the two powers continued to deteriorate as a result of the succession crisis in the duchy of Ferrara that arose when Alfonso II d'Este, Duke of Ferrara, died in 1597, naming his cousin, Don Cesare d'Este, as his successor. Refusing to recognize the transfer of power, given the alleged illegitimacy of Don Cesare's claim, Clement VIII sought not only to take the duchy by force but to secure Venice's aid in this endeavour. Venice understandably saw little to be gained from having Rome so near and especially in control of the Po delta, which remained vital to Venetian commercial interests. Offering her diplomatic services in lieu of military support, Venice sought to put off the inevitable. Clement VIII's superior forces and excommunication of Don Cesare, however, soon convinced him to lay down his arms, thus ending the conflict and bringing the duchy of Ferrara under the dominion of the papacy. Now bordering Venice's frontier, Rome parlayed this victory into a more ambitious campaign.

Soon after Rome's acquisition of Ferrara, pressing issues regarding clerical independence and the taxation of the clergy within the cities of the *terraferma* brought Rome into confrontation with a recalcitrant Venice, which, fearful of setting a dangerous precedent, refused to cede its authority. Although Clement VIII failed to press the matter, the opening of the debate regarding Venice's authority over ecclesiastical matters within the Republic's own domains presaged the crisis that would bring Venice into direct confrontation with the Church.[13]

Much of the enmity between Rome and Venice had arisen from the many occasions when the Republic's political independence and mercantile interests, and particularly the laxity of regulation over the Venetian press, conflicted with the papacy's desire for orthodoxy and control. As Venetian authorities were well aware, an atmosphere of relative tolerance remained essential to the city's continued economic prosperity, as did the principle of diplomatic freedom, which provided Venice with ample room to cultivate allies within an increasingly uncertain geopolitical milieu. Rome, however, frequently protested that Venice's liberal policies, often disguised under the cloak of benign negligence, constituted an abnegation of the Republic's religious obligations.[14]

The atmosphere grew only more tense in 1605 upon the election of Paul V, whose pretensions to papal supremacy and animosity towards Venice in particular made conflict between the two states all but inevitable. In particular, Paul V deplored Venice's recent legislation regulating the acquisition and transfer of property, which had had the effect of limiting the growth of ecclesiastical power within Venetian territory. Judging the extent of the Church's possessions excessive, Venice forbade bequests of secular property in Venice to the Church and took the further measure of placing a moratorium on the construction of any new churches or monasteries without state approval. What Venetian authorities saw as the necessary and legitimate exercise of political power constituted in the eyes of the papacy an assault on the Church.

Relations between the states continued to worsen until a *cause célèbre* involving the heinous acts of two Venetian prelates and their subsequent arrest led to a confrontation that Wotton would soon seek to exploit. Writing to Sir Thomas Edmondes, Wotton described the break between Venice and Rome in the following terms:

> The causes of this breach have been denial of *decime*, prohibition of immovable legacies to holy use, and the like. But especially the laying of secular hands upon men of the clergy, as on an abbot accused of many foul crimes, and a *Canonico* of Vicenza for dishonouring a virgin; which last is, in this corrupted country esteemed the most heinous and prejudicial to papal authority of all imaginable cases.[15]

The issue had little to do with the nature of the defendants' crimes *per se*, but rather revolved around the question of jurisdiction. Seeking to abrogate the Church's right to adjudicate matters involving members of the clergy, the Council of Ten chose to try the accused as ordinary criminals. In this manner, the iniquity of two otherwise unremarkable men provided for the eruption of a diplomatic war.[16]

Seeking to affirm its authority in all secular matters, Venice dispatched Leonardo Donà, a staunch defender of Venetian independence and an implacable foe of papal power, as her emissary to Rome in protest; however, before Donà had reached Rome, Paul V issued two ultimatums with the intent of cowing Venice into submission. Specifically, he demanded that Venice immediately rescind its legislation dealing with Church property and surrender the accused to the Church. The doge at the outbreak of the crisis, Marino Grimani, died on Christmas Day 1605, thereby leaving the crisis in the able hands of Donà, who would succeed him to the ducal throne (fig. 97). Described by Wotton as "a wise and beaten man in the world, eloquent, resolute, provident", Donà had served as ambassador to Rome on several occasions and proved a resolute leader throughout the crisis.[17]

Although Venice took the threat of military action from Rome's surrogates seriously, the conflict was ultimately juridical in nature. Accordingly Venice sought the services of a theologian who could defend the Republic's rights as a secular authority against the peremptory demands of the Church in a battle that would take place not on the battlefield but rather in print. For this task, Venice turned to the Servite friar and prominent scholar and theologian Paolo Sarpi, who remained a close associate of Wotton's (fig. 102).[18] Indeed, Wotton revered Sarpi, whom he described in a dispatch to the Secretary and Lord Treasurer to James I, Robert Cecil, 1st Earl of Salisbury, as "the most deep and general scholar of the world", and whose life he deemed "the most irreprehensible and exemplary that hath ever been known".[19] Yet, of all of Sarpi's talents, it was specifically his expertise in canon law that recommended him to the Senate.

As the official theological counsellor to the Senate, Sarpi had the delicate and unenviable task of responding to Paul V's ultimatums. With regard to Paul V's demand that Venice repeal its decree concerning Church property, Sarpi insisted that the pope had no jurisdiction in this and other secular matters, for temporal authority remained the preserve of princes by divine right. With regard to the pope's demand that Venice deliver the two

clerical reprobates to the Church for judgement, Sarpi's response was of the same substance and tenor. However, it was his characterization of the pope's actions as an abuse of papal power within the secular realm that carried the greatest sway among his contemporaries. Knowing that the crisis was ultimately a battle of ideas, Sarpi published his arguments in his *Considerazioni sopra le censure della Santità di Papa Paolo V contra la Serenissima Republica di Venetia* (1606), a widely disseminated text that encouraged sympathy for Venice and emnity towards Rome. Unswayed by Sarpi's reasoned arguments, and unable to bring the Venetian government to heel, Paul V promulgated on 17 April 1606 a papal bull of Interdict and Excommunication if the republic should not capitulate within twenty-four days.

Wotton relished the crisis. Eagerly relating these developments to the Earl of Salisbury, he confessed his joy in seeing "a Pope notoriously despised by a neighbour state",[20] and in a later dispatch related that "I must not be transported with the secret comfort that I take in these things, and in mine own relation of them".[21] Indeed, as Wotton was aware, Paul V's actions had not had the intended effect of bringing Venice to heel. In a brilliant display of brinksmanship the Venetian Senate passed an edict, signed by Doge Donà, in which all prelates within the republic were absolved from compliance with papal demands and ordered to continue services as usual. Knowing that such a precedent could easily threaten to take root in other nominally Catholic states, Venice took the further measure of dismissing the papal nuncio and banishing those orders, including the Theatines, Carmelites and, most notably, the Jesuits, whose allegiance to the pope was thought to preclude their loyalty to the state.[22]

Loathed by his enemies and adored by Venetians, Sarpi unleashed a diplomatic battle in which the major powers of Europe soon engaged. Spain remained steadfast in its support of the papacy, whereas Spain's rivals, including most notably Great Britain, looked on Venice as a potential proxy and ally. Seeking to profit from the crisis, Wotton saw Venice's struggle with Rome as a timely opportunity permanently to separate the two states.[23] As the only state in Italy that remained truly free of the domination of Spain and Rome, Venice seemed to Wotton a natural ally for England, which remained the most powerful Protestant kingdom in Europe. This ideological conflation of England's and Venice's geopolitical interests, however, would lead Wotton to pursue a course of action that would ultimately satisfy neither state.

Recognizing that Paul V had left himself with little room to manoeuvre, Spain sought to resolve the crisis quickly and with as little damage to papal authority as possible. Yet, whereas the Spanish ambassador encouraged negotiation if not conciliation, Wotton fanned the flames. Seeking permanently to separate Venice from Rome, Wotton publicly professed peace while secretly promoting war.[24] Reminding the Venetians of the Church's possession of excessive property within her domains, Wotton wasted no opportunity to convince his hosts that the Church controlled by the Jesuits would stop at nothing short of complete domination of the Continent, an intent made manifest, he alleged, by the recently foiled Gunpowder Plot. Appealing to Venice's mythical inviolability while calling into the question the sincerity of papal representatives seeking peace, Wotton shared intelligence with Venetian authorities regarding the hostile movements of papal and Spanish forces. Furthermore, and without explicit instruction or authorization from the English court, he foolishly insinuated that James I desired and would actively seek to establish a secret defensive league comprising largely English, French, Swiss and German Protestants.

Although other heads of state, including Henri IV of France, prevaricated in the face of Venetian appeals for help, James I responded enthusiastically promising Venice the support of English forces, albeit with the vague caveat that they would intervene only insofar as they were able. Emboldened by the king's response, the subtlety of which was conveniently not conveyed by his ambassador, Wotton addressed the Doge and the Collegio on 5 September 1606, an event that may indeed have inspired Odoardo Fialetti's painting now at Hampton Court (figs. 96, 105).[25] Although he was certainly authorized to communicate James I's sympathy for Venice's plight, Wotton's promise of military support extended far beyond the symbolic overture that James and his advisors probably intended. Indeed Wotton had on this occasion, as he would on many of those to come, overplayed his hand. Reproached by his superior, the Earl of Salisbury, for his rashness and indiscretion, Wotton regretfully informed the Collegio of James I's reservations regarding the formation of a defensive league, suggesting that Venice should take the initiative in its formation.[26] As the promise of a Protestant league thus vanished, so too did any confidence in England's ability or desire to come to Venice's aid. With her hopes in England as an ally much eroded as a result of English equivocation, Venice soon acquiesced to Henri IV's timely offer to help to negotiate a peaceful resolution to the conflict.

Venice's defiance had revealed the impotence of Rome's most powerful weapon to the world, and, cognizant of the crisis's damage to papal authority, Paul V and the Curia quickly sought to bring the impasse to an end through French mediation. Having won the moral battle, the Venetian Republic remained unapologetic throughout negotiations, granting not even the most minor of concessions to the Church. For instance, Venice refused to readmit the expelled orders, retained the offending laws, and relinquished no

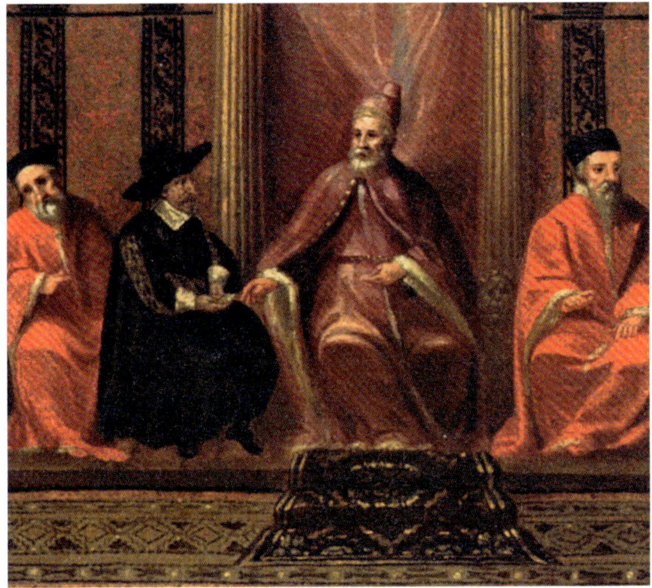

authority in secular matters. Furthermore, although
by the terms of the agreement Venice had agreed to
transfer the ecclesiastical culprits whose arrest had
provoked the crisis into the custody of French officials
– who of course hastily delivered them to Church
authorities – Venice insisted that this was done out
of respect for the French kingdom and in no way
constituted an acknowledgment of Rome's jurisdiction
in this and other secular matters. In a further insult to
papal authority Venice even refused the public lifting
of the Interdict, judging that this would provide tacit
recognition of the pope's right to have issued the
proclamation in the first place. Eager to end the debacle,
Rome agreed to the humiliating terms in April 1607.

For Wotton, however, the battle was not yet over.
In the wake of the Interdict, Wotton redoubled his
efforts, cultivating contacts with prominent Venetians,
including Sarpi, who was transformed by the quarrel
into a secular saint in the eyes of Venetians and into the
Antichrist in the eyes of the Church. Sarpi remained
essential to the success of Wotton's plans, and the two
appear to have met in secret on multiple occasions at the
Fondaco de' Zechinelli, a counting-house in the Mercerie
belonging to a group of Flemish merchants referred
to as the 'Golden Ship', which had long since provided
a gathering place for foreigners and liberally minded
Venetians.[27] Contact with Sarpi was also maintained
through the offices of the chaplain of the English
embassy, William Beddell, who had arrived in the city
shortly after the conflict's resolution.

As a relentless opponent of papal supremacy, Sarpi
seemed to Wotton a valuable ally in the battle to separate
Venice from Rome. In the wake of the Interdict Wotton
frequently wrote to Salisbury of his dealings with Sarpi
and lionized the friar for his heroic achievements and
friendliness towards England. For instance, he described
Sarpi as "a sound Protestant as yet in the habit of a friar"

in a letter to Salisbury that was accompanied by a portrait
of the prominent Venetian for the king as well.[28] When
the portrait was seized by the Inquisition in Milan,
Wotton took it upon himself to have a second version
executed that had the added benefit of depicting Sarpi
with the disfiguring scars he had received as a result of
a recent assassination attempt that he only narrowly
survived.[29] A copy of the portrait survives at the Bodleian
Library, University of Oxford (fig. 102).[30]

Wotton's enthusiasm for the friar, however, led him
to see Sarpi as the Protestant revolutionary he wished
him to be rather than as the Venetian patriot that he
most certainly was. Despite his personal antipathy
towards papal usurpation of secular power, Sarpi
remained acutely aware of the repercussions such a break
would entail for Venice's political and economic interests,
and therefore he remained far more circumspect
than Wotton in his outlook and actions. Even Wotton
was forced to concede that the friar "seemeth a fitter
instrument to overthrow the falsehood by degrees than
on a sudden; which accordeth with a frequent saying of
his own, that in these operations *non bisogna far salti*" (no
need to make leaps).[31] Despite such misgivings, Wotton
continued to cultivate Sarpi as an ally in his ideological
crusade against Rome in the wake of the Interdict.

In Britain, the failed assassination attempt on
James I known as the Gunpowder Plot had resulted

in the administration of an Oath of Allegiance to all Catholics in the realm, requiring that they abjure as heresy the notion that an excommunicated monarch could be deposed or assassinated with moral impunity. As an instrument providing for the clear and complete separation of secular and ecclesiastical authority, the oath set a precedent that threatened papal pretensions to temporal power. Vituperatively attacked in print by the Church, the oath was subsequently defended by James I in his *Apologia pro Juramento Fidelitatis*, copies of which were quickly sent to Venice at Wotton's request. Despite its placement on the Index of Forbidden Books, Wotton thought it appropriate to present a copy to the Doge; however, in so doing, Wotton had once again severely miscalculated.[32] Reluctant to precipitate another diplomatic crisis with the papacy, the Republic allowed the copy to languish unopened, and under increasing duress finally acquiesced to papal demands to hand all copies over to the Inquisition, a decision that provoked Wotton's threat of resignation.[33]

Although Wotton's anger was soon assuaged, his overt attempt to enlist Venice's support in England's battle with Rome was seen as an unwelcome provocation by Venetian authorities. Indeed, Wotton's machinations and warmongering did little to endear him to Venetians, who, desirous of peace and prosperity, wanted no part in Wotton's chimerical vision of a grand pan-European Protestant alliance. Considered in this context, the peaceful resolution of the Interdict, although a great diplomatic success for Venice, represented a resounding defeat for Wotton. Not only had he patently failed in his attempt to separate Venice from the papacy, he had undermined his own credibility and that of his sovereign as a result of his excessive zeal.

Nevertheless, Wotton's embassy was not a complete failure. Although his ambitious plan to recruit Venice into an alliance of Protestant states had come to naught, his promotion of the possibility of such a union had provided Venice with a degree of leverage and room to manoeuvre, without which the conflict might have ended very differently. The success of Wotton's embassy cannot be judged in diplomatic terms alone. Through his activities as an ambassador, agent, correspondent, architectural theorist and procurer of art, Wotton did much to promote a vision of Venice that would fascinate and endure long after the ideologically charged battles of his age would cease to rage. The bond he forged between Venice and England, although born of the exigencies of *Realpolitik*, would continue to grow ever stronger in the decades and centuries to come. Considered in this light his embassy was not a failure, for indeed our vision of Venice owes a great debt to that first glimpse of the city as it was seen through Wotton's eyes and consolidated through his acquisition of Fialetti's *View*.

NOTES

1   L. Pearsall Smith's *The Life and Letters of Sir Henry Wotton*, 2 vols., Oxford, 1907, remains the essential source for reconstructing Wotton's activities as ambassador to Venice. Consisting of many hundreds of Wotton's letters to a variety of correspondents, this text in conjunction with Wotton's letters and writings, posthumously published in *Reliquiae Wottonianae*, ed. I. Walton, London, 1651, and other material in the *Calendar of State Papers and Manuscripts, Relating to English Affairs Existing in the Archives and Collections of Venice and in Other Libraries of Northern Italy*, ed. R. Brown *et al.*, 38 vols., London, 1864–1947, has provided the basis for subsequent accounts of Wotton's life, including most recently G. Curzon, *Wotton and His Worlds: Spying, Science and Venetian Intrigues*, Bloomington, 2003. For other documents related to Wotton's diplomatic activities, see E. Chaney, 'Documentary Evidence of Anglo-Italian Cultural Relations in the Sixteenth and Seventeenth Centuries', in *The Evolution of the Grand Tour: Anglo-Italian Cultural Relations Since the Renaissance*, London 2000, pp. 161–66; and A.M. Crinò, 'Lettere autografe inedite di Sir Henry Wotton nell'Archivio di Stato di Firenze',

in *Fatti e figure del Seicento anglo-toscano*, Florence, 1957, pp. 7–40.

2 Wotton inscribed the definition in Latin as "*Legatus est Vir bonus, peregre missus ad mentiendum Reipublicae causa*" in an album belonging to Christopher Fleckmore in 1604 while in Augsburg *en route* to Venice. The translation of the definition into Latin robbed it of its *double entendre*, and thereby set the stage for its appropriation by Wotton's adversaries: Pearsall Smith, *Life and Letters*, I, pp. 49n., 126–27.

3 Wotton to Robert Cecil, 23 May 1603, *ibid.*, I, pp. 317–19.

4 I. Walton, 'The Life of Sir Henry Wotton', in *Reliquiae Wottonianae*, [B10v].

5 Pearsall Smith, *Life and Letters*, I, pp. 49–51.

6 Wotton vacated the palace after a brief stay of only six weeks. On Wotton's renting of the palace, see Wotton to Sir Dudley Carleton, 2 September 1616, *ibid.*, II, pp. 101–2.

7 *Ibid.*, I, p. 57.

8 Recent studies have shed much light on Wotton's embassy. See especially M. Netzloff, 'The Ambassador's Household: Sir Henry Wotton, Domesticity, and Diplomatic Writing', in *Diplomacy and Early Modern Culture*, ed. R. Adams and R. Cox, Houndmills, 2011, pp. 155–71; M. Ord, 'Returning from Venice to England: Sir Henry Wotton as Diplomat, Pedagogue and Italian Cultural Connoisseur', in *Borders and Travellers in Early Modern Europe*, ed. T. Betteridge, Burlington 2007, pp. 147–67; *idem*, 'Venice and Rome in the Addresses and Dispatches of Sir Henry Wotton: First English Embassy to Venice, 1604–1610', *The Seventeenth Century*, xxii, 2007, pp. 1–23.

9 On Wotton's activities as a procurer of art, see R. Hill, 'Art and Patronage: Sir Henry Wotton and the Venetian Embassy, 1604–1624', in *Double Agents: Cultural and Political Brokerage in Early Modern Europe*, ed. M. Keblusek and B.V. Noldus, Leiden, 2011, pp. 27–58; D. Howarth, *Images of Rule: Art and Politics in the English Renaissance, 1485–1649*, Berkeley 1997; *idem*, 'The Patronage and Collecting of Aletheia, Countess of Arundel, 1606–54', *Journal of the History of Collections*, x, 1998, pp. 125–37; F. Portier, 'Collections d'art et mécénat: formation des agents au XVIIe siècle', *Bulletin de la société d'études anglo-américaines des XVIIe et XVIIIe siècles*, xxxiv, 1992, pp. 47–55; T. Wilks (ed.), *Prince Henry Revived: Image and Exemplarity in Early Modern England*, Southampton, 2007.

10 Netzloff, 'The Ambassador's Household', pp. 163–64.

11 Pearsall Smith, *Life and Letters*, I, pp. 77–78. On Wotton's activities as an Protestant proselytizer in Venice, see Thomas Coryate, *Coryat's Crudities: Hastily Gobled up in Five Moneths Travells* (London, 1611), 2 vols., Glasgow, 1905, I, p. 380.

12 P. Preto, *I servizi segreti di Venezia*, Milan, 1994, pp. 197–233.

13 On the devolution of the Duchy of Ferrara, see especially E. Callegari, 'La devoluzione di Ferrara alla S. Sede', *Rivista storica italiana*, i, 1895, pp. 1–11. For a discussion of the topic and thorough bibliography, see T. Ascari, 'Cesare d'Este, Duca di Modena e Reggio', in *Dizionario biografico degli italiani* (hereafter *DBI*), vol. 24, Rome, 1980.

14 P.F. Grendler, *The Roman Inquisition and the Venetian Press, 1540–1605*, Princeton, 1977.

15 Wotton to Sir Thomas Edmondes, 17 February 1605 [1606], in Pearsall Smith, *Life and Letters*, I, p. 341.

16 On the Interdict, see especially W.J. Bouwsma, *Venice and the Defense of Republican Liberty: Renaissance Values in the Age of the Counter Reformation*, Berkeley, 1968. Also see G. Benzoni, *Lo stato marciano durante l'Interdetto, 1606–1607*, Rovigo, 2008; G. Cozzi, *Venezia barocca: conflitti di uomini e idee nella crisi del Seicento veneziano*, Venice, 1995.

17 Wotton to Sir Thomas Edmondes, 20 January 1605 [1606], in Pearsall Smith, *Life and Letters*, I, p. 340.

18 On Sarpi, see especially D. Wootton, *Paolo Sarpi, between Renaissance and Enlightenment*, Cambridge, 1983. For a recent reassessment of Sarpi and the repercussions of the Interdict, see the collection of essays in *Ripensando Paolo Sarpi*, ed. C. Pin, Venice, 2006.

19 Wotton to Salisbury, 13 September 1607, in Pearsall Smith, *Life and Letters*, I, p. 400.

20 Wotton to Salisbury, 28 April 1606, *ibid.*, I, p. 345.

21 Wotton to Salisbury, 12 May 1606, *ibid.*, I, p. 347.

22 On relations between Venice and the Venetian clergy, see A. Menniti Ippolito, 'La Repubblica di Venezia e il clero veneto. Un eterno Interdetto?', in Benzoni, *Lo stato marciano*, 2008, pp. 51–66.

23 Pearsall Smith, *Life and Letters*, I, p. 79.

24 *Ibid.*, I, pp. 79–80. Also see Ord, 'Venice and Rome', pp. 9–10.

25 The painting was bequeathed by Wotton to Charles I. For a discussion of the painting and of Fialetti's work more generally, see L.M. Walters, 'Odoardo Fialetti (1573–c. 1638): The Interrelation of Venetian Art and Anatomy, and His Importance in England', Ph.D. thesis, University of St Andrews 2009, pp. 160–64. Also see E. Law, *The Royal Gallery of Hampton Court*. London, 1898, p. 191, and Pearsall Smith, *Life and Letters*, I, pp. 48bis, 52–53; F. Yates, 'Paolo Sarpi's *History of the Council of Trent*', *Journal of the Warburg and Courtauld Institutes*, vii, 1944, p. 136.

26 Pearsall Smith, *Life and Letters*, I, p. 83. On the deficiencies of England's diplomatic corps as a result of the ambiguity separating the ambassador from the court he represented, see G. Mattingly, *Renaissance Diplomacy*, London, 1955, pp. 192–93.

27 Pearsall Smith, *Life and Letters*, I, pp. 86–87.

28 Wotton from Venice, 13 September 1607, *ibid.*, I, pp. 398–400.

29 Wotton, in Venice, to Salisbury, 19 October 1607, *ibid.*, I, pp. 407–8.

30 On the portrait, see *ibid.*, II, pp. 478–79.

31 Wotton to Salisbury, 13 September 1607, *ibid.*, I, p. 400.

32 Wotton to Salisbury, 31 July 1609, *ibid.*, I, pp. 463–65. Also see Wotton to James I, 14 August 1609, *ibid.*, pp. 465–67.

33 Wotton to Salisbury, 28 August 1609, *ibid.*, I, pp. 468–70. On Wotton's threat of resignation, see Wotton to Salisbury, 18 September 1609, *ibid.*, I, pp. 471–74. On the reception of James I's text in Venice, see Ord, 'Venice and Rome', pp. 11–12.

OF
THE ELEMENTS
OF
ARCHITECTVRE.

The I. part.

IN *Architecture* as in all other *Operatiue* Arts, the end must direct the Operation.

The *end* is to build well.

Well building hath three Conditions. *Commoditie, Firmenes,* and *Delight.* A common diuision among the Deliuerers of this *Art,* though I know not

 how,

9. The Learned Art of Architecture: Henry Wotton's *Elements of Architecture* (1624)

CHRISTY ANDERSON

WHEN SIR HENRY WOTTON RETURNED from his time abroad, in the service of the British crown, he continued in England as an ambassador of architecture, presenting the principles of Continental building to an eager and growing audience. Architecture was a sideline of his seventeen years in Venice, yet while there he observed not only the products of the great architects but also their methods of design. Wotton's treatise, *The Elements of Architecture*, published in 1624, the year after he returned to England, contains ample evidence of his study of Italian architecture from both books and the buildings themselves (fig. 106).[1] The combination of learned references to the treatises of Leon Battista Alberti, Daniele Barbaro, Giacomo Barozzi il Vignola, Guillaume Philandrier and Philibert de l'Orme are tempered with first-hand observations and his own opinions on buildings he knew. The treatise is personal and yet easily accessible to his intended audience – courtiers and country gentry with a new-found passion for architecture and the desire to build.

Even while he was still in Italy Wotton had served as a conduit of information on Continental architecture. As ambassador, and with connections to European nobility, he was in a unique position to provide information on architecture for English patrons. The Duke of Buckingham had requested from Wotton a drawing of the celebrated Villa Farnese at Caprarola, remodelled by Vignola between 1559 and 1575. The drawings Wotton sent were detailed enough that the Duke "may easily have a model made thereof in pasteboard" from the plans and elevations.[2] Great houses like Caprarola were known from the reports of travellers but the distance and difficulties of travel made seeing the most recent aristocratic houses difficult. In sending drawings back to England, Wotton was continuing a common English practice for a gentleman to send his mason to the house of another in order to obtain plans and details that might then serve as a model to emulate.[3]

This interest in Continental architecture indicates a shift in taste during the early decades of the seventeenth century among those at court. With the accession of King James I in 1603, England gradually returned to a more inclusive cultural policy that welcomed innovations in style from abroad. Under Queen Elizabeth architects (and artists to some degree) had looked to the English past for inspiration, eschewing Continental classicism as suspect for its use in Catholic countries and with little relevance to current English building practice.[4]

Wotton's short, unillustrated book offered practical advice on building and a set of principles for architectural criticism. Like other English advice books, for example Henry Peacham's *The Complete Gentleman* (1622), Wotton synthesized foreign literature to make it more accessible and relevant for his audience. He deprecated his reliance on the Italian and French treatises by saying at the outset that he was "but a gatherer and disposer of other mens stuffe", yet the book's synthetic quality ensured its popularity.[5] Foreign treatises were often difficult to find in England and few had been translated.

Henry Wotton, title page, *The Elements of Architecture*, 1624, Eton College

While craftsmen may have cared more about the illustrations as sources for new designs, both images and text were important to the new class of architectural enthusiasts as architecture increasingly came to be seen as part of a broader education based in the classics. At the beginning of the seventeenth century, books that did address the practical concerns of the patron, such as Andrea Palladio's *Quattro libri dell'architettura* (1570), had not yet been translated into English, and the more detailed guides to the Orders such as Hans Blum's *Quinque columnarum exacta descriptio*, though translated into in English in 1601, were too particular, and aimed at the craftsman. Wotton avoided those aspects of architecture that were only relevant to the specialist or scholar, what he called the "Mysteries of Proportion", but wrote rather about the practical mathematics necessary for the design of an elegant and functional staircase, for example.[6]

Wotton's method in his treatise was also not historical, as he notes, unlike Giorgio Vasari in his *Le vite de' più eccellenti pittori, scultori, ed architettori* (Lives of the most eminent painters, sculptors, and architects; 1550, revised 1568). Rather, he decided to adopt a "Logicall" approach, "by casting the rules and cautions of this Art, into some comportable Methode … though in practicall knowledges, every complete example, may beare the credite of a rule."[7] Even if Aristotelian in approach, as expressed even in its title *The Elements of Architecture* (though never stated in such explicit terms), Wotton's book aimed to chart an approach to building that would accord with Alberti's proposition that building began first in the mind before work ever began on the building site.

Almost a century before, Andrew Boorde had discussed architecture as part of medicine in his *Dyetary of Helth* (1542), and like Wotton saw the house as an active participant in the well-being and prestige of its owners:

A man of honoure, or worshyp, or other estate, the whiche dothe pretende, to buylde a howse or any mansyon place, to inhabyte hymselfe: Or els doth pretende to alter his howse, or to alter olde buydynge in to comodyous and pleasaunt buyldyng, not onely for his owne proper commodyte, welth and helth, But also for other men, the whiche wyll resorte to hym, hauynge also a respect to his posteryte.[8]

Boorde links the body of the house and the body of the owner, and understands the demands of the English climate and building practices.[9]

Wotton must have known these earlier English publications and certainly saw his book as a further commentary on architecture as part of general advice on a healthy and godly life. The most recent architectural publication, before Wotton, was an English translation of Sebastiano Serlio's *Architettura* (1611; fig. 107). The Serlio edition had been commissioned by Robert Peake, court painter to Prince Henry, and was part of a vibrant culture of the arts supported by the Prince.[10] Henry's own interest in architecture and the related arts had spurred several publications by those at his court, including a treatise by his tutor in perspective, Salomon de Caus.[11]

In Wotton's dedication of his book to Prince Charles, Henry's younger brother, he may have hoped for a similar level of artistic patronage, although Charles did not create the same innovative cultural milieu. Surviving copies of *The Elements*, in special presentation bindings and with dedicatory inscriptions, indicate how much Wotton hoped that his work would ensure his continued success in England.[12] After his successful career in Venice, Wotton may have seen the publication of the book as the route to his next employment, as Provost of Eton College, which he hoped would be, as he wrote, "a pretty cell for my fortune".[13]

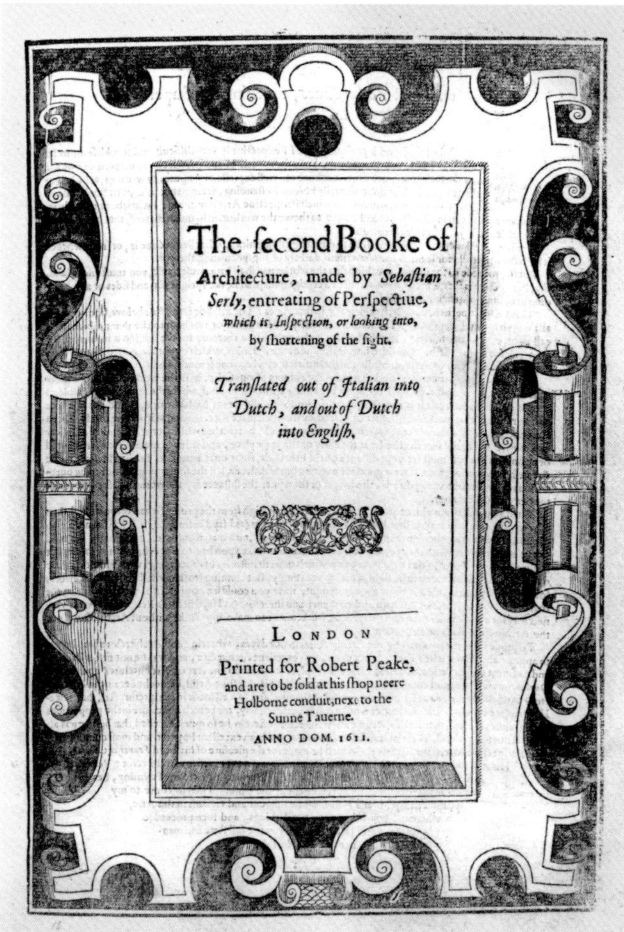

He defended the choice of architecture as his subject
in the first line of the book: "For architecture, can want
no commendation, where there are Noble Men, or Noble
Minds".[14] Yet in England the study of architecture had
only recently been raised to the level of an appropriate
subject for humanistic study. Fifty years earlier the
mathematician John Dee had had to make the case for
architecture as a learned subject in his preface to a new
translation of Euclid's *Elements of Geometrie* (1570), for
"Architecture, to many may seme not worthy, or not
mete, to be reckoned among the *Artes Mathematicall*".[15]
Dee argued for architecture's place as a proper liberal
discipline by invoking the ancient writer Vitruvius,
who urged the architect to study astronomy, medicine,
music, philosophy and painting. "Seying therefore",
according to Dee, "this ample Science, is garnished,
beautified and stored, with so many sundry skils and

knowledges: I thinke, that none can iustly account
themselves Architectes, of the suddeyne. But they onely,
who from their childes yeares, ascendying by these
degrees of knowledges, beying fostered up with the
atteynyng of Many Languanges and Artes, have wonne
to the high Tabernacle of Architecture."[16]

Wotton understood that architecture was, by the
1620s, perceived by the educated English public as a
learned endeavour, increasingly fashionable at court
and beyond. It demanded specialized knowledge, yet the
principles of good building could be made accessible to a
broader audience, especially one that had been broadly
educated in classical culture. *The Elements of Architecture*
was, in that way, like many books that synthesized
ancient history, language, literature, rhetoric and
sciences for use in the classroom and for the general
reader.[17] Architecture was also a matter of style and
identity, much as dress and language were understood
to connect people to a specific place and identify their
status. Wotton uses language that connects architecture
with social customs and easily understood human
experience. In determining where to place a house,
for example, he writes that "in the seating of our selves
(which is a kinde of Marriage to a Place) Builders should
bee as circumspect as Wooers".[18]

The challenge for Wotton was to translate what
he knew and had observed into categories that would
make the information relevant and useful for his
audience. Throughout the book he repeatedly places
classical architectural theory into an English context.
General statements, easily remembered, are then
tempered by local building concerns: "In Architecture
as in all other Operative Arts, the end must direct
the Operation. The end is to build well. Well building
hath three Conditions. Commoditie, Firmenes, and
Delight (fig. 106)."[19] *Sententiae*, short pithy sayings, were
common in humanist educational texts derived from

classical sources, and helped to commit the material to memory.[20] Taken from his own reading of Italian and French architectural treatises, Wotton's book was the printed and published version of his own architectural education. One book that survives from his collection is a copy of Philibert de l'Orme's *Le Premier Tome de l'Architecture*, with copious annotations in his own hand. Like many early modern readers, Wotton made notes in the margin of his books which were then incorporated into his own writings.[21]

Wotton wrote to educate his reader, and to present the essential qualities of good architecture. Although he dedicated the book to Prince Charles, he was not writing necessarily for a royal reader but rather for any potential patron, offering the principles of classical building that would be useful in judging architecture and commissioning his own:

> Every Mans proper Mansion House and Home, being the Theater of his Hospitality, the Seate of Selfe-fruition, the Comfortablest part of his owne Life, the Noblest of his Sonnes Inheritance, a kinde of private Princedom; Nay, to the Possesors thereof, an Epitomie of the whole World: may well deserve by these Attributes, according to the degree of the Master, to be decently and delightfully adorned.[22]

Alberti and Palladio had discussed the concept of decorum, the need for buildings to be appropriate to the qualities of their owners, and Wotton would have seen this principle in action in Palladio's buildings in the Veneto. Yet here Wotton puts that idea into a very English context. A man's house is the "Theater of his Hospitality", according to Wotton, the place where the owner participates in a social practice of generosity and entertainment that was part of his duty as a landowner and a marker of his rank and status. The great house (Wotton's "mansion house and home") obliged the owner to feed, support and protect the extended household as well as the visitor.[23] This largesse was as much a sign of nobility as were the coat of arms and the licence to crenellate his house bestowed on him by the crown. Social obligations were increasingly reflected in the physical structure of the house, in the sequencing of rooms and in the decoration, as Wotton goes on to describe in the second part of his treatise.

National differences in behaviour determine differences in architecture, Wotton observes, and much of his book is an exercise in cultural translation. Into the discussion of architecture he weaves amusing Italian anecdotes ("I must shrinke up my shoulders, as I have learn'd abroad"), and elsewhere makes telling observations about the nature of Italian culture and architecture: "For I observe no Nation in the World, by Nature more private and reserved, then the Italian, and on the other side, in no Habitations lesse privacie; so as there is a kinde of Conflict, betweene their Dwelling and their Being".[24]

The choice of ornament and the sequence of rooms evolve over time, according to Wotton, as do language and other forms of communication and gestures. When judging a work of art Wotton warns the reader not to worry about who made it, because even great artists sometimes create inferior art. Instead one should try to understand it by the standards of the artisans who, according to Wotton, rank a work on three levels – "*Con diligenza, Con studio and Con amore*", that is with care, with diligent study and ultimately with love.[25]

Climate, customs and geography all shape national building styles. In contrast to Italian habits, the English practice of hospitality required the service areas of the house to be closer to the great hall and the entrance court where guests were welcomed and food bestowed. In Italy, the kitchen was often placed below ground, but

Wotton writes that in "our owne Countrie, where though all the other pettie Offices (before rehearsed) may well enough bee so remote, yet by the naturall Hospitalitie of England, the Buttrie must be more visible; and wee neede perchance for our Raunges, a more spacious and luminous Kitchin, then the foresaid Compartition will beare; and with a more competent neerenesse likewise to the Dyning Roome".[26] If English customs required a centrally located kitchen, then, too, the lack of marble in England meant that builders "must be contented with more ignoble materials" and columns must be made of brick covered with stucco, as Palladio himself made them.[27]

Wotton was trying to shape English architectural practice by offering a modified view of classical theory and practice as he understood it. The benefit to patrons would be a house that expressed classical learning in the use of classical architectural ornament. More profoundly, however, *The Elements of Architecture* presented principles for building that could readily be adapted to local practice, for, as Wotton states, "all Nations doe start at Novelties, and are indeede married to their owne Moulds".[28]

The great innovation of Wotton's treatise was his ability to integrate classical architectural theory into the practice of English building, using images and references that would be well known to his readers. Alberti, Wotton's main source, had divided all architecture into two rather vague categories, '*materia*' and '*lineamenta*'. '*Materia*' was the physical substance of building, and '*lineamenta*' a less easily defined term, but broadly including the conceptualization of architecture, its theory and planning. Wotton, however, divided architecture into the "Seate" and the "Worke". In the first half of the book, where he discussed the "Seate", he offered advice as to the location of the house, the choice of the site, and the preparation before building.

For an English reader the house was inconceivable

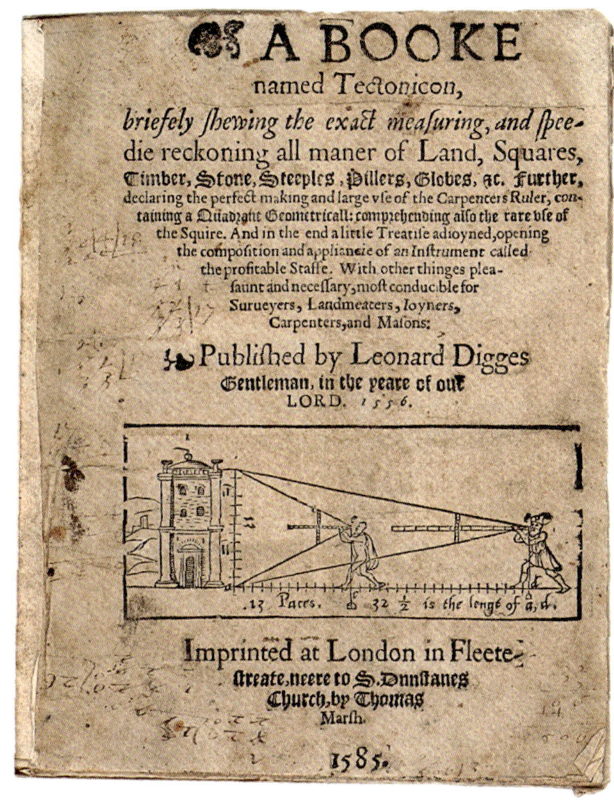

without the land and estate of which it was a part. From the first pages of the book, following Vitruvius and Palladio, Wotton advised the patron to select the site of the house carefully, choosing a healthy location with good air. These physical requirements, however, were matched by the psychological expectation of an English patron to master and manage his land as part of his aristocratic privilege. Books on accurate land-surveying were popular and satisfied a very real need for the accurate measurement of property (fig. 108). Yet Wotton went beyond those practical aspects in order to touch on the implications of land measurement as but one facet of territorial ambitions. For, as Wotton writes, there are also:

Optical … Properties of a well chosen Prospect: which I will call the Royaltie of Sight. For as there is a Lordship (as it were) of the Feete, wherein the Master doth much ioy when he walketh about the Line of his owne Possessions: So there is a Lordship likewise of the Eye which being a raunging, and imperios, and (I might say) an usurping Sence, can indure no narrow circumscription; but must be fedde, both with extent and varietie.[29]

Also in the first half of the book are sections on materials, construction, columns and arches, doors and windows, stairs, roofs, fireplaces, and drains. These are practical matters, important for anyone planning a house and usually determined by craftsmen following accepted practice that had evolved over many years. Wotton included practical advice of this kind alongside more abstract principles, thus merging these two aspects of architectural thinking in a single volume. Like similar books addressed to women on the running of the household, Wotton warned against false economy. He reviewed the process of design with drawings and models, noting that "in a Fabrique of some 40 or 50 thousand pounds charge, I wish 30 pounds at least layd out beforehand in an exact Modell".[30]

Wotton offered specific advice on judging good building but he was also proposing a more general vision of the patron as an active participant, engaged and interested in the whole building process. The knowledgeable patron supervised all aspects of the project, from the design through construction, guarding against wasteful craftsmen or shoddy workmanship. But more importantly, for Wotton, the act of building was a noble one, and all aspects of the work, both intellectual and manual, deserved the patron's attention, in order to ensure a final product that was conceived and executed appropriately for the status of the owner.

Although Wotton never mentions the translation of Serlio by Robert Peake (1611) he surely shared some of his criticisms of English building. In the dedication of his translation, "To the Lovers of Architecture", Peake had counselled English "Architects and artificers of all sorts [to study] these Necessary, Certaine, and most ready Helps of Geometrie; The ignorance and want whereof, in times past (in most parts of this Kingdome) hath left us many lame Workes, with shame of many Workemen".[31] In private houses, however, Wotton condemned the practice of designing houses with circular, oval or triangular plans, for "it is in truth a very unprofitable Figure in private Fabriques" because of the expense of building walls in that shape and the effect on the rooms within.[32] This fashion for houses designed in geometrical patterns or in the shape of the owners' initials was popular in the late sixteenth century; Wotton might have been thinking of the designs by the surveyor John Thorpe (fl. 1570–1618) for houses in the shape of circles, triangles (fig. 109) and even in the shape of Thorpe's own initials.[33]

In the brief essay 'Of Building' (1625) Sir Francis Bacon (1561–1626) famously wrote that "Houses are built to live in, and not to look on", embodying a reaction to the great and opulent houses that had recently been built by some Jacobean courtiers. In a similar vein, the poet Ben Jonson praised the medieval castle Penshurst for being "an ancient pile" without the columns and marble of newly built houses.[34] Like Wotton, Bacon offered practical advice: select a healthy site with good air, plan the rooms for function first, and build modestly. The house was a mirror of the society that builds it, and as much an emblem of the healthy life as a tangible object in the world. For Bacon advised that "neither is it ill air only that maketh an ill seat, but ill ways, ill markets; and, if you will consult with Momus, ill neighbors".[35]

For an English reader, and non-specialist, the most arcane aspect of classical architecture was the attention given to the nuances of the Orders. In the sixteenth century, John Shute had described the Orders and shown their construction in large and detailed plates. Yet Wotton was the first English author to offer standards to critique that ornamental system. Orders had been used in England since the time of Henry VIII but their details and use were part of the domain of the craftsmen as both inventors and makers. Wotton offered his readers guidelines by which to judge a good and appropriate use of this ornament in English architecture. The first

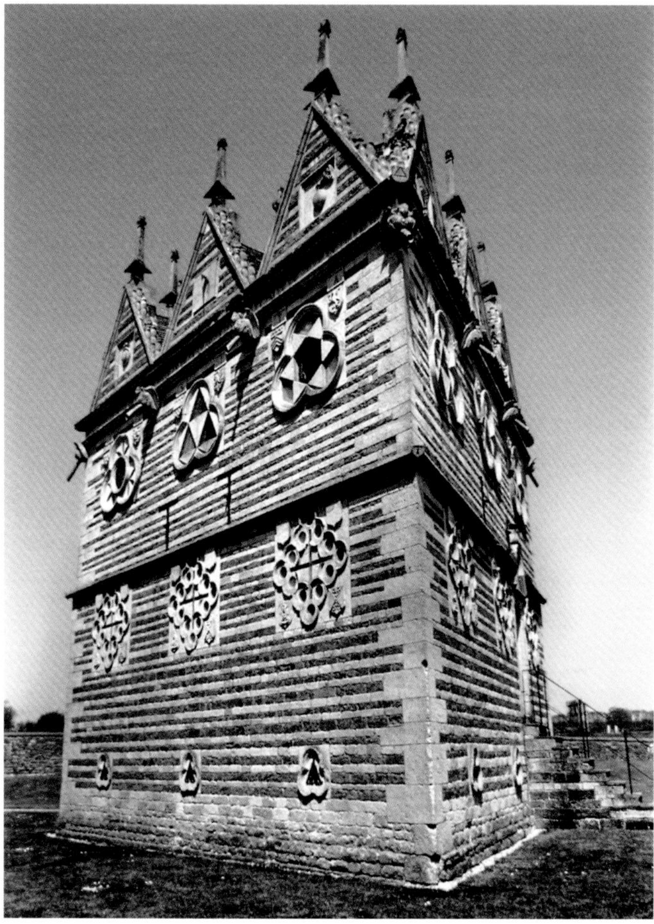

difference that he presented in his approach to the Orders was to see them as a system, a coherent and unified community of ornament and not a disjunctive collection of individual bits.

The introduction of the Orders into England was a linguistic challenge. How could craftsmen or patrons understand what they did not have words for? Columns and the system of the Orders with their accompanying ornament of bases, mouldings and entablatures were the most specialized aspect of classical architecture and the most foreign aspect for English craftsmen. Wotton acknowledged the problem of terminology right at the start of this section. Within the span of the wall, he wrote that there were "intermissions ... by Pillars, or Pylasters" which are also called columns, "for the word among artificers is almost naturalized".[36] Or in the discussion of painting as a form of architectural ornament, which Wotton advises against given the damp English climate, he acknowledged that it was common both in the north and the south but known by different names, "Grotesca (as the Italians) — or Antique worke (as wee call it)".[37] The difficulty simply of ascribing names to the various parts of the Orders presented a problem for craftsman and patrons alike. In a contemporary English translation of Palladio's *Four Books* there is a glossary of Italian architectural terms with their English equivalents. For some words there is no easy translation, and '*loggia*', for example, is given the lengthy definition of "a gallerie, a dyning rome, a faire hall, a walking place, a faire porch upon the streate side, a lodge, a banquetting house".[38] The translator searched in vain for an English equivalent for an architectural space better suited to a warmer climate; none of the northern rooms was a perfect fit.

The Orders operated as a system of discernment allowing for subtle distinctions between the various types of ornament.[39] All orders have columns,

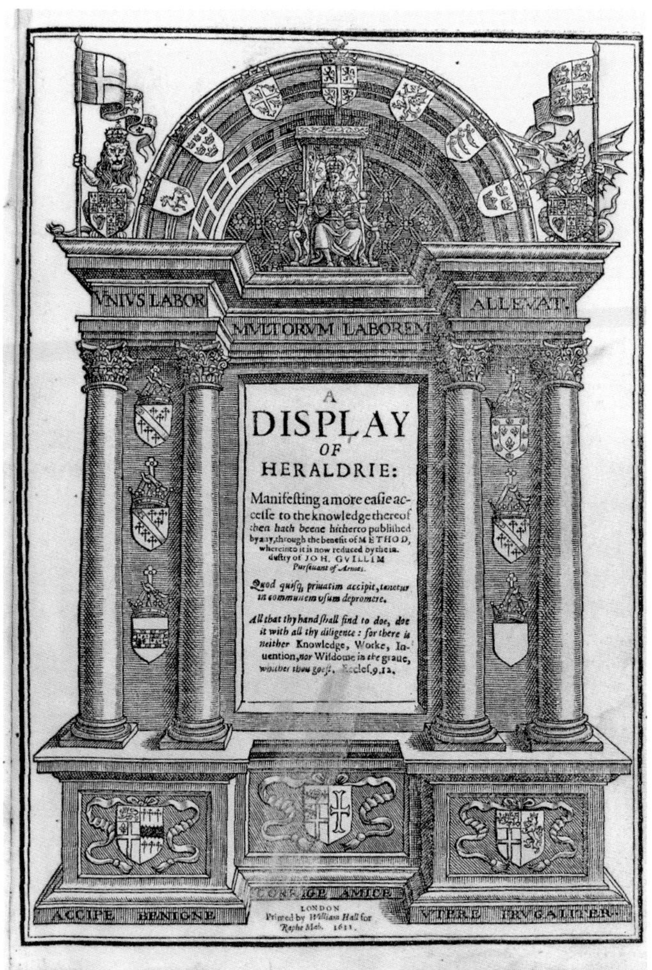

John Guillim, title page, *A Display of Heraldrie*, London, 1611

corresponding supports above and below, and related ornament. Yet the differences between the Orders are subtle but significant. The slightly shorter columns and plainer capitals of the Doric, for example, might evoke more masculine attributes and thus would be appropriate for rural buildings or the more public parts of a large house in the city. These gradations between sorts allow classical architecture to reflect the various uses of buildings and their desired effects. Palladio referred to the correspondence between architecture and the status of the owner as 'decorum', an active quality of buildings that could correlate in the mind of viewers the qualities of the residents with the design of the architecture.

In order to give the discussion of the Orders resonance for an English reader, Wotton described them in terms of heraldry, that most potent system of demarcating status and class. Heraldry was an ancient and tightly managed classification that codified rank through visual means, and books on the topic were published in increasing numbers in the seventeenth century (fig. 110). So, too, were the Orders within classical architecture. Using the language of heraldry, Wotton presented classicism as another system of signifying social and political difference. The Doric order, for example, was shorter and simpler than the other orders. "The length, seven Diameters. His ranke or degree, is the lowest by all Congruity, as being more massie then the other three, and consequently abler to support .... To discerne him, will bee a peece rather of good Heraldry, then of Architecture."[40] In the sixteenth century Sebastiano Serlio had been the first to describe the Orders as a community, much like the actors in a comedy each playing their role on a public stage. Wotton shaped that metaphor for his English reader, aligning the orders with ideas of hierarchy and nobility. "There are five Orders of Pillers, according to their dignity and perfection, thus marshalled".[41]

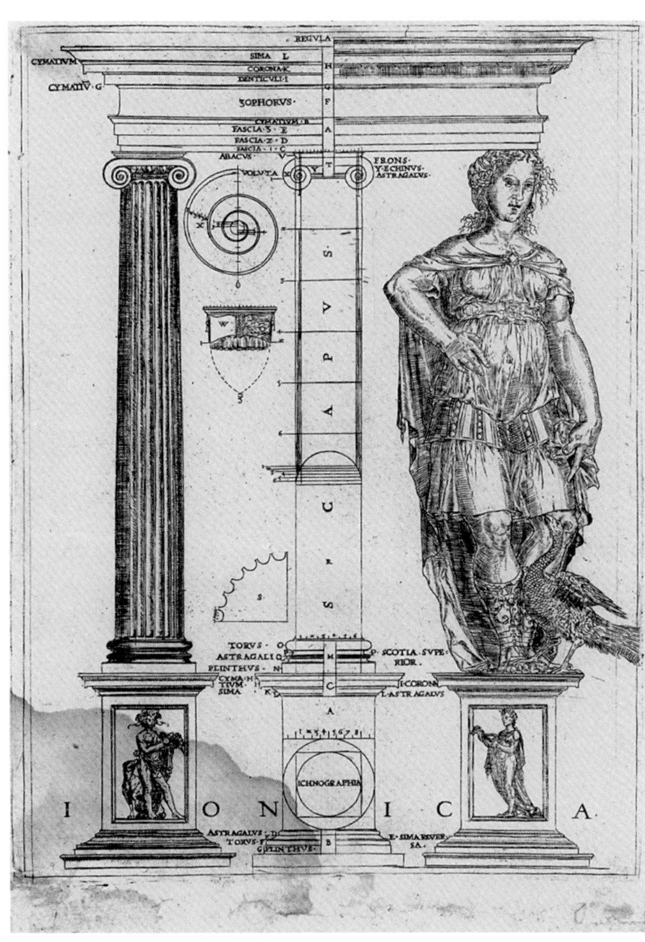

In Ben Jonson's 1640 play *A Tale of a Tub* (IV, 1), the system of modules, proportions and dimensions that distinguished one architectural order from another would also distinguish one sort of person from another:

(Clench) The Squire is a fine Gentleman!
(Medlay) He is more:
A Gentleman and a halfe; almost a Knight;
Within zixe inches: That's his true measure.
(Clench) Zure, you can gage 'hun.
(Medlay) To a streake, or lesse:
I know his d'ameters, and circumference:
A Knight is six diameters, and a Squire
Is five, and zomewhat more: I know't by compasse,
And Skale of man. I have upo' my rule here,
The just perportions of a Knight, a Squire;
With a tame Justice, or an Officer, rampant,
Upo' the bench, from the high Constable
Downe to the Head-borough, or Tithing-man;
Or meanest Minister o' the peace, God save 'un.

Distinctions between the ornament of the Orders could then be seen as like the differences in dress – plain in the Doric like the masculine worker the order resembled, or delicate and fine in the Ionic like a woman. Sixty years earlier John Shute had shown the orders as embodied figures, making that connection between clothing and ornament explicit (fig. 111).

At the end of his book, Wotton promised a second publication, this one on education, "a kinde of Morall Architecture".[42] This next assignment might have been a nod towards his wish to become Provost at Eton, yet it was also a recognition of the new place that architecture had assumed in the hierarchy of the disciplines. A decade before, in honour of King James's visit to Oxford, a tower of the Orders had been built across from the

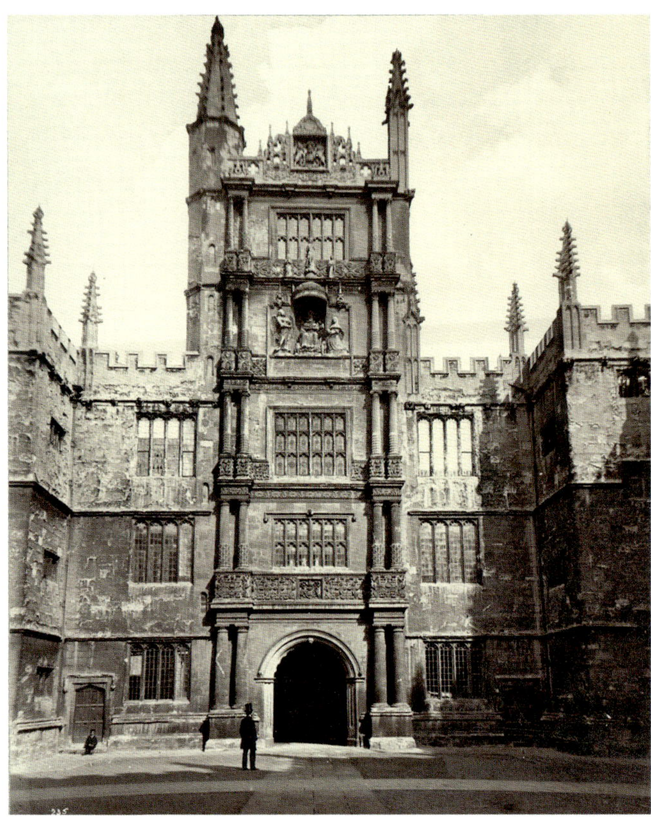

entrance to the Bodleian Library (fig. 112). Architecture was a learned art, drawing on all of the disciplines, and requiring a deep knowledge of ancient culture. It was also, by the beginning of the seventeenth century, the mark of a gentleman.[43] In his understanding of the principles and practices of Italian architecture, Henry Wotton offered a new way of building that could be merged with English traditions and ultimately become part of the English landscape.

NOTES

1 Among the most useful studies of Wotton's treatise are G. Beasley, s.v. 'Wotton', in *The British Books. Seventeenth through Nineteenth Centuries. The Mark J. Millard Architectural Collection*, ed. R. Middleton, G. Beasley and N. Savage, Washington, D.C., 1998, pp. 366–68; H. Burns, s.v. 'The Elements of Architecture', in *Palladio and Northern Europe. Books, Travellers, Architects*, ed. G. Beltramini and H. Burns, Milan, 1999, pp. 62–63; F. Hard, 'Introduction', in *The Elements of Architecture by Sir Henry Wotton*, Charlottesville, 1968, pp. xi–lxxxiii; E. Harris, *British Architectural Books and Writers 1556–1785*, Cambridge, 1990, pp. 499–503; M. Perry, '*Commoditie, Firmenes, and Delight*: The Sources and Significance of Sir Henry Wotton's *Elements of Architecture*, 1624', M.A. thesis, University of London, 1969.

2 Letter to Sir Albertus Morton, probably December 1624: L. Pearsall Smith (ed.), *The Life and Letters of Sir Henry Wotton*, Oxford, 1907, II, pp. 286–87.

3 On English building practices and patrons, see M. Howard, *The Building of Elizabethan and Jacobean England*, New Haven and London, 2007.

4 A.T. Friedman, 'Did England have a Renaissance? Classical and Anticlassical Themes in Elizabethan Culture', in *Cultural Differentiation and Cultural Identity in the Visual Arts*, ed. S.J. Barnes and W.S. Melion, Washington, D.C., 1989, pp. 95–111.

5 Henry Wotton, *The Elements of Architecture*, London, 1624, sig. 3.

6 Wotton, *Elements*, pp. 55 and 57–59. Also see C. Anderson, 'The Secrets of Vision in Renaissance England', in *The Treatise on Perspective: Published and Unpublished*, ed. L. Massey, Washington, D.C., 2002, pp. 323–47.

7 Wotton, *Elements*, p. 1.

8 Andrew Boorde, *Hereafter foloweth a compendious regiment or a dietary of helth*, London, 1542.

9 M. Howard, 'The Ideal House and Healthy Life: The Origins of Architectural Theory in England', in *Les traités d'architecture de la renaissance*, ed. J. Guillaume, Paris, 1988, pp. 425–33.

10 On Prince Henry, see the recent exhibition catalogue, ed. C. MacLeod, *The Lost Prince. The Life and Death of Henry Stuart*, National Portrait Gallery, London, 2012.

11 See A. Marr, 'A Duche graver sent for: Cornelis Boel, Salomon de Caus, and the production of *La perspective avec la raison des ombres et miroirs*', in *Prince Henry Reviv'd: Image and Exemplarity in Early Modern England*, ed. T. Wilks, London, 2007, pp. 212–38, and L. Morgan, *Nature as Model: Salomon de Caus and Early Seventeenth-Century Landscape Design*, Philadelphia 2007.

12 Presentation copies were given to, among others, King James I (now lost), Charles, Prince of Wales (now in the British Library), the Earl of Middlesex, the Lord Treasurer, the Archbishop of Canterbury (Lambeth Palace) and Sir William Boswell (New York Public Library). See Hard, 'Introduction', pp. xlviii–xlx.

13 C. Hollis, *Eton, a History*, London, 1960, p. 76; quoted in Hard, 'Introduction', p. xliv.

14 Wotton, *Elements*, sig. 3.

15 John Dee, 'Preface', in Euclid, *Elements of Geometrie*, London 1570; quoted in C. van Eck and C. Anderson, *British Architectural Theory, 1540-1750: An Anthology*, Ashgate 2003, pp. 11-15.

16 *Ibid.*

17 See K. Charlton, *Education in Renaissance England*, London, 1965.

18 Wotton, *Elements*, p. 6.

19 Wotton, *Elements*, p. 1. Here he reiterated the famous Vitruvian triad of the three qualities required in a good building.

20 On the use of aphorisms in architectural spaces see E. McCutcheon, *Sir Nicholas Bacon's Great House Sententiae*, Honolulu, 1977. Also see A.M. Blair, 'The rise of note-taking in early modern Europe', *Intellectual History Review*, 20, 2010, pp. 303–16.

21 H. Mitchell, 'An Unrecorded Issue of Philibert Delorme's "Le premier tome de l'architecture", Annotated by Sir Henry Wotton', *Journal of the Society of Architectural Historians*, 53/1, 1994, pp. 20–29.

22 Wotton, *Elements*, p. 82.

23 F. Heal, *Hospitality in Early Modern England*, Oxford, 1990.

24 Wotton, *Elements*, pp. 73–74.

25 *Ibid.*, p. 85.

26 *Ibid.*, p. 71.

27 *Ibid.*, p. 43.

28 *Ibid.*, p. 14.

29 *Ibid.*, p. 4.

30 *Ibid.*, pp. 65-6.

31 Robert Peake, 'To the Lovers of Architecture', in Sebastiano Serlio, *The first Booke of Architecture*, London, 1611; quoted in van Eck and Anderson, *British Architectural Theory*, pp. 182–83.

32 Wotton, *Elements*, p. 17.

33 M. Girouard, *Elizabethan Architecture. Its Rise and Fall, 1540-1640*, New Haven 2009, pp. 218–54.

34 On Jonson and Penshurst see D.E. Wayne, *Penshurst. The Semiotics of Place and the Poetics of History*, Madison, 1984.

35 Francis Bacon, 'Of Building', in *The Essays of Francis Bacon*, ed. C.S. Northup, New York, 1908, p. 137.

36 Wotton, *Elements*, pp. 29–30.

37 *Ibid.*, p. 97.

38 The same glossary of architectural terms occurs in all known copies of this English translation of Palladio's treatise. None of the translations was printed, yet all seem to be related to one another or to a common *exemplum*. See the discussion of these translations in C. Anderson, *Inigo Jones and the Classical Tradition*, Cambridge, 2007, p. 5.

39 N. Levine, 'Castle Howard and the Emergence of the Modern Architectural Subject', *Journal of the Society of Architectural Historians*, 62, 2003, pp. 326–51.

40 Wotton, *Elements*, p. 35.

41 *Ibid.*, p. 30.

42 *Ibid.*, p. 122.

43 C. Anderson, 'Masculinity and English Architectural Classicism', in *Gender and Art*, ed. G. Perry, New Haven, 1999, pp. 130–53.

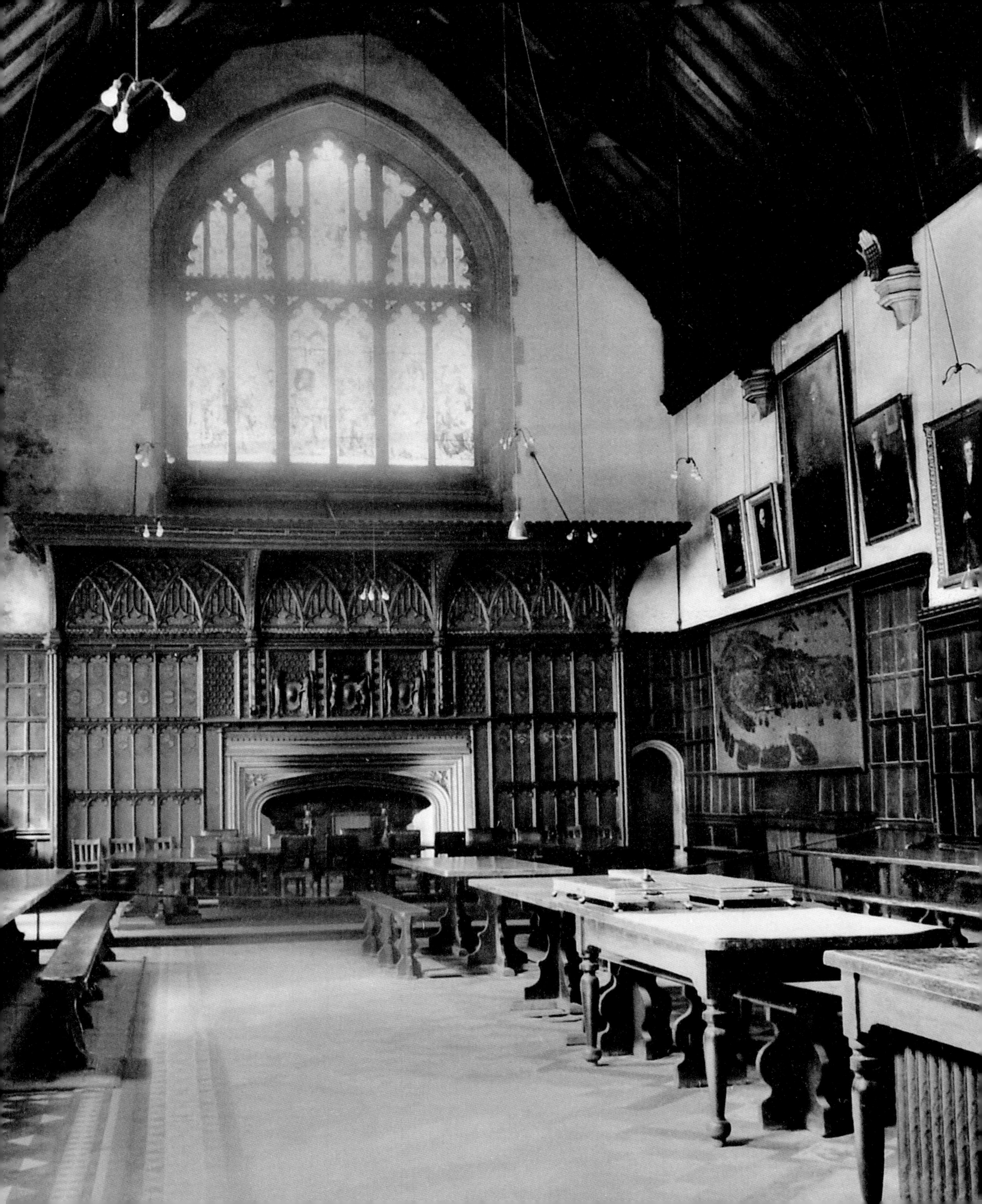

10. "This wonderful picture of a city that seems to float": Sir Henry Wotton's Gift to Eton of Fialetti's View

HENRIETTA MCBURNEY

Henry Wotton, after serving three times as ambassador to Venice, grew old in the happy bosom of Eton College. After twelve years as Provost, passed in most agreeable amity with the Fellows, hung in 1636, near the Fellows' table in memory of himself, this wonderful picture of a city that seems to float.[1]

So RUNS THE TRANSLATION of Sir Henry Wotton's Latin 'memorial' that he had painted on a long wooden tablet and displayed beneath Fialetti's *View*, his gift to Eton which he hung by the Fellows' table in College Hall (fig. 113).[2] There he could look at it each day as he presided over meals and conversed with the Fellows and his guests. Izaak Walton tells us that Wotton, after spending his mornings in meditation and private prayer and studying divinity, "when he was once sate to dinner, then nothing but cheerful thoughts possessed his mind; and those still increased by constant company at his table, of such persons as brought thither additions both of learning and pleasure".[3] Hanging in pride of place where it could be seen by visitors as well as members of the College, Fialetti's *View* was an object of admiration designed to delight the eye, stimulate the imagination and educate the mind.

It is perhaps difficult for us to realise quite what a dramatic impact the vast painting must have had on Wotton's audience of the College's fellows and scholars and his learned guests and visitors.[4] Both for its size (*c.* 2 × 4.25 metres), and for its subject, the *View* was an object of great novelty. Few of Wotton's contemporaries would have visited Venice at that date – although the

"Learned Society" of his colleagues, and his "other Friends of choicest Breeding and Parts"[5] would doubtless have been familiar with the written descriptions of travellers such as Thomas Coryate – so this painted image of the legendary city "that seems to float" must have been a remarkable sight. It was also probably the first large-scale image of Venice they would have seen. Moreover, up until this time, the only works of art to have been displayed in the College (apart from those of a religious nature in the College Chapel) were confined to portraits of monarchs, provosts and other worthies, and a number of tapestries.[6]

Wotton's choice of College Hall as the room in which to hang the *View* was no doubt dictated partly by the size of the painting, but also by considerations of hospitality and education. He notes in his *Elements of Architecture* under the section of 'Distributio' – or "that useful casting of rooms for office, entertainment, or pleasure" – that "chearefull Paintings" should be hung in "Feasting and Banquetting Roomes".[7] It is easy to imagine how the *View* would have prompted Wotton to converse with his guests about his foreign travels, his life in Venice as ambassador, and the language and customs of the place. Just as he had delighted in pointing out the sights of the city to visitors from his gondola, how he might equally have enjoyed describing its art and architecture to Eton pupils or his visitors while gazing at Fialetti's "wonderful picture".[8]

113
Eton, College Hall, photograph, 1922, showing Fialetti's
View with Wotton's memorial tablet hanging below it

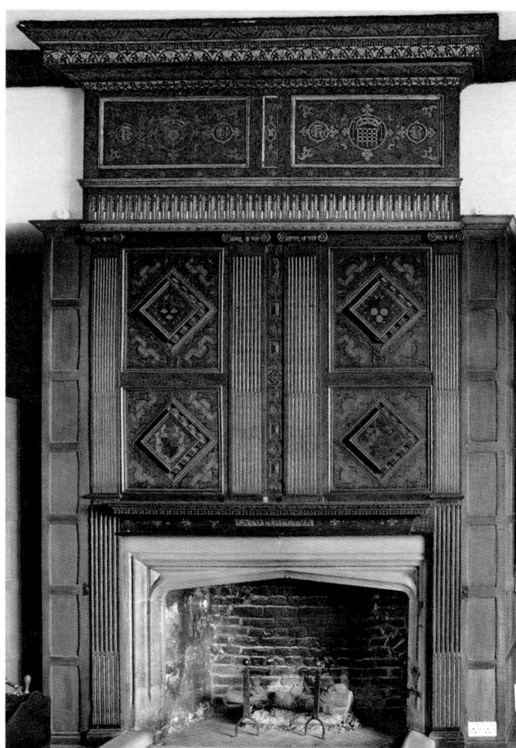

Art, architecture and education at Eton under Wotton
In 1623, following his third embassy, Wotton returned
from Venice for the last time. After his election as
Provost in 1624, Eton became his home until his death
in 1639. We must assume, therefore, that he brought
his Italian paintings, his books and the other objects in
his collection to Eton at that date. As noted in Chapter 7,
the first documentation of Fialetti's *View* – since the date
on the picture itself of its completion in 1611 – occurred
twelve years into Wotton's provostship, when, in 1636,
he presented the painting to the College, hanging it
together with his memorial plaque in College Hall. If
the *View* had been brought to Eton before that date, the
only place he could have hung a painting of such vast
scale would have been the room then known as the
provost's "large dining room", later also described as
the "Provost's Hall", and from the nineteenth century
called 'Election Hall'.[9] If the painting had already been
part of his collection – and had hung in this room in his
private apartments in the College – might it have been
an illness in 1636 which prompted him to start to plan
how his collection should be disposed of at his death,

beginning with the decision to give the *View* to the
College? It was indeed after an illness the following year
that Wotton made his will; and it is thanks to his will
that we have details of his other paintings and where
some of them were hung. In that document he tells us
that he displayed his collection of Venetian paintings
in his "great ordinary Dining-Room" – i.e. the "large
dining room" or present-day Election Hall.[10] These
works included "a Table of the Venetian College, where
Ambassadors had their Audience, hanging over the
Mantle of the Chimney in the said Room, done by the
same hand, which containeth a draught in little,
well resembling the famous D. Leonardo Donato"
(fig. 96).[11] Although he did not mention it, this scene
recorded Wotton's own audience with Doge Donà;
Wotton can be seen sitting on the doge's right in
his ambassador's hat (fig. 105). The painting shows
characteristics of Fialetti's style and method, especially
in the rather sketchy, free handling of the architectural
details, the highlighting of decorative details of the
cornice mouldings, rugs and draperies, and in the
borrowing of various elements from other sources, such
as the group of three figures at a table in the right-hand
foreground copied from Giacomo Franco's engraving of
the Sala del Collegio (fig. 95).[12]

The portraits hung in the room included "four
Pictures at large of those Dukes of Venice, in whose
time I was there imployed, with their names written on
the back side … done after the Life by Edoardo Fialetto"
(figs. 97–100).[13] These four life-size, three-quarter-length
portraits of Doges, wearing their gold brocade robes
and ducal bonnets, must have been an unusual sight.
Despite Wotton's attribution of all four of the portraits of
Doges to Fialetti, it is clear that three of them – Bembo,
Donà and Priuli – are by a different, rather more precise
hand (figs. 98–100). The portrait of Grimani, however
(fig. 97), bears the hallmarks of Fialetti's style, with

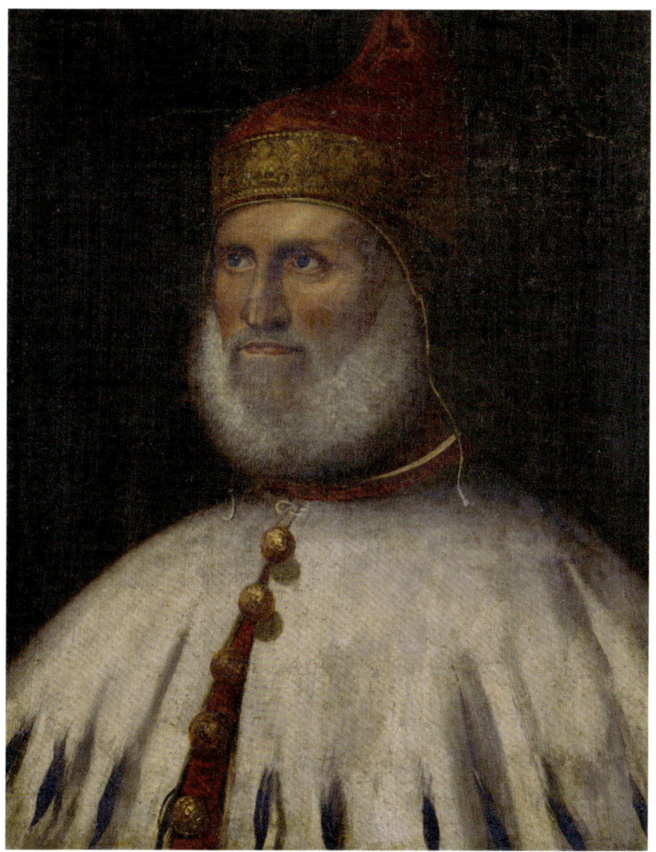

its freer handling and more sketchy brushwork (as for instance in the lacy brocade of the doge's robe, indicated with dabs of white paint); there is also a noticeable similarity between the handling of the curtain drapery in the background of the Grimani portrait and that covering the walls in the background of the *Sala del Collegio* scene (fig. 96).[14] Doge Grimani was the first doge Wotton worked under (he died the year after Wotton arrived in Venice), and if Wotton met Fialetti early on in his first embassy, as suggested in Chapter 7, Fialetti might have been an obvious choice of artist for Wotton to commission for this portrait. He could well have employed Fialetti to act for him as agent, rather than artist, in acquiring the later portraits.[15] The fact that the portrait of Doge Bembo appears to be a copy of one by Domenico Tintoretto suggests that the portraits of the three later doges may all have been copies commissioned by Wotton from existing portraits.[16]

The final painting mentioned as hanging in the room was a smaller portrait of a Doge which was hung above a door, "The Picture of a Duke of Venice hanging over against the door, done either by Titiano, or some other principal hand long before my time" (fig. 115).[17] The door in question may have been one of the two on the north side of the room behind Sir Thomas Smith's screen leading to the Provost's Parlour (see fig. 120). As the east and west sides of the room were taken up by the sixteenth-century library windows, the spaces left for the Doges' portraits would have been the south wall, either side of the *Sala del Collegio* scene above the sixteenth-century fireplace, and the north wall behind the screen. If Wotton owned the *View* before 1636, when he hung it in College Hall, the north wall would have been the only place large enough to hang it, with space perhaps for the two other Doges' portraits either side. By his hanging in one room pictures of all the doges "in whose time I was there imployed", together with a scene showing himself in audience with one of them, Wotton appears consciously to have been creating a 'memorial' or 'souvenir' of his time in Venice. Ruth Bubb points out the connection between the portraits of Doges and views of Venice;[18] in a number of the engraved 'souvenir' images of Venice portraits of Doges occur in vignettes as borders to the view of the city (fig. 74). Wotton's acquisition of the *View* may thus have been the logical counterpart to this collection of portraits.

When Wotton arrived in Eton, he was "so ill provided" with money that "the Fellows were fain to furnish his bare walls".[19] The room in the Provost's Lodge known from medieval times as the 'Great Parlour' (*Magna Parlura*) – later referred to as the 'Provost's Parlour' – was used at various times (as at present) by provosts as their private dining-room.[20] Edward Hussey notes that this first-floor room, at the north-west corner of the Cloisters, with its "arrangement of a pair of windows on either side of the fireplace, is typical of all the Founder's first-floor rooms".[21] In 1624–25 the walls of the Parlour were

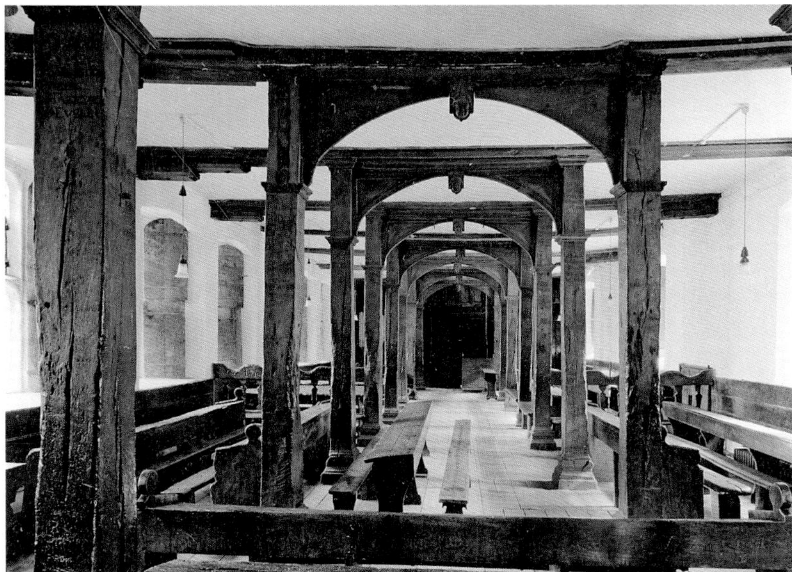

"wainscoted" in oak panelling, and an elaborate architectural fire-surround and overmantel, carved with two pairs of fluted pilasters surmounted by Ionic capitals, was erected to encase the fifteenth-century fireplace (fig. 114).[22] Wotton had recently published his *Elements of Architecture* with its celebration of the classical orders, and the carved fire-surround and overmantel was surely a visual reference to this work and his deep interest in Italian architecture.[23]

Wotton's architectural legacy to Eton also included a colonnade of pillars in Lower School, likewise erected soon after his arrival at Eton in 1624 (fig. 116).[24] It was here that he created a gallery of portraits of historical figures that could be used for educational purposes. The round arches of this colonnade, at the apex of each of which there is a pendant-shaped cartouche incorporating a carved head, are borne on Spanish chestnut columns.[25] While serving the necessary purpose of supporting the floor of Long Chamber (the boys' dormitory) above, Izaak Walton states that Wotton set up these pillars for an educational reason – in order that the "choicely drawn pictures" on them of "divers of the most famous Greek and Latin poets, historians and orators might persuade [the scholars] not to neglect retorick because Almighty God hath left mankind affections to be wrought upon".[26] The tradition of adorning walls with texts or images for teaching

was one that went back to medieval times; the early sixteenth-century school scene painted on the wall of the adjacent Head Master's Chambers, with its numerous inscriptions from classical authors, is an earlier example of such a tradition at Eton.[27] From Izaak Walton we know that Wotton was a dedicated and inspiring teacher, keen to stimulate a love of classical literature in the boys, and "a constant Cherisher of all those youths in that School, in whom he found either a constant diligence, or a Genius that prompted them to Learning".[28] Walton also records that Wotton "was pleased constantly to breed up one or more hopeful Youths, which he picked out of the School, and took into his own Domestick care, and to attend him at his Meals, out of whose Discourse and Behaviour, he gathered Observations for the better compleating of his intended work of Education".[29] As well as attempting to inspire pupils to study classical authors by visual means, "he would also often make choice of some Observations out of those Historians and Poets: and would never leave the School, without dropping some choice Greek or Latin Apothegm, that might be worthy of a room in the memory of a growing Scholar".[30] Wotton's planned *Philosophical Survey of Education or Moral Architecture* was designed to complement his *Elements of Architecture* but was left unfinished at his death.[31]

Wotton's legacy to Eton also included an important collection of Renaissance manuscripts and books

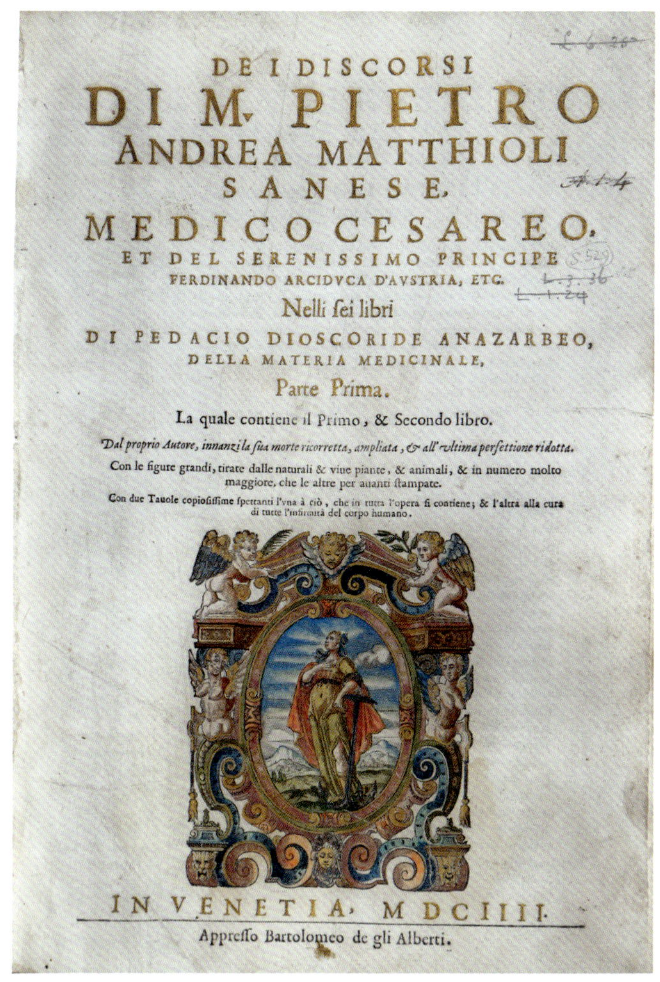

collected in Italy. This was something new for Eton:
Wotton was the first there to collect books for their
artistic and antiquarian interest, and with his
bequest College Library – up until then essentially a
working library – began its superb collection of Italian
Renaissance manuscript and printed books. Amongst
those left by Wotton were a significant number from
the collection of Bernardo Bembo, father of Cardinal
Pietro Bembo, which may have come from the library of
Cardinal Giovanni Delfino, who had died in 1622 during
Wotton's last embassy to Venice.[33] Wotton's artistic as
well as his literary interests are evident in the finely
illustrated title pages of some of the manuscripts,
including a copy of *Bucolica* by the Florentine poet Naldo
Naldi, with the Medici arms on the first page and an
illuminated initial showing Daphnis chasing a nymph.[33]
Wotton's interest in natural history was demonstrated
by his owning a richly coloured copy of Pier Andrea
Mattioli's *Commentarii* on Dioscorides's *De medica materia*,
first published in Venice in 1548 (fig. 117);[34] this he gave
in his will to "our most Gracious and Vertuous Queen
Mary … for a poor token of my thankful devotion, for
the honour she was once pleased to do my private study
with her presence".[35]

Wotton's will further indicates that amongst the
collections he had formed were several items typical of
a cabinet of curiosities. During his travels through the
Continent, including Italy, he would have seen a number
of courtly and other collections of rare objects, man-
made and natural, which no doubt inspired his own
small assemblage of such things.[36] Wotton's rarities
comprised both minerals and artificial objects, including
a "great Loadstone"; "a piece of Amber of both kinds
naturally united, and only differing in degree of
Concoction, which is thought somewhat rare"; "a piece
of Crystal Sexangular (as they grow all) grasping divers
several things within it, which I bought among the

Rhaetian Alps, in the very place where it grew"; and "my
chest, or Cabinet of Instruments and Engines of all kinds
of Uses". Walton noted that the latter contained "many
things of worth and rarity" as well as some surprisingly
utilitarian items – "Italian Locks, Picklocks [and] Screws
to force open doors".[37] Further paintings in his collection
– he does not note their location in his lodgings – were
"the four Seasons of old Bassano … (being in little form)
which I bought at Venice"; a "Picture of the elected
and crowned Queen of Bohemia";[38] "a Picture of Divine
Love, rarely copied from one in the King's Galleries";[39]
and "a Picture of Heraclitus bewailing, and Democritus
laughing at the world".[40] Finally, there is a charming
mention of his "Viol de Gamba, which has been twice
with me in Italy".[41]

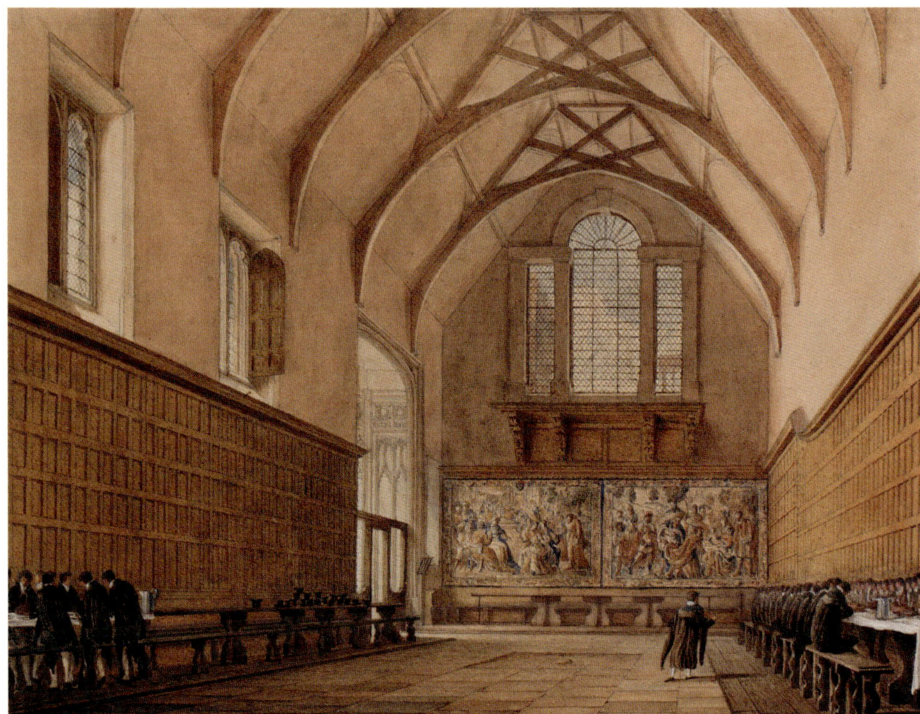

The fortuna of Fialetti's View at Eton

In 1636 when the *View,* together with Wotton's memorial tablet, was placed in College Hall by the "Table of the Fellows", it must have been hung on the sixteenth-century panelling on the north side of the Hall, opposite the bay window, as the early seventeenth-century tapestries occupied the west wall behind the table (fig. 118).[42] This was the position it continued to occupy during its life in College Hall and where it was seen in 1666 by Samuel Pepys, for whom it was one of the memorable features of his visit. His diary entry records:

At Eton … to the College, and there all mighty and fine. The school good, and the custom pretty of boys cutting their names in the struts of the window when they go to Cambridge …. To the Hall, and there find the boys' verses 'De Peste', it being their custom to make verses at Shrove-tide …. Here is a picture of Venice hung up, given, and a monument made of Sir H. Wotton's giving it to the College. Thence to the porter's, in the absence of the butler, and did drink of the College beer, which is very good; and went into the back fields to see the scholars play ….[43]

The *View* apparently continued to hang in College Hall during the next century. The first major restoration of the Hall occurred in 1719–20, when more than £1300 was spent in repairs.[44] However, we know the painting remained *in situ* as it was noted as hanging there by the antiquary George Vertue, together with a printed map of Venice. On his three-day visit to Eton in May 1737 "with Lord Colerane to see Mr Tophams famous collection of drawings in his library",[45] he noted "in the Hall a large view of Venice painted – given by Sr. H. Wooton. 1636. A large map printed of Venice, with Views of the palaces churches, &c. Very good manner".[46] The large printed map with views of palaces and churches seems to fit Lodovico Ughi's *Pianta Topographica di Venezia* of 1729 with its border containing sixteen views of Venetian buildings by Luca Carlevarijs;[47] this is the only reference to a print being framed and hung near the *View,* suggesting a significant interest in the painting at that date and the topography it showed.

A century later the *View* was removed from College Hall and hung in Election Hall. Pugin's 1816 watercolour of College Hall published in Ackerman's *History of Eton*

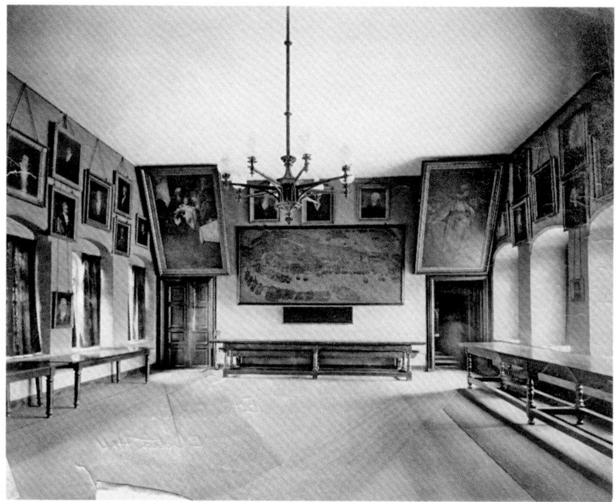

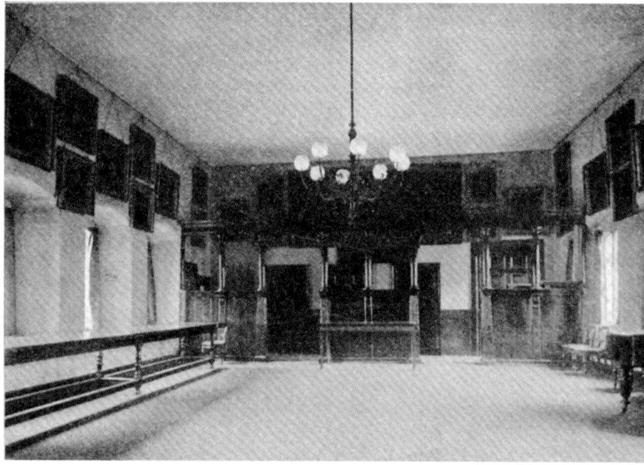

College does not show the *View*, suggesting that it had already been removed by that date (fig. 118).[48] In a photograph of 1879 the *View* can be seen hanging on the south wall of Election Hall, together with Wotton's memorial plaque beneath it, angled between paintings by Benjamin West and William Beechey (fig. 119). By 1900 it had been re-hung on the other side of the room, where it is visible above the Tudor screen in a photograph of that date (fig. 120). It is noted as hanging there in 1907 by Wotton's biographer Logan Pearsall Smith, who wrote that it "now hangs in the Provost's large dining hall with [a] beautiful inscription".[49]

At some date between 1911 and 1922 the *View* was moved back to College Hall and hung in its old position, together with Wotton's plaque, by the Fellows' table (fig. 113). It seems to have remained there until 2008, when the Hall was once again redecorated, necessitating the unhanging of the painting.[50] Following its return from conservation treatment by Ruth Bubb in 2010, the decision was made to hang the *View* once more in Election Hall, not only because of the cleaner and more stable environment, but also in recognition that it warranted a more prominent and visible position in the College (fig. 3).[51]

Conservation history

At some date after 1704 the painting underwent drastic and disfiguring treatment, with the whole area of the lagoon and the canals being overpainted in a deep Prussian blue, giving it a flat and uniform appearance (fig. 72).[52] At the same time, elements of the original painting were covered over (for instance, some gondolas, rigging and the edges of buildings and ships), and a few new boats were painted on top. Although there is no record of who ordered this 'restoration' of the painting, we must assume it was authorized by a provost who was interested enough in Eton's artistic heritage to believe treatment was needed. A likely candidate is Provost Hawtrey (provost 1853–62; previously head master 1834–52), during whose time the second major restoration of College Hall took place, in 1858. Hawtrey, caricatured as an aesthete ("He had a weakness for fine clothes, perfumes, and gold chains"),[53] was responsible for other restoration work in the College, including the repainting of Wotton's overmantel in the Provost's Parlour.[54] If the overpainting of the *View* did indeed occur during Hawtrey's time as provost or head master, it may have coincided with the decision to remove it to Election Hall – a possible reason being that it was judged by Hawtrey or his advisors that the atmosphere of College Hall with its hot food, dirt, grease and huge open fires had contributed to the discoloration of the painting.

By 1978, Wotton's plaque had become almost illegible, partly again no doubt because of dirt and grease from

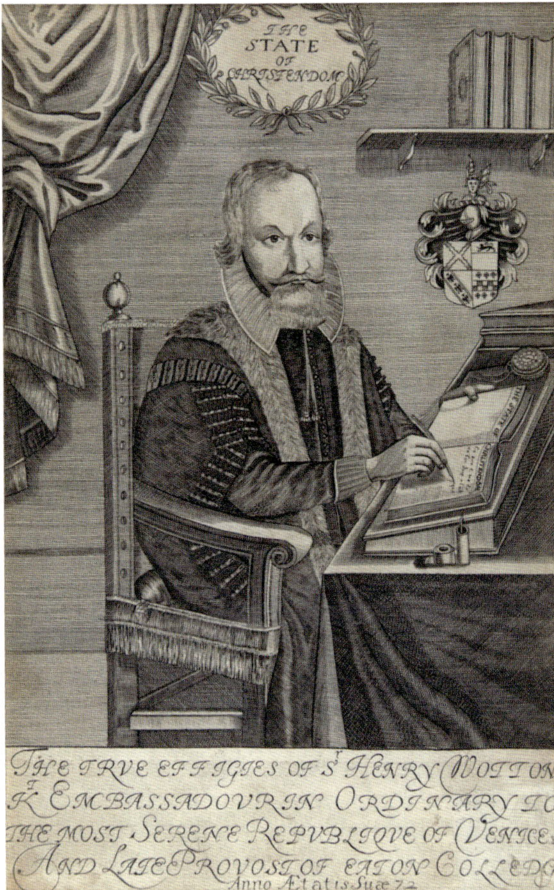

121
Unknown artist, *Sir Henry Wotton aged seventy-two*, line engraving, 228 x 143 mm, *c.* 1639
Eton College

the poor environment.[55] It was cleaned, repainted and hung "as it used to be", although at some date after this it disappeared and has not been traced since.[56] In 1989 the *View* was sent to the Hamilton Kerr Institute in Cambridge for conservation. The treatment was undertaken in preparation for the painting being shown in an exhibition to mark the 400th anniversary of Eton's foundation in the Brewhouse Gallery at Eton.[57] Although removal of the blue overpaint was recommended by the Hamilton Kerr Institute (see fig. 72), the necessary time and money were not available at that date.[58]

In 2009 the *View* was re-examined by Ruth Bubb after having being removed for storage while College Hall was being redecorated. Bubb recommended a programme of conservation, in particular strengthening the stretchers, re-lining the painting and removal of the overpainting, funding for which was made possible thanks to the Friends of Eton College Collections. After a year of conservation work the *View* came back to Eton in 2010,

restored to something near its original appearance. Meanwhile the old frame, which was not strong enough to support the painting,[59] was replaced with a new black and gold frame made by John Davies Ltd.[60] A reconstruction of Wotton's missing plaque, or "monument" as Pepys called it, lettered in black on gold with Wotton's wording, and an additional phrase in Latin to acknowledge the gift of the Friends, was designed by Charles Young and also made by John Davies; this new memorial plaque now hangs near the *View*.[61]

Conclusion

Wotton died at Eton and was buried in Eton College Chapel, having specified that his epitaph should carry not his name but "an useful Apothegm . . . to preserve his Memory".[62] Pepys's visit to Eton in 1666, during which he had admired Fialetti's *View* and Wotton's "monument", ended with his visiting the Chapel, where he singled out Wotton's tombstone for particular note: "And so to the chappell, and there saw, among other things, Sir H. Wotton's stone with his Epitaph: *Hic jacet primus hujus sententiae Author: Disputandi pruritus fit ecclesiae scabies*". The phrase (translated as 'The itch of disputation will prove the scab of the Church') had been used by Wotton in his *Panegyric on Charles I*. There Wotton had praised the king's love of Italian art, suggesting that through the "excellent Artificers, and Works, wherewith in either Art both of Picture and Sculpture you have so adorned your Palaces ... Italy (the greatest Mother of Elegant Arts) or at least ... the principal Nursery, may seem by your magnificence to be translated into England".[63] Wotton's own significant part in this "translation" of Italian art into England might be seen in little at Eton through his artistic, architectural and literary legacies to the College, and not least in his gift of Fialetti's *View of Venice,* a portrait of a city which for him epitomized the essence of Italian culture.

NOTES

1   "*Henricus Wottonius, post tres apud Venetos legationes ordinarias, in Etoniensis Collegii beato sinu senescens, eiusque, cum suavissima inter se sociosque Concordia, annos iam 12 praefectus, hanc miram urbis quasi natantis effigiem in aliquam sui memoriam iuxta socialem mensam affixit. 1636.*"

2   Wotton's original tablet is now missing (though visible in the photograph at fig. 113). It was still extant in 1978 when a framed typescript label hung by it, providing a translation and the following information: "The legend on the board below the picture was repainted in 1978 from the original text, which had faded so badly as to be almost illegible. The old board has been cleaned and hung as it used to be." In an appreciation of Wotton P.E. More observed that "If any connection be sought between [Wotton's] diplomatic and academic careers it may be found in [this] inscription'": More, 'Sir Henry Wotton', in *Shelbourne Essays*, New York and London, 1908, pp. 228–61.

3   Izaak Walton, *Reliquiae Wottoniae*, London, 1685, unpaginated.

4   The seventy 'King's Scholars' or Collegers, as well as the Commensals (selected sons of noblemen who were fee-paying), ate all their meals in College Hall.

5   Quotations from Walton, *Reliquiae Wottoniae*, unpaginated.

6   Including the two tapestries in College Hall of *The Flight into Egypt* and *Christ sitting amongst the Doctors*, given to the College in 1613 by a Fellow, Adam Robyns (fig. 118). Existing portraits include at least one of Henry VI, Gheerardt's portrait of Provost Sir Henry Savile given by his widow in 1622, and one of the Earl of Essex given by Savile during his time as Provost.

7   Wotton, *Elements of Architecture* (1624), London, 1903, p. 99. Not only was Wotton particular about where he hung his own collection at Eton (see below), but he gave careful advice to others, such Lord Salisbury and the Duke of Buckingham, for whom he also collected pictures (see, for example, L. Pearsall Smith, *The Life and Letters of Sir Henry Wotton*, 2 vols., Oxford, 1907, I, letter 125 [4 April 1608 to Salisbury]). A bequest of paintings by Bassano in his Will to Sir Francis Windebank is made with an instruction "to hang [them] near the Eye in his Parlour" (Walton, *Reliquiae Wottoniae*, unpaginated).

8   Thomas Coryate was one of those to whom Wotton gave advice "to take special observation" of the sculpture on the Doge's palace while he was taking him around in his gondola (*Coryat's Crudities: Hastily Gobled up in Five Moneths Travells*, London, 1611, p. 190).

9   Originally built by Roger Lupton as the Fellows' library in c. 1520, it had, since the time of Sir Thomas Smith, provost of Eton 1547–54, been used as the provost's formal dining room. From the nineteenth century it was the room used for the election of scholars entering the College, as well as for scholars proceeding from Eton to King's College, Cambridge, and was accordingly renamed Election Hall.

10 Transcriptions of his will – where he lists his paintings – are included in Walton, *Reliquiae Wottoniae*, unpaginated, and Pearsall Smith, *Life and Letters*, I, pp. 215–19.

11 M. Levey, *The Later Italian Pictures in the Collection of Her Majesty The Queen*, Cambridge, 1991, no. 484, as 'Attributed to Fialetti'. Levey points out that this is one of several versions of the 'Sala del Collegio' composition, derived from the engraving by Giacomo Franco in his *Habiti d'huomini et donne venetiane* (fig. 95). The painting is now in Hampton Court Palace.

12 Levey (*ibid.*) remarks that Fialetti's is "one of the least good" of the several painted versions of the scene derived from Franco's engraving.

13 *Ibid.*, nos. 485–88, as 'Attributed to Fialetti'. Levey notes that "Wotton apparently believed that the four pictures were by Fialetti, and they are therefore retained here, with some reservation, under his name" (p. 83). The four portraits, together with one of Doge Andrea Gritti (fig. 115) were described in 1649 as "five Dukes of Venis: by Tintoret" (L.R. MS., fol. 123).

14 Levey notes, "the technique of this portrait is so different from the other three as to isolate it stylistically. Its slightly 'free' handling of paint suggests some influence of Tintoretto, and it ... could be by Fialetti" (*ibid.*, p. 83). Of note is the similarity of the treatment of the brocade tunic worn by the doge with that of the underskirt worn by St Agnes in Fialetti's *Saint Agnes* (fig. 52).

15 Levey (*ibid.*) suggests that Wotton might have considered the artist less important than the subject of the paintings: see Chapter 7. Wotton himself writes that "when a Piece of art is set before us, let the first Caution be not to aske who made it, lest the Fame of the Author doe Captivate the Fancie of the Buyer": Wotton, *Elements of Architecture*, 1624, pp. 84–85.

16 For Tintoretto's portrait of Bembo, see Sotheby's, New York, *Old Master Paintings*, 24–25 January 2008, lot 217.

17 This, the one earlier painting acquired by Wotton (which was "done ... long before my time"), is now at Hampton Court Palace: J. Shearman, *The Pictures in the Collection of Her Majesty the Queen: The Early Italian Pictures*, Cambridge, 1983, no. 283: "Copy of Titian, Portrait of Doge Andrea Gritti". Andrea Gritti was doge 1523–38; however, Shearman believes it "is unlikely to be itself a product of Titian's studio, and may even have been painted after 1600".

18 See Bubb, p. 79 above.

19 H.C. Maxwell Lyte, *A History of Eton College (1440–1990)*, London, 1911, p. 213, quoting *Calendar of State Papers, Domestic*, James I, vol. clxxi, no. 25, and ECR Audit Book, 1624–25, recording a payment "to Mr. Provost by consent at the end of the Auditt 1624, towards the furniture of his lodging, 40l.".

20 See R. Willis and J. Willis Clark, *The Architectural History of the University of Cambridge, and of the Colleges of Cambridge and Eton*, 4 vols.,

Cambridge, 1886, I, p. 458, who note that the *Magna Parlura* "was mentioned in the early deeds".

21 C. Hussey, *Eton College: with an Account of Oppidan Eton*, London and New York, 1952, p. 54. As Hussey, observes, however, this room "has been more lived in than any other in the house, and has therefore undergone more alteration. It is, none the less, one of the best preserved in its original planning .... The door opening onto the Gallery is untouched, and beside it there remains one of the little two-light windows, placed so as to light an interior porch or lobby which would have projected some 6 or 8 ft into the room." In the 1960s, however, the pair of windows to left of fireplace was replaced by the door built to connect the room with a new kitchen.

22 For the panelling, see Willis and Clark, *Architectural History*, I, p. 458, and note 54 below for the nineteenth-century painting of the overmantel.

23 *The Elements of Architecture* was printed in April 1624 by John Bill; the five classical orders are described in the section on 'Ornaments', pp. 29–46.

24 Lower School was from earliest days until middle of seventeenth century the principal schoolroom at Eton.

25 Tradition had it that the timber was the wreckage of a galleon run aground from the Armada and presented by Queen Elizabeth: see Hussey, *Eton College*, p. 18.

26 Walton, *Reliquiae Wottoniae*, unpaginated. Maxwell Lyte, *A History of Eton College*, cites an entry in the Audit Book, 'To the waterman bringing from London to the Colledge six pictures in frames for the Schoole and Library, given by Mr. Provost, 3s. 6d' (ECR Audit book, 1639-40); although this was the last year of Wotton's provostship, it may indicate a continuation of a tradition already started by him.

27 See McBurney *et al.*, 'Part II: The early sixteenth-century school scene in the Head Master's Chambers', in E. Howe *et al.*, *Wall

Paintings of Eton*, London, 2012, p. 164 and fig. 27.

28 Walton, *Reliquiae Wottoniae*, unpaginated.

29 Robert Boyle, future scientist, was one of the pupils placed under Wotton's particular care; he later described Wotton as "a person that was not only a fine gentleman himself, but very well skilled in the art of making others so": Maxwell Lyte, *History of Eton College*, p. 232.

30 Walton, *Reliquiae Wottoniae*, unpaginated.

31 The first chapter of Wotton's *Survey of Education*, together with 'The Aphorisms of Education', was published by Walton in *Reliquiae Wottoniae*, pp. 75–99.

32 In his will Wotton bequeathed "to the Library at Eaton College all my Manuscripts not before disposed"; he further left "all my Italian Books not disposed of in this will" to his friend and kinsman, Isaac Bargrave, Dean of Canterbury (although, as Birley notes, apart from the manuscripts left to Eton, he only disposed of one book in his will: R. Birley, *The History of Eton College Library*, Eton, 1970, p. 27).

33 *Ibid.*, pp. 26-7. Wotton's MSS from Bembo are described in detail in Nella Giannetto, *Bernardo Bembo: umanista e politico veneziano*, Florence: Olshki, 1975; several of these MSS are described and illustrated in P. Quarrie, *Treasures of Eton College Library*, exh. cat., Pierpont Morgan Library, New York, 1990.

34 Wotton's finely coloured and illuminated third Italian edition of Matthioli's version of Dioscorides "with the plants naturally coloured and the text translated by Mathiolo, in the best language of Tuscany" came into the possession of Thomas Bargrave, Wotton's chaplain in Venice in 1616–18. Thomas's nephew John Bargrave bequeathed the two-volume work to Peterhouse in 1680 (Perne Library, L. 3. 36-7). Many of the drawings of plants have been annotated with their English names. For other evidence of Wotton's interest in plants and gardens, see Pearsall Smith, *Life and Letters*, II, p. 365.

35 Although no visit of Charles I to Eton is recorded, Queen Henrietta Maria visited the College in 1628 or 1629: Maxwell Lyte, *History of Eton College*, p. 224.

36 Wotton must, for instance, have been familiar with the collection of Rudolf II, with whose librarian, Dr Hugo Blotius, he lodged for some months in Vienna in 1590, and that of Daniel Nijs, described by Gigli as the "*sede della Meraviglia*" (Gigli's collection is described in M. van Gelder, 'Daniel Nijs and his contacts with artists in Venice', in M. Keblusek and B.V. Noldus (eds.), *Double Agents: Cultural and Political Brokerage in Early Modern Europe*, Leiden, 2011, pp. 111–24, at p. 119).

37 Pearsall Smith, *Life and Letters*, I, pp. 215–19. Locks, however, were not uncommonly found in curiosity cabinets; see for example the section of Manfredo Settala's museum in Milan devoted to "mathematical and physical instruments": O. Impey and A. MacGregor (eds.), *The Origins of Museums: the Cabinet of Curiosities in Sixteenth- and Seventeenth-Century Europe*, Oxford, 1985, p. 26.

38 By Gerrit van Honthorst, bequeathed to Prince Charles, future Charles II. It is now at Hampton Court Palace (see C. White, *The Dutch Pictures in the Collection of Her Majesty the Queen*, Cambridge 1982, no. 76, pl. 71).

39 Wotton notes that the original was given by himself to Charles I (Pearsall Smith, *Life and Letters*, I, p. 217).

40 A subject favoured by Dutch artists; two paintings of these subjects at Knole are by Paulus Moreelse.

41 Pearsall Smith, *Life and Letters*, I, p. 218. Wotton also enjoyed singing and he "haunted churches ... to listen to the music" (*ibid.*, pp. 59, 375).

42 See note 6 above.

43 Pepys Diary (www.pepysdiary.com), Monday 26 February 1665/66.

44 Willis and Clark, *Architectural History*, I, p. 452 n. 4.

45 For the collection of drawings after the Antique assembled by Richard Topham see A. Aymonino with L. Gwynn and M. Modolo,

Paper Palaces: the Topham Collection as a source for British Neo-Classicism, exh. cat., Eton College, 2013.

46 George Vertue, *Note books*, 6 vols., Walpole Society, 1930–55, VI, p. 101.

47 S. Biadene and G. Romanelli (eds.), *Venezia: piante e vedute. Catalogo del fondo cartografico a stampa, Museo Correr*, Venice, 1982, no. 72, p. 69; G. Cassini, *Piante de vedute prospettiche di Venezia 1479–1855*, Venice, 1982, no. 72, pp. 138–40.

48 Pugin's watercolour shows College Hall before the second major restorations in 1858, largely paid for by John Wilder (Fellow 1840–85), when alterations were made to the roof and west window, and the three original medieval fireplaces were rediscovered on the west, north and south walls. Pugin could of course have omitted to show the paintings hanging in the Hall because of his primary interest in the architectural features.

49 Pearsall Smith, *Life and Letters*, I, p. 210.

50 According to Lytton Sells, however, it was hanging "in the Provost's Dining Room" in 1964 (A.L. Sells, *The Paradise of Travellers*, 1964, p. 74, n. 72), suggesting there might have been another period in the twentieth century when it was moved into Election Hall.

51 Election Hall, although still strictly speaking part of the Provost's Lodge, is used regularly for receptions, lectures, concerts and other gatherings of the College and School.

52 Prussian blue was not available until 1704; the original blue pigment was indigo and smalt (which had turned brown): see Chapter 11.

53 A.D. Coleridge, *Eton in the Forties*, London 1896, pp. 372–73.

54 The overmantel was repainted with decorative foliation and armorial bearings on the escutcheons; the painting is signed *H. Jones* and dated 1853 just above the mantelpiece. See Hussey, *Eton College*, p. 54. Hawtrey, "known to be a scholar of liberal views, as well as a refined and courteous man" (Maxwell Lyte, *History of Eton College*, p. 436), took a keen interest in the history and art of the College.

55 See note 2 above.

56 Several people connected with the College remember the plaque, although there is disagreement about what colour it was painted, some suggesting blue.

57 T. Card (ed.), *Eton: 1440-1990. Portrait, Programme and Catalogue*, Eton College, 1990.

58 See J. Wardius, 'Analytical report 1478, Hamilton Kerr Institute, Cambridge, April 1990, unpublished.

59 The old, possibly nineteenth-century, painted deal frame is in storage in the College.

60 Wotton was concerned that pictures should be framed appropriately; for example, the portrait of Paolo Sarpi he sent to Dr Samuel Collins, Provost of King's, he had framed in "plain deal, coloured black like the habit of his order" (Pearsall Smith, *Life and Letters*, II, p. 370). I would like to record Eton's gratitude to Charles Young of John Davies, who, although seriously ill at the time, advised on and saw through the framing of the *View*.

61 *Haec tabula donis comitum renovata est MMX* (This painting was restored through the gift of the Friends, 2010).

62 Walton, *Reliquiae Wottoniae*, unpaginated. The full epitaph reads: *Hic jacet hujus Sententiae primus Author. Disputandi Pruritus, Ecclesiarum Scabies. Nomen alias quaere.*

63 Wotton, *A Panegyrick of King Charles*, p. 155.

11. Technical Appendix

RUTH BUBB

The conservation treatment of Fialetti's painting, initiated in 1990 by the Hamilton Kerr Institute, Cambridge, was resumed by the studio of Ruth Bubb in 2009. Some technical analysis, minimal structural repairs, selective cleaning and in-painting had been carried out at the Hamilton Kerr Institute. The poor structural state of the painting support and the unsatisfactory appearance of the extensive opaque blue overpaint on the water remained to be addressed.

Close examination and analysis of the material object informed treatment decisions throughout both interventions. The project also yielded information about the making of the painting, and the way this corresponded to contemporary practice and also to Fialetti's sources.

CANVAS

The painting was executed on five pieces of plain-weave canvas stitched together (figs. 122, 123). A sample of original canvas fibre was mounted in methyl metha-crylate resin[1] and identified as linen under polarizing light at ×400 magnification. The pieces were cut so that the minimum length necessary was cut from the bale.[2] The average warp thread count on all five pieces is 14 threads/cm. The weft varies from 14 to 16/cm. All five pieces are thus of similar weight, slightly coarser than either of the paintings by Tintoretto examined by the National Gallery, London,[3] but this is unsurprising as the *View of Venice* is larger. Although the turn-over edges are damaged, it is possible to see that selvages are still extant around the perimeter of the painting (fig. 122). They were trimmed from the seam allowances as they would cause seams to pucker. The seam allowances themselves would have been removed before the canvas was lined. Since only one selvage is present on each piece of canvas, it is impossible to know the exact loom width. Measuring from the outside of the turn-over edge to the

seams, widths ranging from 96 cm to 99 cm were found. The standard loom width of sixteenth-century Venetian painters' canvas was generally between 106 cm and 110 cm.[4]

PAINT LAYERS

Minute flakes of paint were removed from sites adjacent to damages or cracks and mounted in resin.[5] The mounted samples were ground down so that the layer structure of ground, paint and overpaint could be viewed in cross section under high magnification in visible, polarized and ultra-violet light. The sequence in which the ground, paint layers and subsequent restoration had been applied could then be deduced.

A sample taken from water in the canvas addition at the right of the painting (fig. 122; cross section 081A: fig. 124) appeared to show all of the layers. The first three layers consisted of the dark brown ground, a light blue and a coarse beige-coloured layer, all fairly intimately attached to each other, indicating application in fairly close succession. These layers were therefore identified as original. A thin blue layer could be seen above the beige layer, with a thin dark brown separation layer between the two. This was followed by a thicker dark brown translucent layer and lastly the thick blue layer of visible overpaint. The apparently unpigmented layers (fig. 124, layers 4 and 6) dividing the upper paint layers (fig. 124, layers 5 and 7) from the first three and from each other made it more likely that the upper layers consisted of restoration. Brian Singer concluded from elemental analysis that the translucent brown layer was largely organic.[6] A sample taken by the Hamilton Kerr Institute from the water between Dorsoduro and the Giudecca tested positive for starch with iodine. Solubility tests also suggested the presence of resin, from which they concluded that the translucent brown layer consisted of residues of old glue and varnish.[7] Staining tests on

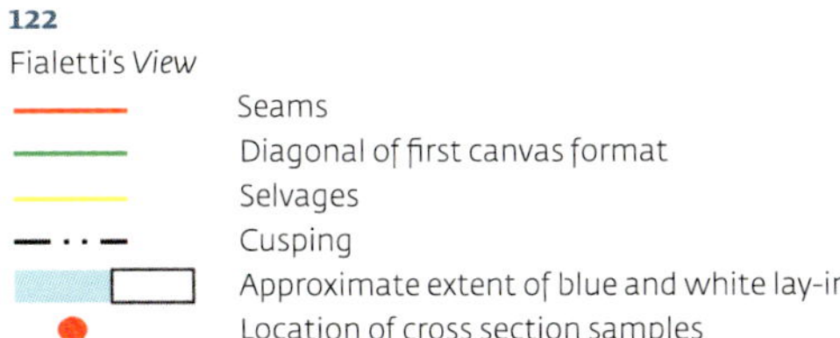

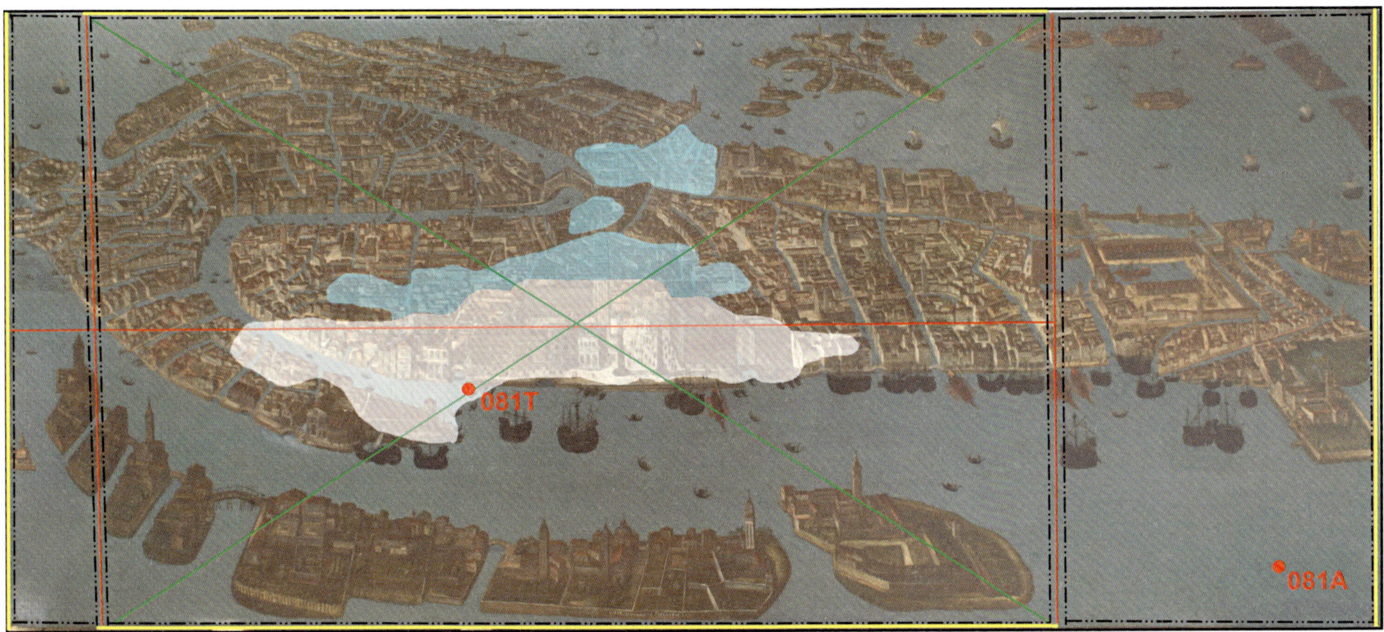

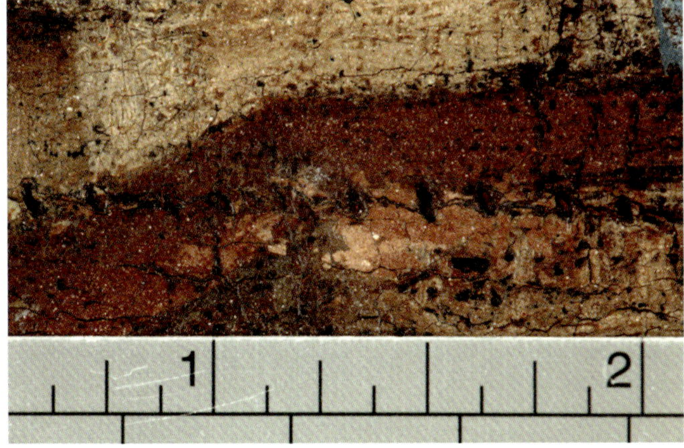

123
Fialetti's *View*, macro detail of stitched canvas seam

sample 081A were also positive for protein in these layers,[8] which would be consistent with the presence of animal glue (fig. 125).

Cross sections from the central canvas were at first more puzzling to interpret. The same brown ground was present, but in the centre of the painting it was followed by a lead-white layer containing a small number of particles of vermilion,[9] then another dark brown layer strongly resembling the first ground layer. Sometimes there was also a light blue layer between the white and the second brown layer (cross section 081T: fig. 128). Specks of white and blue are visible on the surface through abrasion in the upper paint layers (figs. 129, 130). Because both of these layers contain lead white, they also show up on the X-radiograph of the central area. The white paint is slightly denser in X-ray than the blue (fig. 69). The same stratigraphy was observed by the Hamilton Kerr Institute in a sample taken from the

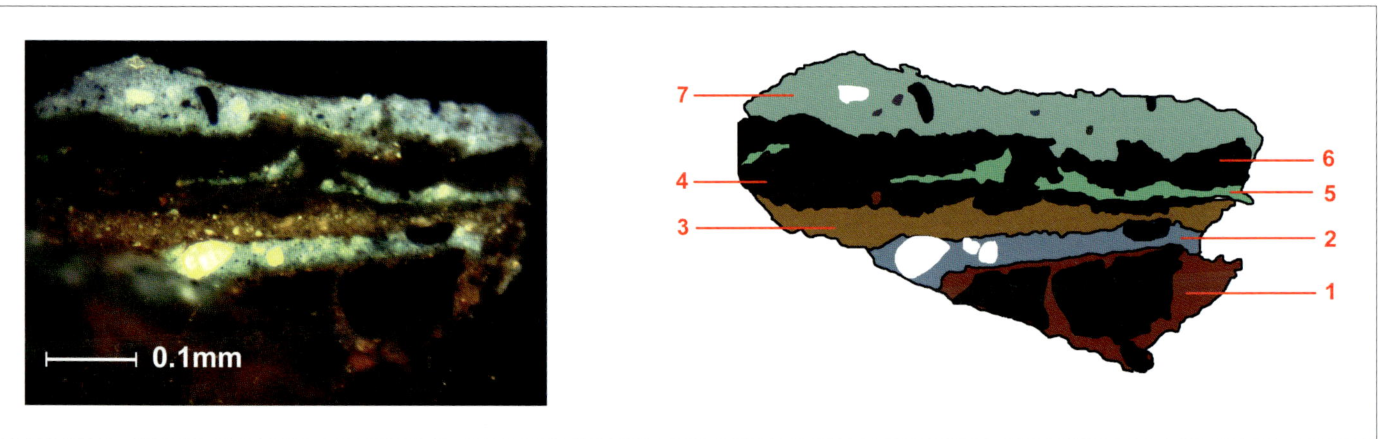

124
Fialetti's *View*, cross section 081A, paint and ground
from open water, lower right in area of added canvas

KEY
1 Reddish brown ground
2 Light blue layer containing indigo, lead white, chalk and carbon black
3 Coarse beige-coloured paint containing smalt
4 Dark brown translucent layer (adhesive residue?)
5 Blue layer containing Prussian blue and lead white
6 Dark brown layer (adhesive residue?)
7 Blue overpaint containing Prussian blue and lead white

pavement of the Piazzetta.[10] The similar appearance of
the two brown layers was also noted,[11] as well as the fact
that blue paint was present under parts of the image that
were not eventually painted blue, such as buildings
(fig. 130).

The likely explanation for the repetition of the brown
layer is that the first white and blue layers represent the
initial broad lay-in. When the canvas was extended, the
additions were primed to match the first ground layer,
and this second priming was also brushed thinly over the
existing paintwork for a fresh start. The initial sketching
out does not appear to have been repeated, presumably
because the preliminary brushstrokes would still have
been more or less visible.

PIGMENTS AND PAINTING TECHNIQUE
Elemental analysis (EDX) of the pigments in each layer
of cross section 081A was carried out by Dr Brian Singer
of Northumbria University.

The brown ground layer of the cross section (fig.
124, layer 1) contained only lead, silicon, sulphur and
iron. This indicates that the ground consists of earth
pigments with lead white. A dark particle in the ground
was mainly carbon and sulphur with a trace of iron and

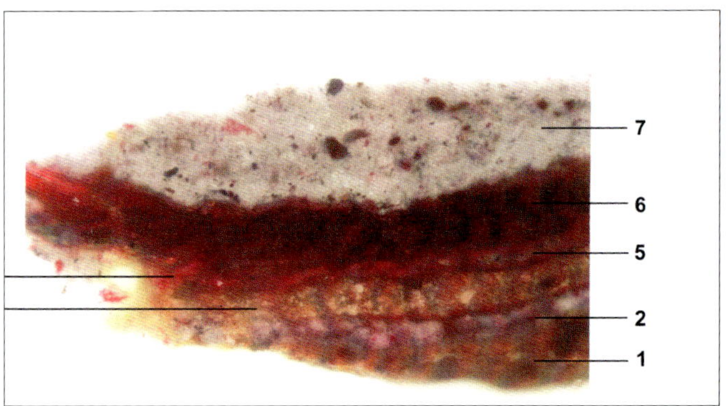

125
Left side of cross section 081A, stained with Acid Fuchsin
Key: See fig. 124

calcium, indicating charcoal. The charcoal particles in
the ground varied greatly in size, some being very large.

The EDX spectrum of the earliest blue paint layer in
the same sample (fig. 124, layer 2) showed a peak for
iron. This can indicate either Prussian blue or indigo.
The date of the painting is too early for Prussian blue,
which was introduced in the first years of the eighteenth
century.[12] Since Prussian blue is almost impossible to
differentiate from indigo using simple light microscopy,

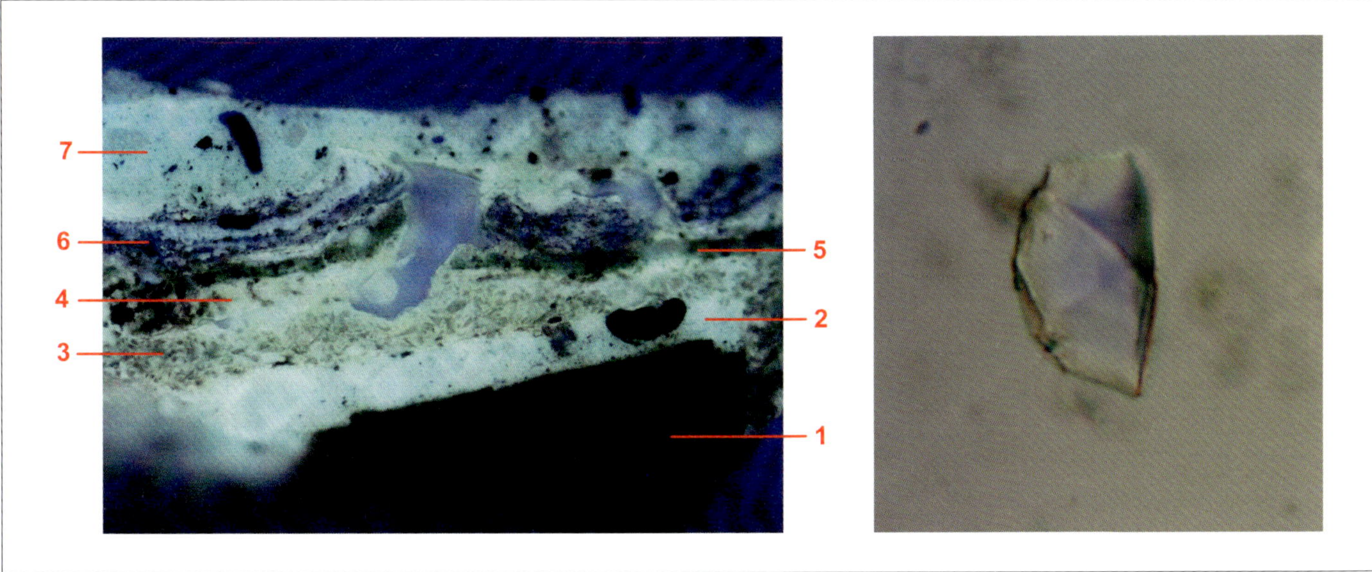

polarized light microscopy was carried out on dispersed samples of pigment. This gave a positive identification of the blue as the dyestuff indigo,[13] confirmed by the microchemical tests previously carried out by the Hamilton Kerr Institute.[14] Singer also found lead white and carbon black in this blue layer.

The layer immediately above the original blue paint in cross section 081A appears beige in colour (fig. 124, layer 3). Elemental analysis of this layer showed the presence of silicon, potassium, cobalt, aluminium and arsenic, all of which are indicative of the blue pigment smalt, made from "a cobalt containing potash glass".[15] The brown layer does not appear to contain any blue particles, but in ultra-violet light the characteristic shard-like particles, resembling broken glass, can be seen, confirming the presence of smalt (fig. 126). The glassy particles can also be seen in dispersion (fig. 127).

Cross sections from different areas of the blue water show indigo used alone, or the two blues used alternately as base coat and glaze for different effects. Where indigo forms the upper layer, it does not seem to have been subject to fading. The blue colour in cross section appears equally intense throughout the depth of the layer. However, where a smalt layer is uppermost, it appears completely brown (fig. 124). The brown colour is that of the discoloured binding medium, though, not the pigment. Deterioration of smalt is thought to occur by means of a reaction promoted by the acidic drying oil binder, which leaches alkaline components from the glass.[16] The particles slowly lose their blue colour and finally become completely translucent (fig. 127).

Where smalt has been used as an underlayer, the blue colour has been better preserved (fig. 128, layer 6), although the discolouration of the smalt itself is not thought to be a photochemical process. There are a number of factors which

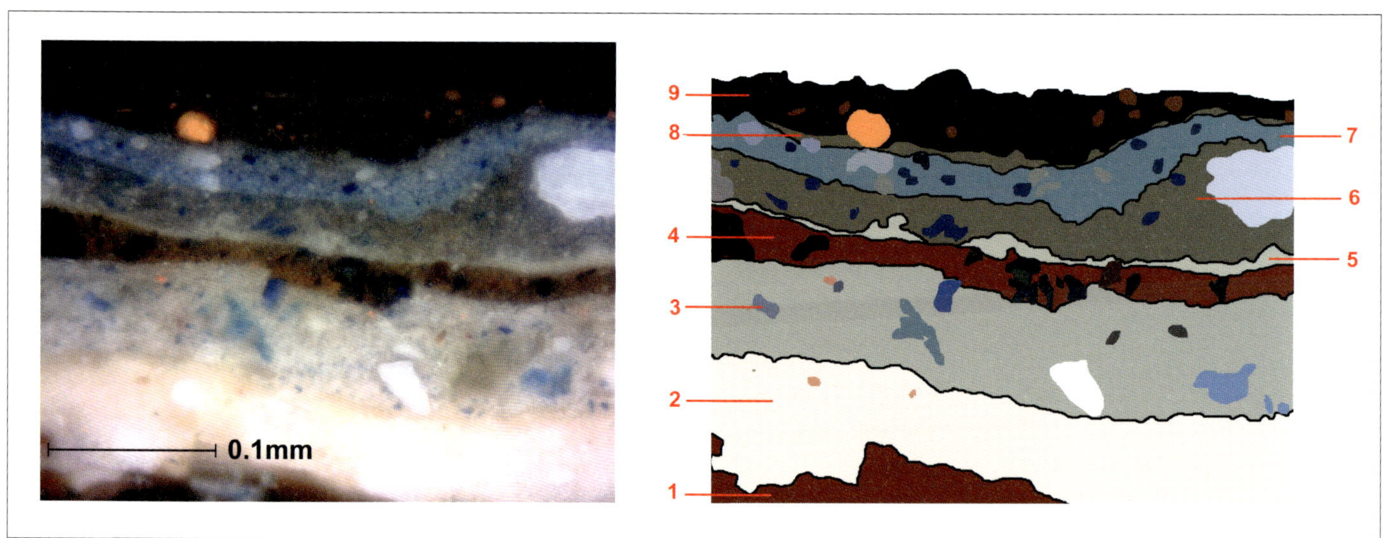

could have caused the difference in deterioration observed. The glaze layer may be richer in medium than the smalt used in underlayers, thus allowing for more leaching of the alkaline components. Where the smalt is mixed with a larger proportion of lead white in the underlayers (fig. 128, layer 3) the lead white may have helped to preserve the blue colour, inhibiting the leaching by reacting preferentially with the oil itself.[17]

Near the opening of the Grand Canal, the artist had obscured his first blue layer with a second coat of brown ground before repainting the blue canal. Since smalt does not have good covering power, he needed to paint a thin layer of white over the brown before applying the blue (fig. 128, layer 5). Here the white and blue layers appear to have been applied in fairly rapid succession, wet in wet, and then finished with a layer of indigo.

PAINT MEDIUM

Cross sections were stained with Acid Fuchsin solution in order to detect proteins (fig. 125) and with Sudan Black B, a stain for lipids.[18] All of the layers stained blue/black,

indicating an oil based binder, although the dark brown layers were too dark for it to be certain whether any stains were taken up. The type of oil was not identified. Tintoretto almost always used linseed oil for its relatively speedy drying, which was sometimes further accelerated by boiling in order partially to pre-polymerize the medium.[19]

Some patchy red staining of the cross sections by Acid Fuchsin was observed. The red staining was more concentrated in the brown layers believed to consist of old lining adhesive (figs. 124 and 125, layers 4 and 6). There also appeared to be a thin layer of material underneath the first layer of smalt (figs. 124 and 125, layer 3) that stained strongly for protein. The handling of smalt, which had to be left coarsely ground in order to appear blue, was notoriously tricky in oil. It did not remain well suspended in the medium, and the excess yellowish oil spoilt the blue colour, a fact acknowledged by Armenini.[20] Seventeenth-century sources indicate that this could be counteracted by mixing the pigment with lead white, and by particular techniques such as

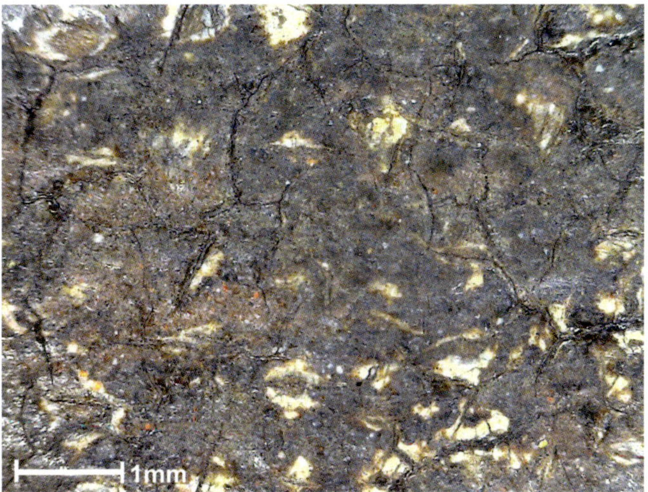

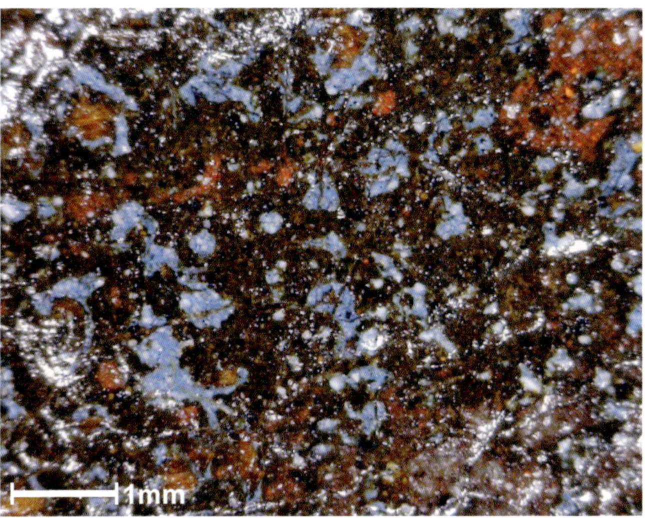

blotting excess medium with paper, drying the painting flat or face down,[21] or strewing the pigment on to the surface of a sticky medium.[22] It was also suggested repeatedly that handling problems and discoloration could be mitigated by incorporating a proteinaceous medium such as egg or glue into the binding medium.[23] This practice has not so far been widely corroborated by medium analysis of extant paintings. Results of staining tests alone should be treated with caution since the uptake of stain can be influenced by other factors such as the porosity of the material and the fact that samples are usually taken adjacent to damages and are therefore liable to be contaminated with later consolidants. It is difficult to draw firm conclusions about the protein content of original materials in this painting because of its repeated relining and consolidation with adhesives based on animal glue.

PREVIOUS TREATMENT

Examination of the painting during treatment showed that it had been the subject of a number of restoration campaigns in its history. The last lining is thought to have been carried out in about 1800–30. This dating is based on the design of the stretcher (fig. 131) and the composition of the lining adhesive. The adhesive consists of animal glue, probably rabbit-skin glue, with a large proportion of flour, a possible source of the starch identified in cross-sections by the Hamilton Kerr Institute. The degradation of the adhesive, which could be removed mechanically without softening with water, is another indication of its age.[24] The glue-paste mixture would have been applied to the reverse of the canvas and lining would be carried out quickly before the glue could cool and dry. Pieces of dried grass and straw were discovered embedded in the glue on the reverse of the canvas, suggestive of the haste with which the process was performed.

Before lining, patches of blue paper had been applied to the reverse of larger damages in the canvas and along the seams (fig. 134). Reinforcement of the seams was necessary once the stitching had been cut away on the reverse to reduce thickness and avoid the formation of a ridge on the front after lining. This method is still commonly used by liners today. Some of the larger losses in the canvas had been inlaid with canvas pieces before the paper was attached. The paper fibres were identified as dyed and undyed cotton fibres, possibly mixed with another undyed fibre, such as hemp. Other fibres in the sample were too damaged by the paper-making process to be identifiable. A mix of cotton and hemp is typical of papers from the late eighteenth century into the nineteenth century. Earlier European paper would have been made from linen fibres. Blue paper was made from blue rags already dyed with indigo for clothing. It was used for wrapping, especially of groceries such as loaf sugar. [25]

A number of patches in different materials on the back of the lining canvas are evidence of local repairs carried out on the lined canvas (fig. 132). Dried liquid staining running down the centre of the canvas on the back indicates that there may have been some water damage. Black staining on the reverse of the lining canvas may have been caused by smoke from the fireplace in the College Hall, where the painting last hung until 2008. No sign of smoke damage was found on the reverse of the original canvas when it was exposed during re-lining. There was evidence of insect damage in the stretcher.

Losses in the paint, ground and canvas had been filled. Six or seven distinct types of filling materials, including the white polyvinyl alchohol and chalk gesso recently applied by the Hamilton Kerr Institute, were found in the course of investigating the painting, giving an indication of the number of interventions the painting has undergone in its history. The earliest filling material was found underneath the translucent brown layer identified as adhesive residue from the last re-lining. It was therefore possible that this orange material might belong to an even earlier intervention.

Elemental analysis and polarized light microscopy of the pigments in dispersion found the earliest extant layer of overpaint to be composed of Prussian blue and lead white. The presence of Prussian blue in the mixture means that it cannot predate 1704, but it could have been applied in the eighteenth century. The earliest layer of overpaint was found mostly in the areas of deep water, such as that at the lower right of the painting, where smalt had been applied as a glaze and had discoloured. It was not found on any of the smaller canals, where

the indigo blue is well preserved. Two further layers of overpaint were applied to all of the water in the painting after the last lining. Elemental analysis and examination in cross section confirmed that they were similar in their pigment content and structure and were composed mainly of Prussian blue and lead white. When the sample is examined in cross section, the two distinct layers are not easily distinguishable, but in ultra-violet they fluoresce slightly differently. This indicates that both coats of paint were probably applied within a short time of each other, but they may have a slightly different medium content. The medium of all three layers of overpaint is probably a drying oil, as indicated by staining with Sudan Black B. Sometimes great care was taken to respect the finer details such as the outlines of the gondolas or spaces between the ships' rigging, but elsewhere original details were disregarded and completely painted over.

CONSERVATION TREATMENT

Before carrying out the structural consolidation of the painting, a yellowish brown film of surface dirt was removed. Paper labels were removed from the back of the stretcher and conserved. It is usual to remove old varnish and restoration from the painting before lining, to avoid carrying non-original material deeper into the layer structure of the painting by the heat and vacuum pressure used in the lining process. The MS2A reduced ketone resin varnish applied by the Hamilton Kerr Institute in 1990 was removed. This inevitably disturbed some of their retouching carried out with pigments bound in the same resin, but the base-coat retouching in egg tempera was not dissolved and was intentionally retained.

After extensive testing, the most successful method for removing the blue overpaint from the sea and canals was found to be the use of timed sequential applications

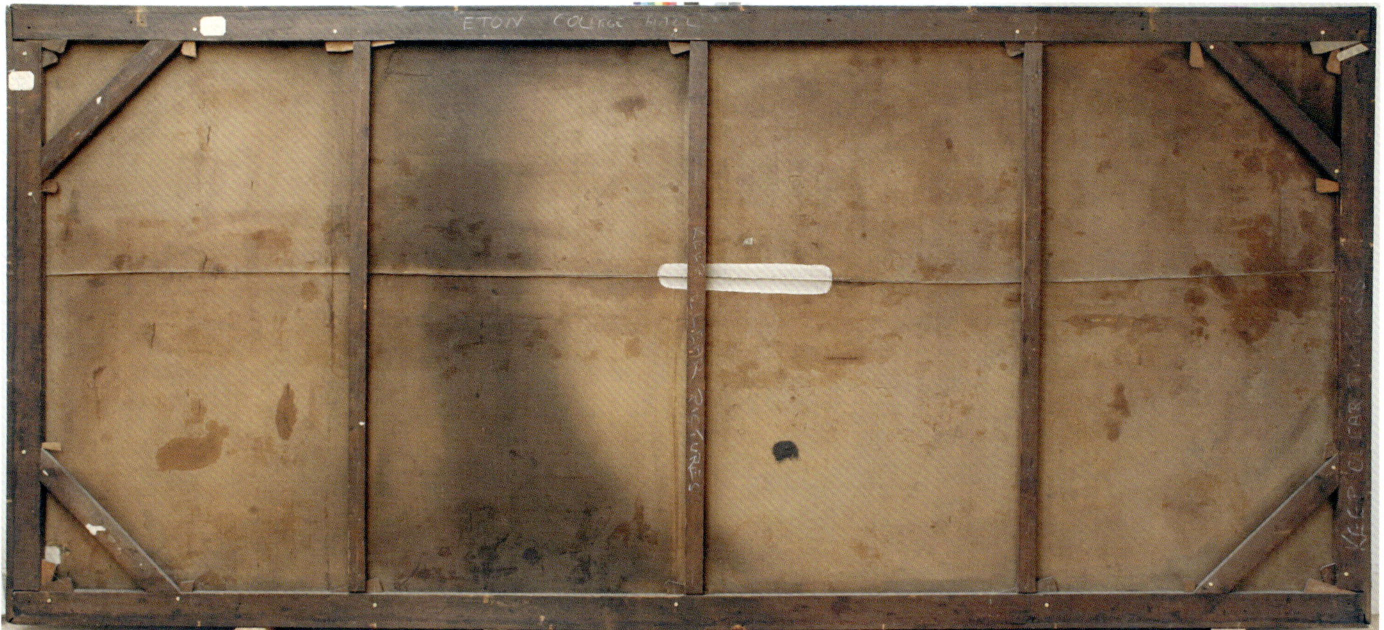

of solvent gels, cleared with solvent mixtures. The contact time was reckoned empirically, depending on the observed thickness and number of layers of overpaint in each area. Where two layers were present, or where a single layer was particularly thick, the application was repeated. The dirt and glue residue found underneath the blue overpaint was removed separately, often revealing a well-preserved original blue layer (fig. 132).

The older, greenish blue overpaint was extremely resistant to all solvents, solvent mixtures and solvent gels. It was therefore difficult to remove this layer completely without affecting the original blue underneath. In areas where the original blue was in poor condition the greenish blue overpaint could only be thinned (fig. 133). It proved easier to remove the greenish overpaint in areas where the original paint layer was in better condition, as in the central part of the lower half of the painting. In areas where the original blue was painted more thinly or had been subject to more abrasion, the process of overpaint removal had to be slow and tailored to each particular area. Where old filling materials extended over original paint they were softened with a solvent gel and removed mechanically with a scalpel under magnification.

In the process of removing the overpaint, a small number of features that had been added on top of the overpaint by restorers, including two gondolas, were removed after having been recorded in photographs. Removal of carelessly applied overpaint also exposed the original outlines of the islands and buildings. Delicate, albeit abraded, original details, such as fish in the fishing nets, and numerous small vessels, were revealed (figs. 64, 65).

All the materials subsequently applied to the painting were selected for their stability and reversibility. The painting was relined by Trevor Cumine. The front of the painting was protected by sheets of soft acid-free tissue adhered with dilute BEVA 371 (ethylene vinyl acetate co-polymer) heatseal adhesive. The canvas was removed from its stretcher and the lining canvas removed. Old adhesive residues were scraped off the back of the canvas with a scalpel. The paper patches were removed after the old adhesive. The painting was then relined with BEVA 371 on to linen canvas and restretched on to a new stretcher with copper tacks. The expansion keys were secured with nylon line.

After removing any residues of lining adhesive from the front of the painting, an isolating varnish of Paraloid B72 acrylic resin was applied by brushing. Losses in the paint and ground were filled with a proprietary acrylic putty (chalk and butyl methacrylate dispersion) (fig. 135). A base coat of casein paint was applied to the

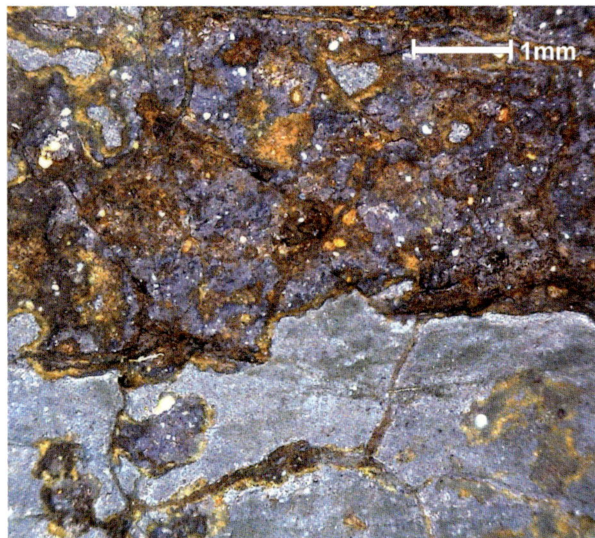

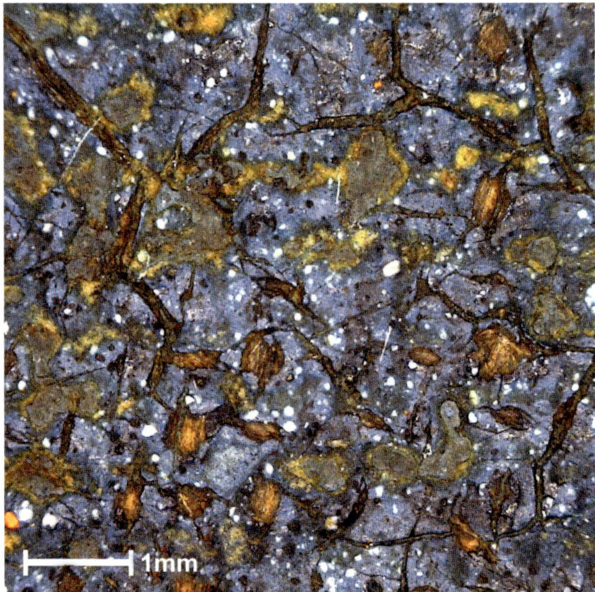

132
Fialetti's *View*, original blue (top) with overpaint (bottom)

133
Fialetti's *View*, original blue with remains of older,
greenish overpaint

front of the tower were present to show that it did not
have the appearance it has today, as there appeared to be
a figure alongside the winged lion. This was confirmed
with reference to the history of the Clock Tower[27] and by
examination of the detail on the de' Barbari print. Until
it was removed at the end of the Venetian Republic in
1797, there was a statue of Doge Agostino Barbarigo, who
inaugurated in the clock in 1499, next to the Lion. The
intended appearance of other details, such as the jetties
in the Arsenale basin, and a boat at the lower right that
had been uncovered by removal of the overpaint, was
also reconstructed from the printed map. The boat might
have been painted out because it appeared to be leaning at
a strange angle. A study of the corresponding vessel in the
printed maps clarifies why this should be. De' Barbari's
boat is careened in shallow water while several figures are
cleaning or painting her bottom from a pontoon.

A varnish of MS2A reduced ketone resin in
Stoddard solvent with approximately 1% Cosmolloid
80H microcrystalline wax was applied by brushing.
Retouchings were adjusted as necessary with dry
pigments bound in MS2A and a final varnish of the same
with approximately 1% microcrystalline wax was applied
by spraying. The lined canvas was re-tensioned to
compensate for any shrinkage of the new stretcher and
creep in the canvas, by tapping out the expansion keys.

FRAMING AND HANGING

A new frame was supplied by John Davies Ltd. In view
of the limited access to the location, the new frame
was designed to be assembled and fitted on site. Henry
Wotton cared about the practical aspects of hanging and
framing paintings. A letter of 1636 described a painting
as being "ready to sett up, being in a gilded frame
already".[28] The following year he sent a portrait of Paolo
Sarpi to the Provost of King's College, Cambridge, "and
had sent the frame withal if it were portable, which

fills to imitate the brown colour of the ground layer.
Retouching was carried out in dry pigments bound in
Paraloid B72 acrylic resin. Pthalocyanine (monastral)
blue was used to match the indigo blue paint, for its
superior stability with a reflectance curve similar to that
of indigo. Manganese blue was used for the glazes.[26]

The upper part of the Torre dell'Orologio, a key feature
of Piazza San Marco, is located on a horizontal split in
the canvas, and the detail was considerably abraded. The
upper part of the bell was visible, but the statues of the
Mori were illegible. Sufficient traces of the image on the

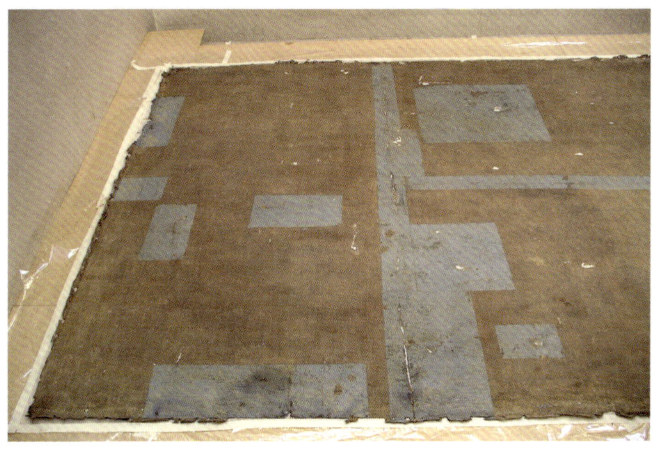

is but of plain deal, coloured black like the habit of his order".[29] From descriptions in the Mantua inventory, maps and landscapes generally seem to have had wooden frames, sometimes embellished with gold.[30] In 1621, Balthazar Gerbier paid £15 in Venice for two frames "karven after the Italian faschion, beloing to the great peece of Titian and Tintoret ar sendet bee sea".[31] He paid a further £7 for gilding both of them. The paintings have comparable dimensions to the *View of Venice* but the Titian had cost the exceptional sum of £275, the Domenico Tintoretto £50.[32] It seems most likely that a frame would have been made for the *View of Venice* in England after it had been unrolled and re-stretched, and that, if Wotton was responsible for the framing, the frame would have been relatively modest.

In *The Elements of Architecture*, Wotton considered a north aspect best for "Repositories for works of rarity in Picture or other Arts". The direction of the light, according to a man who had visited artists' studios, should take account of "how the painter did stand in the Working", "so as Italian pieces will appear best in a Roome where the Windowes are high; because they are commonly made to a descending Light".[33] A painting that had been "done truly and naturally but roughly, alla Veneziana" was "to be set at some good distance from the sight".[34] Some paintings, on the other hand, such as the Bassanos he left in his will to Francis Windebank, were suitable for hanging "near the eye" in the intimate space of a parlour,[35] in order to appreciate the detail.

The *View of Venice* was returned to Eton College on 1 June 2010 and hung in the Election Hall.

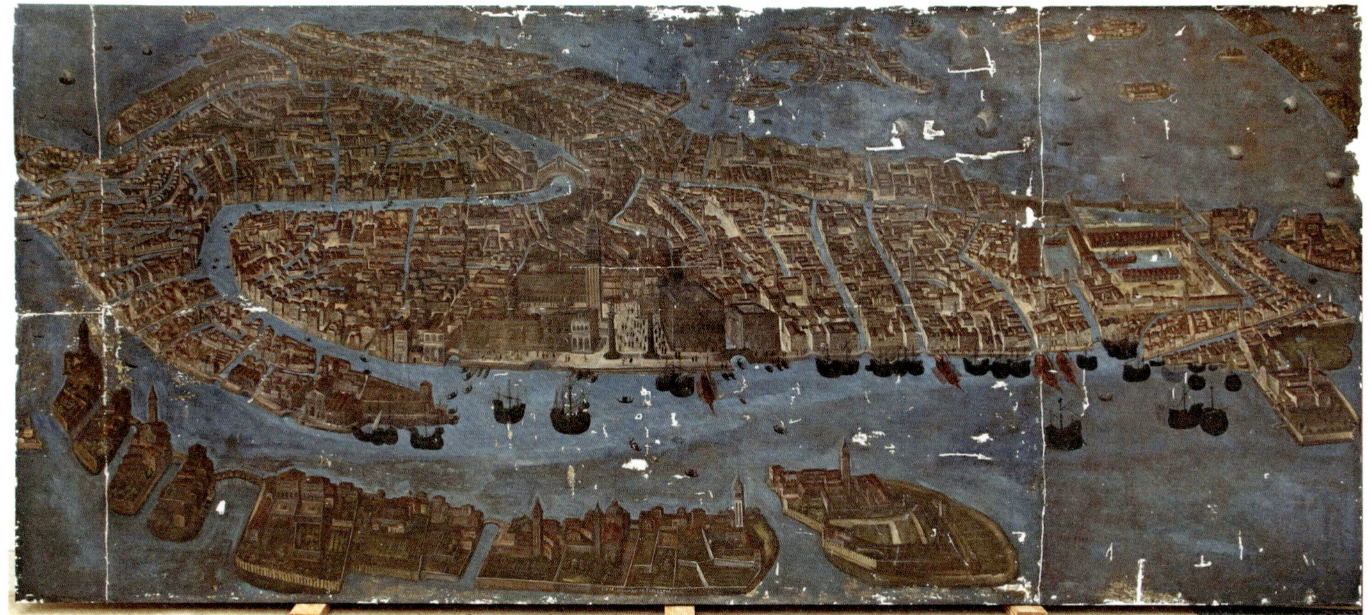

NOTES

1 Meltmount, Cargille, USA, refractive index = 1.662.

2 See J. Dunkerton, 'Tintoretto's Painting Technique', in M. Falomir (ed.), *Tintoretto*, exh. cat., Museo del Prado, Madrid, 2007, at p. 152, and E. Weddigen, 'The Works of Tintoretto: Sewn, Designed, Patched and Cut – the uncertainty of canvas measurements', in M. Falomir (ed.), *Jacopo Tintoretto: Proceedings of the International Symposium*, Madrid, 2009, pp. 151–64.

3 J. Plesters, 'Tintoretto's Paintings in the National Gallery', *National Gallery Technical Bulletin*, 4, 1980, pp. 32–48, at p. 34, fig. 5.

4 *Ibid.*, p. 37.

5 Meltmount, Cargille, USA, refractive index = 1.662.

6 B. Singer, unpublished report prepared for Ruth Bubb, Northumbria University, July 2009.

7 J. Wardius, unpublished analytical report 1478, Hamilton Kerr Institute, Cambridge, April 1990, samples 9 and 10.

8 Singer, unpublished report.

9 *Ibid.*

10 Wardius, report 1478, sample 7.

11 *Ibid.*, samples 1, 6.

12 R.D. Harley, *Artists' Pigments c. 1600–1835*, 2nd edn, London, 1982 pp.70–71, also E. West Fitzhugh (ed.), *Artists' Pigments. A Handbook of Their History and Characteristics*, 3 vols., III, Washington, D.C., 1997, pp. 193–95.

13 P. and A. Mactaggart, *A Pigment Microscopist's Notebook*, 7th revision, privately published, 1998, p. 4.

14 Wardius, report 1478, p. 2.

15 M. Spring, C. Higgitt and D. Saunders, 'Investigation of Pigment-Medium Interaction Process in Oil Paint containing Degraded Smalt', *National Gallery Technical Bulletin*, 26, 2005, pp. 56–70, at p. 56.

16 *Ibid.*, p. 57.

17 *Ibid.*, p. 61.

18 This work was carried out by Brian Singer, Northumbria University.

19 Dunkerton, 'Tintoretto's Painting Technique', pp. 149–51.

20 Armenini, *On the True Precepts*, , pp. 194–95.

21 M. van Eikema Hommes, 'Indigo as a Pigment in Oil Painting and its Fading Problems', in *Changing Pictures, Discolouration in C15th-C17th Oil Paintings*, London 2004, pp. 24–27.

22 Theodor Turquet de Mayerne, *Pictoria sculptoria et quae sub alternarium artium ...*, 1620, cited in H. Binger, 'Das Blaupigment Smalte', *Restauro*, 102/ 1, 1996, pp. 36–39.

23 For this practice in seventeenth-century Venice, Eikema Hommes, 'Indigo as a Pigment', p. 22, cites Marco Boschini and Filippo Baldinucci's *Lives* of Veronese (1664 and 1681), also Richard Symonds's *Secrete intorno la pittura* (1650–52).

24 Personal communication, Trevor Cumine, liner.

25 Personal communication, Clare Reynolds, paper conservator.

26 S. Staniforth, 'Retouching and Colour Matching: the Restorer and Metamerism', in *Studies in Conservation*, 30/3, August 1985, pp. 101–11.

27 R. and F. Zamberlan, 'The St Mark's Clock, Venice', *Horological Journal*, January 2001, pp. 11–14.

28 L. Pearsall Smith, *The Life and Letters of Sir Henry Wotton*, 2 vols., Oxford, 1907, II, p. 365.

29 *Ibid.*, p. 371.

30 See the inventory in A. Luzio, *La Galleria dei Gonzaga venduta all'Inghilterra nel 1627–28*, Milan 1913, pp. 89–127.

31 I.G. Philip, 'Balthazar Gerbier and the Duke of Buckingham's Pictures', *Burlington Magazine*, xcix, May 1957, pp. 155–56.

32 *Ibid.*

33 Henry Wotton, *The Elements of Architecture*, 1624, p. 79.

34 Pearsall Smith, *Life and Letters*, II, p. 419.

35 *Ibid.*, I, p. 218.

BIBLIOGRAPHY

Ackerman, James, 'Palladio, Michelangelo and publica magnificentia', *Annali di architettura*, 22, 2010, pp. 63–78

Adams, Percy, *Travelers and travel liars 1660–1800*, Berkeley: University of California Press, 1962

Allen, Joanne, 'Radical innovation or conventional afterthought? Dating the San Giobbe retrochoir', in Nebahat Avcioglu and Emma Jones (eds.), *Architecture, Art and Identity in Venice and its Territories 1450–1750*, Aldershot: Ashgate, 2013 (forthcoming)

Ames-Lewis, Francis, 'Model books and drawing-books', *Apollo*, 144, 1996, p. 59

Ammerman, A.J., and C.E. McClennen (eds.), *Venice before San Marco: Recent Studies on the Origins of the City*, Hamilton, NY: Colgate College, 2001

Ammerman, Albert, 'Venice before the Grand Canal', *Memoirs of the American Academy in Rome*, 48, 2003, pp. 141–58

Anderson, Christy, *Inigo Jones and the Classical Tradition*, Cambridge: Cambridge University Press, 2007

Anderson, Christy, 'Masculinity and English Architectural Classicism', in G. Perry (ed.), *Gender and Art*, New Haven and London: Yale University Press, 1999, pp. 130–53

Anderson, Christy, 'The Secrets of Vision in Renaissance England', in L. Massey, *The Treatise on Perspective: Published and Unpublished*, Washington, D.C., 2002, pp. 323–47

Anderson, Christina M., 'Daniel Nijs's cabinet and its sale to Lord Arundel', *Burlington Magazine*, cliv, 2012, pp. 172–76

Armenini, Giovanni Battista, *On the True Precepts of the Art of Painting*, ed. and transl. E.J. Olszewski, New York: Burt Franklin, 1977

Lilian Armstrong, 'Benedetto Bordon, "Miniator", and Cartography in Early Sixteenth-Century Venice', *Imago Mundi*, 48, 1966, pp. 65–92; republished in *eadem*, *Studies of Renaissance Miniaturists in Venice*, 2 vols, London, 2003, vol. 2, pp. 591–643

Ascari, Tiziano, s.v. 'Cesare d'Este, Duca di Modena e Reggio', in *Dizionario biografico degli italiani*, vol. 24, Rome: Istituto della Enciclopedia Italiana, 1980

Auerbach, Erna, and Charles Kingsley Adams, *Paintings and Sculpture at Hatfield House*, London: Constable, 1971

Austen-Leigh, Augustus, *King's College*, London: F. E. Robinson & Co., 1899

Aymonino, A., with L. Gwynn and M. Modolo, *Paper Palaces: the Topham Collection as a Source for British Neo-Classicism*, exh. cat., Eton College, 2013

Azzi Visentini, Margherita, 'Venezia in una sconosciuta veduta a volo d'uccello del Seicento', *Antichità viva*, 17/4, 1979, pp. 31–38

Azzi Visentini, Margherita , 'Ancora un'inedita pianta prospettica di Venezia in un dipinto di Odoardo Fialetti per Sir Henry Wotton', *Bollettino dei musei civici veneziani*, 35/1, 1980, pp. 19–25

Bacon, Francis, 'Of Building', in *The Essays of Francis Bacon*, ed. C.S. Northup, New York, 1908

Balistreri, E. (ed.), *Venezia città mirabile. Guida alla veduta prospettica di Jacopo de' Barbari*, Verona: Cierre, 2009

Barber, Peter, '"Procure as Many as You Can and Sent Them over": Cartographic Espionage and Cartographic Gifts in International Relations, 1460–1760,' in *Diplomacy and Early Modern Culture*, ed. Robyn Adams and Rosanna Cox, Basingstoke: Palgrave Macmillan, 2011, pp. 13–29

Bassi, Elena, *Tracce di chiese veneziane distrutte: ricostruzioni dai disegni di Antonio Visentini*, Venice: Istituto Veneto, 1997

Bassi, Elena, *Tre palazzi veneziani della Regione Veneto: Balbi, Flangini-Morosini, Molin*, Venice: Stamperia di Venezia, 1982

Bate, Jonathan, and Dora Thornton, *Shakespeare: Staging the World*, exh. cat., British Museum, London, 2012

Beasley, G., 'Wotton', in *The British Books. Seventeenth through Nineteenth Centuries. The Mark J. Millard Architectural Collection*, ed. R. Middleton, G. Beasley and N. Savage, Washington, D.C., 1998, pp. 366–68

Benezit, Emmanuel, *Dictionary of Artists*, vol. 5, Paris: Grund, 2006

Benvenuti, Feliciano, 'Fialetti, Odoardo', in *The Dictionary of Art*, ed. Jane Shoaf Turner, 34 vols., London: Macmillan, 1996, vol. 11, p. 51

Benzoni, Gino, *Lo stato marciano durante l'Interdetto, 1606–1607*, Rovigo: Minelliana, 2008

Bettley, John, 'The Office of Holy Week at St Mark's, Venice, in the late 16th century, and the musical contributions of Giovanni Croce', *Early Music*, 22/1, 1994, pp. 45–62Biadene, Susanna, and Giandomenico Romanelli (eds.), *Venezia: piante e vedute. Catalogo del fondo cartografico a stampa*, Museo Correr, Venice: La Stamperia di Venezia, 1982

Biadene, Susanna, and C. Tonini (eds.), *A volo d'uccello: Jacopo de' Barbari e le rappresentazioni di città nell'Europa del Rinascimento*, Venice: Arsenale, 1999

Białostocki, Jan, 'Doctus Artifex and the Library of the Artist in the XVIth and XVIIth Centuries', in *De Arte et Libris: Festschrift Erasmus, 1934–84*, Amsterdam, 1984, pp. 11–22

Binger, H., 'Das Blaupigment Smalte', *Restauro*, 102/1, 1996, pp. 36–39

Birley, Robert, Sir, *The History of Eton College Library*, Eton: Eton College, 1970

Blair, A.M., 'The rise of note-taking in early modern Europe', *Intellectual History Review*, 20, 2010, pp. 303–16

Boni, F. de, *Biografia degli Artisti*, Venice: co' Tipi del Gondoliere, 1840 (British Library, Rare Books, 1402.k.5)

Bonora, Elena, *Ricerche su Francesco Sansovino: imprenditore, libraio e letterato*, Venice: Istituto Veneto, 1994

Boorde, Andrew, *Hereafter foloweth a compendyous regyment or a dyetary of helth*, London: John Gowghe, 1542

Boucher, Bruce, Howard Burns and Lynda Fairbairn, *Andrea Palladio 1508–80: The Portico and the Farmyard*, exh. cat., Arts Council of Great Britain, London, 1975

Bourne, Molly, 'Francesco II Gonzaga and Maps as Palace Decoration in Renaissance Mantua', *Imago Mundi*, 51, 1999, pp. 81–52

Bouwsma, William J., *Venice and the Defense of Republican Liberty: Renaissance Values in the Age of the Counter Reformation*, Berkeley: University of California Press, 1968

Bouwsma, William J., 'Venice and the political education of Europe', in J.R. Hale (ed.), *Renaissance Venice*, London: Faber, 1974, pp. 445–66

Bracken, Susan, 'The Early Cecils and Italianate Taste', in Edward Chaney (ed.), *The Evolution of English Collecting: The Reception of Italian Art in the Tudor and Stuart Periods*, New Haven and London: Yale University Press, 1993, pp. 201–19

Brown University, *Children of Mercury: The Education of Artists in the Sixteenth and Seventeenth Centuries*, Providence, RI, 1984

Brown, Horatio F., *The Venetian Printing Press*, London: J.C. Nimmo: 1891

Brown, Horatio F., *Studies in the History of Venice*, 2 vols., London: John Murray, 1907

Brown, Rawdon, *Calendar of State Papers and Manuscripts, Relating to English Affairs, Existing in the Archives and Collections of Venice and in Other Libraries of Northern Italy*, 38 vols., London: Longman Green, 1864–1947

Browne, A. (ed.), Fialetti, O[doardo], *The whole art of drawing, painting, limning and etching. Collected out of the choicest Italian and German authors*, London, 1660 (British Library, Rare Books, C.123.f.22)

Burns, Howard, s.v. 'The Elements of Architecture', in *Palladio and Northern Europe. Books, Travellers, Architects*, ed. Guido Beltramini and Howard Burns, Milan: Electa, 1999, pp. 62–63

Bury, J.B., 'El Greco's Books', *Burlington Magazine*, cxxix, 1987, pp. 388–91

Bury, Michael, *The Print in Italy 1550–1620*, exh. cat., London: British Museum Press, 2001

Caccin, A.M. (ed.), *La Basilica dei SS.. Giovanni e Paolo in Venezia*, Venice: Zanipolo, 1964

Calabi, Donatella, and Andrew Hopkins, 'Progetto per il ponte di Rialto a Venezia (1588)', in Franco Barbieri and Guido Beltramini (eds.) *Vincenzo Scamozzi 1548–1616*, exh. cat., Museo Palladio, Vicenza, 2003, pp. 285–88

Calendar of State Papers and Manuscripts, relating to English Affairs existing in the Archives and Collections of Venice, ed. Rawdon Brown *et al.*, London: Longman …, 1864–

Calendar of State Papers, Domestic Series of the Reigns of Edward VI, Mary, Elizabeth, (James I), ed. R. Lemon and M.A.E.Green, 12 vols., London: Longman, 1856–72

Callegari, Ettore, 'La devoluzione di Ferrara alla S. Sede', *Rivista storica italiana*, 1 , 1895, pp. 1–11

Campbell, James Dykes, *Samuel Taylor Coleridge: Narrative of the Events of His Life*, London: Macmillan, 1896

Campbell, Thomas (ed.), *Tapestry in the Renaissance: Art and Magnificence*, exh. cat., Metropolitan Museum of Art, New York, 2002

Campbell, Thomas, *Tapestry in the Baroque: Threads of Splendor*, New Haven: Yale University Press, 2007

Canella, S. , 'Odoardo Fialetti, 1573–1638', tesi di laurea, Padua University, 1974–75 (supervisor: Rodolfo Pallucchini)

Card, Tim (ed.), *Eton 1440–1990: Portrait, Programme and Catalogue*, Eton, 1990

Carile, A., and G. Fedalto, *Le origini di Venezia*, Bologna: Patron, 1978

Casper, Andrew, 'A taxonomy of images: Francesco Sansovino and the San Rocco *Christ Carrying the Cross*', *Word and Image*, xxvi, 2009, pp. 100–14

Cassini, Giocondo, *Piante e vedute prospettiche di Venezia (1479–1855)*, Venezia: La Stamperia di Venezia, 1982

Ceccarelli, Francesco, and Nadja Aksamija (eds.), *La Sala Bologna nei Palazzi Vaticani: Architettura, cartografia e potere nell'età di Gregorio XIII*, Venice: Marsilio, 2011

Cecchini, I., *Quadri e commercio a Venezia durante il Seicento*, Venice: Marsilio, 2000

Cellauro, Louis, 'La biblioteca di un architetto del Rinascimento: la raccolta di libri di Giovanni Antonio Rusconi', *Arte veneta*, 58, 2001, pp. 224–37

Chaney, Edward, *The Evolution of the Grand Tour: Anglo-Italian cultural relations since the Renaissance*, London: Frank Cass, 1998

Charlton, K., *Education in Renaissance England*, London: Routledge, 1965

Coleridge, Arthur Duke, *Eton in the Forties*, London: R. Bently & Son, 1964

Concina, Ennio, *L' Arsenale della Repubblica di Venezia*, Milan: Mondadori, 2006

Cooper, Tracy E., *Palladio's Venice: Architecture and Society in a Renaissance Republic*, New Haven and London: Yale University Press, 2005

Corner, Flaminio, *Notizie storiche delle chiese e monasteri di Venezia, e di Torcello tratte dalle chiese veneziane, e Torcellane*, Padua: Stamperia del Seminario, 1758

Coryate, Thomas, *Coryat's Crudities: Hastily Gobled up in Five Moneths Travells*, London: printed by W.S., 1611; republished, 2 vols., Glasgow: MacLehose, 1905; online at http://www.archive.org/details/coryatscrudities01coryuoft

Cosgrove, Denis, 'The myth and the stones of Venice: an historical geography of a symbolic landscape', *Journal of Historical Geography*, 8, 1982, pp. 145–69

Cosgrove, Denis, 'Mapping New Worlds: Culture and Cartography in Sixteenth-Century Venice', *Imago Mundi*, xliv, 1992, pp. 65–89

Cozzi, Gaetano, *Venezia Barocca: Conflitti di uomini e idee nella crisi del Seicento veneziano*, Venice: Cardo, 1995

Crinò, Anna Maria, 'Lettere autografe inedite di Sir Henry Wotton nell'Archivio di stato di Firenze', in *Fatti e figure del Seicento anglo-toscano*, Florence: Olschki, 1957

Crouzet-Pavan, Elisabeth, *'Sopra le acque salse': Espaces, pouvoir et société à Venise à la fin du Moyen Age*, Rome: Ecole française de Rome, 1992

Crouzet-Pavan, Elisabeth, *Venice Triumphant: The Horizons of a Myth*, Baltimore: Johns Hopkins University Press, 2002

Curzon, Gerald, *Wotton and His Worlds: Spying, Science and Venetian Intrigues*, Bloomington: Xlibris Corporation, 2003

Dal Mas, Mario, 'Contributo alla conoscenza dell'opera architettonica di Alessandro Vittoria', in *Atti del XXIII Congresso di storia dell'architettura* (Conference proceedings, Rome 1988), 2 vols., Rome: Centro di Studi per la Storia dell'Architettura, 1989, II, pp. 255–63

Dee, John, 'Preface', in Euclid, *Elements of Geometrie*, London: John Daye, 1570

della Dora, Veronica, 'Denis Cosgrove (1948–2008)', *Imago Mundi* 61/1, 2009, pp. 97–100

Dunkerton, J., 'Tintoretto's Painting Technique', in Falomir (ed.), *Tintoretto*, pp. 139–58

van Eck, C., and C. Anderson. *British Architectural Theory, 1540–1750: An Anthology*, Aldershot: Ashgate, 2003

ECR: Eton College Records

van Eikema Hommes, M. , 'Indigo as a Pigment in Oil Painting and its Fading Problems', in *Changing Pictures, Discolouration in C15th-C17th Oil Paintings*, London: Archetype, 2004

Eton: 1440–1990. Portrait, Programme and Catalogue, Eton: Eton College, 1990

Fabri (Faber), Felix, *The Wanderings of Felix Fabri*, transl. Aubrey Stewart, London: Palestine Pilgrims' Text Society VII-X, 2 vols. in four, 1892

Falomir, Miguel (ed.), *Tintoretto*, exh. cat., Museo Nacional del Prado, Madrid, 2007

Falomir, Miguel (ed.), *Jacopo Tintoretto: Proceedings of the International Symposium*, Madrid, 2009

Favaro, Elena, *L'arte dei pittori in Venezia e i suoi statuti*, Florence: Olschki, 1975

Federici, D.M., *Memorie trevigiane delle opere di disegno dal mille e cento al mille ottocento, per servire all storia delle belle arti d'Italia*, Venice: Presso Francesco Andreaola, 1803 (British Library, 786.g.7-8)

Fenlon, Iain, *Music, Ceremony and Identity in Renaissance Venice*, New Haven and London: Yale University Press, 2006

Fialetti, Odoardo, *Il uero modo et ordine per dissegnar tutte le parti et membra del corpo humano*, small edition, Venice, 1608 (British Library, Rare Books, 1560/3394)

Fialetti, Odoardo, *Scherzi d'amore*, Venice, 1617 (Biblioteca Apostolica Vaticana, Cicognara. IV.2113(b), 69-83)

Finlay, Robert, 'The Immortal Republic: The myth of Venice during the Italian Wars (1494–1530)', *The Sixteenth Century Journal*, xxx, 1999, pp. 931–44

Finocchi Ghersi, Lorenzo, *Alessandro Vittoria: architettura, scultura e decorazione nella Venezia del tardo Rinascimento*, Udine: Forum, 1998, pp. 170–79

Fletcher, Jennifer, 'The Arundels in the Veneto', *Apollo*, 144/414, 1996, pp. 63–69

Fortini Brown, Patricia, 'Measured Friendship, calculated pomp the ceremonial welcomes of the Venetian Republic', in Barbara Wisch and Susan Munshower (eds.), *'All the world's a stage …', Art and Pageantry in the Renaissance and Baroque*, University Park: Pennsylvania State University, 1990, pp. 136–86

Fortini Brown, Patricia, *Venetian Narrative Painting in the Age of Carpaccio*, New Haven and London: Yale University Press, 1988

Frajese, Vittorio, *Sarpi scettico: stato e chiesa a Venezia tra Cinque e Seicento*, Bologna: Il Mulino, 1994

Franco, Giacomo, *Habiti d'huomini et donne venetiane …*, Venice: G. Franco, 1610

Franzoi, Umberto, *Le prigioni di Palazzo Ducale a Venezia*, Milan: Electa, 1997

Franzoi, Umberto, and D. Di Stefano, *Le chiese di Venezia*, Venice: Alfieri, 1976

Friedman, A.T., 'Did England have a Renaissance? Classical and Anticlassical Themes in Elizabethan Culture', in S.J. Barnes and W.S. Melion (eds.), *Cultural Differentiation and Cultural Identity in the Visual Arts*, Washington, D.C., 1989, pp. 95–111

van Gelder, Maartje, 'Daniel Nijs and his contacts with artists in Venice', in Keblusek and Noldus, *Double Agents*, pp. 111–24

van Gelder, Maartje, *Trading Places: The Netherlandish Merchants in Early Modern Venice*, Leiden: Brill, 2009

Gianighian, Giorgio, and Paola Pavanini, *Venice: The Basics*, Venice: Gambier & Keller, 2010

Giannetto, Nella, *Bernardo Bembo: umanista e politico veneziano*, Florence: Olschki, 1975

Gigli, Giulio Cesare, *La pittura trionfante*, Venice: Giovanni Alberti, 1615 (fascimile edn, ed. Barbara Agosti and Silvia Ginzburg, Porretta Terme: Il Quaderni del Battello Ebbro, 1996)

Girouard, Mark, *Elizabethan Architecture. Its Rise and Fall, 1540–1640*, New Haven and London: Yale University Press, 2009

Goy, Richard J., *Venetian Vernacular Architecture: Traditional Housing in the Venetian Lagoon*, Cambridge: Cambridge University Press, 1989

Goy, Richard J., *The House of Gold: Building a Palace in Medieval Venice*, Cambridge: Cambridge University Press, 1992

Goy, Richard J., *Building Renaissance Venice: Patrons, architects and builders, c. 1430–1500*, New Haven and London: Yale University Press, 2006

Greist, Alexandra Arvilla, 'A rediscovered text for a drawing book by Odoardo Fialetti', *Burlington Magazine*, clvi, January 2014, pp. 12–18

Grendler, Paul, 'Francesco Sansovino and Italian Popular History 1560–1600,' *Studies in the Renaissance*, xvi, 1969, pp. 139–80

Grendler, Paul F., *The Roman Inquisition and the Venetian Press*, 1540–1605, Princeton: Princeton University Press, 1977

Griffiths, Antony, *The Print in Stuart Britain*, 1603–1689, exh. cat., British Museum, London, 1998

Grubb, James S., 'When Myths Lose Power: Four Decades of Venetian Historiography', *The Journal of Modern History*, 58, 1986, pp. 43–94

Guidarelli, Gianmario, 'Venice's Cathedral of San Pietro di Castello, 1451–1630', in Nebahat Avcioglu and Emma Jones (eds.), *Architecture, Art and Identity in Venice and its Territories 1450–1750*, Aldershot: Ashgate, 2013 (forthcoming)

Hammond, Norman, 'Bellini's birds: avifauna in the Frick 'St Francis', *Burlington Magazine*, cxlix, 2007, pp. 36–38

Hard, F. 'Introduction', in *The Elements of Architecture by Sir Henry Wotton*, Charlottesville: University of Virginia, 1968, pp. xi–lxxxiii

Harley, R.D., *Artists' Pigments c. 1600–1835*, 2nd edn, London: Butterworth, 1982

Harris, E., *British Architectural Books and Writers 1556–1785*, Cambridge: Cambridge Uniersity Press, 1990

Heal, F., *Hospitality in Early Modern England*, Oxford: Clarendon, 1990

Hill, Robert, 'Art and Patronage: Sir Henry Wotton and the Venetian Embassy, 1604–1624', in Keblusek and Noldus, *Double Agents*, pp. 27–58

Hill, Robert, 'Works of Art as Commodities. Art and patronage: the career of Sir Dudley Carleton 1610-1625', PhD thesis, Nottingham Trent University, 1999

Hill, Robert, 'Ambassadors and art collecting in early Stuart Britain: the parallel careers of William Trumbell and Sir Dudley Carleton, 1609-1625', *Journal of the History of Collecting*, 15/2, 2003, pp. 211–88

Hochmann, Michel, *Peintres et commanditaires à Venise (1540–1628)*, Rome: École française de Rome, 1992

Hodgkin, Thomas (ed.), *The Letters of Cassiodorus*, London: H. Frowde, 1886

Hollis, Chistopher, *Eton, a History*, London: Hollis and Carter, 1960

Hopkins, Andrew, *Santa Maria della Salute: Architecture and Ceremony in Baroque Venice*, Cambridge: Cambridge University Press, 2000

Hopkins, Andrew, 'Completamento delle libreria sansoviniana (1581–1588)', and 'Procuratie Nuove in piazza San Marco (1581)', in Franco Barbieri and Guido Beltramini (eds.), *Vincenzo Scamozzi 1548–1616*, exh. cat., Museo Palladio, Vicenza, 2003, pp. 202–20

Hopkins, Andrew, 'Architecture and Infirmitas: Doge Andrea Gritti and the chancel of San Marco, Venice', *Journal of the Society of Architectural Historians*, 57, 1998, pp. 182–97

Hopkins, Andrew, 'Combating the plague: devotional paintings, architectural programs and votive processions in early modern Venice', in Gauvin Bailey *et al.* (eds.), *Hope and Healing: Painting in Italy in a time of plague*, exh. cat., Worcester Art Museum, Worcester, MA, 2005, pp. 137–52

Hopkins, Andrew, 'The Influence of Ducal Ceremony on Church Design in Venice', *Architectural History*, 41, 1998, pp. 30–48

Hopkins, Andrew, 'Longhena proto e architetto: disegni e documenti per le aree attorno alla Piazza', *Arte veneta*, 60, 2003, pp. 199–206

Hopkins, Andrew, *Baldassare Longhena and Venetian Baroque Architecture*, New Haven and London: Yale University Press, 2012

Howard, Deborah, *Jacopo Sansovino: Architecture and Patronage in Renaissance Venice*, New Haven and London: Yale University Press, 1975; 2nd edn 1987

Howard, Deborah, 'Ritual space in Renaissance Venice', *Scroope*, 5, 1993–94, pp. 4–11

Howard, Deborah, 'The Scuola Grande della Misericordia di Venezia', in Gianni Fabbri (ed.), *La Scuola Grande della Misericordia di Venezia: storia e progetto*, Milan: Skira, 1999, pp. 13–58

Howard, Deborah, 'Venice as a Dolphin: Further Investigations into Jacopo de' Barbari's View', *Artibus et historiae*, 18/35, 1997, pp. 101–11

Howard, Deborah, *Venice and the East: The Impact of the Islamic World on Venetian Architecture*, New Haven and London: Yale University Press, 2000

Howard, Deborah, *The Architectural History of Venice*, revised edn, New Haven and London: Yale University Press, 2002

Howard, Deborah, *Venice Disputed: Marc'Antonio Barbaro and Venetian Architecture, 1550–1600*, New Haven and London: Yale University Press, 2011

Howard, Maurice, 'The Ideal House and Healthy Life: the Origins of Architectural Theory in England', in J. Guillaume (ed.), *Les traités d'architecture de la Renaissance*, Paris: Picard, 1988, pp. 425–33

Howard, Maurice, *The Building of Elizabethan and Jacobean England*, New Haven and London: Yale University Press, 2007

Howarth, David, *Lord Arundel and his Circle*, New Haven and London: Yale University Press, 1985

Howarth, David, 'The Patronage and Collecting of Aletheia, Countess of Arundel, 1606–54', *Journal of the History of Collections*, 10, 1998, pp. 125–37

Howarth, David, *Images of Rule: Art and Politics in the English Renaissance, 1485–1649*, Berkeley: University of California Press, 1997

Howe, Emily, Henrietta McBurney, David Park, Stephen Rickerby and Lisa Shekede, *Wall Paintings of Eton*, London: Scala, 2012

Humfrey, Peter, *The Altarpiece in Renaissance Venice*, New Haven and London: Yale University Press, 1993

Hussey, Christopher, *Eton College: with an Account of Oppidan Eton*, London and New York: Country Life and Scribner, 1952

Impey, Oliver, and A. MacGregor (eds.), *The Origins of Museums: the Cabinet of Curiosities in Sixteenth- and Seventeenth-Century Europe*, Oxford, 1985

James I, King of England, *Triplici Nodo Triplex Cuneus, Sive, Apologia pro Juramento Fidelitatis*, London: Robert Barker, 1607

Johnson, Eugene J., 'A window in the Venetian mint and the Libreria di San Marco 2010', *Journal of the Society of Architectural Historians*, 69/2, 2010, pp. 190–205

Keblusek, Marike, and Badeloch Vera Noldus (eds.), *Double Agents: Cultural and Political Brokerage in Early Modern Europe*, Leiden: P. Brill, 2011

Kirby, J., 'The Price of Quality: Factors influencing the cost of pigments during the Renaissance', in G. Neher and R. Shepherd (eds.), *Revaluing Renaissance Art*, Aldershot: Ashgate, 2000, pp. 19–39

Landau, David, and Peter Parshall, *The Renaissance Print, 1470–1550*, New Haven and London: Yale University Press, 1994

Lane, F.C., *Venice: A Maritime Republic*, Baltimore and London: Johns Hopkins University Press, 1973

Law, Ernest, *The Royal Gallery of Hampton Court*, London: G. Bell and Sons, 1898

Leonardo e Venezia, exh. cat., Palazzo Grassi, Venice, Milan: Bompiani, 1992

Levey, Michael, *Painting in Eighteenth-Century Venice*, New Haven and London: Yale University Press, 1994

Levey, Michael, *The Later Italian Pictures in the Collection of Her Majesty The Queen*, Cambridge: Cambridge University Press, 1991

Levine, N., 'Castle Howard and the Emergence of the Modern Architectural Subject', *Journal of the Society of Architectural Historians*, 62, 2003, pp. 326–51

Lieberman, Ralph, 'Real architecture imaginary history: the Arsenale gate as Venetian mythology', *Journal of the Warburg and Courtauld Institutes*, 54, 1991, pp. 117–26

Loh, Maria, *Titian Remade: Repetition and the Transformation of Early Modern Italian Art*, Los Angeles: Getty Research Institute, 2007

Loomie, A. J., 'Wotton, Henry', in *Oxford Dictionary of National Biography*, ed. H.C.G. Matthew and Brian Harrison, vol. 60, Oxford: Oxford University Press, 2004, pp. 377–82

Luzio, Alessandro, *La Galleria dei Gonzaga venduta all'Inghilterra nel 1627–28*, Milan: L.F. Cogliati, 1913; reprint Rome, 1974

McAndrew, John, *Venetian Architecture of the Early Renaissance*, Cambridge, MA, and London: MIT Press, 1980

McBurney, Henrietta, *et al.*, 'Part II: The early sixteenth-century school scene in the Head Master's Chambers', in Howe, McBurney *et al.* 2012

McCutcheon, E., *Sir Nicholas Bacon's Great House Sententiae*, Honolulu, 1977

MacGregor, Arthur (ed.), *Tradescant's Rarities: Essays on the Foundation of the Ashmolean Museum, 1683, with a catalogue of the surviving early collections*, Oxford: Clarendon Press, 1983

MacGregor, A., 'King Charles I: a Renaissance Collector?', *Royal Stuart Papers*, Paper LVIII, 2001, p. 11

MacLeod, Catherine (ed.), *The Lost Prince. The Life and Death of Henry Stuart*, exh. cat., National Portrait Gallery, London, 2012

Mactaggart, P. and A., *A Pigment Microscopist's Notebook*, 7th revision, privately published, 1998

Maier, Jessica, 'A "True Likeness": the Renaissance City Portrait', in *Renaissance Quarterly*, 65, 2012, pp. 711–52

Malvasia, Carlo Cesare, *Felsina pittrice. Vite de' pittori Bolognesi*, 2 vols., Bologna: Per l'Erede di Domenico Barbieri, 1678

Mann, Thomas, *Death in Venice; Tristan; Tonio Kröger*, transl. H T. Lowe-Porter, Harmondsworth: Penguin, 1955

Marina, Areli, 'From the myths to the margins: the Patriarch's piazza at San Pietro di Castello in Venice', *Renaissance Quarterly*, 64, 2011, pp. 353–429

Marr, A., 'A Duche graver sent for: Cornelis Boel, Salomon de Caus, and the production of *La perspective avec la raison des ombres et miroirs*', in Wilks, *Prince Henry Reviv'd*, pp. 212–38

von Martels, Zweder (ed.), *Travel fact and travel fiction: Studies on fiction, literary tradition, scholarly discovery and observation in travel writing*, Leiden: Brill, 1994

Martineau, Jane, and Charles Hope (eds.), *The Genius of Venice 1500–1600*, exh. cat., Royal Academy of Arts, London, 1983

Masini, A. de Paolo, *Bologna perlustrata*, Bologna: Per l'Erede di Vittorio Benacci, 1666 (British Library, Rare Books, 660.a.6)

Mason Rinaldi, Stefania, 'Il Tabernacolo della chiesa dei "Giesuiti" alla Dogana di mare', *Arte Veneta*, 36, 1982, pp. 211–16

Matthew, L.C. , 'The Painter's Presence: Signatures in Venetian Renaissance Pictures', *Art Bulletin*, 80/4, 1998, pp. 616–48

Matthew, L.C., '"Vendecolori a Venezia": the Reconstruction of a Profession', *Burlington Magazine*, cxliv, 2002, pp. 680–86

Mattingly, Garrett, *Renaissance Diplomacy*, London: Cape, 1955

Maugeri, V., 'I manuali propedeutici al disegno, a Bologna e Venezia, agli inizi del Seicento', *Musei ferraresi bolletino annuale*, 12, 1982, pp. 147–56

Maugeri, Vincenza, 'Fialetti, Odoardo', in *Dizionario biografico degli italiani*, vol. 47, 1997, Rome: Rome: Istituto della Enciclopedia Italiana, pp. 322–24

Maxwell Lyte, H.C., Sir, *A History of Eton College (1440–1910)*, London: Macmillan, 1911

Mazzi, Giuliana, 'La cartografia per il mito: le immagini di Venezia nel Cinquecento', in Lionello Puppi (ed.), *Architettura e utopia nella Venezia del Cinquecento*, Milan: Electa, 1980, pp. 50–58

Menniti Ippolito, Antonio, 'La Repubblica di Venezia e il clero veneto. Un eterno Interdetto?', in Gino Benzoni (ed.), *Lo stato marciano durante l'Interdetto, 1606–1607*, Rovigo: Minelliana, 2008, pp. 51–66

Merrifield, M.P., *Medieval and Renaissance Treatises on the Arts of Painting*, New York, 1999

Millar, Oliver, *Abraham van der Doort's Catalogue of the Collections of Charles I*, Walpole Society 37, 1958–60

Mitchell, H., 'An Unrecorded Issue of Philibert Delorme's "Le premier tome de l'architecture", Annotated by Sir Henry Wotton', *Journal of the Society of Architectural Historians*, 53/1, 1994, pp. 20–29

More, Paul Elmer, 'Sir Henry Wotton', in *Shelbourne Essays*, New York and London, 1908, pp. 228–61

Moretto, Gino (ed.), *Venetia. Le immagini della Repubblica. Piante e vedute prospettiche della città dal 1479–1797*, Piazzola sul Brenta: Papergraf, 2001

Morgan, L., *Nature as Model: Salomon de Caus and Early Seventeenth-Century Landscape Design*, Philadelphia: University of Pennsylvania Press, 2007

Morolli, Gabriele, *Le procuratie nuove in Piazza San Marco*, Rome: Editalia, 1994

Mowl, Timothy, and F. Earnshaw, *Architecture without Kings: The rise of puritan classicism under Cromwell*, Manchester and New York, 1995

Moz, Adriano, 'Francesco Sansovino, a Polygraph in Cinquecento Venice. His Life and Works', PhD diss., University of Carolina at Chapel Hill, 1985

Mozo, A.G., 'El concepto de dibujo en Jacopo Tintoretto Análisis de los recursos técnicos utilizados en algunos cuadros del Museo Nacional del Prado', in Falomir, *Jacopo Tintoretto: Proceedings*, pp. 165–77

Muller, J.M., and J. Murrell (eds.), *Edward Norgate: Miniatura or the Art of Limning*, New Haven and London: Yale University Press, 1997

Nepi Sciré, Giovanna, P.C. Mariani et al., *Leonardo e Venezia*, exh. cat., Palazzo Grassi, Venice, 1992

Netzloff, Mark, 'The Ambassador's Household: Sir Henry Wotton, Domesticity, and Diplomatic Writing', in Robyn Adams and Rosanna Cox (ed.), *Diplomacy and Early Modern Culture*, Houndmills: Palgrave Macmillan, 2011, pp. 155–71

Nuti, Lucia, 'The Perspective Plan in the Sixteenth Century: The Invention of a Representational Language', *Art Bulletin*, 76, 1994, pp. 105–28

ODNB: *Oxford Dictionary of National Biography*, ed. H.C.G. Matthew and B. Harrison, Oxford, 2004

Ord, Melanie, 'Venice and Rome in the Addresses and Dispatches of Sir Henry Wotton: First English Embassy to Venice, 1604–1610', *The Seventeenth Century*, 22, 2007, pp. 1–23

Ord, Melanie, 'Returning from Venice to England: Sir Henry Wotton as Diplomat, Pedagogue and Italian Cultural Connoisseur', in Thomas Betteridge (ed.), *Borders and Travellers in Early Modern Europe*, Burlington, Vermont: Ashgate, 2007, pp. 147–67

Orsini, Laura, 'Gli architetti Contin da Lugano: dal ponte dei Sospiri alla chiesa di S. Maria del Pianto', in *Arte e storia*, 8/40, 2008, pp. 150–55

Ottenheym, Konrad, *et al.* (eds.), *Public Buildings in Early Modern Europe* (Architectura Moderna 9), Turnhout: Brepols, 2010

Panzarin, Francesca, 'Il collezionismo inglese a Venezia nel Seicento: Henry Wotton letterato, agente, collezionista, mecenate e il suo rapporto con Odoardo Fialetti', *Arte in Friuli, arte a Trieste*, 20, 2000, pp. 37–60

Peacham, Henry, *The Compleat Gentleman*, London: Constable, 1622

Pearsall Smith, Logan, *The Life and Letters of Sir Henry Wotton*, Oxford: Clarendon Press, 2 vols, 1907; reprinted 1966

Pepys, Samuel, *The Diary of Samuel Pepys: A New and Complete Transcription*, ed. Robert Latham and William Matthews, 11 vols., London: Harper Collins, 1995

Perry, M., 'Commoditie, Firmenes, and Delight: The Sources and Significance of Sir Henry Wotton's Elements of Architecture, 1624', unpublished M.A. Thesis, University of London, 1969

Philip, I.G., 'Balthazar Gerbier and the Duke of Buckingham's Pictures', *Burlington Magazine*, xcix, May 1957, pp. 155–56

Pignatti, Terisio (ed.), *Le scuole di Venezia*, Milan, 1981

Pin, Corrado (ed.), *Ripensando Paolo Sarpi*, Venice: Ateneo Veneto, 2006

Pizzigoni, Vittorio, 'I tre progetti di Palladio per il Redentore', *Annali di architettura*, 14, 2003, pp. 165–78

Placentino, Paola, 'Politica ed economia nella riconfigurazione tardocinquecentesca di piazza San Marco: il cantiere delle Procuratie Nuove', *Mélanges de l'École Française de Rome. Italie et Méditerranée*, 119/2, 2007, pp. 321–40

Plant, Margaret, *Venice: Fragile City 1797–1997*, New Haven and London: Yale University Press, 2002, pp. 124–31

Plesters, Joyce, 'Tintoretto's Paintings in the National Gallery', *National Gallery Technical Bulletin*, 4, 1980, pp. 32–48

Poole, R.L., revised Kenneth Garlick, *Catalogue of Portraits in the Bodleian Library*, Oxford: Bodleian Library, 2004

Portier, F., 'Prices paid for Italian Pictures in the Later Stuart Age', *Journal of the History of Collections*, 8/1, 1996, pp. 53–69

Portier, François, 'Collections d'art et mécénat: Formation des agents au XVIIe siècle', *Bulletin de la société d'études anglo-américaines des XVIIe et XVIIIe siècles*, 34, 1992, pp. 47–55

Potterton, Homer, 'Aspects of Venetian Seicento Painting', *Apollo*, 110, 1979, pp. 408–15

Preto, Paolo, *I servizi segreti di Venezia*, Milan: Il Saggiatore, 1994

Puppi, Lionello (ed.), *Le Zitelle: Architettura, arte e storia di un'istituzione veneziana*, Venice: Albrizzi, 1992

Paul Quarrie, *Treasures of Eton College Library*, exh. cat., Pierpont Morgan Library, New York, 1990

Radclyffe, Charles Walter (draughtsman and lithographer), *Memorials of Eton College*, Eton: T. Ingalton & Son, 1844

Reed, S.W., and R. Wallace, *Italian Etchers of the Renaissance and Baroque*, exh. cat., Museum of Fine Arts, Boston, 1989

Ridolfi, Carlo, *Le meraviglie dell'arte: ovvero le vite degli illustri pittori veneti e dello stato* (Venice, 1648), reprint, 2 vols., Bologna, 2000

Ridolfi, Carlo, *Le maraviglie dell'arte: ovvero le vite de gl'illustri pittori veneti* (Venice, 1648), ed. Detlef Freiherr von Hadeln, 2 vols., Berlin: G. Grote, 1914–24

Roca de Amicis, Augusto, 'Il primo Seicento e l'architettura dei proti', in Augusto Roca de Amicis (ed.), *Storia dell'architettura nel Veneto: il Seicento*, Venice: Marsilio, 2008, pp. 20–35

Rosand, David, 'The Crisis of the Venetian Renaissance Tradition', *L'Arte*, 11–12, 1970, pp. 4–53

Rosand, David, *Myths of Venice: The Figuration of a State*, Chapel Hill: University of North Carolina Press, 2001

Rosand, David, 'Venetia Figurata: the iconography of a myth', in D. Rosand (ed.), *Interpretazioni veneziane: studi di storia dell'arte in onore di Michelangelo Muraro*, Venice: Arsenale, 1984, pp. 177–96

Rößler, Jan-Christoph, 'Da Andrea Palladio a Francesco Contin: i palazzi Mocenigo a San Samuele e Contarini degli Scrigni', *Arte veneta*, 66, 2009, pp. 53–63

Rye, William, *England as seen by Foreigners in the days of Elizabeth and James I*, London, 1865

Sansovino, Francesco [under the name of Anselmo Guisconi], *Tutte le cose notabili che sono in Venetia*, reprint Venice: Tipografia Emiliana, 1861

Sansovino, Francesco, *Delle cose notabili che sono in Venetia*, Venice: Comin da Trino, 1561

Sansovino, Francesco, *Venetia, città nobilissima et singolare*, Venice: Iacomo Sansovino, 1581; reprint Venice, 1998

Sanudo, Marin, il giovane, *De origine, situ et magistratibus urbis Venetae, ovvero La città di Venetia (1493–1530)*, ed. Angela Caracciolo Aricò, enlarged and revised edn. Venice, 2011

Sanudo, Marin, *Venice Cità Excelentissima: Selections from the Renaissance Diaries of Marin Sanudo*, ed. H. Labalme, L.S. White, transl. L.L. Carroll, Baltimore: Johns Hopkins University Press, 2008

Sanuto (Sanudo), Marin, *I diarii*, ed. R. Fulin *et al.*, 58 vols., Venice, 1879–1903

Sarpi, Paolo, *Considerazioni sopra le censure della Santità di Papa Paolo V contra la Serenissima Republica di Venetia*, Venice: Roberto Meietti, 1606

Savoy, Daniel, *Venice from the Water*, New Haven and London: Yale University Press, 2012

Scamozzi, Vincenzo (?), 'Descrittione di alcune fabriche moderne', in Giovanni Stringa, *Venetia città nobilissima, et singolare … ampliata dal M. R.D. Giovanni Stringa*, Venice: Altobello Salicato, 1604, fols. 426v–432v

Scamozzi, Vincenzo, *L'idea dell'architettura universale*, 2 vols., Venice: Scamozzi, 1615

Schulz, Juergen, 'Cristoforo Sorte and the Ducal Palace of Venice', *Mitteilungen des Kunsthistorischen Institutes in Florenz*, 10/3, 1962, pp. 193–208

Schulz, Juergen, 'The printed plans and panoramic views of Venice (1486–1797)', *Saggi e memorie di storia dell'arte*, 7, 1970

Schulz, Juergen, 'Jacopo de' Barbari's View of Venice: Map Making, City Views, and Moralized Geography before the Year 1500', *Art Bulletin*, 60/3, 1978, pp. 425–74; republished in *idem*, *La cartografia tra scienza e arte: Carte e cartografi nel Rinascimento italiano*, transl. T.D. De Zuliani, Modena, 1990, pp. 13–63

Schulz, Juergen, 'The Origins of Venice: Urbanism on the Upper Adriatic Coast', *Studi Veneziani*, n.s. LXI, 2010, pp. 15–56

Sciamberg, Scott, 'Palladio's lost, rejected, and found porticos: façade projects for San Giorgio, the Redentore, and San Petronio', *Annali di architettura*, 22, 2010, pp. 79–88

Sells, Arthur Lytton, *The Paradise of Travellers: The Italian influence on Englishmen in the Seventeenth Century*, Bloomington: Indiana University Press, 1964

Sénéchal, Philippe, 'Justus Sadeler Print Publisher and Art Dealer in Early Seicento Venice', *Print Quarterly*, 7, 1990, pp. 22–35

Serlio, Sebastiano, *The First–Fifth Booke of Architecture*, London, 1611

de Seta, Cesare (ed.), *L'immagine della città europea dal Rinascimento al secolo dei Lumi*, exh. cat., Museo Correr, Venice: Skira, 2014

Shakeshaft, Paul, '"To Much Bewiched with Thoes Intysing Things": The Letters of James, Third Marquis of Hamilton and Basil, Viscount Feilding, concerning Collecting in Venice 1635–1639', *Burlington Magazine*, cxxviii, 1986, pp. 114–134

Shearman, John, *The Pictures in the Collection of Her Majesty the Queen: The Early Italian Pictures*, Cambridge: Cambridge University Press, 1983

Sloan, Kim, *A Noble Art: Amateur Artists and Drawing Masters, c. 1600–1800*, exh. cat., British Museum, London, 2000

van der Sman, Gert Jan, 'Prints and Printmakers in Later Sixteenth-Century Venice', in Bernard Aikema and Beverly Louise Brown, *Renaissance Venice and the North: Crosscurrents in the Time of Dürer, Bellini and Titian*, exh. cat., Palazzo Grassi, Venice, 1999, pp. 150–59

van der Sman, Gert Jan, 'Print Publishing in Venice in the Second Half of the Sixteenth Century', *Print Quarterly*, XVI, 2000, pp. 235–47

Smith, Logan Pearsall: see Pearsall Smith, Logan

Smuts, Malcolm, 'Prince Henry and his World', in Catharine MacLeod (ed.), *The Lost Prince*, pp. 19–29

Spieghel, A., *De Humani Corporis Fabrica Libri Decem*, Venice: Euangelistam Deuchinum, 1627 (Biblioteca Nazionale Marciana, 097.D.012)

Spring, M., C. Higgitt and D. Saunders, 'Investigation of Pigment-Medium Interaction Process in Oil Paint containing Degraded Smalt', *National Gallery Technical Bulletin*, 26, 2005, pp. 56–70

Staniforth, S, 'Retouching and Colour Matching: the Restorer and Metamerism', *Studies in Conservation*, 30/3, August 1985, pp. 101–11

Strong, Roy C., *Henry Prince of Wales, and England's lost Renaissance*, London: Thames & Hudson, 1986

Tafuri, Manfredo, *Venezia nell'età di Andrea Gritti (1523–1538)*, Rome: Officina, 1984

Tafuri, Manfredo (ed.), *Renovatio Urbis: Venezia nell'età di Andrea Gritti*, Rome: Officina, 1984

Tafuri, Manfredo, *Venezia e il Rinascimento: Religione, scienza, architettura*, Turin, 1985; English edn *Venice and the Renaissance*, transl. Jessica Levine, Cambridge, MA: MIT Press, 1989

Tensini, F., *La fortificatione guardia difesa*, Venice: Filippo Sadeler, 1624 (Biblioteca Nazionale Marciana, D.041D.021)

Tessarin, Lucia, 'I Contin: una dinastia di proti nel '500 veneziano', unpublished tesi di laurea, IUAV University, Venice, 1985

Tillotson, Kathleen (ed.), *The Letters of Charles Dickens (1844–46)*, Oxford: Pilgrim edition, vol. IV, 1977

Tramontin, Silvio, 'Le nuove congregazioni religiose', in Giuseppe Gullino (ed.), *La chiesa di Venezia tra riforma protestante e riforma cattolica*, Venice: Studium Cattolico Veneziano, 1990, pp. 77–112

Trincanato, C.B., E. Balistreri, A.M. Ghion and D. Zanverdiani, *Venezia città mirabile: Guida alla veduta prospettica di Jacopo de' Barbari*, Verona: Cierre, 2009

Trincanato, Egle Renata, *Venezia minore*, Venice: Filippi, 1948

Vasari, G., *Lives of the Artists*, vol. I, transl. and ed. George Bull, London: Penguin, 1965

Vasari, Giorgio, *Vasari on Technique*, transl. L.S. Maclehose, ed. G. Baldwin Brown, New York: Dover, 1960

Vertue, George, *Note books*, 6 vols., London: Walpole Society, 1930–55

Vesalius, Andreas, *De humani corporis fabrica*, Basle, 1543 (NLS, NRR, Am.1.23)

Viggiano, Alfredo, *Le procuratie vecchie in Piazza San Marco*, Rome: Editalia, 1994

Wallert, A., and C. van Oosterhout, *From Tempera to Oil Paint – Changes in Venetian Painting, 1460–1560*, Amsterdam: Rijksmuseum Foundation, 1998

Walpole, Horace, *The Duchess of Portland's Museum*, New York: Grolier Club, 1936

Walters, L.M., 'Odoardo Fialetti: The Interrelation of Venetian Art and Anatomy, and his Importance in England (1573 – c. 1638)', unpublished PhD thesis, University of St Andrews, 2009 (supervisor: Peter Humfrey)

Walton, Izaak, *Reliquiae Wottonianae: Or a collection of lives, letters, poems: with characters of sundry personages: and other incomparable pieces of language and art*, London: T. Maxey for R. Marriot, 1651

Walton, Izaak, *The Lives of Dr John Donne, Sir Henry Wotton, Mr Richard Hooker, Mr George Herbert and Dr Robert Sanderson*, 1685, reprinted London: Society for Promoting Christian Knowledge, 1857; online at http://ia311329.us.archive.org/1/items/livesofdrjohndonoowaltrichlivesofdrjohndonoowaltrich.pdf

de Wardius, J., unpublished analytical report 1478, Hamilton Kerr Institute, Cambridge, April 1990

de Wesselow, T., 'Ambrogio Lorenzetti's *Mappamondo*: A Fourteenth-Century Picture of the World Painted on Cloth', in C. Villers (ed.), *The Fabric of Images*, London: Archetype, 2000, pp. 55–65

West Fitzhugh, Elizabeth (ed.), *Artists' Pigments. A Handbook of Their History and Characteristics*, 3 vols., III, Washington, D.C., 1997

White, Christopher, *The Dutch Pictures in the Collection of Her Majesty the Queen*, Cambridge: Cambridge University Press, 1982

Wilks, Timothy, 'The Picture Collection of Robert Carr, Earl of Somerset (*c.* 1587–1645), reconsidered', *Journal of the History of Collections*, 1/2, 1989, pp. 167–77

Wilks, Timothy, 'Art Collecting at the English Court from the Death of Henry, Prince of Wales to the Death of Anne of Denmark', *Journal of the History of Collections*, 9/1, 1997, pp. 31–48

Wilks, Timothy (ed.), *Prince Henry Revived: Image and Exemplarity in Early Modern England*, Southampton: Southampton Solent University, 2007

Wilks, Timothy, 'Princely Collecting', in Catharine MacLeod (ed,), *The Lost Prince*, pp. 118–39

Willis, Robert, and John Willis Clark, *The Architectural History of the University of Cambridge, and of the Colleges of Cambridge and Eton*, 4 vols., Cambridge: Cambridge University Press, 1886

Wilson, Bronwen, *The World in Venice: Print, the City and Early Modern Identity*, Toronto, Buffalo, and London: Toronto University Press, 2005

Wittkower, Rudolf, *The Drawings of the Carracci in the Collection of Her Majesty the Queen at Windsor Castle*, London: Phaidon, 1952

Wood, Jeremy, 'Inigo Jones, Italian Art and the Practice of Drawing', *Art Bulletin*, 74, 1992, pp. 247–70

Woodward, David, *The History of Cartography*, vol. III, *Cartography in the European Renaissance*, Chicago and London: Chicago University Press, 2007

Woodward, David, *Maps as prints in the Italian Renaissance: Makers, distributors and consumers*, London: British Library, 1996

Worsley, Giles, *Inigo Jones and the European Classicist Tradition*, New Haven and London: Yale University Press, 2007

Wootton, David, *Paolo Sarpi, between Renaissance and Enlightenment*, Cambridge: Cambridge University Press, 1983

Wotton, Henry, *A Panegyrick of King Charles*, London: printed for Richard Marriot, 1649

Wotton, Henry, *The Elements of Architecture*, London: John Bill, 1624; reprinted London, 1903

Yates, Frances, 'Paolo Sarpi's "History of the Council of Trent"', *Journal of the Warburg and Courtauld Institutes*, vii, 1944, pp. 123–43

Zaggia, Stefano, '"Far la città": Il ruolo dei Provveditori di Comun nell'evoluzione dell'ambiente urbano di Venezia – Strade, ponti, pozzi, case', *Mélanges de l'École française de Rome. Italie et Méditerranée*, 116, 2004, pp. 665–81

Zamberlan, R. and F., 'The St Mark's Clock, Venice', *Horological Journal*, January 2001, pp. 11–14

Zanardi, Mario (ed.), *I gesuiti e Venezia: Momenti e problemi di storia veneziana della Compagnia di Gesù* (conference proceedings, Venice 1990), Padua: Gregoriana, 1994

Zava Boccazzi, F., *La Basilica dei Santi Giovanni e Paolo in Venezia*, Venice: Ongania, 1965

Zorzi, Alvise, *Venezia Scomparsa*, 2nd edn, Milan: Electa, 1972; 2nd edn 1984

Zorzi, Alvise, *Venice: The Golden Age 697–1797*, New York: Abbeville, 1980

PHOTOGRAPHIC CREDITS

By kind permission of the Provost and Fellows of Eton College: 1, 2, 3, 8, 10, 11, 13, 14, 16, 17, 19, 20, 62, 63, 64, 65, 67, 70, 75, 77, 82, 85, 88, 89, 91, 106, 113, 114, 115, 116, 117, 118, 119, 120, 121 (Roddy Fisher: 3, 114, 116; Dennis Wallis: 1, 106, 121)

Fondazione Musei Civici di Venezia: 4, 5, 6, 27, 35, 39, 41, 46, 47, 49, 50, 51, 54, 68

The Trustees of the British Museum: 7, 9, 30, 34, 42, 59, 74, 86

By kind permission of the Syndics of Cambridge University Library: 12, 15, 18, 40, 57, 58, 73, 95

Royal Collection Trust/ © Her Majesty Queen Elizabeth II 2013: 21, 94, 96, 97, 98, 99, 100, 105

The Bodleian Libraries, University of Oxford: 22, 28, 92, 102

Deborah Howard: 23, 25, 66, 76, 78, 79, 80, 83, 84, 87, 90, 103

Richard J. Goy: 24

Biblioteca Nazionale Marciana, Venice, by permission of the Ministero per i Beni e le Attività Culturali; reproduction forbidden: 26, 29, 38

By permission of the Master and Fellows of Trinity College Library, Cambridge: 31

Professor Juergen Schulz: 32

Cameraphoto Arte, Venice: 36, 37, 52, 53, 55, 56, 57, 81

Stockholm, National Library of Sweden: 44

Berlin, Staatliche Museen: 45

Albertina, Vienna: 60, 61

Hamilton Kerr Institute, University of Cambridge: 69, 72

By courtesy of the Marquis of Salisbury: 93

Sarah Quill: 104

Christy Anderson: 109, 112

By permission of the Master and Fellows of Peterhouse, Cambridge: 117

Ruth Bubb: 122, 123, 131, 135

Brian Singer, University of Northumbria: 124 (photo), 125, 126, 128 (photo)

Ruth Bubb Ltd., Helen Davis: 124 (diagram), 128 (diagram); Chantal Thür: 127, 129, 130, 132, 133

Trevor Cumine: 134

NOTES ON THE AUTHORS

CHRISTY ANDERSON teaches architectural history at the University of Toronto. She is the author of *Inigo Jones and the Classical Tradition* (Cambridge, 2006) and *Renaissance Architecture* (Oxford, 2013).

RUTH BUBB is an accredited conservator of easel paintings in private practice near Banbury, Oxfordshire. She has a BA in English Literature and the History of Art from the University of Cambridge and the Postgraduate Diploma in the Conservation of Easel Paintings from the Courtauld Institute, University of London. She works on a wide range of material, mostly for institutions such as the National Trust, Oxford University and the British Council, as well as private individuals.

ANDREW HOPKINS is Associate Professor at the University of L'Aquila, Italy. His books include *Santa Maria della Salute: Architecture and Ceremony in Baroque Venice* (Cambridge, 2000) and *Baldassare Longhena and Venetian Baroque Architecture* (Milan 2006; New Haven and London, 2012).

DEBORAH HOWARD is Professor Emerita of Architectural History and Director of Research in the University of Cambridge, where she is a Fellow of St John's College. Her latest book is *Venice Disputed: Marc'Antonio Barbaro and Venetian Architecture 1550–1600* (New Haven and London, 2011).

HENRIETTA MCBURNEY was Keeper of Fine and Decorative Art at Eton College 2004–13, having previously been Deputy Curator of the Print Room of the Royal Library, Windsor Castle. Her books include *Wall Paintings of Eton* (London, 2012), and her current research focuses on the history of scientific illustration.

DANIEL MCREYNOLDS is a lecturer in architectural history in the Department of Art and Archaeology at Princeton University and a Fellow of the American Academy in Rome. His research focuses on architectural theory and practice in the Early Modern Veneto.

ALLISON SHERMAN teaches at Queen's University, Kingston, Ontario. Her current research focuses on strategies employed by the Venetian Republic to preserve and display works of art displaced from suppressed monasteries and convents in the seventeenth and eighteenth centuries.

LAURA WALTERS gained her PhD thesis at the University of St Andrews on Fialetti and his impact in England in the early seventeenth century. Subsequently she worked for the Public Catalogue Foundation in Edinburgh.